THE
AGING
EXPERIENCE

THE AGING EXPERIENCE

Diversity and Commonality Across Cultures

Jennie Keith ◆ Christine L. Fry ◆ Anthony P. Glascock
Charlotte Ikels ◆ Jeanette Dickerson-Putman
Henry C. Harpending ◆ Patricia Draper

SAGE Publications
International Educational and Professional Publisher
Thousand Oaks   London   New Delhi

For information address:

SAGE Publications, Inc.
2455 Teller Road
Thousand Oaks, California 91320

SAGE Publications Ltd.
6 Bonhill Street
London EC2A 4PU
United Kingdom

SAGE Publications India Pvt. Ltd.
M-32 Market
Greater Kailash I
New Delhi 110048 India

Printed in the United States of America

Library of Congress Cataloging-in-Publication Data

Main entry under title:

The aging experience: diversity and commonality across cultures/
Jennie Keith . . . [et al.].
    p. cm.
    Includes bibliographical references and index.
    ISBN 0-8039-5866-8.—ISBN 0-8039-5867-6 (pbk.)
    1. Aged—Cross-cultural studies. 2. Aging—Cross-cultural
studies. 3. Old age—Cross-cultural studies. I. Keith, Jennie.
HQ1061.A4578 1994
305.26—dc20   94-21925

94 95 96 97 98 10 9 8 7 6 5 4 3 2 1

Sage Production Editor: Diane S. Foster

Contents

Preface

This book is a result of more than 10 years of collaborative work by a team of seven people. The research project it reports was a collective effort, and the book is that as well. One member of the team carried out the fieldwork in each of our research locations, and the data from each field project are included in *The Aging Experience*. Because we wanted our book to reflect the collaborative and comparative character of our research, we have organized it by topics, not by location. Each chapter addresses a major theme of our research and includes comparative information from all seven sites. Different members of the team took responsibility for coordinating and writing each chapter, and their authorship is indicated in a footnote to the chapter. I had overall responsibility for the book and wrote its Introduction and Conclusion.

Because the project extended over two phases of fieldwork, and more than 10 years, the data were collected at different times, and in the cases of Momence, Swarthmore, and Hong Kong, over 10 years ago. To make the book more readable, most of the discussion is in the present tense. However, dates of fieldwork are specified in the text, and where the time lag might distort understanding of numerical information in particular, more recent data are given as well.

There are many people and institutions to thank for their assistance in sustaining this long and complex project. The National Institute on Aging funded our research through grant #AG 03110. We especially appreciate the personal advice and encouragement of Shirley Bagley, our first Program Officer, and Matilda Riley, who was Associate Director for Social and Behavioral Research at NIA during our study. Mitch Allen, our editor at Sage, has guided and encouraged this book, and, above all, persisted.

I am grateful to my family—Fitz, Kate, Aaron, Robert, and Leslie—who shared not only the fieldwork phase of the project in Swarthmore but the entire 14-year journey from initial idea to final assembly of the book. The research team for the Swarthmore study included three extraordinary people, Alice Brodhead, Isabeth Gross, and Mary Etta Zwell, who gave me strength in areas well beyond our fieldwork. My greatest regret about the project is that Etta isn't here to see the book. Swarthmore College has supported my participation in this research in many ways, including a Lang Faculty Fellowship for a sabbatical in 1981-1982. Swarthmore students: David Bedell, Elizabeth Davies, Will Reese, and Elin Waring were also invaluable research assistants during different phases of our study. I am deeply grateful to the many residents and former residents of Swarthmore who talked with us about their lives and their town. They have added greatly to my understanding of the aging experience, in personal as well as scholarly terms.

Patricia Draper expresses her appreciation to the people of western Ngamiland in Botswana, especially to ≠Oma !Oma, !Xoma Kaeshe, N≠isa Kxau, /"ashe Kumsa, Hwan//a !Xam, Be/Gau, Gakekgosi Isak, Timon Mbatara, and Wakapita Mbatara, and to her "old names" /Asa and Kasupe.

Henry Harpending is grateful for help with data collection from Sarah Harpending, Gakekgosi Isaka, Kaetire Ndjarakana, Kavasana Ndjarakana, Muzeja Korujezu, and Renee Pennington. In addition he had special support with fieldwork from Harry Harpending, Xoma Kxau, and Xashe Kumsa. Data analysis was done with the help of Renee Pennington and Deborah Walker.

Anthony Glascock first and foremost thanks his wife, Judith, and daughters, Denise and Sandra. Although Judith is an anthropologist who has lived and researched in a variety of countries, this was the first time she had to cope with a 15-month-old child while in the field. Anthony also wants to thank Sheila Graham, who not only served as research assistant but truly became a part of the family. Finally, the research could not have been accomplished without the generous cooperation of the people of Clifden. Their willingness to put up with our questions and our general wanderings around their community allowed the team to exceed its original goals. The only thing that can ever surpass the beauty of Clifden is the charm and friendliness of its inhabitants.

Jeanette Dickerson-Putman appreciates the support and participation of her husband, Duncan Putman, who shared her research experience in Blessington. John Ryan of Maynooth University was her research assistant. His skilled, gracious, and reliable colleagueship was essential to the fieldwork. Dickerson-Putman is also especially grateful to the residents of Blessington, who welcomed her into their community and patiently provided the insights into their experience that became the basis of her contribution to *The Aging Experience.*

Christine Fry thanks the many people who were involved in the collection, management, and analysis of the Momence data. Assisting in the Momence community study were Margaret Perkinson, Cheryl Woosnam, and Pam Leinhart. Management, coding, and analysis of Momence data involved a team of sociology graduate students at Loyola University of Chicago. Samir Miari and Lauree Garven were instrumental in the management of both the quantitative and the qualitative data. Shoba Srinivasan, Cheryl Knight, Carmen Quintero, David Shagley, John Demelo, Michael Fleischer, Stephanie Cole, Demayne Murphy, and Debbie vandenHoonard contributed in the coding and entry of data.

Chris is also grateful to her husband Robert, who not only lived with Project AGE for over a decade but also rode a bicycle through Momence recording behavior in public places.

Charlotte Ikels would like to thank especially the staffs of the Kowloon City District Office and the Yang Memorial Social Service Centre for their generosity in providing contacts with community residents familiar with the circumstances of the elderly and allowing her to carry out participant observation in their facilities. She would also like to thank the Universities Service Centre, then under the direction of John Dolfin, for all its logistical and social support. In the most fundamental sense this work could not have been carried out without the efforts of her undergraduate team of seven field assistants from Chinese University—members of which not only helped with the interviewing but also conducted spot observations at nearly every hour of the day and night—and the willingness of 204 residents of Hong Kong to open their doors and accept a foreigner's word that she was a researcher and not a missionary intent on saving their souls. Finally, for support above and beyond the call of duty, Charlotte Ikels thanks her husband, Ezra Vogel, who endured not only the long separations necessitated by the fieldwork phase of this project but also the turbulence of the subsequent years of data analysis and write-up.

Essential contributions to the entire AGE project were made by people working with the two codirectors at Loyola and at Swarthmore. Professor Richard Block, Loyola University, served as statistical consultant to the project. The work of Loyola graduate students facilitated the cross-site analysis. Joanne Adams helped make the comparison of qualitative data possible by getting it into electronic form. Tammy Jones spearheaded the cross-site analysis of reliability of coding and the obituaries from Momence and Swarthmore. Angela Debelo helped with the factor analysis of functionality across the seven sites. Rebecca Morrow-Nye read the entire corpus of textual data from each site, evaluating the coding categories for comparability. Barbara Stucki (Northwestern University) assisted with the cluster analysis of the Age Game.

Philip E. Bartow, of Bartow Associates in Rutledge, Pennsylvania, provided invaluable expertise in database management, as well as in creation of the tables and figures for this book.

Finally, each member of this team thanks the others for making possible Project AGE.

Jennie Keith

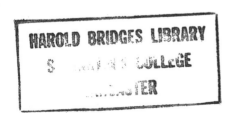

Introduction

*L*ike all human experience, aging has social, cultural, and physical dimensions. This book reports research by Project AGE—Age, Generation, and Experience. We are a team of anthropologists who explored the interweaving of these social, cultural, and physical dimensions into the experiences of old age in seven locations: among the !Kung and the Herero of Botswana; in the towns of Clifden and Blessington in Ireland; in the towns of Momence, Illinois, and Swarthmore, Pennsylvania, in the United States; and in four neighborhoods of Hong Kong.

The "bottom line" question we are most often asked about our study is, "Where is the best place to grow old?" This is not precisely the question we set out to answer, nor the one we did answer, but it comes close. Our goal was to discover the mechanisms through which attributes of different settings shaped pathways to well-being in old age. The question we eventually discovered and answered is better stated as "What are the sources and consequences of the different *meanings* of age in different sociocultural settings?" This restatement of questions represents our gradual realization that although we set out looking for patterns of diversity in aging experiences, our framework for investigation was built on too superficial a notion of variation in the meaning of age. The diversity went deeper than we expected. Attributes of social and cultural settings were not simply contexts that affected aging; they were part of the very meaning of age itself.

Contemporary anthropologists are careful to acknowledge their own participation in creation of knowledge about the settings they study, as well as to avoid reduction of these human contexts to static and univocal tokens in a cross-cultural calculus of comparison. Working as a team of seven anthropologists over the 10 years of this research has made the collaborative and negotiated nature of knowledge creation clear to us, at times painfully clear. In this book we report the process of our research as well as the results. Some of our most important findings, we believe, resulted from our collective scrutiny of the process through which we communicated with persons in the research settings as well as among ourselves.

Another type of communication with important influence on this research is that between our team and other researchers as they are represented in the existing anthropological and gerontological canons of questions and findings about old age. As researchers involved in both of these disciplines, we have tried to be guided by them, to talk back to them with critiques grounded in our field study, and, through example, to make clearer the possibilities for productive exchange between them.

The following sections of this introductory chapter expand on these three themes. First, we place our work in the context of previous research in anthropology and gerontology; second, we describe our methodological strategy; and finally, we sketch an overview of our research questions and findings, and the way they are presented in this book.

Project AGE in the Context of Previous Research

Anthropological Research on Age

There are several broad themes in the history of anthropological research on age, each corresponding to a major theoretical perspective, often associated in turn with a characteristic methodological approach.

Age as a Structural Feature

Focus on age as a structural feature in society has produced research into formal age systems as well as into conditions affecting the status and treatment of elderly persons. The approach to age as an aspect of social structure is characteristic of a period in anthropology that produced not only reports that are still considered classics but also images of the anthropologist in safari suit and pith helmet that persist to this day. In the 1920s and 1930s, intellectuals from British universities did research in countries that were part of a colonial empire. Their books, such as Evans-Pritchard's early classic about the Nuer age system (1940), presented abstract models of social relations in which individuals and their experiences are not prominent. As Evans-Pritchard describes it, the role of the Nuer themselves in his study is almost adversarial. Not only do they not explain their system to him, but they resist giving him any information at all. In exchange for gifts of tobacco Evans-Pritchard extracted from members of the society facts that he then interpreted in a feat of intellectual puzzle solving.

The studies of age systems have typically been carried out by ethnographers and reported in case studies of groups, especially those in East Africa, where these systems ramify into an intricate choreography of ritual transitions through which members of age sets pass from one age grade into another. The question most often asked in these studies is about the *social function* of the groups and life stages defined by age. Early interpretations of age groups as war machines have been replaced by readings that emphasize management of conflict, in particular that between generations, and integration of persons across extensive territories in which there is no centralized political structure (for general discussion of age systems see Almagor, 1978a; Bernardi, 1985; Keith, 1990; Kertzer, 1978; Spencer, 1976; Stewart, 1977; for ethnographic case studies see Almagor, 1978b; Kertzer & Madison, 1981; Legesse, 1973; Spencer, 1965).

Although the golf courses of Florida and Arizona seem unlikely candidates for comparison with the East African deserts, where early work on age systems was done, anthropologists interested in age as a basis for group or community formation have made these connections through studies of retirement residences and continuing care communities. In these settings—responses to increasing numbers of old people in modern, industrial societies—common age appears to promote social integration in several ways that parallel its function in the traditional age systems. Age is an evocative symbol of equality among peers, such as East African youths or American elders, who on the basis of their age are excluded from attaining or maintaining the powerful roles of midlife. The age-homogeneous setting offers insulation from the negative status, as well as an arena in which age-mates may collaboratively create alternative bases of identity. Formalization of intergenerational relations into, for example, management versus residents or residents versus school board provides a channel for management of conflicts that are likely to be more disruptive if played out within families and households (Keith, 1990, reviews these studies and provides additional references).

The status and treatment of older persons in different societies is another focus for research that is carried out mainly on a structural level, with little reference to the life experience of older individuals. In this case the anthropologist is no longer seated in front of a canvas tent in the African sun waiting for locals to provide data, but in front of a computer whose files contain information from societies all over the world. The pursuit of information about status and treatment is characteristically quantitative comparison of attributes of entire social units, such as "societies" or "tribes" (Glascock, 1982a; Glascock & Feinman, 1981, 1986; Maxwell & Maxwell, 1980; Maxwell, Silverman, & Maxwell, 1982; and Simmons, 1945, are examples; Silverman, 1987, is an excellent review). Some generalizable patterns can be extracted from these studies. Older members of human groups usually do well when social life is egalitarian, which is most often the case in groups that have little property at all. However, if subsistence conditions become constrained, older people do better in a group with some social differentiation. Subgroups, usually based on kinship, within which and between which differential rights are defined, offer an opportunity for seniority to provide a basis for privileged access to resources and to care from junior group members. This "cushion" of resources and support is vulnerable, however, to rapid social changes that undermine the principle of seniority, based as it is upon accumulation of social links and experiences in a stable system. If rules change, then having lived many years no longer offers advantages and may become a handicap. In addition, quantitative, comparative research on the treatment of older persons has discovered that different treatment is generally directed toward old people in two distinct life stages, which Glascock (1982b) has labeled "intact" and "decrepit." This distinction opens the possibility that within one social setting high status (for the "intact") and nonsupportive treatment (for the "decrepit") may coexist. These patterns also highlight perceptions of the life course as important influences on the well-being of older persons.

Life Experience of Older Persons

The other continuing broad concern in anthropological research on age is the life experience of older individuals. Life history work with elderly partners has been carried out by anthropologists throughout the history of the discipline (see Langness & Frank, 1981, for review of life history research in anthropology). The purpose of recording these histories has, however, shifted through time from the social to the personal. Earlier life history work was part of efforts to "salvage" as much as possible of cultural knowledge rapidly being obliterated by colonization and modernization. Franz Boas, the founder of anthropology in the United States, and his famous students such as Alfred Kroeber, Margaret Mead, Ruth Benedict, and Robert Lowie collected information as completely as they could about the native American cultures whose days were numbered. These goals were in sharp contrast to the abstract models the British structuralists hoped to produce. Boas's reports on the Kwakiutl, for example, contain details of life down to the recipe for blueberry pie. In this race against time, elderly members of the vanishing societies were of course invaluable allies and their life stories invaluable sources of information.

More recently, life stories have been recorded and interpreted less as a means to an end and more as a worthy focus of research in themselves. Many anthropologists who do this type of work place great emphasis on the significance of making heard the individual voices that tell these stories, often with less concern to generalize to broad populations or to construct structural models. Researchers usually view their role as that of collaborator with the partner whose story is being recorded. Major attention is paid to the personal experiences of the individuals—often older persons—relating life stories, including the shapes and meanings of their narrative process itself. Attributes of life stories may be connected analytically with both individual and collective sources of meaning, such as institutionalization, ethnicity, or cultural requirements for personhood (Gubrium & Lynott, 1985; Kaufman, 1986; Luborsky, 1987; Luborsky & Rubinstein, 1987).

Working to specify the location of Project AGE in the historical stream of anthropological research on age, we realized that a most important goal for us was to bring into the foreground of our models those mechanisms that *link* the structural and the experiential aspects of human aging reviewed above. These two aspects have more often been studied by different researchers, using different techniques, at different times and in different parts of the globe. We believe that the mechanisms linking characteristics of social context to individual experience must be made explicit in order to move to an explanatory or interpretive level in the study of aging as an interweave of social, cultural, and physical dimensions. A major goal for our own project was to reconnect the experiences of older people's daily lives with the characteristics—such as social class, resources, stability, and culture—of the settings in which they live.

Anthropological Research in Gerontology

As a research team of anthropologists, we planned this study as a way to accept what we saw as the most demanding challenge confronting contemporary cross-cultural researchers: that is, to elevate culture from the descriptive to the explanatory level.

Within the gerontological enterprise, anthropologists have most often played a curatorial role, collecting and preserving information about aging in other cultures. At appropriate moments in gerontological debates about activity and disengagement or modernization and the status of the elderly, we have reached into our collections to produce examples to support or, more frequently, to challenge the generalization in question (Keith, 1985, 1988, 1990, reviews anthropological participation in gerontological research). This persistent, and sometimes insistent, documentation of culturally shaped diversity in experiences of aging has been an important contribution. Without it, the scientific view of aging would look even more like the experience of a modern, Western, white, retired male. However, the cost of our success at maintaining the museum of cultural examples has been to limit other types of participation in the development of gerontology. Most critical, we have not often enough gone beyond illustration of cultural influence to the theoretical effort of identifying mechanisms through which culture interacts with social and physiological factors to define the aging experience. Project AGE was dedicated to that effort.

As a practical guide to launch our study, we distilled the following core questions from our review of the field:

- What is defined as a good life for older people, and by older people, in different social and cultural settings? What features of these settings influence these definitions and how?
- How are older people's lives affected by broad characteristics of their social environment, such as scale, economic resources, or residential stability?
- How are the influences of these social characteristics mediated by cultural norms and values, such as filial piety, individual independence, peer bonds, domestic arrangements, and family responsibilities?
- How are the implications of health or functionality shaped by attributes of the social and cultural context, such as definitions of full functionality or availability of care and attitudes toward giving and receiving it?

Research Sites for Project AGE

Choosing research sites from the world of human communities might seem a pleasant task for a team of anthropologists. In fact, it is an embarrassment of riches because the practical possibilities fall so far short of encompassing the universe of variation. Our decision making about locations tacked back and forth between the practical parameters and our theoretical goals. To find answers to our questions, we needed sites that offered variation in scale, subsistence base, social and residential stability, values, perceptions of the life course, family and household structure, age grouping, and provision of medical care. In addition, research designed to investigate social and cultural mechanisms requires units of study within which the operation of these mechanisms can be observed. A survey of individuals without reference to their social environment is not adequate. The research must take place, therefore, within units that have social and cultural meaning to their participants, such as neighborhoods, villages, or towns.

Practical considerations were also compelling. Each research site required a team member already fluent in its language and knowledgeable of its culture. Locations about which extensive and high-quality information already existed also offered the best possibilities for evaluating types and rates of change. We were most likely to recruit team members among anthropologists already interested and experienced in research on age, not a large number of people. Professional and personal schedules of potential team members—*inter alia*, sabbatical dates, spouse's sabbatical dates, children's school calendars, and pregnancy due dates—posed additional constraints. Finally, the limitations of research funding in the 1980s forced us to select the *fewest* sites that we thought could possibly provide the information we needed.

Constantly referring to these practical requirements, we began a speculative tour of the world looking for locations that would provide the variation and the personnel required by our research design. In 1980, "we" were Jennie Keith and Christine Fry, who had met more than once as members of panels discussing the need for cross-cultural research on aging. We decided that if we really believed a coordinated cross-cultural project was as essential as we were preaching, it was time to stop exhorting audiences and begin to plan to do the work ourselves. The number of anthropologists studying old age was small enough then that we usually fit into one session at a professional meeting. Given the less than lofty status of this type of research at the time, these sessions often occurred at times and in places that attracted only the hardiest and most interested participants, so they were a good field for recruitment of possible team members.

Anthony Glascock's stories of the perils of doing research in Irish pubs (buying rounds was somewhat onerous, but drinking them all the real challenge) were unforgettable. He had also done quantitative comparative research on treatment of the elderly, just the type of "homework" on previous research our team would have to carry out before going to the field. When we approached Anthony Glascock he was enthusiastic. He had already planned to return to Ireland, and agreed with us about the importance of creating a project to facilitate systematic comparison. Anthony Glascock introduced the idea of working with pairs of research sites within the same country. The idea of pairing research sites to highlight certain contrasting features was eventually used throughout the project. In Ireland Anthony believed he could select a pair of locations that would represent two major demographic trends affecting old people there, emigration of the young away from rural areas in the west and into the wider Dublin area in the east. The in-migration into former villages has increased the diversity of the population, especially in terms of social class, and has promoted the perception of social categories defined by length of residence: "locals" versus "blow-ins." In addition, research located in Ireland as a culture area could be rooted in ethnographic literature portraying the formerly powerful role of Irish older people. Comparison with those reports provided an opportunity to focus on changes in the worth and control of agricultural land as a resource, as well as in domestic relationships and household composition. The comprehensive national financing of medical care in Ireland was also an important contrast to the U.S. system that would affect the lives of older people in two other study communities.

A talk by Jennie Keith attracted the attention of Charlotte Ikels, who had recently completed her dissertation on aging in Hong Kong. She sent a copy to Keith, who in turn presented our research plans to her. Because of its fame as being supportive of the elderly, Chinese culture was one we knew we wanted to include in our comparison if possible. Charlotte Ikels is fluent in Cantonese and not only had done extensive work on aging in Hong Kong but also hoped to extend her research to the Chinese mainland. She became the fourth member of our team.

The next three people we asked to join us we first had to convert to our cause. They were researchers with expertise in areas of the world and types of societies that we needed, but they had not previously worked on old age. The !Kung (often also referred to as the Bushmen) are the group of people anthropologists usually think of first when asked to exemplify a way of life that is technologically very simple and shared by very small groups of individuals. Because both the technological level and the scale of society were characteristics we expected to have important influences on lives of older people, the !Kung were an excellent possibility for us. We defined scale in terms of complexity, density, and participation in external systems. *Complexity* refers to the numbers of different social principles that categorize people into different roles and groups, as well as the number of roles and groups defined. *Density* refers to the concentration of people in a given space. *Participation in external systems* may occur along several dimensions, such as political control, trade, and cultural institutions such as schools, churches, and organized sports. The contemporary people living in societies of the smallest scale are those in foraging bands. Band societies have little social differentiation, and groups of usually 15 to 25 people move over large areas of land. The !Kung in particular have minimal links to the nation of Botswana or the world beyond. Their children, for example, do not attend school, and adults do not vote in elections. In addition, there was a major research literature about most aspects of !Kung life, upon which our own study of aging could build. We began to ask colleagues for suggestions of anthropologists who had worked with !Kung. Patricia Draper was recommended as a member of the Harvard University project that had carried out a study of !Kung life that extended over more than 20 years. When we looked up her own research, we discovered that she had worked extensively with children, especially on the types of interactions they had with their parents. Surely we could entice her to extend her interest in human development to the further end of the life course?

In fact, Christine Fry did that, and as Patricia Draper explained to us the remarkable changes that had taken place in the !Kung way of life over the last two decades, we realized that work with them would make even more valuable contributions to our comparisons than we had anticipated. Renowned in the ethnographic literature as present-day hunter-gatherers who move across the Kalahari foraging for food, the !Kung in northwestern Botswana have become sedentary. Because Patricia Draper's own research relationship with the !Kung spans much of this transition, she was able to bring to the project a comparative perspective on the ways this profound change affects the lives of older !Kung.

Another recruit to our project was invited because of her expertise in the horticultural (gardening) societies of New Guinea. As an intermediate step between foraging and mechanized agriculture, these societies that have a permanent food supply but achieve it with simple gardening tools seemed to us an important type to include. Particularly interesting about the horticultural groups in New Guinea is their complex ideology about gender. Jeanette Dickerson-Putman was recommended to Jennie Keith by a colleague at Bryn Mawr College, whose department of anthropology was especially known for its training of researchers in the South Pacific. We also invited Jay Sokolovsky, to return to a peasant village in Mexico that he had previously studied, to represent a Latino culture area and an intermediate scale society.

A society with the type of formal age system studied by early British anthropologists also appeared very desirable to us, because the extent and content of formal age ideology had previously been examined as an influence on the lives of *younger* people, but not on the lives of the elderly. A close colleague of Jennie Keith's in the same department at Swarthmore College was an expert on the Boran, a group of pastoralists who ranged across the Kenya-Ethiopia border. Asmarom Legesse had once been the discussant for a session Jennie organized on retirement communities, talking about the similarities and differences in being age-mates for East African warriors and American retirees. He was interested in the possibility of doing more comparative work on age structures by returning to Boran and focusing on the meaning of old age.

The two American towns in Project AGE were chosen both to provide information about the influence of broad American values and of the U.S. system for financing care and, within the American context, to offer contrast in scale, social class, and stability. They are also the residences of the two project directors. Christine Fry lives in Momence, Illinois, and Jennie Keith in Swarthmore, Pennsylvania. The decision to work in these two communities forced us to face difficult issues about objectivity and also about accountability to people who would read and critique whatever we reported about them. Our final choice was influenced by the positive trade-offs in the direction of our previous knowledge of the communities and our current access to key persons and sources of information, as well as by the fact that Jennie Keith was expecting a baby and was not easily able to move to a more distant field site.

A full account of the selection of our research sites also requires inclusion of both political and financial influences. Two of the research sites we originally selected were removed from the study by the National Institute on Aging (NIA): a peasant village in Mexico and the horticultural society in New Guinea. In order to maintain as intact as possible the research team that had developed the project, Jeanette Dickerson-Putman, who had planned to lead the research in New Guinea, took on the fieldwork in Blessington, Ireland. NIA also redefined the temporal aspect of the research by funding it in two phases. The first included Hong Kong and the two towns in the United States. The second included the four sites in Africa and Ireland, and funding for this was contingent on a new application to the institute, which needed to be prepared and submitted during the second year of the first phase of our research. This change excluded Asmarom Legesse from the project because he already had commitments for the future dates. We rather abruptly became six researchers in search of a pastoral African society with age grades.

We met Henry Harpending through Patricia Draper, and he joined us to pursue his interest in the Herero, a cattle-herding group that lives in the same area of Botswana as the !Kung. Harpending's previous research had been primarily with the !Kung, but he had become intrigued by the Herero, who are locally famous for their traditionalism, their wealth in cattle, and their dominating older women. Because many Herero are bilingual in !Kung, he had the language skills needed to begin the research, with the expectation of acquiring more in the field.

Henry Harpending had previous contact with Herero from earlier research trips to the area, and the proximity of !Kung and Herero settlements made it possible for the two Project AGE teams to set up a joint camp in the Mahopa Valley.

We originally planned that Charlotte Ikels would conduct research in a production brigade in Guangdong Province of the People's Republic of China. In 1980 she carried out 3 months of urban research in China as a preliminary step. Chinese official concerns about fieldwork in general, however, resulted in virtual banishment of researchers from rural areas in the early 1980s, and it was temporarily impossible for Charlotte Ikels to obtain a visa at the time Project AGE began, in 1982. We were forced to shift the research location to Hong Kong, where Ikels also had research experience, in order to preserve the Chinese cultural component of the project.

Hong Kong is the highest in scale and has been subject to the most rapid change of all our study sites. It also provides information about Chinese values that have been frequently identified as beneficial for the position of older persons.

In its final form the project had seven sites and extended over 10 years. Figure I.1 shows the location of the seven Project AGE sites.

Methodological Strategies of Project AGE

The methodological challenge for our research is summed up by the implications of two statements that we took as axioms: (a) the experiences of individuals becoming old can be fully understood only *within* their cultural context; (b) the aging process can be fully understood only when its cultural mechanisms are *distinguished from* any specific cultural context. In conjunction, these two statements define demanding parameters for a research design. The information from each setting must at the same time have cultural validity and be comparable to information from other settings. Stated in practical terms, the challenge is even clearer. In order to have cultural validity, measurement of every variable, including those as basic as functionality or even age itself, must be appropriate to the specific research setting. In order to be useful in the systematic interpretation required to identify generalizable cultural mechanisms, measurement of each variable must be comparable, if not standardized.

Project AGE as a research process was continuously defined and energized—sometimes collaboratively and sometimes through conflict—by this tension between cultural validity and comparability. At the outset of the study we committed ourselves to an overall strategy that we saw as our methodological gyroscope, designed to keep us in balance between the pull of these two demands. Through the years of research, especially at the times when data collection began in new settings, we reviewed and negotiated the tension between

Figure I.1. Location of Research Sites in Project AGE

validity and comparability again and again. We believe that among our more important findings are those that emerged from this metaprocess of debating how to learn what we needed to know, not always the same thing as what we initially wanted to discover (Draper & Glascock, n.d.).

Researchers, such as anthropologists, who rely extensively on qualitative methods have also invested considerable professional time and energy in the attempt to persuade other gerontologists that their techniques are adequately "scientific" (see Gubrium & Sankar, 1994, for papers on qualitative methods in gerontology). In this report on Project AGE, our intent is to provide a methodological commentary that will make two contributions to concluding this exercise. First, we hope to demonstrate the necessity and the productivity of qualitative methods in research including cultural variables. Second, we intend to emphasize the benefits of a multimethod approach that regards qualitative versus quantitative as a choice of most appropriate measurement strategy rather than as an existential statement.

A multimethod approach was assumed from the time our first research questions were formulated. The need to obtain holistic information about contexts for aging indicated ethnographic case studies. The data required to document individual experiences of aging necessitated both formal interviewing of a representative sample in each setting and collection of in-depth, personal information from selected individuals. Our methods therefore included long-term participant observation; a formal interview including questions about kinship, domestic arrangements, work and educational experience, health, functionality, well-being, and perceptions of the life course; and the recording of life histories. The specific sampling units for observation and interview were necessarily different in these very diverse settings. Details about sampling are included in Chapters 1 through 4, which present the research sites.

As we prepared to launch a set of far-flung, yet comparative, community studies, it was clear that the most crucial links between cultural validity and cross-site comparison would be ourselves. Communication posed a tremendous challenge in that we were separated by great distances not only during our field studies but also during the periods of data analysis when we returned to our separate institutions in the United States. During the years of our study, several new technologies became available, and we eagerly adopted each one. Ethnographic notes and succeeding drafts of interview guides were exchanged on diskette. Laptops were carried to Africa and operated from solar panels. Electronic mail was used for the next best thing to conversations between institutions in the United States. Telephone contact was useful within the United States, but for many logistic reasons it was only minimally practical between the United States and the other sites. Discussion of research strategy with a colleague in the United States while standing at a phone box on the main street of an Irish community, for example, is constrained by lack of privacy as well as lack of unlimited funds. Letters, printed forms, and field notes also, of course, traveled in many directions by old-fashioned, and often very slow, postal service.

We learned repeatedly that there was no technological substitute for personal contact of fieldworker to fieldworker, and between each fieldworker and the other field sites. Our distance in time from some of the earliest lessons makes a few of them almost humorous. The "op scandal," for example, was a miscommunication based on the parallel, but not identical, assumptions by one American researcher in the United States and one Chinese research assistant in Hong Kong about the "only way" it made sense to fill in spaces on an opscan (optical scanning) sheet. It was only after 500 sheets had been hand coded in Hong Kong and returned to the United States that we realized there *was* more than one way to do this, and consequently a need to make this aspect of research culture explicit.

Visits by each of the two project directors (Fry and Keith) to each of the field sites was the most direct, personal contact across field sites that our budget could afford. Each location was visited twice during the study, once by each director, once early in the fieldwork and once near the final stage. It was during these visits that much of the most difficult negotiation between cultural validity and the demands of comparability was accomplished.

The methodological balance we sought was needed in both data collection and data interpretation phases of our work. The overall guide for data collection that we adopted at the beginning of the project distinguished specific measurement of variables from the strategy used to discover these specific measures (Fry & Keith,

1986, present results of a conference at which team members and consultants discussed these issues in terms of specific data collection techniques). The same distinction between validity and reliable comparability emerged again as we developed ways to code and interpret textual data.

In initial plans for data collection, demands of validity were assigned priority in decisions about specific measurements; demands of comparability were assigned priority in decisions about the strategies used to discover those measures. Perception of the life course and well-being, for example, were key concepts in our research questions. Measurement of these concepts, like all the measurement decisions we made, will be discussed in detail in the chapters devoted to each concept. Here we present a brief summary of the decisions we made and remade about collecting data on well-being and on the life course as concrete examples of our general approach to balancing validity and comparability, and of ways we learned from methods that at first glance "didn't work."

To begin with, what we wanted to know about perceptions of the life course included how it was differentiated internally into stages, how many stages of life there were, how these were marked, how they were evaluated, what attributes, behaviors, and meanings signaled transitions between stages, how much consensus there was in all of these perceptions, and with what attributes (sex? age?) diverse perceptions about the life course were associated. An especially pressing need for us was a way to discover what the boundaries of "old" were within each of these settings so that our comparisons could be done not only in terms of standardized chronological categories but also according to the age definitions valid for each research site.

The fieldworker in search of culturally valid data faces an Archimedean problem. Archimedes said, "Give me a place to put my lever and I can move the earth." Students of culture face a parallel lack of a culture-free place to stand while employing their instruments of observation. We could not use our own framework of life stages to pose questions about people's own perceptions. We could not ask Herero or Chinese at what age a person becomes old, or to give us their evaluation of middle age, without giving them a template for their answers.

Our choice of technique for eliciting views of the life course was a sorting task that asked participants in our study to categorize by age or life stage items that described culturally plausible but imaginary persons. Then, using the elicited categories representing their *own* view of the life course, we could ask questions about bases of categorization, evaluations of the various stages, and actual social contact with individuals of different ages. In the settings where almost everyone was literate, we planned to ask people to sort cards with printed descriptions of people. Among the !Kung, where almost everyone is not literate, we planned to design visual portrayals of people with different attributes, indicated, for example, by clothing, activities, and presence of children of different sizes.

In Hong Kong, in the two American towns, in Blessington, Ireland, and among the Herero, our card sorting worked quite smoothly. For the !Kung and most residents of Clifden, however, it turned out to be an awkward, uncomfortable—and, at least in terms of our initial expectations, unproductive task. In Clifden we discovered what Anthony Glascock labeled "the kitchen table factor." People laid out their card deck of imaginary people one by one until they reached the edge of the table and then, of necessity, made a pile of cards. They also responded to each card as if it described a real person: "Ah, that's so-and-so, and she's about 35, so she goes between these two."

Patricia Draper began her work on the card sort with sketches showing !Kung individuals in clothing, settings, and behaviors she expected to be recognized as attributes of different ages and used as a basis for clustering the individuals portrayed into life stages. Instead, the drawings elicited detailed comments and questions about the pictures—why the people were doing what they were doing, and the respondent's opinion of people who did things like that (lazy young men who lie around camp during the day)—but little generalization about age categories or life stages.

Deciding that the drawings were a distraction, Draper shifted to asking people directly what were the different stages of life. !Kung willingly gave her three to five labels and defined them in mainly physiological terms: for example, "she has not menstruated yet," "she has menstruated but does not know men," "he can no longer hunt," or "he can no longer chew meat." However, when the interview progressed to questions about the supposed age categories, !Kung respondents did two unsettling things. First, during the course of an interview, some people shifted the numbers of "stages" they had originally identified several times, sometimes talking about the third as oldest, sometimes adding a fourth, and so on. Second, the people Draper interviewed persistently referred to actual individuals they knew rather than to age categories.

Intense discussions about why the card sort "didn't work" took place by the campfires in Mahopa and in front of the peat hearth in Clifden during the visits to Ireland and Botswana made by the project directors. The two poles of validity and comparability seemed stretched impossibly far apart at these times, and it was difficult to avoid a lineup of fieldworkers as defenders of validity versus directors waving the banner of standardization and comparison. The strenuous process of resolving this issue continued throughout the fieldwork and into the interpretation of our data. It also led us to what we view as major findings of our research. The details of what we learned from the card sort, both when it worked and when it did not, are presented in Chapter 6. Here we can say that using the card sort, viewed as this entire process of frustration, critique, and reevaluation, led to some of our most important findings. First, the type and degree of variation in not only shape but also salience of the life course is greater than previously documented or even hypothesized. In addition, comparison of our experiences with the sorting task in our seven research sites points to specifiable characteristics of social settings that promote lack of salience for the life course as a unit and/or fluidity of its internal differentiation. Variable life course salience and structure also have consequences for the lives of older persons.

Measurement of well-being presented a similarly challenging tightrope walk between cultural validity and comparison. We selected the Cantril Self-Anchoring Ladder (Cantril, 1965) as a key instrument for measuring well-being. It offered a standard strategy for eliciting both definitions and evaluations of well-being, with validity on both individual and community levels. Presenting a ladder with six rungs, of which the top rung represented the best possible life people could imagine for themselves and the bottom rung the worst possible life, we asked participants to place themselves on a rung. This numeric rank was then "anchored" by their description of the best and worst possible lives represented by the ends of the ladder, and of the reasons they placed themselves where they did.

Although we faced less dramatic challenges with the use of the Cantril ladder than with the card sort, we did recognize important cultural caveats to interpretation of the results. Our awareness of these was stimulated by patterns we perceived in answers within certain sites and by the contradictions that sometimes appeared between these answers and our own ethnographic observations. For example, Chinese respondents were uncomfortable placing themselves on rungs represented by integers. They preferred to be *between* rungs. Eventually Charlotte Ikels transformed the ladder to a set of steps, and interviews proceeded more smoothly. A tendency to choose middle-level scores did, however, persist. Annotated by the comments people made ("I'm worse than some, better than some"), this tendency seemed to be linked to the Confucian ideal of moderation. Among Herero, by contrast, the tendency was to give oneself a low score, in many cases to the consternation of the fieldworker who knew he was interviewing one of the richest and most influential men in a village. For Herero, the cultural "interference" is from pressure on those individuals with above-average resources to redistribute them to others in the group. There appears to be a corresponding tendency to minimize one's strengths and assets in order to decrease one's visibility as a potential target of demands.

The implication of these cultural patterns for interpretation of data is that comparison of raw numerical scores for well-being will not be meaningful across cultures. The well-being data are a good example of the reason why most of our quantitative data can be analyzed with inferential statistics only within a research location. The patterns of association between well-being and other attributes of persons within a setting can then very usefully be compared to patterns within the other sites. Similar combinations of within-site and cross-site analysis will appear for other variables whose numeric ratings are influenced by cultural factors, such as functionality and health.

The texts elicited by the questions about why people evaluated their well-being as they did, on the other hand, provide appropriate and informative data for *both* within-site and cross-cultural comparison. These texts, like those elicited by many of the questions about life stages in the card sort, were coded thematically. Presence, absence, and frequency of themes in the aggregate responses of people from the different research locations can then be examined. In addition, patterning of the reference to various themes by persons with specific characteristics such as sex, age, or functionality was described within each site as a basis for cross-site comparison of the patterns of association.

The coding goals and procedures are another aspect of our measurement strategy that required arduous negotiation and revision throughout many years of the project. However, this process too led to deeper understandings of the cultural differences we set out to explore, as well as of the methods most appropriate for including them in comparative analyses. The core tension between cultural validity and the need for comparison reappears particularly clearly in this aspect of our methods. Having begun the coding enterprise with an emphasis on standardization that would facilitate comparison, we were pulled back to concerns about validity and eventually redefined both our goals and our procedures for interpreting textual data. We started out to define a numeric codebook of general themes and specific subthemes (e.g., family = general theme; children, grandchildren = subthemes), with the intent to use it on all texts from all sites. The addition of necessary sub- and sub-subthemes mushroomed as the researchers from each site tried to make the codebook workable ("conflict with daughter-in-law" for Chinese; "children's divorce interferes with grandparenting" in Swarthmore). This very cultural specificity then made it impossible for us to code each other's texts with any reasonable level of agreement. Did "active" as used by North Americans mean the same thing as *jingsahn* (usually translated "energetic, active") used by Hong Kong Chinese? Did "nursing home" mean dependence (likely code by U.S.-based researcher) or "health care" (likely code by Hong Kong-based researcher)? As we haggled and argued, the talk among researchers about why certain themes were or were not the same was inevitably more informative than the results of counting numeric codes.

Return of the fieldworkers from Africa and Ireland, each with his or her own voluminous texts, finally forced us to face the fact that we had come close to translating our texts word for word into a Byzantine numeric code without achieving either validity or reliability. The talk was more productive than the manipulation of the numbers because the explicit comparison of cultural meanings was lost in the standardized scheme.

The redefinition of text coding took us back to the first principles of our project. In our efforts to participate as far as possible in the multidisciplinary discourse of gerontology, we had come close to forgetting our own disciplinary culture. Our zeal to quantify and compare had pulled us dangerously far away from the goal of cultural validity. The reasons why our research required long-term, ethnographic case studies were the same reasons why a universal coding scheme was impossible. Codes, like the measures we originally defined, could be comparable but not standardized either across questions or across sites.

The new approach to our texts was more grounded in those texts and proceeded up from each researcher's immersion in the texts from a specific site, rather than down from an attempt at standardization. For each question, each of us read and reflected on texts, then proposed major themes as well as possible broader clusters into which these might be combined. This material, along with translations of the texts, was sent to the coordinator of a particular writing project, such as a chapter for this book. The coordinator read all the texts and all the proposed coding schemes. Processed through one central nervous system, sets of themes often showed considerable commonality. The coordinator verified this with each researcher and defined common coding categories wherever appropriate. So, for example, "My cattle are dead" from a Herero is agreed to indicate lack of material security, equivalent to "I've been laid off" in Momence. On the other hand, the psychic lost and found ("I found myself"; "When he retired, he lost his sense of self") of personal development as described by middle-class Americans has no equivalent in any other of our settings. In comparison across sites, of course, such unique themes are as meaningful as the varying manifestations, frequencies, and correlates of themes that occur everywhere.

With this revised strategy, our coding efforts came into line with our other measurement decisions. The validity of each code was rooted in the common strategies used by all team members to discover cultural meanings and had to be judged by the researcher expert in a particular site. Intercoder reliability of assigning numeric codes to texts was relevant within the research group for each

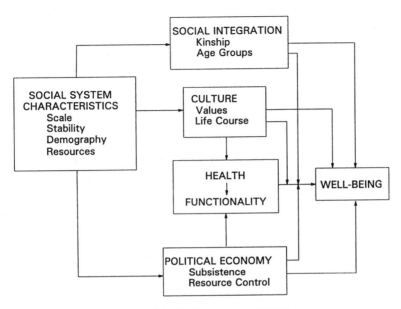

Figure I.2. Schematic Model of Influences on Well-Being

site. Across the sites, comparability, rather than reliability in the usual sense, was our goal. To expect that the researcher expert in Herero culture would code the data from Hong Kong in the same way as the person who did research there was a denial of the very need to discover cultural meanings upon which our research strategy was based. Comparability, as described above, was established through coordinated assessment of cultural meanings by the team of researchers, each expert in the culture of one site. Talking about cultural meanings thus became the focus of our coding efforts, and the numeric codes assumed their proper place as convenient counters for those meanings (Keith, 1994, discusses the use of qualitative methods in comparative research with examples from Project AGE).

Interpretive Model and Plan of the Book

Culture and explanation are the essential ingredients of this book. We plan to show how culture influences lives in old age, as cultural mechanisms carry and mediate the influence of contextual features such as scale, resources, and stability. Figure I.2 shows in its most schematic form the model that guided our research.

The next four chapters and their photographs provide a description of each research site and its older residents. Chapter 5 begins Part Two of the book, in which each chapter is centered on a major variable, and includes data from all the research settings. Chapter 5 reports our methods for discovering evidence about well-being of older persons and the sources and levels of well-being we discovered in the seven sites. The next three chapters each focus on a social or cultural variable, or cluster of variables, our strategies for discovering information about them, and the ways they influence well-being of the elderly: perceptions of the life course in Chapter 6, political economy in Chapter 7, and health and functionality in Chapter 8. The conclusion in Chapter 9 gives our summary of what Project AGE taught us about meanings of human aging and also our reflections about what this cross-cultural study offers as guidance toward well-being in old age for those of us who will experience it in complex, modern societies.

Part One

The Research Sites

Photo 1.1 A !Kung Woman

1

Botswana

T he locations where we lived and worked as field researchers are presented more fully in the following four short chapters. Each describes the sites in one country, with special attention to characteristics that made them particularly interesting as places to study old age and to features that posed special challenges for research methodology. When these site descriptions are read together as a set, they show the major dimensions of variation in terms of which our comparisons are structured throughout the book: societal scale, demography, subsistence strategy, resource level, perceptions of the life course, family and household organization, values, and the political economy of the larger society in which the community or neighborhood is included.

The two African sites in Project AGE represent the smallest scale social groups and also offer important cultural information about sedentary versus nomadic lifestyles, lineal kinship, and the sacred role of ancestors. In addition, the location of the !Kung and the Herero in the same geographic area highlights their different social, cultural, and economic adaptations to the same environment.

We defined scale in terms of complexity, density, and participation in external systems. The contemporary people living in societies of the smallest scale are those in foraging bands. Band societies have little social differentiation, and groups of usually 15 to 25 people move over large areas of land. The band society about which the best and most extensive information already exists is that of the !Kung of Botswana and Namibia, often referred to as Bushmen. Although they are now citizens of these two nation-states, the !Kung are still relatively tenuously linked into their political, economic, or educational systems. Pat Draper had a research relationship with !Kung stretching back 20 years, spoke their language fluently, and was intrigued by the possibility of extending her research on familial relationships from its earlier focus on young children to include older people. Especially important for our interest in change, her 20 years of contact with !Kung in western Botswana spanned the period of their transition from a subsistence strategy based on foraging to a sedentary life of food production.

Living in small, kin-based villages, and subsisting largely by food and tools they produced themselves, the !Kung were the quintessential small-scale, face-to-face society, in which social relationships based on kinship and marriage governed much of daily life. Social roles in this population were minimally differentiated (primarily by age and sex), and economic, educational, occupational, and status differences among people were of very low magnitude. Family ties were the primary basis for residence, and all older people stayed in the community, continuing to live with the same kin they had known and worked with most of their lives.

On the basis of what we already knew about !Kung culture, we expected that it would offer both advantages and disadvantages for older people. We expected that as older people living in a technologically simple society with limited material resources, the !Kung would be disadvantaged relative to elders in societies with more material abundance. The most difficult thing for aging !Kung was the fact that as their strength weakened, there were relatively few buffers or compensations (except, of course, help from relatives) to ease their losses. On the positive side, we expected that the elderly would have good social support as they grew older in locales where they were well known and where many relatives still lived. We also anticipated that older people would fare better under the sedentary lifestyle that all of the Botswana !Kung had adopted by the time the age research began. In earlier times when many !Kung bands were mobile and lived by hunting and gathering, the infirm elderly had poor prospects. The rigorous demands of moving and walking in search of food posed challenges that older people could not meet as their physical capacities failed. In the most extreme cases, !Kung groups were forced to abandon frail elderly to die. Once the !Kung abandoned foraging and settled around permanent water, some of the most taxing features of the elders' lives were removed. Furthermore, we believed that once !Kung assumed the more complex set of economic practices associated with growing their own food, the social and economic roles would become more differentiated, opening up new types of labors and supervisory responsibilities that older people could fill despite their reduced physical capacity. One of the surprises in our findings was that for reasons we only gradually came to understand, *no* !Kung of any age had anything positive to say about old age.

The pastoral Herero occupy the same territory in southern Africa as the !Kung. Herero offered us important contrasts to the !Kung and to the other non-African sites in kinship organization, values, scale, and resources. A notch higher in societal scale than the !Kung, Herero social organization, like that of !Kung, is patterned by kinship and age, but among Herero these principles differentiate corporate groups and also channel individuals into more distinct subsistence activity. Herero also participate more in the external social system; most Herero children, for example, attend primary school and are literate in the national language of Setswana as well as in Ojitherero. Older Herero, who did not go to school, are still likely to be literate in Ojitherero because of the activities of German missionaries who translated the Bible into that language. Herero are nevertheless particularly known in southern Africa as a conservative group who have preserved their "traditional" values and changed their way of life very little. They maintain their considerable wealth in large herds of cattle, for example, rather than translating it into modern paraphernalia.

Characteristic of most Bantu groups, Herero share values that emphasize the role of ancestors, who remain significant members of their kin groups after death. The place of the ancestors is a continuation of the tree of seniority that places the senior male and his spouse in the role of leadership in a village, symbolized in part by their responsibility for preserving the sacred flame of the ancestors between their own house and the opening of the corral. It is particularly interesting for Project AGE that although both children and elders are recognizable categories in Herero social life, it is the children who are less individualized and more interchangeable. The custom of fostering children from one household to another allows an older relative to request a child from the household of a younger relative, with the realistic expectation that one will be sent to live with them and to provide necessary services such as fetching water and firewood.

!Kung, Botswana

Description

The !Kung who participated in Project AGE live in the northwestern area of Botswana, near the Namibian border. (!Kung are also known in the anthropological literature as Bushmen, Zhun/wasi, or Basarwa.) The country is savannah-woodland, the type common throughout central and southern Africa. It is an area of gently rolling sand dunes, covered with a vegetation that is surprisingly thick to be found in an area officially classified as a desert. To an unpracticed eye, the local terrain is monotonous. There is little relief to the landscape, and the plant communities are not highly varied. Driving or walking in this area, the observer rarely glimpses a vista or a prominent landmark by which to mark distances or to establish direction. Because the land is almost flat and the vegetation dense, the impression one gains as a traveler, either by foot or by vehicle, is of continuously pushing one's way through kilometer after kilometer of heavy sand and tall stands of grass interspersed with heavy bush and the very occasional taller tree.

A more accustomed viewer, however, perceives more variation and can discern in the vegetation patterns that alternate regularly across the sand dunes over a scale of 3 to 6 miles.[1] In the shallow valleys of the sand dunes (called *molapos* in the Tswana language) are clumps of grasses and low bushes. In these low places the ground is harder because water collects here during the few months of rainfall. Moving in the direction of the "crests" of dunes, the grasses give way to stands of broad-leafed bushes, often laden with berries in the rainy season, and groves of nut-bearing trees such as mongongo and marula.

The climate in the Kalahari is severe, and this fact, together with the extremely simple technology employed by !Kung, needs to be acknowledged in understanding the rigors of daily life for people in this society. In the winter months of May to July, temperatures drop to nighttime lows in the range of 25 to 35 degrees Fahrenheit. In the hottest months of October and November, temperatures are regularly above 100 and occasionally as high as 115 or 120 degrees Fahrenheit. The !Kung accommodate to these temperature ranges by adjusting their habits. They live in small, insubstantial mud and thatch houses that offer little protection from wind and cold. On long winter nights people sleep as close as possible to their fires, trying to stay warm while not setting their blankets on fire. On very cold nights many people stay up much of the night hunched over their fires and talking to other wakeful people who are also too uncomfortable with cold to sleep. In the daytime, temperatures rise into the 80s, and the sky is invariably clear and blue. In general the cold season and the dry season coincide. However, as September and October arrive, average temperatures rise sharply, and the rains (not due until December) have not yet come to break the heat cycle.

In this hot season people reduce their activity during the heat of the day, rising early to collect water and accomplish various tasks, then retiring to the shade of their huts or nearby trees until the heat lifts in the late afternoon. The months of September to December are the hardest time of the year, not only in terms of heat stress but in terms of the availability of food. By this time cattle are no longer giving milk, and the grazing areas located close to the water sources have been consumed. Cattle, goats, and other domestic stock must walk farther and farther to find food. The men who own the cattle (or work for owners of cattle) must spend long hours in "bucket brigades" at the hand-dug wells. Up to three men stand at intervals beginning at the bottom of the well and pass buckets of water from hand to hand to the surface for long lines of milling cattle, goats, donkeys, and horses.

The hot dry season is also a time when hunting is least rewarding for the !Kung living in permanent settlements. Many species of grazing animals that require standing water for drinking retreat from the dry bush country to the north and east where the waters of the Okavango Swamp are available year round. There are other game species, such as kudu, gemsbok, and duiker, that remain in the bush year round because they can get by with moisture from roots and dew. However, even these animals retreat from the areas close to human habitation because the domestic animals, in their relentless pursuit of anything edible, have trampled the area within 6 to 10 miles of the wells, leaving poor grazing for the wild species. Some men go after more distant game by taking pack animals and carrying water. Sometimes these hunts are successful; however, one consequence of the shift to sedentary life of food production is that men must balance the desire for fresh meat with the increased labor requirements of watering stock by hand from deep wells.

The !Kung live in a series of scattered villages or hamlets located along the dry river beds of ancient watercourses that are laid out in a roughly east-west pattern in this part of the western Kalahari. These fossil rivers no longer have running water, although in some of the molapos such as those of !Angwa and N!aun!au, where we worked, water can be found in subterranean channels by digging wells 30 or more feet. Villages are situated at intervals of 3, 6, and 15 miles, each within 1.5 or 2 miles of one of these permanent water sources.

!Kung live in extremely small villages, which are typically extended family compounds composed of 25 to 30 people. As a consequence of the isolation and small size of villages and the low overall population density, there is little overall community feeling among the !Kung living in this region. People are well informed about their relatives in their own villages, and to some extent they are up on the affairs of people living in other villages at the same water hole. When asked to compare life at their own village with life at another !Kung village, perhaps 20 miles away, or to generalize about the quality of life in the whole region, informants disclaimed having any knowledge or basis for offering an opinion.

Most villages have five or six permanent buildings and numerous storage platforms, often arranged in a crescent or half-circle shape. The houses are "rondavels," round, mudded structures, stuccoed with mud made from a mixture of water, earth from termite hills, and cow dung. Conical roofs for the rondavels are constructed of saplings, the vertical and horizontal poles generally lashed together with a supple fiber made from a common plant. When completed, the roof structure is lifted into place atop the walls of the rondavel. Lastly, the roof framework is fitted with bundles of dried grass for thatch. Dwellings assembled in this manner seem to last about 3 or 4 years. Toward the end of this time people complain that their roofs are leaking and that the sand in and around the huts is infested with biting insects. After prolonged discussion, people agree on a new village site, almost always located at the same water source. Together the people of the village undertake a new round of construction that may go on for several weeks. Despite these moves, the social composition of villages is for the most part constant, except for the changes brought by marriages and deaths. Most !Kung settlements have a ramshackle air about them, with a mixture of completed houses, half completed houses that have stood unfinished for some time, and simple grass huts identical to the ones !Kung used some years ago when they lived in the bush as foragers. These beehive-shaped, grass huts (sometimes called "scherms") are frankly preferred by many old people who claim they are cooler in the summer and easier to maintain than the "new style" Bantu rondavels. Other adults build grass huts as temporary housing in the new village location.

Another feature of most villages is the animal enclosures. These are circular corrals made of thorn brush piled 7 to 8 feet in height. Each evening men and boys herd the stock into these pens, closing them in until the next morning when the cows are milked, after which all stock are driven to the wells for watering. The precaution of enclosing stock is necessary because animals left out overnight are prey to attacks by predators such as lions, leopards, hyenas, and wild dogs.

Perhaps one third of the 30 or more villages that were visited during our fieldwork in 1987 to 1988 had active gardens. Gardens were located a few minutes' walk from the villages and, in all cases, because of the threat posed by domestic stock, had to be enclosed by thorn brush fences. Gardening is a laborious task in the Kalahari and also one of uncertain rewards, for the rainfall from one year to

Photo 1.2 !Kung Village With Mongongo Nut Harvest

10

the next is extremely unpredictable. At the time of the Project AGE study an 8-year drought had gripped this region of southern Africa, and many people who had been active gardeners in the past had become discouraged.

Demography

It is difficult to estimate population figures with any accuracy from the Botswana census because ethnic or tribal origins are not differentiated in their interview forms. However, on the basis of Draper's own demographic and census interviewing in the !Angwa and N!aun!au molapos, she estimated that there were approximately 750 !Kung living in the study area with another 500 people of Herero, Tswana, and Hambukushu tribal origins. People are vastly outnumbered by domestic stock in this part of the Kalahari (as elsewhere in Botswana), and there were approximately 8,000 domestic animals in the study area at the time of our work.

The !Kung population lacks the broad base common among Third World peoples owing to the low fertility rate that has long been characteristic in this population. The fertility rate has increased somewhat in the last 20 years of sedentary life, but not in a dramatic fashion. Children under 15 constitute about 39% of the total population, with people 60 years or older composing 14%.

Old People in !Kung Villages

Older people are visible at the same tasks and activities as other !Kung. Aside from the fact that they do less heavy physical labor, they are present in all other types of social and work activities. A consequence of the heterogeneous mixing of ages is that everyone is familiar with several old people, and everyone can see on a daily basis how particular old people deal with the physical losses that coincide with aging. When we asked !Kung people of all ages to think of a person who was having a difficult time in old age, people readily responded with names. This is because old age and, in particular, the physical debilities that occur with old age are universally seen as bad; old people by definition are having a hard time because they lack physical strength and vigor. Conversely, when !Kung were asked to think of or to name an old person who was doing well in old age, they responded less quickly. Many people answered this question with a flat "There is no person like this. There is no good in old age."

Among the !Kung, older people were by no means rare, and they were distributed rather uniformly among the different villages. There is no custom, such as is common in Western societies, for old people to band together with other people their own age for recreation and residence. The older people we observed lived with their kin, and their most frequent interactions were with people dissimilar to them in age. It is fair to say that no older person "lived alone" in any meaningful sense. Most adults, including older adults, were married except for the very aged, decrepit old. Among the !Kung, older men were somewhat more likely to be married than old women, but the sex discrepancy was not marked. Among men 60 years and over, 80% were married, and about 69% of women of the same age were married.

Of course there were some elders who were unmarried and technically "living alone" in a separate rondavel or grass hut. However, in these small, kin-based villages, their separate dwellings were placed only a few feet from the huts of various other kin, usually one or more adult children. Elders shared meals with their younger kin and at night often shared their blankets with grandchildren or young nieces and nephews. In sum, though unmarried old people among the !Kung were technically "living alone" (in a separate house), the house was a simple, one-room structure placed in very close proximity to the houses of their village coresidents, many of whom were relatives. During the day old people could directly observe and participate in the many different activities that went on in the village.

Economics and Scale

The !Angwa and N!aun!au molapos have administrative centers in villages named for the molapos. Here are located the clinic, a police station, the headman's office, and an elementary school that teaches the equivalent of grades 1 through 7. Another important draw for these centers is a one-room store selling soap, matches, tobacco, tea, sugar, ground cornmeal, and a small selection of canned food. Representatives of the central government make calls to these communities as they begin canvassing the entire region. For example, the veterinary officials and the agricultural development officer make rounds of the outlying hamlets but often call first at the regional centers, where they can be housed overnight at one of the government rest houses built for this purpose. Maun, the nearest town, offering several stores, an airport, garages for vehicle repair, and a fully staffed post office, is 210 miles to the east of the valleys where we worked. Travel over much of this distance is by sand track, and although the drive can be accomplished in 2 days, it is necessary to allow 3 because of the high likelihood of breakdowns. In the rainy season, deep puddles and water-sodden, black soil make travel by four-wheel drive a necessity; in the dry season the wet bogs are replaced by long tracts of deep sand that also isolate the area from all but specially equipped conveyances. For the more prosperous Herero and Tswana residents of the area, the ability to travel in and out of the bush is unpredictable, inconvenient, and tiring, but not impossible. Money, language skills, and contacts in distant towns are the things a rural person must have to plan travel outside the study area. Anyone who has the money sometimes can "hitch" a ride on a truck to more populous settlements to the east such as Nokaneng, Tsau, Sehitwa, and Maun. Similarly, if one wants to travel far from the study area, good knowledge of the Bantu languages is necessary to make arrangements with the owners of trucks or government-employed drivers of vehicles. These types of people are typically from the eastern part of Botswana and have no knowledge of the !Kung language. Once en route, a traveler needs to know people along the way or at the destination who will take the traveler in and provide food and shelter. !Kung lack the cash, the language ability, and the social contacts necessary to travel frequently and widely out of their immediate area. For example, of the over 100 !Kung interviewed in the Project AGE study, most had not been more than 20 miles from their home villages during the last year. Ironically enough, these !Kung, many of whom could remember earlier times when they were frequently on the move as hunter-gatherers, are not only sedentary but village-bound.

The !Kung have a long history of association with neighboring pastoral peoples, including the Herero and Tswana, although the pace of acculturation has accelerated markedly since the 1960s

when Botswana (formerly British Bechuanaland) became independent from Britain. The Botswana government did not bring
schools into the study area until the 1970s. From the beginning
Tswana and Herero children were well represented at the schools.
!Kung children, however, were slower to enter the classrooms and
to complete the elementary years during which basic skills of
reading, writing, and arithmetic were taught. !Kung adults, therefore, are neither literate nor numerate in the sense of being able to
write numerals or make arithmetic calculations with paper and
pencil. Some !Kung men have worked for local pastoralists for
years and have acquired good knowledge not only of the Tswana
or Herero language (often both) but also of the skills necessary for
successful gardening and stock raising. At the time of our study,
most young and middle-aged men and about half the women
understood the denominations of currency, known as *pula* ("rain"
in seTswana) in Botswana, and could make change accurately in
coins and in bills of small denominations. Old people were less
adept at making change in bills and coins and said they call on a
relative for help in doing this.

Kinship and Domestic Arrangements

The village is the center of social as well as economic life, and
!Kung spend much of their time in their own village or at the nearby
water hole. The rondavels, described above, are dark and small
enough (about 7 to 9 feet in diameter) that people spend most of
their waking hours when they are at home out of doors, sitting in
the sun; carrying out some task, such as beading leather, cleaning
a weapon, or cooking cornmeal; and conversing with neighbors or
visitors from other villages. Much of everyday life takes place in
public in full view of other villagers or passers-by.

The house structures, whether of mud stucco or grass thatch, are
used mainly for storage, and it is not customary for people to spend
long stretches of time actually inside their houses. Exceptions to
this rule are during the cold season, when people may sleep inside
their huts to shelter from a cold wind, or during rainy periods,
when the ground outside the houses is wet and people want to
avoid rainfall at night. In this way, although most marriages are
monogamous, and although most rondavels are associated with a

married couple and their dependent children, the nuclear family is not the private, self-contained entity familiar to people who live in Western societies. On an average day !Kung men, women, and children have regular contact with people of all ages, ranging from infants to elders in their 70s.

On a given day, if one were to drop in on a typical !Kung village one would see at a glance that perhaps one-third to one-half of the residents were at home. The people most likely to be at home in the middle of the day would be children, young adults, and old people, but some middle-aged men and women would be found there as well. As described above, villages are physically small and visually quite "open," with virtually no barriers to casual observation.

Values shared by !Kung are closely linked to the characteristics of their villages. Having enough to eat, being in good physical health, and maintaining good relations with kin are the values that !Kung described in response to many different types of questions. From their point of view, physical vigor is a prerequisite of full personhood. Children and old people are consequently seen as not quite "whole" persons because they have to depend on the bodily strength of others. However, when we paid close attention to what elderly !Kung said to us, it was clear that their version of independence had a cooperative aspect to it. Although they said that they were glad they could still "do their work," such as fetching water or gathering firewood, they could not do it if it weren't for the help from their younger relatives. Independence was valued in the sense of satisfaction in the physical ability to carry out familiar activities, but there was no implication of a corollary value placed on social or economic independence. !Kung elders had experienced interdependence in these senses throughout their lives, and although they vehemently expressed their regret at losing the physical aspect of independence, they did not perceive adjustment to social or economic reliance on others as problematic or even unusual.

Research Among !Kung

Both physical and sociocultural aspects of !Kung communities presented some special challenges for field research. Participant observation among !Kung required from our team major investments of energy and ingenuity to meet the needs of daily existence.

Because the ethnographers responsible for the !Kung and Herero research were working in the same geographic area, they set up a joint camp compound with five large tents for researchers, children, and assistants. Water was hauled in 50-gallon drums from !Angwa in the two Toyota Land Cruisers. Most food was purchased about once a month in Maun, although gifts of game from !Kung neighbors sometimes provided a supplement. Cooking was done over an open wood fire, which also heated water for bathing and washing clothes. The camp was surrounded by a thorn brush fence, and the pit latrine was beyond this fence, inside its own brush walls.

Soon after the team's arrival, a !Kung named ≠Oma !Oma who had worked for Harpending 20 years earlier appeared with the gleeful greeting, "My European has returned! Now I will live!" After many years in the army, ≠Oma !Oma had become a licensed driver and skilled mechanic who was a valuable aide-de-camp. He also helped with cooking, gathering firewood, and cleanup. Draper was assisted in her research by another !Kung named Kxau, who was very unusual in having had many years of schooling. He spoke and wrote English well and assisted with the construction of the !Kung interview guide, as well as carrying out interviews himself. The !Kung set up their own camp just outside the research compound.

Climate also exerted its effects on research. During the hottest season, the field team, like the !Kung, had to retreat to shelter and shade for several hours a day. In addition, there was a severe malaria epidemic during the research period. Because this was a strain of the disease resistant to the usual medication, Pat Draper was incapacitated with fever and chills for over a week. Eventually the district nurse at !Angwa gave our research team a quick course in diagnosing malaria and relied on them to distribute medication to more !Kung than he could possibly reach himself. Another medical emergency interrupted the research schedule when one of the children became so ill with tonsillitis that he had to be driven 350 miles to Windhoek (Namibia) for surgery.

From a social point of view, !Kung neighbors treated the AGE camp much like one of their own villages, assuming that activities there were open to the public. Visitors, including friends and relatives of the !Kung employees, came frequently and stayed long, sitting by the fire to chat and observe. The generous sociability characteristic of the !Kung participants in our work was in general a major advantage. However, it also presented some difficulties. For example, withdrawal to the tent for research "business," such as typing field notes, was often awkward. As Pat Draper said, the !Kung were always home when she came to visit with her interviews; how could she not be "at home" for them? The more subtle problem was that structured strategies for gathering information, such as interviews or card sorts, were stiff and awkward intrusions into !Kung-style communication, which is more spontaneous and uses more soliloquy. (!Kung responses to the sorting task will be discussed more completely in Chapter 6.)

One hundred and five !Kung, 54 men and 51 women, participated in the formal AGE interviews. Almost the entire adult (approximately 20 years and older) population in the !Kung villages was interviewed. Selection was routinely required only among younger persons, approximately 20 to 30 years old. In each village Draper first made a special effort to talk with the oldest people, then shifted to the middle-aged adults. In all but the largest village, which had 18 adults, she interviewed everyone over about 30 years old. Younger people were selected last because they were the most numerous. The principle for choosing among these was to "fill in" the overall sample for the village by favoring the sex and/or the households underrepresented so far. An additional 202 adults were also interviewed by Pat Draper during her fieldwork on the subject of their own and their parents' reproductive histories.

Herero, Botswana

Description

Herero live in Ngamiland, the northwestern corner of the Republic of Botswana in southern Africa. Their villages are interspersed with those of the !Kung in the western and northern parts of our study area and along the delta and throughout the desert. Herero also interact with Tswana, Yei, Mbukushi, and other Bantu-speaking groups. Ngamiland is famous for its beautiful topography, including both the swampy Okavango Delta and the dry northern Kalahari sandveld, its large herds of game, and the ethnic diversity of its inhabitants.

Although many people maintain houses in one or more of the larger towns of Ngamiland, most Herero live most of the time at rural homesteads where the family cattle herds are kept. Scattered along the fossil river valleys of western Ngamiland, these homesteads may consist of 2 to 20 round mud and thatch huts, a large *kraal* where homestead cattle are kept, and several smaller kraals for calves, goats, and other small stock. If the owner of the homestead maintains the holy fire of his family, it occupies a prominent hearth on the path between the hut of his senior wife and the gate of the cattle kraal.

The drab, grayish mud huts blend visually with Kalahari sand and the white earth of the termite mounds scattered everywhere. Enlivening this monochromatic landscape, Herero women move slowly around the homestead in brilliantly patterned Mother Hubbard dresses and elaborate, two-pointed turbans, also made of colorful cloth. Their long, flounced dresses are the most visible legacy of German missionaries who lived among the Herero in Southwest Africa in the 19th century.

Demography

Figure 1.1 shows the age and sex composition of the Herero population in 1988. The proportion of the population over age 60 is 14%. The shape of the age-sex pyramid of a population is determined mostly by the birthrate, and the high proportion of old people among Herero, as among !Kung, is a consequence of the relatively low fertility rate in both groups. A detailed examination of Herero age structure and demographic history (Harpending & Pennington, 1991) shows a recovery from infertility in the 1960s, a pattern shared with many central African peoples. The resulting shape of the Herero demographic pyramid is column-like except for the base, which is broadened by large numbers of children.

Old People in Herero Villages

Herero have a rich set of terms for people of various ages, and they know birth years because gregorian years are named by events

Photo 1.3 A Herero Family

19

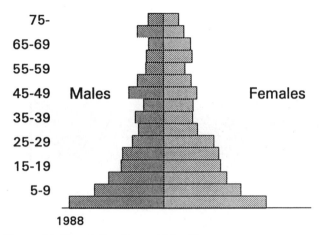

Figure 1.1. Population Pyramid for Herero

occurring in them, such as "year of the drought," "year of the eclipse," and "year of the man who asks questions." However, neither terms for life stages nor chronological ages have much function in daily life. Rural Herero society is a face-to-face society, and there is little or no reason to resort to age categories, or any other type of category, for describing people or groups of people.

Aging among Herero is regarded as a slow, inexorable process of physical decline, but the tempo of this process varies widely among individuals. One 70-year-old man we met was up at the crack of dawn every day and off to the well to supervise the watering of his cattle. Another was partially crippled, inactive, dependent on relatives and children to prepare his food, bring him tobacco, tea, and water, and help with his toilet. As people age, their activities gradually become more and more restricted, but there are no standard or stereotyped activities of the elderly. A person who retains health at age 70 does much the same thing every day as a 50-year-old.

Seniority is, however, a meaningful principle among Herero. Older people receive deference and respect. It is the senior wife of the senior man in the homestead who occupies the "great house," in front of which she maintains the sacred flame for the ancestors. Visitors to the village are taken to meet old persons, and village members themselves enjoy sitting with elders and listening to them

Photo 1.4 Watering the Cattle

21

reminisce about Herero life in the "old days." Care for older people is also a source of prestige and of pride. Whereas in North America one hears that someone is a "wonderful parent," among Herero one hears that someone "takes wonderful care of his uncle." When Herero told us their life stories, they provided extensive details about the care they had given to elderly members of their families, but often had to be prodded for similar information about their marriages and children. The Herero practice of fostering children into households other than the one they are born into is an important source of young helpers for the elderly. Herero feel that old people "ought" to be given children to care for them. A scene characteristic of Herero villages is of an old woman seated in her floral finery under a tree, surrounded by several children who scurry to obey her requests to feed the fire, push the churn, bring water, wash clothes, make tea, and do anything else she needs. Herero women do not make sharp distinctions among their children in terms of which they bore and which were fostered to them. This became clearer to us, for example, as we came to know well many of the people we interviewed. As we gradually learned about past histories of fostering, we realized that fostered children had been included without comment in the lists women provided in answer to our questions about their reproductive histories.

Economy and Scale

The Herero are known as a prosperous, although "traditional," ethnic group. They are self-consciously ethnic and endogamous while participating fully in the developing educational and economic systems of Botswana as a nation. Herero prosperity rests on their cattle and the market for beef, and in Botswana this market in turn depends on arrangements with the European Economic Community (EEC). On an economic dimension, therefore, the scale of Herero society is worldwide. Local communities, on the other hand, are remote and isolated, and there are few signs of modernity in either social or technological aspects of village life. Water is carried from wells 2 miles or more away. Cooking is done over open fires. Travel is on foot, or occasionally by donkey or horseback; there is no electricity to provide light or heat. Homesteads are located where there is grazing and water for herds, so, like ranches in the western United States, they are widely spaced. All Herero children attend school. Although there is always a school within 100 kilometers of the homestead, the distances are great enough and travel conditions rugged enough to require all children to board with relatives near the school during the week.

Kinship and Domestic Arrangements

Herero have both patrilineages and matrilineages—that is, they belong to one social group defined by descent from a common ancestor traced through males and to another social group defined by descent from a common ancestor traced through females. Social personhood is rooted in these kinship affiliations. The patrilineages are local, weak, and of mostly ceremonial significance. Many younger people were unsure of their patrilineage prohibitions on marriage partners, for instance, and had to check with older people about them before they could complete our interviews. Matrilineages, on the other hand, are well known to everyone and of great social significance. Members of the same matrilineage view each other as kin and treat each other differently than they treat nonrelatives.

Although Herero villages are theoretically patrilineal, they appear more like matrilineal groupings. A typical homestead includes an adult male owner with a wife or several wives in residence, plus his sisters and children of his wives and sisters. There is often tension in the homesteads of prosperous men between wives and their children on the one hand, and sisters and their children on the other. This skewing toward matrilineal villages occurs for several reasons. The divorce rate is high, and many women return to live with their parents and/or their brothers following a divorce or separation. Many women never marry but remain home instead and bear children for the patrilineage of their own father. Marriage appears to have economic and political importance for Herero, but it has little to do with patterns of reproduction. Marriage also seems to have little salience to Herero in personal terms. People were puzzled by the numerous questions about marriage in our interview and had trouble giving us information about dates or about spouses. Informants who readily told us the years of birth of all four of their grandparents, both their parents, and all their siblings had no idea in what year they married or divorced, and they had little knowledge of any kind about their spouses, either current or past.

Research With Herero

The Herero research team was headed by Henry Harpending. His American research assistant was Renee Pennington, then a graduate student in anthropology at Penn State University. Harpending spoke !Kung because of his previous fieldwork in the area, and many Herero speak !Kung. In the earlier stages of the fieldwork, interviews were done with the help of an interpreter so that both Herero and !Kung languages could be used. By the later stages of the fieldwork, Harpending and Pennington could also carry out an interview in OjitHerero. The Herero who worked at various times as research assistants to Harpending and Pennington were Timon, Hakegoshi, Prince, and Kavesana, all of whom lived in nearby Herero villages. Hakegoshi, whose mother was Tswana and father Herero, spoke SeTswana and !Kung along with Herero. Timon spoke some English and fluent !Kung as well as his native OjitHerero. The reason Timon was available to work for us is revealing of Herero values. He had worked with a team of archaeologists about 15 years earlier and through one of them had gotten a job at the National Museum in Gaborone. There he worked on his high school equivalency degree and received the promise of a government scholarship to an overseas university when the degree was finished. When Timon became engaged to a Tswana woman with a university education, his mother appeared in full Herero costume at the Museum office and demanded that he return to the country to marry the child bride she had chosen for him. He shortly thereafter did what she demanded.

The Herero team shared the !Angwa Valley camp with Pat Draper. There were approximately 400 Herero in the valley, so Harpending also visited Herero in other regions of northwestern Ngamiland. Renee Pennington also continued interviews with Herero near Sehitua, a large settlement at the southern end of the Okavango Delta. All the old Herero in the !Angwa Valley were interviewed, as well as every additional adult who could be located, for a total of 176. Our initial goal of enumerating a systematic census of Herero in the area, from which a sample could be drawn, was early revealed to be impossible because of the extreme mobility of Herero. Herero commonly make extended visits over great distances for social tasks such as funerals, marriage arrangements, or attending the ill. Close family members of someone deceased may stay at the site of a funeral for 6 months to a year. There are several adults listed as residents in our initial census of the region near our camp that we never saw again in a year and a half of fieldwork. Repeat visits to local homesteads regularly revealed new faces, people who were visiting or simply traveling through.

Everyone the team encountered was given a brief demographic interview and added to the database of people we knew about. This database grew to include nearly all the Herero living in western Ngamiland because, in the last few months of the study, the team rarely encountered anyone whom they did not already have listed in some way, for example, as the parent or offspring or sibling of someone else.

Note

1. Kilometers are the usual unit of distance in Botswana, as well as in Ireland. In this volume, kilometers are translated into miles at the ratio of 0.6 kilometers to 1.0 mile.

Photo 2.1 An Older Man of Clifden

2

Ireland

*I*n many ways Ireland is an ideal place to study the aging process and old age. Even though the elderly have for generations held positions of prominence within the rural community, this authority has been accompanied by tensions between generations that have been frequently portrayed in Irish literature, as well as in storytelling and song. However, at the same time, Ireland has the youngest population of the 12 EEC countries and is experiencing economic development that is dramatically transforming the country. In addition, research in Ireland as a culture area can be rooted in extensive ethnographic literature dating back to the 1930s, affording the opportunity to compare current conditions, such as the worth and control of agricultural land as a resource, domestic relationships, and household composition, to the situation in the past. Finally, the existence of a comprehensive national financing of medical care in Ireland provides an important contrast to the health care system in the United States and its impact on the lives of older people in the two north American communities.

Thus where better to search for answers to the major questions raised by Project AGE than Ireland, but where best to study? This question was partially answered by the nature of the major Project AGE variables: scale, geography, demographic characteristics, economics, and degree of integration with the state. Although the two Irish communities were to be of approximately equal size—no more than 2,000 inhabitants each—they were to contrast on the other variables: one was to be far, both in miles and in degree of integration, from Dublin, whereas the other was to be part of the Dublin urban fringe; one was to be experiencing emigration resulting in a high percentage of the community's population being made up of older people, whereas the other was to be undergoing population increase resulting in a relatively low percentage of elderly inhabitants; and one was to be enduring economic decline accompanied by high unemployment, whereas the other was to be undergoing economic growth and low unemployment.

A review of the census and economic reports of Ireland combined with his own research experience in Ireland led Tony Glascock to select 14 Irish communities as potential research sites. A visit to each of these communities during which brief interviews were conducted narrowed the list to two: Clifden, County Galway, nestled on the western Atlantic coast 180 miles from Dublin in the area known as Connemara, a community that has been losing population for decades because of limited economic opportunities; and Blessington, County Wicklow, on a direct bus route to central Dublin only 18 miles away, a community that has experienced in-migration of younger people because of economic growth and an attractive lakeside environment. The contrast between the two communities is evident in more ways than just cold, hard statistics. A walk through Clifden in the winter provides stark evidence of the impact of emigration brought about by limited economic opportunities—the streets, the shops, the pubs are all filled with older people, and everyone knows everyone else. By contrast, in-migration has increased the diversity of Blessington's population, especially in terms of social class, and has promoted the perception of social categories defined by length of residence. Not only are there noticeably fewer older people on the streets of Blessington than in Clifden, but in many ways Blessington does not appear to *be* a single community.

A major reason for selecting Clifden as one of the pair of Irish sites was its demographic pattern, characteristic in western Ireland, of a decline in total population and an increase in the proportion of the elderly. Blessington, the other Irish location, by contrast has experienced in-migration of younger residents, and a corresponding decrease in the elderly proportion of its population. Residents of both these Irish communities participate in the national health plan, which provided an important contrast to the financial organization of U.S. health care. Clifden also offered us the opportunity to observe the contemporary social circumstances of older people in an area that in earlier times was characterized in both dramatic and ethnographic literature as almost gerontocratic. In these descriptions of the past, 40-year-old men were referred to as "boys" unable to become fully adult until "da" allowed them to marry and become head of the household. When or if this marriage occurred, the West Room in the farmhouse was reserved for the elderly couple, who were entitled to live there and receive support from their son.

Rapid changes occurring in Ireland in the 25 years preceding our study can be at least roughly indicated by figures from the 1971 census. That enumeration reports that for the first time in the history of Ireland, more people lived in town areas than in rural areas. Blessington was included in our project to represent the kind of town area to which people were moving when they left isolated rural villages such as Clifden. Blessington has experienced population increase and has a relatively small proportion of older persons. Clifden has lost population, and the proportion of older persons is very large. Because of the immigration, Blessington is also more differentiated socially than Clifden.

In Blessington at the time of our research in 1987-1988, two of the most salient social categories were "local" and "blow-in." People who were born, raised, and settled in the Blessington area were called locals. They owned most of the shops and the land and tended to live along the main street of Blessington town in terraced (attached) houses or in the old-style houses outside of town. Most natives worked locally in shops, on farms, or as laborers. They had attended local schools and sent their children to school locally as well. Locals were 35% of our sampled population and 40% of the residents over age 65.

Blow-ins, by contrast, were born and raised outside of Blessington. They had typically been attracted to the area by the scenic beauty of the lakes and saw Blessington as a good place to settle and establish a family. Those viewed as classic examples of the blow-in category were people who had moved to Blessington in the 1970s and 1980s, built fancy bungalows around the lakes or along the Dublin road, and commuted daily to work in the city. Such classic blow-ins were 18% of our sampled population.

The polarization of locals and blow-ins in Blessington represents a pattern of differentiation appearing in many formerly rural Irish towns. It was articulated to us in various ways. Many locals, especially those over 65, said that Blessington was no longer a community at all. They said that blow-ins did not act like members of the community because they sent their children away to school and shopped outside the town. Newer arrivals, on the other hand, said that local people often did not support, and sometimes actively opposed, the efforts of blow-ins to introduce constructive new ideas, services, and organizational forms into Blessington.

Clifden, Ireland

Description

Clifden is located on the storm-swept and enigmatically beautiful western coast of County Galway. This area, known as Connemara, is dominated by the majestic Twelve Bens mountain range, dotted with clear, cold lakes and fringed by the rocky and deeply indented Atlantic coastline. The barren and desolate landscape varies between rocky outcrops, large expanses of bog, and small, stone-fenced fields. The area has figured prominently in both the political and artistic history of Ireland and has often been characterized as "the wild lands." It has known famine, emigration, and failed rebellions, and yet, perhaps because of this adversity, it was the birthplace of one of the great literary movements of the 20th century. William Butler Yeats, John Synge, and Liam O'Flaherty are among the best known of the writers who used the barren landscape of Connemara as a backdrop for their literary works. Their

Photo 2.2 Clifden, Ireland, With Twelve Bens

stories are peopled with the stubborn, independent-minded, and myth-laden inhabitants of this desolate land.

The town of Clifden sits perched above an inlet of Ardbear Bay, nestled between the ocean and the foothills of the Twelve Bens. The town is made up of two main streets with two- and three-storied connected terraced buildings that meet at the western end of town at "the square." The buildings are a mix of businesses and residences, with people living behind and above the main shops, pubs, and restaurants, as well as in purely residential structures. One-half dozen smaller streets, on which single-family residences are prevalent, radiate from this central town area. The skyline of Clifden is dominated by the town's two churches: the Catholic church at the eastern edge of the town, built in 1830, and the Protestant church further to the west, built 10 years earlier.

The town of Clifden is part of the Clifden District Electoral Division, which includes, in addition to the town, 29 townlands and stretches approximately 4 miles from north to south and 3 miles at its widest from east to west. Irish District Electoral Divisions are the smallest administrative area for which census population figures are published and are the units in which people register to vote. The Clifden DED was the research area for our study. The vast majority of the people living "outside" of town in one of the 29 townlands live in single-family dwellings that are built on the three main roads running east, north, and south of the town. The townlands range from the peninsula formed by Ardbear and Faul in the south to Doon—overlooking Streamstown Bay and almost devoid of population—in the north, from the now uninhabited islands of Inisturk and Turbot in the west to Shanakeever, which sits on the edge of an extensive peat bog in the east and extends into the foothills of the Twelve Bens. In between, one finds some of the most starkly beautiful country in all of Ireland.

Clifden, known as the unofficial capital of Connemara, is connected to Galway City, 50 miles to the east, by a single road and is 180 miles from Dublin, about as far away as one can get in Ireland from the seat of government, industry, and commerce. This isolation and the raw beauty of Clifden and Connemara are a magnet for tourists from the rest of Ireland, Europe, and North America during the 2 to 3 months of summer. However, during the winter the gale force winds from the Atlantic, when combined with rain and darkness, drive the tourists away, and Clifden becomes isolated from the rest of Ireland. It is during these winter months that Clifden turns in upon itself and the dark, foreboding, and often morose nature of the land and its people reemerges.

Demography

In 1988, the population of the Clifden DED (1,656) was divided almost equally between the inhabitants of the town (805 people) and the surrounding townlands (851 people). Figure 2.1 indicates the demographic profile of the DED and illustrates the impact of emigration on the area. Like much of the west of Ireland, Clifden since the famine of the late 1840s has had a long tradition of the emigration of young people to the United States, England, Australia, and, most recently, continental Europe. Prior to the famine, Connemara and Clifden were part of the "Congested Districts," the euphemistically named region of western Ireland into which the English transported the Irish after the Cromwellian conquest of the mid-17th century. This movement raised the population of the "West" and created the circumstances for the devastating effects of the famine and massive emigrations that followed. This emigration has resulted in a steady decline in the population of the Clifden DED; although fluctuating economic and political conditions in the area have caused peaks and valleys over the last two decades, the general trend has been down, and the DED has lost slightly over 15% of its total population between 1966 and 1985. This reduction in the total population of the DED has been accompanied by an increase in both the absolute number of the elderly and the proportion of elderly in the total population. In absolute terms the number of elderly within the DED increased from 198 in 1961 to 272 in 1988, and as a percentage of the total population the increase was from 12.2% in 1961 to 16.5% in 1988.

The population pyramid for Clifden depicts the specific impact of emigration on the community. The relatively large base is the result of the moderate fertility rate found in the west of Ireland combined with the bulge in the 30 to 44 age category, the main reproductive ages for women in the area. The small number of individuals between the ages of 20 and 29 reflects the out-migration of young people caused by the dismal economic conditions of the

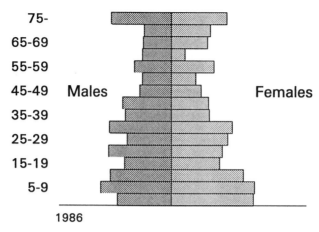

Figure 2.1. Population Pyramid for Clifden

country and the DED during the mid-1980s—19% unemployment nationwide during the research period in 1987 and 1988. The increase in the number of 30- to 44-year-olds in Clifden reflects three conditions: the better economic conditions in Ireland during the late 1960s and throughout the 1970s, which provided jobs for these individuals when they were otherwise most likely to emigrate; the growth of tourism in Clifden, which provided new jobs during the 1970s; and a certain amount of return migration of people who wanted to raise their families in Connemara. The noticeable decline in the number of individuals aged 45 to 59 can be explained by the fact that many of them reached the age of 20, the crucial age for emigration, during the late 1940s and early 1950s. This was a horrendous economic period in Ireland, and the country experienced the largest out-migration of young people since the famine. The large number of people over 65 was primarily the result of failed emigration of many members of this cohort during the worldwide depression of the 1930s and the return migration of a few older people coming "home" to retire.

This pattern of emigration resulted in over 16% of the 1,656 people living in the DED in 1987-1988 being over the age of 65. When children are excluded, over 25% of the adult population was 65 and older. Thus Clifden was a community of older people and children with an incredibly high dependency ratio of 0.98:1. A pattern of return migration is clearly indicated in the findings—just slightly less than 60% of the 130 people interviewed in the study had lived overseas for at least a year and had returned to Clifden for a variety of reasons. If internal migration is included, 70% of the respondents had moved away from Clifden for at least 1 year. In fact, because some of the individuals interviewed had moved to Clifden for business opportunities or marriage, only 20% of the respondents had lived all their lives in Clifden. A full 70% of respondents had had at least one sibling emigrate, and 75% had had at least one adult child leave Clifden.

Old People in Clifden

Almost everyone interviewed in Clifden agreed that for the purpose of obtaining the pension, old age was defined as 66. Once a person reached this age, he or she was entitled to either a contributory or a noncontributory pension, and depending upon financial status, the individual might also have been entitled to the medical card and associated benefits. However, defining old age in Clifden was not as straightforward as this consistency in response might appear to indicate. Although everyone agreed that 66 was an important age for the government, no one said that it was important for people living in Connemara. In fact, during the early stage of the research, when key individuals were being interviewed, the only people in Clifden described as being old were at least in their late 80s. Interestingly, these "old" individuals were never designated by their age—"you should speak to Pat, who is 95, or Mary, who is in her 90s"—but instead by some physical description associated with functionality—"you should speak to Pat, who cannot get around much anymore"; "you should speak to Mary, whose daughters cook her meals." It was only during the later stages of the research that it became evident that these individuals were all 88 or older.

These suggestions were the first clue that among the inhabitants of Clifden, age was not as important a factor for defining people as old as were functional capabilities and physical characteristics. This view was reinforced throughout the research period by the results of participant observation, the answers to questions in the formal interviews, and the life histories. When respondents were asked, "How do you know when a person is old?" over 85% of them gave an answer related to health, physical appearance, and/or functionality. No responses were given that pertained to retirement, children being raised, or having grandchildren. Only a handful of people answered that chronological age, dependency, loneliness, or any other state of mind defined a person as old. Well over 50% of the individuals responded that some form of functional decline was the main defining characteristic of old age—when a person had lost the ability to get around town, to be seen in the shops, or to take care of him or herself, he or she was old. These findings were reinforced by the conclusions derived by the analysis of the relationship between the answers to a series of questions concerning activities of daily living (ADLs) and the well-being of older people. Tasks requiring mobility and muscular effort—bringing in fuel, walking to town, carrying groceries, walking up and down stairs, riding a bicycle, doing laundry—were positively associated with the well-being of all people: that is, when people could bring in their own fuel, walk to town, and carry their own groceries, they considered themselves as "doing well." When they could no longer accomplish these tasks without help, they were worse off and considered old. Interestingly, declines in vision, hearing, or memory were not strongly associated with well-being. Declines in these characteristics did not, by themselves, define a person as old, and when they were a factor, they were always associated with one of the functional activities of daily living.

If a person had not experienced functional decline, there was little to outwardly distinguish an elderly individual from someone younger. Because few people in Clifden were employed in a conventional sense, retirement from work was not a marker for old age. Part-time work in the tourist industry, government assistance, or a bit of farming or fishing was the norm for people of all ages. Except for the day of the week to pick up the assistance funds from the post office, there was no real difference between receiving the dole and receiving the pension. In addition, almost no one in Clifden, either male or female, had a "career" through which to advance, and therefore career stages as indicators of age were completely lacking.

This lack of differentiation between old and young people was also present in dress and social activities. Men over the age of 30 tended to dress similarly. If they were working outdoors, an old dark-colored sport coat over a jumper (sweater), an old dress shirt, and, depending on the weather, several layers of shirts and vests (undershirts) topped by a cloth cap were the most common clothing. For church or an evening out, a newer sport coat with a newer shirt was worn, but the colors would still be dark, and eventually the "good" suit would be used for work. There was a bit more variation in the clothing worn by women. Younger women, especially those who had moved to the community from outside Connemara, often wore more "fashionable," more brightly colored dresses, but for the most part, women over the age of 40 wore dresses with floral patterns or of dark colors. Younger women also wore pants, whereas women over 40 almost always wore dresses or skirts.

Likewise, there were few places or social events in Clifden that were clearly age segregated. Older men could be seen habitually standing in twos or threes in the square, but younger men might join them for a talk. Older women were seen in shops more frequently than younger women, but most people who lived in town visited one or more of the shops each and every day. Even people living in the rural areas of the DED made regular trips to town to shop, converse, and socialize. Some of the pubs in town, especially in the summer because of the music played, were frequented by people in their 20s. Nevertheless, even in pubs filled with tourists and young people, one found middle-aged and older people who regarded the pub as their "local." The clientele of the pubs was based much more on geography, habit, and kinship ties than on some type of age distinction.

Economy and Scale

Connemara and Clifden were areas in which locally based economic opportunities were limited to small-scale farming, livestock raising, fishing, and small shopkeeping. Other income sources—tourism and welfare—depended on links to external systems. Land in Connemara was primarily rock, bog, or meadow. Thus farming was limited to the raising of vegetables and hay, with farms averaging less than 10 acres in size. Cattle, sheep, and Connemara ponies were raised in the area, but locally only a few individuals could survive on the income derived from livestock, let alone become rich. Livestock was much more important as an economic activity in communities to the north and east, although Clifden had served as a livestock market in the past. By the mid-1980s, the majority of the livestock trade had moved to other parts of County Galway, and local "fairs" were small, with comparatively few animals changing hands. Fishing, primarily lobstering, did provide work for some residents, but the number of people in the Clifden DED who could earn a living from it was small. A few salmon farms had been developed in the Connemara area, but their impact on Clifden was negligible.

The major economic activity in the area was tourism, and much local effort was focused on the 3-month tourist season. A wide range of businesses were dependent on both Irish and foreign tourists: pubs, restaurants, bed and breakfasts, small hotels, individuals who rented out houses, and a variety of shops selling sweaters, linen, and other "tourist" goods, few of which were produced locally. It is difficult to estimate the total number of individuals in the DED who were directly or indirectly dependent on tourism for their livelihood or the total amount of money that came into Clifden during the tourist season, but well over 50% of all individuals who worked earned a part of their income from tourism. The distribution of this tourist-derived income, though, was not even throughout the Clifden DED. The majority of tourist-related businesses were located in the town itself, and many of them were owned by people who had moved to Clifden from outside Connemara for the purpose of operating them. In general, older, locally born inhabitants did not gain income from tourism. In addition, the vagaries of local weather made tourism for everyone a risky endeavor, and the town experienced several disappointing seasons in the mid- and late 1980s.

The most dependable source of income, especially for older residents of Clifden, was derived from the Irish social welfare system. The extensive Irish social welfare system affected all people in Clifden in some way through one of four programs: (a) the dole, paid to all unemployed individuals in the community, approximately 35% of males between the ages of 18 and 65 during the research period; (b) the pension, paid to all eligible individuals over the age of 65 who did not have contributory pensions, approximately 94% of the individuals in the study area; (c) the medical card, primarily for older people, which provided free medical care and a variety of other services, such as free fuel, a free television license, and free prescription medication, approximately 95% of the older people in Clifden; and (d) a series of other social welfare payments, the most important being the child allowance paid to all children under the age of 18 regardless of the economic condition of the parents. The impact of this type of social welfare system on a community with limited economic opportunities was dramatic, and without such a system, emigration would have been even higher than it was.

Kinship and Domestic Arrangements

Contrary to the pattern of late marriage for the west of Ireland frequently described in earlier research and literature, people in Clifden tended to marry while in their 20s. The majority of both males and females married local people; if an area comprising the Clifden Parish, which is about three times larger than the DED, is considered, over 70% of the people interviewed obtained their spouses from the area. Emigration had had an impact on marriage in general: There were older people in the DED who stated that they had never married because there just had not been any eligible spouses around, and an often-expressed concern among females in their 20s was that there was a shortage of males caused by emigration. One characteristic of the study area that was caused partially by emigration and partially by the poverty of the area was the large number of older people who never married. It was common in the Clifden DED to find two never-married brothers living in the same house, or a never-married brother and sister living together. A relatively large number of these never-married individuals lived alone, and when they are combined with the older widows and widowers in the area, the result is that over 16% of people over the age of 65 lived completely alone. However, the average household size, both within Clifden and in the more rural townlands, was approximately three and one-half people.

Research in Clifden

The Clifden research team consisted of Dr. Anthony P. Glascock, Principal Investigator, and Sheila Graham, Research Assistant. Ms. Graham, a graduate in anthropology from St. Patrick's College, Maynooth, lived in a flat on one of the main streets of the town of Clifden for the full 15 months, June 1987 through August 1988, of the research. Dr. Glascock rented a house for him and his family in Derrygimlagh, approximately 3 miles south of the town, and spent 12 months in the area. The research was divided into four main segments. An initial period of slightly more than 3 months was spent discussing the research project with key individuals in the community, Connemara, and Galway City, deciding on the appropriate research area, mapping the community, and gaining familiarity with the entire area of western Connemara through a wide-ranging participant observation. The second stage, lasting approximately 2 months, consisted of developing the formal interview schedule and card sort, pretesting the instruments, and selecting the samples of adults and older individuals to be interviewed. The pretest was conducted in areas adjacent to the north and south of the Clifden DED and resulted in some significant modification in the instruments. The third period of 9 months consisted of interviewing the selected respondents, completing business and voluntary organization surveys, undertaking extensive participant observation in specialized settings, and selecting individuals for life history interviews. During the fourth period of approximately 1 month, life histories were conducted, and the team carried out exit interviews in Clifden, western Connemara, and Galway. Throughout the 15 months of research, participant observation was used, as anthropologists have used it in many small communities, to ascertain the type of interaction of individuals and groups within a large number of settings and locations.

Our initial objective, consistent with the activities in other project sites, was to interview 200 individuals within the Clifden DED and to employ two samples: a representative sample of 150 individuals consisting of adults 19 years and older and a focused sample of 50 individuals that included only individuals 65 years of age and older. The representative sample was drawn from the electoral list of the Clifden DED. The electoral list was compiled and updated, because of a national election in 1987, by a local individual and was therefore extremely accurate even though the community was experiencing a large amount of emigration. The focused sample of older individuals was drawn from the medical card list, which, it was estimated, included at least 95% of the elderly in the Clifden DED. Individuals were selected for interviewing through the use of a table of random numbers. Two caveats were employed in creating both of the samples. First, if two or more individuals from the same household were selected, only the first individual designated was included in the sample. Second, only two individuals living in each of the two religious communities were included in the sample, and any additional members designated by the table of random numbers were eliminated.

After approximately 100 individuals had been interviewed, it became apparent that it would be impossible to reach the goal of 200 respondents, not because of a reluctance of the residents of Clifden to be interviewed, as the total refusal rate was less than 4%, but because of the nature of the community itself. Although the residents of Clifden were friendly, hospitable, and open, conducting extensive and lengthy interviews in such a close-knit community had its challenges. Privacy in a community in which everyone knows almost everything about everyone else made confidentiality a continuing problem. Our team learned firsthand about the effectiveness of communication in Clifden when one researcher, suffering from a headache, purchased aspirin at 11 p.m. one night. At 9 a.m. the next morning a Clifden resident whom the researcher had not seen for 2 days greeted him with the query, "And how's your headache this morning?" The problems of confidentiality posed by this village-wide lack of privacy became especially apparent when more than one member of a large extended family was interviewed or when individuals from adjacent houses were included in the sample. Because of the vagaries of random sampling, it was not uncommon for people from every house on a small road in one of the rural townlands to be selected for interviewing. Thus after 7 months of interviewing it was clear to us that our research was becoming intrusive on the community, and the interviews were concluded after 130 individuals—94 from the representative sample and 36 from the focused sample. Because respondents from roughly one of every three households in the DED had been interviewed at this stage, there was no indication that this decision in any way jeopardized the reliability of the samples or the ability to generalize from the samples to the inhabitants of the DED.

In addition to privacy, several other features of Clifden and its inhabitants presented challenges. Unlike the stereotypical characterization of Irish Americans as loud, boisterous, and perennially happy, the residents of Clifden were quiet, private, and even taciturn. It was typical for respondents to be friendly and helpful, but not expansive in their answers to questions. Seldom did respondents anticipate questions or add to basic answers. Probing to explore interesting or important aspects of answers during the interviews, a well-respected and useful technique in the United States, made respondents in Clifden nervous and uneasy because follow-up questions were often seen as challenges to their original answer.

People in Clifden were also reluctant to generalize about groups of people, speculate about the future, or respond to questions concerning emotions and feelings. Most individuals responded to questions concerning groups of people by saying, "How would I know what these people do, each one is different." This is perhaps understandable given the face-to-face nature of Clifden, where everyone knows everyone and relationships go back generations. More important for our interests, age itself did not appear to be a salient factor in the respondents' view of themselves and their relatives, neighbors, and friends. Questions that asked people, "How will your life be in 5 years?" were largely ineffectual, as were questions that asked people, "How do you feel about being this age?" The most awkward and least effective questions were those that asked people to speculate about the feeling of groups of people—for example, "How do you think people of this age feel about . . . ?" Finally, at this site, unlike the other research sites, it was impossible to ask people to speak about individuals in the community. The surest way to end research in a small community in Ireland is to begin to discuss specific people, and thus questions that asked respondents to name older people who were doing well or poorly and to discuss the reasons why, for example, were not asked in Clifden. It was appropriate to ask about a person's parents, but certainly not about neighbors, friends, or people living in the community. There are sound historical and cultural reasons for this reluctance on the part of the Irish to discuss other people with an

Photo 2.3 The Lakes, Blessington

outsider, and they relate to why one never refers to someone in Ireland as an "informant"—it is just too close to "informer" for comfort. In Clifden, consequently, the research team relied more on participant observation and "guided conversation" than on the formal interviews for information about these culturally sensitive topics.

Blessington, Ireland

Description

In 300 years Blessington has evolved from an estate settlement into a heterogeneous rural town. Very little is known about the early history of the Blessington area. In the 13th century Blessington was included as church land in the parish of Burgage. The area was just outside the final boundaries set for the Pale established in 1494, and local mythology includes accounts of guerrilla-style attacks by the native Irish against the English settlers. Later in the 1600s the parish was divided, and what is now Blessington was granted to Archbishop Boyle.

The contemporary town of Blessington is located 18 miles south of Dublin in the Baltinglass Rural District of County Wicklow. There is bus service to Dublin (45 minutes) and to Naas (20 minutes) in County Kildare. The dominant physical features of the area are the vast desolate uplands, the deciduous woodlands, the Pollaphuca Reservoir, the gently rolling hills, and fertile lowland farms. The Wicklow Mountains, bordering Blessington to the east, are a vast wilderness of bog and rock, the most extensive uplands in Ireland. Many area residents have inherited rights to boglands from which they harvest peat to burn for additional heat in the winters when gale force winds and horizontal rain buffet Blessington.

The Pollaphuca Reservoir is referred to locally as the "Blessington Lakes." The 6 square miles of reservoir were created in 1943 and represent the largest manmade lake in the country. The reservoir is a source of water and electric power and also a recreational area that attracts tourists, for instance, to the annual 3-day regatta.

Early interviews with Catholic priests, the minister for the Church of Ireland, various *garda* (policemen), the Local Councilor, and other officials suggested to the research team that the boundaries of Blessington as locally perceived did not coincide with the administrative unit (DED) of that name. Further interviews with other residents with diverse perspectives elicited a consensus that our study area should include the town of Blessington, with 1,322 residents, as well as an additional 618 persons residing in surrounding administrative districts in County Wicklow and County Kildare. The total population on which our Blessington research focused was 1,930.

Demography

Between 1870 and 1929 Blessington remained a small market village whose population increased only gradually. Many workers migrated to the area during the construction of the reservoir in the 1930s and 1940s. Some of these workers, as well as others employed at the newly created Roadstone Quarry, remained permanently when two tracts of low-income housing were opened. Development of the lakes promoted new employment and recreational opportunities that contributed to sustained population growth that peaked in an increase of 45% between 1971 and 1979. Greatest growth occurred in the age categories under 40 years old, and the resulting broad-based population pyramid is shown in Figure 2.2. Development reached a plateau in Blessington in the early 1980s, and an overall decline in local employment opportunities is reflected in the population between the ages of 20 and 40. The loss of population through emigration is greater among young women than young men, a pattern characteristic of the Republic as a whole.

Old People in Blessington

Older persons were 7% of the population of the Blessington DED, 6% of the population of Blessington town, and 10% of our study area that was locally referred to as Blessington. Over half of the older residents were widowed—68% of the women and 38% of the men; 35% of the older residents were married.

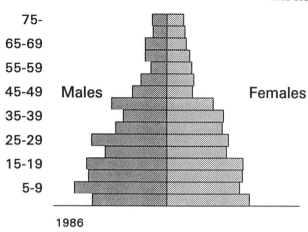

Figure 2.2. Population Pyramid for Blessington

Perhaps because of their small numbers, older people were not highly visible in the Blessington community. Only occasionally did we see an older person going to the shops or walking to or from one of the two churches. There were no age-homogeneous organizations for older people, although older women did predominate in two officially mixed-age groups, the Irish Countrywomen's Association and the Mother's Union (women's group within the Church of Ireland Protestant).

Older residents we talked with commonly described Blessington as a "quiet, caring community." Most of the elderly (55%) in Blessington had daily contact with local relatives. Children were the main source of support for all elderly, helping, for example, with grocery shopping and transportation to the doctor and to church. Older people received this kind of support whether they shared a household with children or lived alone. Informal and formal organizations in the Blessington community further expanded sources of support to elderly residents.

Most older people gave high praise to the Blessington Area Senior Citizens Committee. The group was started in the 1960s by two members of the Irish Countrywomen's Association who volunteered to prepare a Christmas dinner at the Catholic Community Center. At the time of our study there were 12 members of the committee, each of whom monitored the welfare of old persons in

Photo 2.4 Portrait of a Blessington Woman

his or her area. (Committee members also tended to be caregivers within their own families.) The group sponsored both a Christmas party and a summer outing and also organized and partially subsidized a local chiropody clinic. Members also visited local residents who were in the nearest nursing home. Bimonthly trips to the adult day care facility in a nearby town were also arranged by the committee. Money for all these activities came from a small government grant and from local money-making activities, such as home auctions.

Economy and Scale

Blessington is more integrated into urban and national economic systems than Clifden because of its proximity to Dublin, where some Blessington residents find employment, education, and amenities. At the time of our research Blessington provided a healthy economic climate for its residents. Only 7.3% of those between the ages of 15 and 65 were unemployed. The main tree-lined street of Blessington was home to about 35 businesses, including pubs, banks, petrol stations, fast food shops, and the Downshire Hotel. Additional businesses, including an industrial estate with seven small-scale industries, a snooker hall, and six bed and breakfast establishments, were located outside of town along the roads to Dublin and to Baltinglass. Most of the businesses were owned and operated by families.

Though there has been a decline in agricultural involvement since the 1960s, about 15% of the Blessington population was involved in agriculture when we were there. The average agricultural holding was 50 to 60 statute acres. Sheep were tended in the hill areas on smaller properties, and dairy cattle were kept on larger lowland farms. Many of these larger farms had been handed down through generations of Protestant families. Thirty-six percent of the Blessington population commuted to work in Dublin as professionals, managers, salaried employees, and intermediate nonmanual workers.

Kinship and Domestic Arrangements

Most people in Blessington lived in nuclear family households. The second most common type of domestic arrangement was living alone, and the next most frequent was living as a couple. Most of the older people who did not live alone were blow-ins. Thirty-nine percent of them lived with their spouse, 19% lived in a nuclear family, 15% lived in extended families, and 12% lived with siblings. Local old people were more likely to live alone than blow-ins, but of the locals who did live with others, a larger proportion (80%) lived as part of nuclear or extended families than was true for blow-ins.

Family life was a central value for people in Blessington. Although friendships among men were important, most people preferred to socialize with family members. The primary significance of family was communicated to us in many ways. In the section of our interview that asked about perceptions of the life course, family stage was a key criterion in people's differentiation of life stages. In addition, the majority of people in Blessington told us that they were involved in giving some type of care to a family member. One of the losses that locals described to us with most regret was of feelings shared in earlier times that the entire community functioned as an extended family whose members looked out for and depended on one another.

Research in Blessington

The research team in Blessington was led by Jeanette Dickerson-Putman, who was joined by John Ryan, a recent graduate of Maynooth College when our project began. Dickerson-Putman and her husband rented a two-room apartment from a local couple who lived in the modern house to which the rental was attached. John Ryan rented a room in a home on the edge of town.

As is true for all ethnographic research, the team needed to spend time becoming "visible" in the community before beginning any direct questioning. They established social relations within various segments of Blessington by shopping at local businesses and by joining various organizations. Interesting challenges were posed by the heterogeneity of the community. It was important to select shops, organizations, and clubs that tapped the needs and interests of *all* the categories of people in Blessington. Before it was possible to make those choices, it was necessary to confer with a wide range of key individuals to discover what the relevant social categories were.

The team was also introduced to Blessington in more formal ways. Both researchers visited community leaders to present the project, answer their questions, and ask for their cooperation. Articles explaining the research were placed in various local and regional newspapers. Copies of these articles were then enclosed in the introductory letter sent to each person drawn into the random sample. This sample of 170 adults (18 and over) was drawn from the electoral lists. The team spent the first months working with individuals from different informal and formal groups to develop a "map" of the boundaries of Blessington as well as of the social differentiation within it. The next efforts were to create the set of hypothetical individual descriptions to be used in the sorting task and to pretest these and the interview. The middle stage of the research accomplished the interviews and the participation and observation in community organizations. As an Irish person, John Ryan felt less comfortable as a participant observer than Dickerson-Putman, whose American identity made her researcher role more apparent and appropriate. They resolved this by dividing their responsibilities so that Ryan did a greater number of formal interviews and Dickerson-Putman carried out more of the participant observation. In the final months of the study, both researchers concentrated on collecting life stories, which was an activity that fit smoothly into the Irish storytelling mode and gave mutual pleasure to participants and researchers.

Photo 3.1 Winner of the Momence Sesquicentennial Baking Contest

3

United States

*F*rom the very beginning of our discussions about a cross-cultural comparative study of aging, it was clear that at least two of the sites should be in the United States. In the first place, the researchers were American, and the National Institute on Aging was paying the bill. Theoretically it was important to include in our comparisons American cultural values as well as the unique American system for financing health care and income payments to the elderly. The problem was, of course, which of the thousands of possible American communities were to be selected. The two communities to be chosen had to provide, within the American context, a contrast in scale, social class, economic base, and stability, while at the same time being small enough to be studied from an anthropological perspective. Finally, the axiom that all researchers included in Project AGE should be familiar with their study communities had to be respected. The communities we selected were Momence, Illinois, and Swarthmore, Pennsylvania. In addition to meeting the other criteria, these towns were home to two of our research team; Chris Fry lived in Momence and Jennie Keith in Swarthmore. Momence, located on the Kankakee River to the south of Chicago, represents the small farming/manufacturing community so common throughout the Midwest. The town's nickname "The Old Border Town" emphasizes the permanence that characterizes the community and highlights the residential stability of its inhabitants. Its population is predominately blue-collar, and important roles, whether for the Gladiolus Festival or in various other committees and associations in the town, are filled by older residents who gain status, positions of prominence, and authority because of their age and length of residence in Momence. In addition, Momence was of a size that allowed the use of the desired research techniques.

In contrast, for the Philadelphia suburb of Swarthmore, residential stability was lower, and the residents were mainly upper-middle-class professionals. Many older Swarthmoreans reached a point in their lives where they had to decide between staying in town and leaving to enter a retirement community or to be nearer to children. However, Swarthmore was also characterized by the movement of older people into the community because some elderly individuals moved into Swarthmore to be near a younger relative. For these people, developing a new basis of personhood was a challenging task that was often accomplished most successfully in groups of age peers. Jennie Keith, like Chris Fry, had the advantage of over 10 years of residence in her "field site," and the community was of the desired size.

Momence was selected as a site in the AGE project primarily because it is a small, stable, and blue-collar town that contrasts sharply with the upper-middle-class and suburban nature of Swarthmore. We expected that residential stability in Momence would be beneficial for the social integration, care, and possibly even prestige of older persons. We were also curious about what differences in the lives of old people might correspond to the social class difference between the two communities, especially as these might be channeled through access to resources and choices regarding work.

Residents of Momence are by no means wealthy, and a significant number are working poor, as is evidenced by the use of food stamps in the local food markets. Minimum wage jobs and second jobs and households with both spouses working are the norm. At the time we interviewed people in the community, unemployment in the county was officially estimated as high as 19%, with unofficial estimates running as high as 25%. Although Momence is a community in which aspirations for the American Dream run high, at the time of our study financial constraints (per capita income was around $10,000 in 1980) forced people to make painful compromises.

Momence is also a relatively stable community in terms of population dynamics. Since the Second World War, population has steadily increased, but at a modest rate of around 200 residents per decade. Prior to our research we knew that younger people were leaving the community in search of education and jobs, but that there was a core of kin who remained in the community. The 1980 census indicated that Momence had a population shift of about 16% per decade.

Swarthmore was included as a site in the AGE project partly because it is a suburb. In the earliest days of fieldwork this definition was challenged with considerable vehemence by residents who preferred to define Swarthmore not as a suburb but as a small town. Throughout our research, we continued to discover contradictions coiled within the definitions of this community. Many of these contradictions we learned to see through the eyes of older persons who could no longer ignore inconsistencies between the small town it seemed to be and what, as a suburb, it could actually provide.

Residents of Swarthmore were upper-middle-class Americans who in their own terms were "comfortable" although not wealthy. They had successfully followed many American norms and successfully achieved many American values. We believed that understanding the good and bad aspects of being old for such people would offer especially clear insights into the ways American culture shapes experiences of later life. Put another way, we anticipated that people who had striven for and achieved what American culture defines as good could help us understand whether maximizing American values earlier in life also pays off in a good old age. The other, more disconcerting, possibility was that the techniques producing maximal "cultural fitness" in earlier years might lead to undesirable side effects in later life.

As a community, Swarthmore also offered an interesting mix of features that we expected to promote well-being for older persons and features that we expected to constrain it. Its high position in social scale and high level of residential mobility, for example, had been associated in the research literature with lower status and less informal social support for the elderly. Nuclear family households and widely scattered kin, typical of most older persons in Swarthmore, are also assumed to limit status and availability of care. The core American values of independence and achievement, also proposed in the AGE model as problematic for older persons, are both realized and celebrated in this community.

On the other hand, there are characteristics of Swarthmore that we expected to contribute positively to the well-being of its older residents. For example, quality and availability of health care in the area are high. The sophistication of technology available to middle-class Americans also facilitates many domains of life for the physically frail, including transportation, communication, and home maintenance. Census data also showed high per capita income and high levels of home ownership in Swarthmore, suggesting that older individuals there controlled substantial economic resources. Finally, the large percentage of older people in the Swarthmore population offered the possibility of old-age peer groups that in other residential settings have been shown to promote socialization as well as new bases of personal identity and reciprocal support.

Momence, Illinois

Description

The phrases most commonly used to describe Momence are "Cosmopolitan Small Town" and "Old Border Town." Unlike many small towns in the Midwest, it is more than a community of retired farmers. Agribusiness is certainly a major component of the local economy, and the fields surrounding Momence are in the core of the world's largest corn- and soybean-producing area. However, in addition Momence has for many decades also participated in wider networks of trade and manufacturing. Momence has always been

Photo 3.2 Downtown Momence, Looking up the Dixie Highway

57

near major transportation routes that attracted industry and commerce. At first it was the Kankakee River and the ledges that permitted easy crossing in the absence of a bridge. The Vincennes Trail blazed by Gurdon Hubbard connected Fort Dearborn (Chicago) with Fort Vincennes on the Wabash River in Southern Indiana. Early settlers were attracted by trade as well as by opportunities for homesteading the prairie wilderness. Later the railroads came (three passed through Momence) and then the Dixie Highway (Illinois, Route 1), which was the first hard road. By the 1960s two interstate highways were constructed within 15 miles of Momence: Interstate 57 to the west and Interstate 65 to the east in Indiana. Momence has benefited from its location on these increasingly efficient trade routes through both light manufacturing and provision of redistribution services.

Since its origin over 150 years ago, Momence residents have viewed it as a cultural center of Kankakee County. As a community forged out of the wilderness, Momence was visualized as being on the border between civilization and outlaws. The early days were rough and tumble. To the east was the Grand Marsh of the Kankakee, which provided hideouts for horse thieves or other undesirables. As recently as the 1930s Chicago mobsters were known to have hideaways in the marshes south of Momence before these areas were drained for agricultural land.

Momence is no longer a cultural outpost, yet it has maintained a sense of identity. Settlement is nucleated into a political entity bridging the Kankakee River and bounded by two railroads on the east and north. Just to the north of the river is the downtown area clustered around the intersection of the Dixie Highway and Washington Street. Surrounding this hub is a grid of over 100 city blocks. Beyond the city itself, settlement is dispersed into cottages along the river, subdivisions, and farms. The boundaries here—less visible, but nevertheless well known—embrace all of Momence Township and the eastern half of Ganeer Township, a 72-square-mile area. The borders do not neatly correspond to postal zip codes, telephone exchanges, school districts, or even the 36 square miles of the township plat maps. Yet the boundaries are quite sharp. To the east lie the former marshland and the state of Indiana, which maintains a different environmental policy on management of the river. Differences over this border escalated in 1917, when the men of Momence were mobilized into a militia to prevent Indiana from dredging the river to the Momence ledges. To the south is the African American town of Pembroke. To the west is Kankakee, where a border was sharpened in an election over the location of the county seat, which, according to Momence accounts, Kankakee won through fraud. Finally, to the north is the "up north" of Chicago with its opportunities and also its dangers of crime and expressway driving.

Regardless of which of the three entry ways to town one uses, there is a welcoming sign, erected during the Sesquicentennial, to "Momence, An Old Border Town, 1834." Immediately one is impressed with the tree-lined streets in contrast with the cleared farmland. Situated on the floodplain of the Kankakee, Momence is flat. To find the nearest hill, one must travel 6 miles to the north to "Six Mile Ridge," which is the first terrace of the river. The town was platted into equal-sized blocks in the 1850s and subsequently developed by individuals constructing their houses until the blocks were fully occupied. Public buildings within the town consist of the predominantly two-story commercial architecture in the center, three school complexes on the western edge of town (elementary, junior high, and high school plus two parochial elementary schools), a city hall and fire station, and a public library. Along the Dixie Highway a "strip" of commercial establishments are scattered along the six blocks zoned as commercial. Also dispersed throughout the town are a dozen churches. On the island separating the north and south channel of the Kankakee is a large park with picnic facilities, band shells, and recreational equipment.

Small towns have traditionally been a haven for older people, and Momence is no exception. To the first-time visitor, the impression is of a safe place to live and to raise children—broad streets lined with tall trees, sidewalks, and spacious lawns. A closer look reveals people of all ages in the streets, especially in the downtown area. Children can be seen walking to and from school in the early morning and mid-afternoon, along with parents driving students to and from the three school complexes. Young people forage for fast food at the local grocery stores and three drive-ins around lunchtime. Older adults take over the daytime restaurants at breakfast and lunch. Owners and waitresses know their patrons' preferences and events happening in their lives. In the evening teenagers "cruise" the Dixie Highway to the Island Park, and on summer evenings they can be found in groups in the downtown area. Older people are not generally residentially separated from the young, although some blocks are recognized as older blocks occupied primarily by widows or older couples. In addition, at the edge of one of the larger subdivisions are four small federally subsidized apartment buildings (four units in each) that are occupied by older adults.

Momence is an intact community. Although the social field is over 3,000 and ranges upward of 7,000 when one considers the surrounding area, the major players, both male and female, are well known to the majority. Social networks of kin, friends, and neighbors are tight knit. The dozen churches, the schools, the voluntary associations, and, above all, the Gladiolus Festival integrate the community beyond the household level. In the year following our research in Momence, a summer-long Sesquicentennial celebration was held that intensified identification with historical roots and identity. Annually in early August a 3-day harvest/fertility festival is held to celebrate the gladiolus growers to the south of town. Preparations for and enactment of this festival stimulate reactions to the town's identity, both positive and negative.

Old People in Momence

One of our key informants volunteered that when he returned from an expedition to Kankakee, he noted there were a lot of old people on the streets in Momence. Old people were also easily visible to us—in the downtown restaurants and shopping areas and also either walking on the residential blocks or working in their yards. Some groups in Momence were clearly age graded, such as the subunits of church organization, which promote age homogeneity. Other formal groups were officially age heterogeneous, but most of their members were decidedly older. A principle of seniority was observable in the community. With longer-term membership and participation made possible by stable residence, the leaders tended to be older, and the past leaders were also included in decision making. Unlike most bureaucratic structures, which promote turnover in personnel, Momence organizations favored long-term occupation of offices (sometimes over 25 years). The limits were the willingness of the occupant and his or her continued competence.

Observation of the daily rhythm of life in Momence showed us how older people used the town as their arena. Most restaurants opened around 5 a.m., and one remained open for 24 hours. Following the initial rush of tradesmen and delivery men for coffee and breakfast, the school bus drivers took over. After the bus drivers (all women) left, the older people made their appearance, clustered in different restaurants by commonalities such as occupation. At the restaurant favored by farmers, for example, older people arrived shortly after the sun was up. Once the stores opened, there was usually a lull, and then five men, all in their mid- to late 80s, came in for coffee and conversation. The noontime crowd was more age heterogeneous, but many tables were occupied by older people who were regulars partaking of what appeared to be their main meal of the day. The "farmer" restaurant, unlike most others in Momence, was open 24 hours.

Older people in Momence were visible and active. In describing a person who is doing well in old age, over 25% of our sample used the word *active*, which meant a combination of visibility and physically able. We wondered about those older people who were no longer able to be active and engaged. Would they become invisible? Would they leave the community? As we learned more about the town, we discovered that frailer old people did not disappear. They retained their presence in the community in a less direct way. Because older people were embedded in diverse networks of kin, neighbors, church, and services, they were regarded as community members even if they were not visibly present. Their situations were closely monitored through inquiries made to people who were in contact with the frail old person. Passings out of the community into nursing homes and hospitals were tracked. When an older person finally did leave the community, through death or entrance to a nursing home, the transition was marked by a traditional Midwestern event—the auction. Seldom was this conducted in the impersonal surroundings of the sale barn. Instead, the material artifacts of a lifetime were displayed in the front and back yard of the person's former home. Neighbors, peers, kin, and strangers bid for the treasures, which were dispersed through the community as the departed individual's social identity was disassembled.

Demography

At the time of our study there were 3,294 people living in the city of Momence and an estimated 3,000 to 4,000 people living in the 72 square miles surrounding the town. Population has been relatively stable over many decades. Census reports of this stability were confirmed by our own review of phone number listings for the Momence exchange. We found that over a 5-year period two thirds of the phone numbers remained with the same people at the same address. In our sample of 210 people, over one-third reported being born in Momence. The average percentage of life lived in Momence was close to 66%. As the pyramid in Figure 3.1 shows, the Momence population is aging. In 1980, 22% of the population was over the age of 60, and 17% were over the age of 65. The majority of the over-60 population was married (53%), and 38% were widowed. Most of these older people lived as couples or alone.

The educational level of Momence residents at the time of our study reflected the blue-collar nature of the community. Seventy percent of our sample had a high school education or less. On the Treiman Prestige scale (Treiman, 1977), 75% ranked under 50 on the 100-point scale, and no one exceeded 71. The nature of stratification in Momence was localized. There was a local elite consisting of professionals (lawyers, educators) and merchants as well as the descendants of the pioneer families who arrived in Momence as middle-class people with resources to invest in land. However, with increased integration into the regional and national economy, the local definitions were declining in importance.

Economy and Scale

Momence's incorporation into regional and national economies increased markedly following World War II. The agricultural sector of the town's economy persisted, but with a shift in the direction of agribusiness. As mechanization and the use of chemical fertiliz-

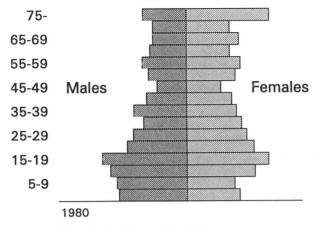

75-
65-69
55-59
45-49   **Males**   **Females**
35-39
25-29
15-19
5-9

1980

Figure 3.1. Population Pyramid for Momence

ers increased, the number of individuals engaged in farming decreased. Factories and food production enterprises had been present
in Momence for many years. The Momence Ice House harvested
ice from the Kankakee. The brick factory produced glazed bricks
used for construction in Chicago, and a textile mill made basketball
nets sold within the region. However, after the war, ownership of
Momence factories was less often local, and a greater proportion of
their products was distributed on a national basis. Both the local
dairy and the local bakery closed, and national products replaced
the local brands. Several corporations in other states opened branch
factories in Momence to make household chemicals, plastics, and
medications.

By the time of our research in the early 1980s, Momence was
suffering from the recession. Several of the remaining local businesses closed, and the downtown area had noticeable empty spots.
Younger people were more likely to leave Momence in search of
work, although most of them still eventually returned. Like other
Americans, residents of Momence participated in the national Social Security program. The lower average income levels in Momence gave Social Security a different significance here than in the
more prosperous community of Swarthmore. In Momence, Social
Security was seen as a very important advantage for older people

because it gave them some insulation from the economic uncertainties plaguing other adults.

Kinship and Domestic Arrangements

Although kinship connections were strong and numerous, most older persons in Momence did not live in extended family households but lived either alone or as part of a married couple. In the small and stable social field of Momence, older people were still well connected in networks of local relatives. Two of three people over 60 had at least one child living in Momence, and three fourths of the older people had at least one child living within half an hour's drive. Over half of the people over 60 had one or more grandchildren living in Momence, and 75% had a grandchild living within a 30-minute drive. When we asked about siblings, almost one-third of the older residents of Momence said they had a sibling living in the town, and almost one-half had a sibling living within half an hour's drive.

Kinship was the most salient identity on the social map of Momence. At the time we did our study, adult women were still often referred to by their mother's names—that is, they were identified as "so-and-so's daughter." The most insurmountable barrier to assimilation into the community for newcomers to Momence was that they had no kinship link to place them on the map. An important consequence of the centrality of kinship connections was that even if frailty forced an older person to withdraw from more public arenas of participation, the private contacts of kinship domains were a solid basis for maintaining a role in the community.

Research in Momence

Because Momence is a small town with a known social field, we were able to use a multiple method research strategy. Participant observation was used to learn about aspects of community life in which the researchers could appropriately take part. In addition we interviewed a sample of adults (over the age of 18) concerning their views of the life course, residential patterns, dispersal of kin, occupation, health and functionality, and well-being. Participant observation was facilitated by the accident that the anthropologist was appointed to a committee of community residents to research and plan the events for the 1984 Sesquicentennial celebration. The visibility of Chris Fry in this role allowed her to transcend the divisive nature of most formal groups because the Sesquicentennial Committee was a pan-community organization that had the single purpose of celebrating the community and its origins.

The core members of the research team in Momence were Chris Fry, the anthropologist, who had lived in town for about $4\frac{1}{2}$ years, and Margaret Perkinson, a graduate student in Human Development who lived in Momence during her employment by the project. The other two team members were longer term residents of the town—Pam Lenhart, a teacher in the parochial school, and Cheryl Woosnam, who was born and educated in Momence, a homemaker who was completing her college degree on a part-time basis.

All members of the field research team were involved in the formal interviews. On a weekly basis we held team meetings to discuss our progress and problems. Observations of public places and the survey of local businesses and groups were carried out by all members, but more were done by the anthropologist and the graduate student. The observations of public spaces involved three team members mounted on bicycles to tour the town and establish a 24-hour baseline. Then random days and times were selected for continued observation of certain locations. Public meetings of the Women's Club, the Chamber of Commerce, the two Senior groups, the Hospital Auxiliaries, the Car Club, the City Council, the School Board, and the Park Board were attended as well as those of the Sesquicentennial Committee. Where possible, we became involved with these groups and helped out on a number of projects.

Our research was introduced to the Momence community in several ways. First, a news release was published in the *Momence Progress Reporter*. This was followed up by an interview in the *Kankakee Journal*. Prior to the research Chris Fry had talked with the mayor and several merchants about the research and elicited their support and suggestions. In the letters to participants we referred to the newspaper coverage and included copies of the articles. The *Kankakee Journal* article was especially supportive in that it had a photograph of one of Momence's oldest residents doing our card sort. She was known to nearly everyone because she had been the town librarian for years.

For the interview/Age Game part of the research, we selected a two-part sample drawn on a probability basis to represent the adult population of Momence. There was a community sample of 150 adults and an additional sample of 60 adults over the age of 60 for a total of 210 interviews. The community sample was constructed by cluster sampling based on city blocks and township sections. For those drawn in the city, the Haines Criss-Cross Directory was used to link addresses and names of occupants. For the townships, each section was first mapped using plat maps, rural directories, tax records, and aerial photographs (from 1963 with a 1970 update). For both the city blocks and the mile square sections, our on-the-ground observation confirmed addresses and where possible the number of households in the house (by number of gas meters, electric meters, and mailboxes). Each of these units was then numbered. Again, a random number table was used to select the unit. For city blocks we selected one in three units. For farmland settlement we selected one in two units because density was lower. For the very dense settlement along the river, we selected one in seven. Once the households were identified, we developed a procedure to randomize the sex of the adult in the household we would interview and a contingency procedure to further randomize selection if there was more than one individual of the selected sex. If there were no adults of the sex selected, we asked for people's ages, and if an individual was over 60 years, he or she was placed in the pool for the older adult sample.

To create this older adult sample, we asked the people we interviewed to give us a census of their block. At the conclusion of the interview we asked the respondent to verbally "walk us around the block" by telling us the composition of his or her neighbors' households and an estimation of their ages. The name and address of each person estimated to be over 60 were placed on a list for the potential sample of older people. The age estimates were confirmed by comparing judgments of various respondents, and in "close calls" by consultation with others. From this list we selected the 60 older adults contacted, again on a probability basis.

Willingness to participate in the research was quite high. The rejection rate was approximately 11%, with considerable variation by location. The highest was in one of the rural subdivisions of wealthier people who, as one of the researchers stated, "had moved out there to get away from people." The lowest rejection rate was among the poorest people living along the river.

Swarthmore, Pennsylvania

Description

Tree City would be the ideal pseudonym for Swarthmore. Swarthmore's trees are both the essence and symbol of special qualities attributed to the town by visitors as well as residents: "You feel the atmosphere change when you turn off the Pike and see all those trees." Swarthmore is bounded physically by several prominent features: a four-lane highway, the 300-acre Swarthmore College campus, and the block-long greenspace adjacent to a church and convent. Socially, the community is perceived to be just as sharply set apart. Although critics and supporters agree on Swarthmore's distinctiveness, they assign it different valences. What residents treasure as "real community" outsiders and newcomers may resent as smugness and inaccessibility.

Important aspects of living in Swarthmore, especially for older persons, are easily visible even to a first-time visitor. The initial turn south off the Baltimore Pike abruptly leaves behind an artificial horizon of mall roofs and service station signs for the green archway of lofty trees that line PA Route 320 as it passes through Swarthmore. At the first traffic light appear lush lawns and playing fields, massive fieldstone buildings, and the arched bell tower of Swarthmore College. Just beyond the campus are the four blocks that form "downtown." At first, or even second, glance, this does appear to be the heart of a classic small town. Most of the buildings are two or three stories, and those on two sides of one block are faced with brick and have dormers surrounded by Tudor-style exposed beams. This "old-fashioned" block and scenes from the college campus are the most frequent subjects for Swarthmore postcards and notepaper sold in local shops. Street-level stairways

Photo 3.3 Swarthmore Borough Viewed From the College Campus
Photo by Grant Heilman.

lead to apartments above all the stores. Several businesses at ground
level have coordinated their awnings in matching blue with white
letters. The borough hall, police station, and public library share
one floor of a more modern red-brick building whose lower level
houses the all-volunteer fire company. The weekly newspaper, to
which 95% of the households subscribe, is published in a bay-
windowed residence next to the grocery. The war memorial stands
on a patch of grass at the meeting point of the two main streets.

Individuals of all ages mix on the streets, although there are tidal
patterns bringing different categories of people to different places
at different times of day. Children between 5 and 11 years old walk
through town on their way to the elementary school around 8:30
and home again after 3:30. Highschoolers fill the pizza parlor
between about 3 and 5. College students in their late teens and early
20s, wearing backpacks and casual clothing, stroll in groups, usu-

ally seeking food, in the late afternoon. By 5:30 the less formal family restaurant attracts many gray-haired clients, most of whom negotiate large cars into parking places along the block and across the street in the borough lot. In warm weather these older people, many in couples, sit on white metal chairs outside the restaurant waiting to get in. Inside the restaurant, waitresses refer knowledgeably to their patrons' preferences for certain dishes or to their health-related restrictions on salt or butter. Between 5 and 7 p.m., when the grocery closes, some middle-aged men and many women, often with children in tow, join the competition for parking and rush into the market to shop for dinner. The atmosphere in this store is chatty and pleasant as many people greet each other and the staff. By 8 p.m. there is no business open downtown except the pizza parlor, which closes at 11 p.m. on weekdays and at midnight on weekends.

The northern edge of the "ville," as Swarthmore College students call the downtown, is separated from the campus by railroad tracks and the gray stone station building that includes the Sidetracks Cafe. Philadelphia is a 26-minute ride from Swarthmore on this railway. From its earliest days, this connection to the city has been essential to Swarthmore. At early morning and late afternoon rush hours, the flood of commuters boarding and leaving the train is a strong reminder of the suburban aspect to this community. Another insight into the tension between the small town image and the suburban identity of Swarthmore comes from an inventory of what is *not* visible in the community. There is no supermarket, no mall, no high school, no gas station, no men's or children's clothing store, no bar, no industry, no nursing home, no funeral parlor. A more careful look at the people also reveals *who* is not visible. It is rare to see someone in a wheelchair on Swarthmore streets, and even canes or walkers are uncommon. The unevenness of sidewalks and the lack of curb ramps would make mobility in these circumstances difficult. It is also not common to see older people with young children. The presence of a grandchild seems rather to be unusual and cause for excited comment by acquaintances who stop to admire.

All of these absences raised questions that became important in our study. Where were older people's kin? Where did people go to meet needs that could not be met in the town? What happened to people who could not meet their needs if they continued to live in Swarthmore?

There are also persons and places that were part of Swarthmore although not featured in its public, or private, images. There is a small but old and stable African American neighborhood, for example. Three percent of the town's population is African American, and most of these residents live within the four blocks that several older white Swarthmoreans told us used to be called "Scrapple Hundred."[1] Also, although the homes that typify Swarthmore are large single-family houses 75 to 100 years old, there are also multiple dwellings: one 13-story building with over 200 condominium apartments, two smaller condominium residences, three large apartment buildings in the downtown area, and one garden apartment complex on the eastern edge of town. In addition, there is a "tract" of postwar split-level houses near the former location of the elementary school.

The large condominium and two of the downtown apartment buildings have large enough proportions of older residents to be considered de facto retirement communities. The condominium runs a van between the building and the train station several times each day, the only collective transportation regularly available within the town. (A public bus runs *through* Swarthmore on a route from Chester to the trolley terminal in Philadelphia.) We discovered that older people in these buildings form the networks of sociability and support characteristic of age-homogeneous settings. We also learned that there are two main paths into these apartments. Some long-time Swarthmoreans move in after selling a home that is too large and too much work for an elderly couple or, more often, an elderly widow alone. Many elderly newcomers to Swarthmore buy or rent an apartment because they have come to live near an adult child, but both they and the child prefer to maintain independent residences.

Demography

At the time of our study almost 6,000 people lived in Swarthmore. Of these, 1,300 were students at Swarthmore College, of

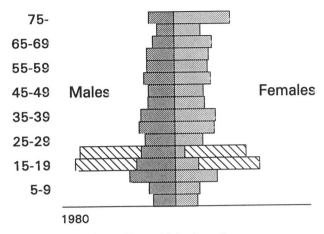

Figure 3.2. Population Pyramid for Swarthmore

whom over 90% lived in dormitories on the campus. The population in town, excluding the campus, therefore totaled approximately 4,700. Population numbers had been stable in the 10 years preceding our research and had increased by about 1,000 since 1950. As Figure 3.2 shows, people over 60 formed a substantial proportion of the Swarthmore population. Twenty-five percent of the residents were over 60, and almost 20% (19.1%) were over 65. Among the older people in Swarthmore, widowed women were numerous, 24% of our sample over 60 and half of our sample over 75.

Three-fourths of our representative sample had college education or more. More than 90 different occupations were reported, but 80% of these were above the midpoint on Treiman's scale of occupational prestige (Treiman, 1977). Almost half were professionals such as teachers, ministers, attorneys, and executives.

Old People in Swarthmore

At the time of our research, the first thing a visitor to Swarthmore would have been likely to remark about older people is that there were a lot of them. The gray-haired people, many of them women, that one saw on the street or in the shops were noticeably well dressed and groomed. Styles of personal appearance were diverse,

i

ncluding a tweedy citified look of tailored suits or dresses as well as the suburban casualness of jogging suits and sneakers or L.L. Bean denim and T-necks.

What the older persons seen by a visitor to Swarthmore would have had in common was their appearance of health and vigor. Downtown, they walked or drove cars, carried packages, paid for their own meals and purchases, and bought tickets for long-distance travel. Outside the business district, they could be seen tending large gardens, chopping wood, raking leaves, and shoveling snow.

Many younger and middle-aged residents told us that they enjoyed seeing old people in Swarthmore: "You see wonderful old ladies tooling around the streets, digging in yards, all dolled up in town." One connection to older persons reported by younger Swarthmoreans was "seeing them on the street."

As Americans, residents of Swarthmore were used to speaking of age in chronological terms. No matter how young they thought someone felt or acted, including themselves, it still seemed appropriate to refer to anyone as older once they entered their 60s. A visitor to various formal and informal groups in Swarthmore would have found many old people in some and very few in others. The observer would also more often have seen, as we did, older women in one hair salon and college students of both sexes in the other; older groups in the family restaurants, and students and parents with young children in the pizza shop.

Public rituals offer an outsider special insights into structures and values of any community. In Swarthmore, many holiday celebrations, including Easter, Fourth of July, and Halloween, featured competitions, which accurately indicates the centrality of achievement as a shared value there. The role of older persons, especially in the all-day town celebration of July Fourth, was not that of participant but that of judge. Members of the Women's Club, many in their 70s and 80s, walked among the costumed children who rode decorated bicycles, walked decorated pets, and pushed or pulled homemade patriotic floats. The women took notes, then conferred under a shady tree and finally decided on three levels of prizes for each category of entry in the parade. This judge's role, carried out by older women once a year, is an effective symbol for the ambivalent position of its older residents. People in Swarthmore perceived the

Photo 3.4 Retired Sisters in Swarthmore

town as a special place to be old, and its older residents as especially active and interesting old people. However, in routine community affairs there was no seniority principle leading to privileged access either to tangible resources or to powerful positions.

Swarthmoreans easily gave examples of actual older persons who were having a good old age. They do indeed sound like special people—optimistic, enjoying life, healthy, independent, and above all, active.

> [She has] college students in the house, still drives, she's very active, delivers the newsletter for Women's International League for Peace and Freedom.

> She has a very positive outlook, she's very independent; she can still get around, goes where she wants to go.

> He seems to be well, comes to church every Sunday, he walks, is active, manages his own affairs.

Asking about an older person having difficulty, on the other hand, stymied our Swarthmore respondents. Over half of them said they knew *no* such person in Swarthmore. When we spoke with people under 60 themselves, the proportion who could name no person having a difficult old age rose to two of three. The puzzle for us was whether these responses meant that we had found our Shangri-La in which the evils of old age never appeared or a set of singularly uninformed informants. Close reading of what people actually said when they "couldn't answer the question" gave us the first clue that neither was the case. Many of the responses specified that what they could not do was name a *current* resident of Swarthmore having difficulty in old age. Most of them could easily name a *former* resident of Swarthmore: "She moved away from Swarthmore to a place where she could get medical care," or "She used to live here, but now she's in a nursing home."

The contradiction revealed by these responses is a characteristic of Swarthmore with important implications for the well-being of its older residents. Although Swarthmore looked and felt like a small town, it lacked the facilities and supports that would allow older people to anticipate enjoying these benefits to the end of their lives.

Economy and Scale

Swarthmore was linked to external social systems tightly and in multiple ways. There had never been industry in the town, and most residents who worked commuted to jobs elsewhere, either by car or by the train and trolley that ran to Philadelphia. Some commuted by train as far as Trenton, New York, or Washington, D.C. Only 19% of the households in our sample were headed by a person whose employment was in Swarthmore. (In the majority of households that were described to us as being headed "jointly," this meant that neither person worked in Swarthmore.)

In addition, many local businesses were branches or franchises of regional or national enterprises, for example, in real estate, insurance, hardware, or banking. Also, most Swarthmore high school graduates went on to college, and the majority attended schools outside Pennsylvania. Swarthmore was part of a unified school district that included three other towns. Swarthmore lost its separate high school in 1983 when it was merged into the larger school in the largest town in the district. Loss of their neighborhood school, with its associated activities and sports teams, was keenly felt by many Swarthmoreans. The extended and bitter fight that preceded the decision also, for some Swarthmore residents, heightened awareness of their "small town's" distinctiveness from what they saw as the more typical suburban qualities (no downtown, no sidewalks, no community spirit) of the other towns.

Swarthmore residents, like other Americans, also participated in a dense web of extralocal regulation, service, and policy, including Social Security and Medicare, federal and state financing of transportation, taxation, and building codes, to name a few. As members of formal organizations, Swarthmoreans also belonged to many groups whose boundaries were national or even international. Several prominent organizations in the town were local branches of much larger entities, such as Rotary, League of Women Voters, and Women's International League for Peace and Freedom. As the description of the Swarthmore business district implies, most residents relied on sources outside the town for many of their needs, including clothing, auto service, groceries, and medical care.

Kinship and Domestic Arrangements

Most Swarthmore households at the time of our study included nuclear rather than extended families. According to the 1980 census, 60% of the households were occupied by couples or families. The average number of persons per household on a block in Swarthmore ranged from 1.55 to 4.0.[2] One third of the households included a person 65 or older. Of these, *all* were headed by a person 65 or older; in two thirds of them this person was the owner, in one-third the renter. In total, 26% of the households in Swarthmore were owned, and headed, by a person 65 or older. Three times more households were occupied by a female alone (21% of all households) than by a male alone (7% of all households).

Residential mobility in Swarthmore was high, and dispersal of kin was correspondingly wide. Visits to and from family were consequently part of the yearly rhythm for most older Swarthmoreans. The modal number of years persons in our adult sample (not including students on campus) had lived in Swarthmore was five.

Although 85% of the older Swarthmoreans at the time of our study had children, three of four residents over 60 years old did not have a child in town, and 86% of the residents 75 years old or older did not. Other kin were similarly far-flung. Less than a third of Swarthmore residents over 60, for example, had a sibling living as close as an hour's drive, although most (over 70%) did have siblings.

The great value placed on independence and achievement was communicated to us in multiple ways by Swarthmoreans, and with intensity. Independence, especially as manifested in a separate household, was what younger people vigorously strove to establish and old people tenaciously attempted to maintain. Any evaluative question we asked, about life stages or older individuals or a person's own well-being, elicited frequent responses about independence versus dependence. The resume in which many Swarthmoreans documented their accumulating public identities would be an appropriate symbol for the value nexus of individuality, independence, and achievement. Individual achievements were observed, recorded, and rewarded in myriad ways here, from trophies for best Halloween costume, to college GPA, to promotions on the job, to T-shirts for swimming 1,000 laps in the community pool.

As Americans, residents of Swarthmore were accustomed to chronological age as a marker of many important social boundaries: eligibility for kindergarten, driving, voting, selective service, drinking, and Social Security, to name a few. Age was so basic to the structuring of social life in Swarthmore that most people perceived age differentiation as "natural." It seemed natural, for example, that most events at the Community Center were either formally or informally age homogeneous. Thursday lunches and Tuesday-Thursday bridge games were for seniors (persons over 55), Friday night dance parties were specified as open to 5th to 7th graders or 8th graders or high school students. Many more groups and activities were not formally labeled as for a specific age category but were de facto age homogeneous. The Women's Club had mainly members over 60, for example, and the Recreational Association had more younger people. Within each church congregation, certain groups were predominantly composed of older or younger adults, and youth and children were separated in turn into their own categories. Both the Episcopalian Altar Guild and the Presbyterian Bandage Group, for example, were in fact groups of older women.

The default option for informal social events was also age homogeneity. Invitations to dinner in a private home, for example, were understood as for adults unless it was explicitly stated that this was a family event where children were welcome. It was also worthy of comment (i.e., not natural) if adults from more than one generation were present. It seemed natural that most people have friends of approximately the same age, although the age ranges included in "same age" expanded from the 1 year typical of school children to about 10 years for most adults. Parents and children alike in Swarthmore remarked as unusual a friendship that spanned as few as two grades in elementary school.

Research in Swarthmore

The combination of small town and suburban attributes in Swarthmore's identity is reflected in our research strategies. Participant observation was used, as anthropologists have used it in many small communities, to learn about the groups and activities in which we could appropriately take part and about which we needed holistic and dynamic information. In addition, we invited a sample of residents over 18 to respond to our formal interview, including the card sort. In contrast to study sites in Botswana and Ireland, it was more difficult for us to explain and justify participant observation than the interview questionnaire format, which is very familiar to middle-class, suburban Americans.

The aspect of research in Swarthmore our team found most difficult was that we were studying our own community. Although this offered us advantages in initial access and background knowledge, it posed problems as well. We had to be alert to avoid being blinded by familiarity with some elements of local culture and to ensure ethical use of information obtained when residents who knew us as friends or neighbors did not know we were "on duty."

The AGE team in Swarthmore had four core members and also several student assistants who joined us for a semester or a summer. The core members were four women, Jennie Keith and Isabeth

Gross in their 40s, Mary Etta Zwell in her mid-60s, and Alice Brodhead almost 70. During our 3 years of research in Swarthmore, four Swarthmore College students joined the project for periods ranging from 3 months to over a year: Elizabeth Davies, David Bedell, Will Reese, and Elin Waring. When work began, the members of the core team were all married, but Alice Brodhead became a widow during the course of the study. Jennie Keith and Beth Gross had children in the local schools, and Etta and Alice were both grandmothers. Beth Gross was a homemaker, Jennie Keith was on the faculty of Swathmore College, Etta Zwell was retired from a secretarial postion at the College, and Alice Brodhead was retired from a faculty position. Our depth of residence in Swarthmore ranged from 4 years for Jennie Keith to almost 50 years for Alice Brodhead. We lived in different areas of town, and there was little overlap in our social networks. We consequently had fairly easy access to most arenas of town life and were able to be unobtrusive participant observers in a wide range of them.

All members of the team carried out some of the formal interviews, participated in a survey of local businesses, and did observations in public spaces and community groups. Some observations, such as those of streets, parks, restaurants, and public rituals, were done by everyone on the team. Extended participant observation in some settings was specialized, so that the team member most appropriate for a particular group or activity became responsible for it. Senior lunch and bridge groups at the community center, for example, were observed for 3 years by the researcher in her 60s (who also knew how to play bridge). One male student joined an early morning gathering of local tradesmen around the coffee urn at the hardware store. Other locations in which we did extensive observations were the Women's Club, Borough Council, Planning Commission, Friendly Open House (monthly program and refreshments sponsored by churches in rotation for elders), Rotary Club, Consumers Cooperative Market, and Council of Republican Women. At our weekly team meetings, journal notes on observations were read by everyone and discussed. The notes from these meetings in turn recorded our developing hypotheses about the significance of age in community life.

We introduced ourselves and Project AGE to the Swarthmore community in several ways. The Swarthmore College news office put out a release that resulted in feature stories in both the *Swarth-morean* and the *Philadelphia Inquirer.* Jennie Keith also spoke to the borough manager and the president of the elected borough council to explain the project to them and offer to include in our interviews specific questions that might be useful to them. We did add a section on how well Swarthmore met residents' needs in various domains such as transportation, shopping, and medical care. During the course of the research, Jennie Keith spoke to various local groups including the Rotary Club, the Quaker meeting, PEO, and the Presbyterian Women. When we wrote letters to each of the persons in our sample, we referred to the newspaper articles, which many people had seen. The letters were signed by all four of us, and we followed these up with telephone calls to ask for interview appointments.

Our goals in creating a sample for the interview part of our study were to select participants who would accurately represent the Swarthmore adult population, to include adequate numbers of persons over 60 to permit the types of analysis we planned, and to maximize the possibility of each interviewer accumulating knowledge about certain social or spatial areas of town. Eventually each interviewer had independent information about specific individuals that helped us interpret, for example, why they were named by others as doing well or having problems in old age.

We created two samples, a representative community sample of 150 persons and an additional probability sample of persons 61 and over. The strategy for constructing the community sample, parallel to that used in Momence, was random selection of blocks that served as the clusters within which we again randomly chose our sampling units, which were households. On the basis of review of the block statistics from the 1980 census, in which Swarthmore constituted a tract within the Philadelphia area, we decided that it was appropriate to select blocks from the entire tract without preliminary stratification. We had included in our background interviews about the town a question about what different types of people we should be sure to include in our study in order to get a full view of the town. Answers to this question did not emphasize location within the town, but social differences such as working versus being retired or membership in different churches.[3] We found no disagreement about the boundaries of the borough in

more than 30 preliminary interviews. The boundaries correspond
to the political unit of borough government and to the census,
although not to the postal code, which extends over a wider area.
To create the sampling frames of households from which to select
within each block, we walked the streets to record addresses and
to locate indicators of separate households under one roof, such as
mailboxes or gas meters. Then we used tax rolls, voting lists, and a
realtor's criss-cross telephone directory to match names with each
address. Households were chosen randomly at a density of one in
three per block. Because we intended to interview only one adult
in each household, we also created a contingency procedure for
choosing that person when there was more than one adult. This
random process identified the sex, which we used to direct our
letters, and the relative age of the person to be invited to participate during the follow-up phone call in case there was more than
one adult of the appropriate sex. Our acceptance rate was 85%,
and it required 31 blocks to fill our community sample of 150
persons.

The frame for the supplemental sample of people 61 and over
was created by the same two methods as used in Momence: age
estimates of neighbors by people we interviewed in the community
sample, and names of people living alone who were not included
in the community sample because they were of the "wrong" sex.
We established a list of 97 people at least 61 years old and living
on our sample blocks, and from this list we randomly selected
names. The refusal rate for this sample was 26%. Reassuring to us
in terms of possible bias was that there was an almost perfect
balance in the reasons for refusing between those who said they
did not feel well enough and those who said they had too many
other activities.

Notes

1. Scrapple is a meat product made from pork scraps and cereal, usually fried
in slices and eaten for breakfast. Some white Swarthmoreans told us that Scrapple
Hundred was a derogatory term derived from the association of eating scrapple
with being poor and black.

2. Presence of the college dormitories does not skew these figures because students living in them were not counted as being in households, but in group quarters.

3. The only two areas we considered using as strata, one including most black residents of the town and one demarcated by a pillared entrance, both contained several blocks, at least one of which was likely to fall into a general sample. A block from each area did fall into our random selection.

Photo 4.1 An Elderly Shoe Repairer Works in His Shop

4

Hong Kong

*H*ong Kong was selected for inclusion in Project AGE because it exemplifies features considered characteristic of modern industrial society and that distinguish this type of society from "simple" or "traditional" societies. First, in 1983 only a tiny fraction of the population—on the order of 2%—was involved in any type of primary production—agriculture, fishing, or mining. Hong Kong's working population of nearly 2.5 million was concentrated in manufacturing, which employed 901,000; shops, restaurants, and hotels, employing 524,800; construction, employing 203,600; and transport and communications, employing 193,900. The range of job categories is enormous (informants themselves listed 101 different occupations either currently held or, if currently out of the labor force, last held), and Hong Kong young people can generally expect to find employment easily, though competition for particular jobs can be intense.

The labor force is increasingly highly trained. Although older workers, most of whom came from China, have had little education and in the case of older women are frequently illiterate, by 1983 young people in Hong Kong were required to complete 9 years of basically free education (6 in primary and 3 in secondary school). Students completing their third year of secondary school took an examination to determine their academic eligibility for upper secondary school placement. In 1983 over 16,000 students were enrolled in postsecondary degree-granting institutions such as the University of Hong Kong, Chinese University of Hong Kong, and Baptist College. The shortage of tertiary educational institutions resulted in many students going abroad for college or university training. During the 1982-1983 academic year, over 12,000 students left Hong Kong for study in Britain, Canada, the United States, and Australia.

From the point of view of scale, Hong Kong's economy extends far beyond its borders in that it is tightly integrated into international markets. Its manufactured products are intended primarily for export or for sale locally to foreign tourists. It is a major transit point for the China trade and the main foreign investor in the Chinese Special Economic Zone of Shenzhen immediately across its northern border. For these reasons even the least educated resident has an interest in political and economic trends affecting Hong Kong's wealth and stability.

As indicated above, in terms of degree of urbanization and population density Hong Kong easily outranks the other sites included in Project AGE. Furthermore, the population is constantly growing from both migration and natural increase. In the early 1980s only 57% of the total Hong Kong population were Hong Kong born, whereas 40% were born in China (the remainder were born elsewhere—for the most part in Great Britain, Europe, or India). Between the taking of the 1981 census and the completion of interviewing in 1983, the total population grew by 300,000. The crude birthrate was 15.7. Internal population movement is also high. According to the 1981 census, 30% of the population (over the age of 4) had not been at the same address 5 years earlier. This figure compares favorably with our own sample, of which 31% had not been at the same address 5 years earlier. These rates, however, conceal major variation by neighborhood and by type of housing. In the two public housing estates in our study, the mobility rates ranged from 4% to 10%, whereas in the two neighborhoods characterized by privately owned housing, the rates ranged from 47% to 68%.

Despite all these characteristics indicative of a modern industrial society, Hong Kong, as a fundamentally Chinese society, is also viewed as atypical of industrial societies. Chinese culture is frequently assumed by officials, the public, and outsiders to provide a kind of immunization against the ills associated with "modernization." Chinese are said to be familistic, to train family members to put the family and not themselves first, and, most importantly from Project AGE's point of view, to respect and care for the elderly. Including Hong Kong in the study added the interesting opportunity to consider how the cultural values of familism derived from a then-obsolete rural way of life would function in a very differently structured environment.

Description

The visitor to Hong Kong (literally "Fragrant Harbor") usually arrives by air, landing at Kai Tak Airport on the Kowloon Peninsula from either the southeast or the west. Those arriving via the southeast flight path descend along the northeast coast of Hong Kong Island, cross the harbor filled with boats and ships from around the world, and touch down on a runway extending out into the water on the eastern side of the peninsula. Those arriving via the more harrowing western flight path skirt the mountains separating Kowloon from the once rural New Territories, execute a sharp turn to line up with the opposite end of the same runway, and descend into the midst of a heavily populated area, so close to residential high-rises that, as one passenger put it, "You could almost snatch the clothes hanging out to dry!"

This initial impression of a densely populated urban area hemmed in by mountains and water on all sides is confirmed by the visitor's experiences on the ground. At the time of the research in 1983, Hong Kong, with an area of only 1,066 square kilometers, had an average population density of 4,972 per square kilometer, but this figure masked the enormous variation between the New Territories on the one hand and the urban areas of the Kowloon Peninsula and the northern fringes of Hong Kong Island on the other. In the New Territories the overall population density was 792 per square kilometer, whereas in the metropolitan districts it was 28,479. Within the urban areas too, density varied enormously, reaching a high of 165,445 per square kilometer in the district of Shamshuipo, which includes one of our research neighborhoods and is adjacent to the district containing the other three. Housing design reflects these population densities. Most new private construction is of high-rise towers reaching 25 stories or more. On The Peak and in affluent neighborhoods elsewhere, baronial single-family homes continue to exist, as do eight- and nine-story postwar dwellings without elevators in less wealthy neighborhoods. Public housing estates, which accommodate nearly half the population, range from very basic units (no self-contained plumbing) in six-story blocks built in the late 1950s to full apartment units in blocks that, in height at least, approach those in the private sector.

Visitors as well as residents are frequently overwhelmed by the ever-present crowds. Traffic is stalled, public buses are jammed, and restaurants are packed with latecomers stationing themselves behind the seats of parties that appear close to vacating them. In a city with a 6-day work week, Sunday is a nightmare as hundreds of thousands of families compete for the limited space in the parks or other amusement places. These problems are most acute for the ordinary Chinese resident of Hong Kong. The wealthy, both foreign and Chinese, can insulate themselves from most of this by living above it—most conspicuously by living on The Peak—and venturing below in quick dashes by private car to their offices in Central.

Living on The Peak or other elevation also offers some small relief from the tropical climate. The annual mean temperature is 23 degrees Centigrade, and the mean relative humidity is 78%. These statistics obscure the fact of a brutal summer climate that from late April through October is characterized by daily highs of 33 degrees (or more) Centigrade—that is, 90+ degrees Fahrenheit. Residents are accustomed to walking close to buildings so as to remain in their shadows, and tourists rapidly become adept at learning how to walk from the Star Ferry terminal to the New World (Shopping) Center via air-conditioned shopping arcades.

The positive side of this climate is the mild winter and a year-round growing season that guarantees an abundance of fresh fruits and vegetables from the bordering Chinese province of Guangdong every day of the year.

Photo 4.2 Victory Avenue Neighborhood

Cantonese, the term used broadly to indicate Chinese whose origins lie in Guangdong and who speak the distinctive language of the province, constitute the overwhelming majority of the residents of Hong Kong. Cantonese is the ordinary medium of instruction in most primary schools as well as the dominant language of radio, television, and locally produced films. Its nearest rival is English. The university educated, those anticipating employment in the tourist or international trade sectors of the economy, and those expecting to emigrate take bilingualism very seriously, but the bulk of the population, including even younger people, who have studied English in secondary school but do not use it in their work easily become tongue-tied when faced with communicating with a non-Cantonese speaker.

Visitors who confine their movements to the tourist areas of Central or Tsimshatsui will be impressed with the ethnic diversity and international flavor of Hong Kong. On their day off from domestic duties, Filipinas congregate in Statue Square. Men in turbans guard the entrances to goldsmith shops, and a mosque stands on the main thoroughfare of Nathan Road. Japanese crowd the duty-free shops, and Europeans and Americans wander about in a semidazed state, unable to decide which camera shop is really offering the best deal. Foreigners resident in Hong Kong live disproportionately on Hong Kong Island, whereas the Kowloon Peninsula is almost entirely Chinese. Once one moves beyond the tourist area on its southern tip following Nathan Road into Yaumadei and Mongkok, English language signs and English-speaking staff seem to vanish. The four neighborhoods chosen for inclusion in Project AGE are all located in the center of Kowloon.

Demography

Hong Kong has been characterized by enormous swings in the size of its population. Although the colony now known as Hong Kong was acquired piecemeal by the British between 1842 and 1898, the vast bulk of the population working in Hong Kong prior to the Second World War was made up of sojourners. Young people migrated to Hong Kong from Guangdong Province to work primarily as laborers, petty traders, or domestic servants. They regularly sent remittances to their parents, spouses, and children who had been left behind in China and returned to visit them several times a year. In old age they expected to return to their home communities and to be supported by remittances from their descendants, who were also likely to be working in Hong Kong.

Beginning in the 1930s political turmoil in China caused many to flee to Hong Kong, first to avoid the Japanese invaders, then to escape the civil war between the Communists and the Nationalists, and finally to avoid persecution by the Communist government itself as it enacted policies to overturn the old social and political order. The population grew from 0.8 million in 1931 to 1.8 million by 1947. In the interim, during the Japanese occupation of Hong Kong, it fell to about three-fourths of the 1931 figure. By 1961 the population had reached 3.1 million, by 1971, 3.9 million, and by 1981, 5.0 million—an increase of 25% in the short space of 10 years. (By the end of 1990 the population reached 5.9 million.)

At the same time the age-sex structure of the population was also undergoing changes. According to the Hong Kong Government Information Service annual publication (1984), the proportion of the population under 15 dropped from 33.7% in 1973 to 23.9% in 1983 while the proportion of those 65 or older rose from 4.9% to 7.1%. Between 1973 and 1983 the sex ratio increased from 1,037 males per 1,000 females to 1,080 and was attributed to the substantial inflow of immigrants over the 10-year period, most of whom were young and male. Among the elderly, however, old women greatly outnumbered old men. (See Figure 4.1 for the population pyramid of Hong Kong.)

Old People in Hong Kong

Though the Hong Kong government uses the age of 65 as the demarcator of the elderly for demographic purposes, it uses other ages for other purposes, such as eligibility for entering a home for the aged, receipt of public assistance on the grounds of age, and retirement. In these cases both the government and the ordinary public generally concur that if a chronological marker is to be used, 60 is a better one than 65, and in this study when the elderly are referred to as a category, it is the population 60 or older that is generally meant. Furthermore, as will become clear in Chapter 6, where we discuss the life course in detail, chronological markers of age are not necessarily the most salient ones for Hong Kong informants.

In Hong Kong, as in most other parts of the world, most individuals have knowledge of or interact with elderly women much more than elderly men. In our sample, for example, 118 informants have surviving mothers, but only 85 have surviving fathers; similarly, 81 have surviving mothers-in-law, but only 50 have surviving fathers-in-law. In the grandparental generation the disproportion is even greater. On the paternal side 19 informants have surviving

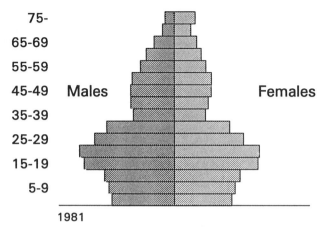

Figure 4.1. Population Pyramid for Hong Kong

grandmothers, but only 4 have surviving grandfathers. On the maternal side 25 have surviving grandmothers, and only 10 have surviving grandfathers.

Older people are highly visible in Hong Kong, especially in the early morning hours when they congregate on hill slopes to absorb the good morning air and carry out their exercises, either tai chi chuan (derived from Chinese martial arts traditions) or a variety of stretching exercises. Our spot observations carried out at 6:30 a.m. certainly confirm that older people do spend time in interaction with each other. At this hour nearly every park and playground in Hong Kong at any time of the year is occupied by older people, who, following their workouts, gather in groups of two or three for leisurely discussion of matters of mutual interest. Fourteen hours later no elderly are to be seen in these locations; instead their places have been taken by numerous amorous young couples.

Later in the morning, old women, some with a grandchild strapped to their back, go off to the street market to buy fresh vegetables and live chickens and fish for the day's meals while old men congregate in teahouses reading the paper or discussing current events, including the results of the previous day's horse races. Ideally, and in reality at least for many men, old age is supposed to be a time of rest and relaxation, a time when one is rewarded for years of hard work by being relieved from work. For women, however, old age is likely

Photo 4.3 Morning Tai Chi Chuan Exercises in the Park in Yau Yat Chuen

to entail considerable domestic work, a fact that stimulates pride
in some and resentment in others. In fact, there are considerable class
differences in how people experience old age in Hong Kong. Those
who are wealthy usually have servants to carry out the necessary
household chores, can travel abroad to visit their dispersed children
and grandchildren, and can play mah jong to their heart's content.

Most elderly remain solidly ensconced in their families. They live
with their adult children, and evenings are spent watching television
together. On Sundays the whole family goes out for dim sum, a kind
of brunch featuring many small dishes. On holidays such as Ching
Ming (when the spring "grave-sweeping" rituals are conducted) or
during folk celebrations such as the Hungry Ghosts Festival, the
elderly, the middle-aged, and the young together burn incense, share
food, and exchange family news. There are elders who are isolated,
having lost their families or become alienated from them, and most
people can recount sad cases they have known of personally, but
the neglected elder living alone is still regarded as the deviant case.

The elderly are not significant actors in the public arena. The rare
elder who is visible is likely to be so despite his or her age rather

than because of it and to be memorable for other qualities such as wealth, articulateness, or a remarkable personality. The typical elder's lack of education and inability to speak English confine him or her to the realms of the family and the immediate neighborhood. Older people who are involved in organized activities outside the family tend to be involved in cohort-specific organizations. These are associations founded to meet the needs of a largely male migrant population with few family members in Hong Kong or, even less frequently, organizations reflecting the political interests of people who were involved in the Chinese civil war. Thus older men, though seldom involved in any organizations, are most likely to be in clan associations, native place associations, or Nationalist Party affiliates. A tiny minority of the elderly, in this case primarily women, participate in the activities of government-supported multiservice centers organized by much younger social workers. Sustained participant observation was carried out at the Yang Memorial Social Service Centre in Mongkok, a center unique for its attempts to involve elderly men in projecting a more positive and activist image than is currently the norm.

Kinship and Domestic Arrangements

Traditional Chinese kinship norms are organized around the central concept of the patrilineage, a group of men descended from a common ancestor and sharing a common surname. In South China, the place of origin of the bulk of the Hong Kong population, villages were normally composed of one or more patrilineages. People with a common surname considered themselves related and could not intermarry. Thus, when a young woman married, she usually had to leave her natal village while her brothers remained and brought their wives in from elsewhere. The resulting typical household was ideally one that contained an older couple, at least one younger couple (a married son and a daughter-in-law), and grandchildren. In old age Chinese expected to live with and be looked after by their sons.

Because of the emphasis on descendants and extending the ancestral line, not marrying was considered deviant at best and unfilial at worst, and few people failed to marry (data from the 1986 by-census revealed that less than 5% of the elderly in Hong Kong had never married). Traditional Chinese marriages were not viewed as romantic or companionate relationships. During the early decades of this century most marriages were arranged by the parents and were known as "blind marriages"—that is, the bride and groom did not set eyes on each other until the wedding. Parents selected their daughters-in-law with an eye to their family reputation, personality characteristics (modesty, obedience, and industriousness), and presumed childbearing capabilities. Failure to bear children could be compensated for by adoption or purchase of a child or by the husband's taking of a concubine (secondary or "little" wife, whose status was below that of the first wife and whose children were technically considered those of the first wife). Concubinage was not abolished in Hong Kong until the early 1970s, and this outlawing did not affect already established unions. Years of living together and coparenting might bring about affectionate ties between a couple, but then again they might not. Divorce was rare (one female informant used the Chinese expression "When married to a dog, follow a dog" to explain the absence of divorce), and most couples focused on their relationships with their children rather than with each other. Women were expected to remain single following the death of a husband and, if they already had nearly adult children, usually did so. Men, on the other hand, were free to remarry.

Most of the older people in Hong Kong come from this background. The more educated may have selected their own spouses on the basis of criteria not so different from those in the West, but they still view children as the main reason for a marriage and expect to live with them in their old age. Although a minority of elderly couples may spend a few years living without children, eventual widowhood usually results in a parent's move to an adult child's home. The 1986 by-census revealed that 11.5% of the elderly lived alone, 17.6% lived with only one other person (usually a spouse), and nearly all the rest lived in some form of family (nuclear, extended, or joint). Only 3.5% of the elderly lived in any kind of group quarters, including hostels and homes for the aged and for the well elderly; and care and attention homes and private nursing homes for the infirm.

As indicated above, familism has long been a core Chinese value. In the past individual family members were expected to put the family's interests ahead of their own under nearly all circumstances. In Hong Kong these norms have been reinterpreted, and the wishes of the individual are given more consideration. Parents do not determine whom their children will marry, nor do they expect to have much influence over their married children's domestic or work affairs. Indeed, many parents find themselves being servants to their daughters-in-law rather than the other way around. Nevertheless, the sheer fact of living together means that most Hong Kong Chinese must consider the impact of their daily actions on others and must remain attuned to the needs of their family members. In the family context interdependence is a higher value than independence. The most frequent responses from younger adults to our requests for descriptions of individuals doing well in old age referred to being easy to get along with, being tolerant, and not being a nag.

The negative side of this familism is that it creates a tightly bounded social unit, whose internal affairs are considered its own business. Victims of abuse or neglect—be they spouses, children, or the elderly—are reluctant to reveal their problems to others. They don't want to be the ones to bring shame to the family by calling attention to their plight. Similarly, most ordinary Hong Kong Chinese are reluctant to become involved in other families' affairs. They may be sympathetic and even indignant about particular situations, but they don't feel it is their right or responsibility to become involved. This reluctance to become involved is also visible in the community domain, although quite apart from the issue of motivation most people in Hong Kong lack both the time and the energy to become active in public affairs.

The minimal welfare security net in Hong Kong means that for most people making a living is a primary preoccupation. Wealth is the key indicator of social status, and most Hong Kong residents believe that there are many unscrupulous people out there who will do anything for money. Consequently wealth may be envied, but it is not necessarily respected. Police officers living beyond their means explain that they have been lucky at the track. The line between what is a gift and what is a bribe is constantly being redrawn. In this morally murky environment people feel safest when they can work through people whom they know personally.

Coming to understand who can be trusted and who is a real friend is a sign that one is growing up and coming to "know society."

Research in Hong Kong

Factors of scale and social stratification based primarily on wealth required modifications of the sampling strategy in Hong Kong. Rather than draw a random sample of the entire population, it was preferable to select an urban neighborhood of manageable proportions as the sampling frame. Selecting a single neighborhood, however, posed the question of its representativeness. To deal with this problem, four neighborhoods known to vary systematically by wealth were selected as the sampling frame. Three of the four neighborhoods, Victory Avenue, Homantin Estate, and Valley Road Estate (the latter two both large public housing estates), are nearly contiguous and administratively fall under the jurisdiction of the Kowloon City District Office. The fourth neighborhood, Yau Yat Chuen, lies less than a mile from Victory Avenue in the adjacent administrative district of Shamshuipo. Familiarity with the four neighborhoods (Charlotte Ikels had lived in Yau Yat Chuen for a month in 1974 and on Victory Avenue for 15 months in 1975-1976) as well as Hong Kong census household income statistics, newspaper and real estate advertisements for rental or purchase of property, and Hong Kong Housing Department rental scales provided the basis for the selection of the four neighborhoods.

The sampling and contact procedures were modifications of those employed in the two U.S. sites. Yau Yat Chuen itself served as one sampling frame. It is located on the leveled top of a hill accessible in 1983 by a single road and was settled in the 1950s when a group of wealthy manufacturers bought the land from the government and attempted to recreate the genteel environment of tree-lined streets and walled villas characteristic of wealthy urban neighborhoods in pre-Communist Canton (Guangzhou). (Yau Yat Chuen translates as "Once Again a Village.") Two square blocks (including both the one in which the researcher had lived in 1975-1976 and the one on the opposite side of the street in which she lived during the 1982-1983 fieldwork) provided the sampling frame for Victory Avenue. One housing block, randomly selected, from each public housing estate provided the remainder of the sampling frame.

Hong Kong residents are wary of strangers. Robberies are far more likely to occur inside buildings (on staircases and in elevators) than outside. Consequently buzzing someone whom one does not know into one's apartment building, let alone letting such a person into one's own apartment, requires enormous trust. Furthermore, a Cantonese-speaking non-Chinese, such as Charlotte Ikels, standing at the door means only one thing to most Hong Kong residents—a missionary bent on saving souls or collecting money. To generate some publicity both just before and during the interviewing stage of the research, we turned to the mass media. First, a short article about the research that included the researcher's picture was published in the largest circulation daily, the *Dung Fong* (*Oriental Daily*). Second, a longer article appeared in the monthly publication, *Pine and Cedar*, of St. James Settlement, a well-known social service agency. This eight-page Chinese-language publication is both for and about the elderly and carries greater legitimacy than the first, though it reaches a much smaller audience. Copies of these articles were included in our initial mailing to all prospective households. Third, about halfway through the interviewing the researcher was a guest on a daytime Cantonese television program aimed at housewives that allotted about 20 minutes to the research and included a clipping of the researcher teaching knitting at the social center where she was conducting participant observation. (This clearly reached a large audience. For about a week after it was shown, heads turned at the market, people smiled at Ikels on the bus, and kids squealed, "It's Dr. Ai!" when she appeared at the door.) Finally, a sympathetic informant in Yau Yat Chuen mentioned her research to a radio talk show host, Aileen Bridgewater, who invited me for a half-hour interview in English. Her informant assured her that the listeners of this program were largely Chinese interested in improving their English and thus likely to belong to that hard-to-reach category of middle- and upper-income residents of private housing.

The original aim was to select 50 informants from each of the four neighborhoods. Logistics made the fulfillment of this aim difficult, and a compromise was effected. Yau Yat Chuen was the wealthiest neighborhood in the study, as well as the one most difficult to access. Residents lived behind high walls or locked building entrances, reducing our initial vocal contact effort to strained introductions over an intercom—often with a low-flying plane headed for the airport screaming over our heads. Yau Yat Chuen was also a neighborhood in transition. A substantial proportion of dwelling units was unoccupied or occupied by inhabitants who spent much time outside of Hong Kong. Furthermore, the residents were turning over rapidly as the old manufacturing families were selling their homes and emigrating and young professionals were moving in. The Victory Avenue neighborhood, the second wealthiest in the study, still had many older families living in privately owned (or rented), though entirely high-rise, accommodations. Consequently we oversampled in Victory Ave, obtaining 60 informants there and 40 in Yau Yat Chuen. Nearly half the Hong Kong population lives in public housing estates with heavily subsidized rents. Homantin Estate, settled 10 years prior to the study, was home to 53 informants, and Valley Road Estate, our lowest-income neighborhood, settled about 20 years prior, was home to 51.

The research team consisted of eight people, the team leader and at one time or another a total of seven local college student assistants, four young men and three young women. Charlotte Ikels as the team leader conducted interviews in all four neighborhoods, and the assistants, in pairs, were responsible for only one neighborhood each. Yau Yat Chuen was the exception to this rule—one assistant and the leader carried out all the interviews there. A random sample of 100 households was selected in each site for each round of interviewing. Each potential informant household was sent a letter in Chinese addressed to "Head of Household" along with the two newspaper articles informing them of the nature of the project, the characteristics of the researcher, and a statement that the researcher would be visiting the neighborhood within the next few days. Upon being received at the door, the researcher selected one member of the household according to its age and sex composition and scheduled an interview at the informant's convenience. Because there was no way of knowing in advance whether a particular household contained a person 60 years of age or older, the team could not easily design a special older person sample to augment the community sample. Instead they preferentially interviewed older people whenever they happened to be members of sample households. If no one was at home, the researchers left a note along with name cards identifying themselves. The assistant would then attempt up to four revisits before eliminating the household from the sample. Six hundred and eighty-one letters were sent for a final yield of 204 interviews. The overall refusal rate (percent of those actually contacted who refused to be interviewed) was 58%—71% in Yau Yat Chuen, 66% in Victory Avenue, 39% in Homantin, and 41% in Valley Road. Much of this variance in willingness to participate can be attributed to the design of the housing in which the informants lived. In the well-to-do neighborhoods, the researchers often could not even get into the lobby of the building and had to try to persuade an unseen person over the intercom to let them in. In the housing estates Charlotte Ikels or an assistant appeared right at the door of the household and negotiated admission face-to-face. There were usually several informants on each floor, and many people had already observed interviews in progress through the grillwork gates behind which most apartment doors were kept open. Also, each new person invited to participate could easily contact someone interviewed earlier and determine whether our team was trustworthy.

Part Two

Cross-Cultural Comparisons

5

Age and Well-Being

*A*s ethnographers about to begin community studies, we viewed the seven settings described above with eagerness to discover every possible detail of the social and cultural features that in combination gave age its meanings in each one. On the other hand, as colleagues in a comparative project we had to maintain, on a metalevel, the more abstract view of our sites as representing different points on several dimensions of variation.

Scale, measured by the size and density of a site, as well as its interdependence with the "outside" world, varies from the minimal level represented by !Kung villages to the teeming streets and international commerce of Hong Kong. From a demographic point of view, our sites include a considerable range of variation in both age distribution of population and residential stability. The paired communities in Botswana, Ireland, and the United States are particularly interesting from this perspective. In Botswana, the recent

AUTHOR'S NOTE: This chapter was written by Charlotte Ikels, using information provided by all members of the research team.

sedentism of !Kung offers important insights into the consequences of varying degrees of mobility for the experience of aging. Clifden and Blessington occupy opposite poles of Irish migration history. Clifden has experienced the pattern characteristic of western Ireland, losing young persons who emigrate in search of work, so that the remaining population has a very high proportion of elderly. Blessington has received young in-migrants, so that the proportion of old persons is smaller and the contrast between "locals" and "blow-ins" is an important basis of social differentiation. Scale has important effects on views of the life course, which also vary substantially across our sites, with implications for older persons important enough to warrant being the sole topic of Chapter 6.

In the United States, Momence and Swarthmore also offer a sharp contrast in residential stability. Although the proportions of their populations made up of older people are similar, the greater stability of residence in Momence offers possibilities of social participation that are lacking in Swarthmore.

Subsistence strategies and levels of material resources also vary across our research locations, from the minimal technological paraphernalia and material accumulation of the !Kung to the complexity of industrial production in Hong Kong and the United States and the economic abundance of Swarthmore as an upper-middle-class American suburb. The variation in individual versus collective bases of allocating resources, seen most clearly in the health care systems of the United States and Ireland, also has powerful consequences for the meaning of old age. The relationship between age and access to power and resources is the focus of Chapter 7 on political economy.

Structures and values of family ties also vary among our sites, with a range representative of that present in human society. The !Kung and the communities in the United States have flexible kinship systems in which relationships are defined by an individual's descent from both parents. One line of descent or the other is not emphasized to the point of becoming a basis of corporate group formation, as is the case for Herero and the Chinese of Hong Kong. In Ireland, the basic principle of kinship is similar to that in our !Kung and American communities, but the range of relationships within which tangible resources and support are shared tends to be wider than in either U.S. town. The Herero and the Chinese, in contrast, participate in familial systems that strongly emphasize lineality, and consequently define groups of kin, in addition to networks of individuals. Membership in these kin groups—patrilineages for the Chinese, both patrilineages and matrilineages for the Herero—brings rights and responsibilities that transcend individual relationships and have important consequences for their older members. These consequences are particularly clear in the sphere of caregiving, and they are discussed most fully in Chapter 8 on health and functionality.

Our book is organized around these dimensions of variation, both in the lives of the old people in the different sites and in the social and cultural attributes of their communities that we believe influenced those lives. In this section, Chapter 5 presents information collected from older persons themselves about their views of their own lives and the quality and sources of their well-being. Chapters 6 and 7 on the life course and on political economy present key features of the research settings and their relationship to the life experiences of their older residents. Chapter 8 brings the other chapters together in an examination of the ways that social and cultural features, in particular structures and values of kinship, mediate the influence of changes in health and functionality on old people's lives. Finally, the concluding chapter summarizes the findings of Project AGE as the basis for an interpretation of the guidance they can give for improving the experiences of aging in our own society.

The most direct of the many ways we attempted to understand the experiences of old age was to ask older people themselves how they felt about their lives. Because we wanted to know whether and how age made a difference in the ways people of all ages looked at their lives, we also asked these questions in our interviews with younger people. Specifically we wanted to know whether well-being, primarily in the sense of life satisfaction, was patterned within societies by such key demographic variables as age and sex as well as the degree to which any such patterning was similar across the societies in our study. As a dependent variable, well-being is presumed to reflect how well or poorly the elderly (or any other segment of a population) are doing. Depending on one's perspective, well-being measures therefore reveal either how well a society meets the needs of the elderly or how well the elderly adapt to whatever society provides.

The evaluations below were made by individuals about their own lives. They offer a flesh-and-blood preview of themes and variations that will be developed in the following sections of this chapter, in which we present theoretical context, measurement strategy, evidence, and, finally, cultural interpretations for the meanings of well-being in the various societies.

- Low Evaluation of Well-Being

!Kung: My life is not good. Even you saw me. Last rainy season I slept in this dwelling you see behind me. It has no top, and when the rain fell, it just fell on me. I have no dwelling. [Female, age 60 or older]

Herero: I am a 1 because I have no cattle, no money, no husband, and no children. My cattle have all died in the drought. My children are gone, and I am all alone with no one to support me. Life 10 years ago was much better because my son was here to help me. Today I have no one. [Female, age 51]

Clifden: I have bad health, but I'm in my own home, so I'm not that bad. [Female, age 78]

Blessington: I'm unemployed and feel financial pressure. [Male, age 44]

Momence: I have lived at poverty level all my life even with my educational level. I feel my life has been wasted except for my kids and my wife. I had to scrimp past 30 before going to college. [Male, age 40]

Swarthmore: Because my wife is not with me. [Male, age 62]

Hong Kong: I'm unhealthy. Living is not good too. Just enough for the two meals. [Female, age 60]

- Moderate Evaluation of Well-Being

!Kung: I live by my own efforts. I keep myself young and no one else supports me. [Male in his 70s]

Herero: I have a few stock, enough to feed myself and to take care of my family. Things have gotten worse lately, though. There used to be rain around here, but there has been none lately. [Male, age 38]

Clifden: My family are all gone and I'm all alone now. [Female, age 55]

Blessington: I'm still able to work and get on. [Male, age 77]

Momence: Though I am sick [right now], I have health and strength. I can get around because I have children and aid. I don't have fancy things, but they're paid for. What I have, I am happy with. Kids are old enough that I don't have to worry about them. I have time to myself. [Female, age 33]

Swarthmore: Because I think I have a good life, beautiful children, nice husband, nice husband's parents, family all close by, but I haven't accomplished all my goals. [Female, age 38]

Hong Kong: In the middle, not so toilsome [as before]. I have no money left to save, but I have enough food to eat. [Female, age 71]

- High Evaluation of Well-Being

!Kung: I have a good life. Bau [another old woman] brings me edible resin and berries. //ushe [her middle-aged daughter] brings me other bush foods. I eat enough to be full, and I have food. [Female, age 60 or older]

Herero: I stay with old people who are really rich. We have a lot of milk and a lot of butter, and there is money to buy things that I need. [Female, age 20]

Clifden: I have as much of life as I can and take a little drink. [Male, age 72]

Blessington: I have a good family. They are grown up. I'm free again. I might travel. [Male, age 45]

Momence: Our home will be paid for next month—we don't want for anything. We're both on social security. Kids are worse off than I am. [Female, age 62]

Swarthmore: If I didn't think it was the best possible life, I'd go out and change it! [Male, age 40]

Hong Kong: I have children who support the family. The children do everything. On the whole everyone treats me very well. [Female, age 63]

Theoretical Context for Evaluation of Well-Being

Key Issues

Two major issues have guided debate among gerontologists on the most appropriate means of measuring well-being. The first has focused on the relative utility of objective versus subjective measures, and the second has focused on the relative merits of quantitative versus qualitative approaches.

Objective Versus Subjective Measures

Objective measures, sometimes referred to as social indicators, usually focus on material, social, or other external conditions thought by the researcher to have a major impact on individual well-being. The variables chosen reflect the beliefs of the investigator that high scores on some, such as income, educational attainment, access to health care, housing, and interaction with kin, and low scores on others, such as number of stressful life events, will indicate high levels of well-being. These measures as well as changes in them over time are relatively easily obtained and more or less quantifiable. The problem for investigators, however, has been that these external measures do not correlate all that well with what individuals themselves say about their well-being—that is, with subjective measures. When individuals are asked global questions (How do you feel about your life now?) or domain-specific questions (How do you feel about your housing? Your health care?) or provide answers to instruments measuring mental health status or affective states, there have been only modest or inconsistent correlations between these subjective measures and the objective ones (Chappell & Havens, 1980; Diener, 1984; Larson, 1978; Lawton, Moss, & Kleban, 1984; Lee & Ellithorpe, 1982; Wan & Livieratos, 1978).

In an effort to resolve these seeming contradictions, investigators at first focused on the measuring instruments themselves (Nydegger, 1977), speculating that perhaps findings were uneven because the different studies employed different types of questions, and indeed, when the nature of the various measures was taken into consideration, some correlations were enhanced. For example, it rapidly became clear that self-assessed health was a better predictor of subjective well-being than physician- or observer-assessed health (George & Landerman, 1984; Zautra & Hempel, 1984). It also became clear that well-being meant different things to different investigators. For some it was equated with "happiness," mood, or a net balance of positive affect (variously referred to as "morale"); for others it was equated with "life satisfaction." The objective indicators generally correlated better with measures of life satisfaction than with those of morale. Because life satisfaction has come to be regarded as a more stable variable than morale (or mood) and to involve a more cognitive component, we chose to ask about life satisfaction rather than morale (Campbell, Converse, & Rodgers, 1976; George, 1981; Horley, 1984; Larson, Mannell, & Zuzanek, 1986).

One of the consequences of the finding that predictions could not be made neatly from objective to subjective well-being has been a massive effort to find out just what does determine subjective well-being. Investigators have spent the better part of the last two decades working backward from subjective well-being scores to a whole host of variables, ranging from basic demographic ones, such as age and sex, to more complex variables, such as the nature of interaction with kin or friends and the recency of exposure to various types of stressors, such as job loss or widowhood. Investigators have also sought to discover which domains, such as family, health, and employment, have the greatest impact on well-being. Computer-assisted analyses have become increasingly sophisticated, moving beyond simple one-to-one correlations to multiple regression, factor analysis, path modeling, and, most recently, hypothesis-testing models using LISREL (see, for example, Chappell & Badger, 1989; Diener, 1984; Ishii-Kuntz, 1990; Krause, 1991; Lance, Lautenschlager, Sloan, & Varca, 1989; Liang, Asano, Bollen, Kahana, & Maeda, 1987; Liang, Lawrence, & Bollen, 1987; McKenzie & Campbell, 1987; Okun & Stock, 1987; Okun, Stock, Haring, & Witter, 1984). Still the amount of variance explained has not been very impressive.

A number of researchers have concluded that the core of the problem lies in the mistaken assumption that different categories of people have the same sources of well-being. Instead they argue that sex, age, life stage, and ethnicity lead to differential saliences for particular domains and that well-being will (or should) correlate most closely with the domains that are most salient to the respondents. Thus, for example, it has been hypothesized that health will be especially salient for the elderly, being married for the newly married, and church-mediated relationships for elderly African Americans (Blandford & Chappell, 1990; Diener, 1984; George, Okun, & Landerman, 1985; Ishii-Kuntz, 1990; Ortega, Crutchfield, & Rushing, 1983; Ryff, 1989b; Weingarten & Bryant, 1987; Zautra & Hempel, 1984). In short, these researchers attempt to specify the variables that are meaningful to the subpopulations in their studies. By and large, however, these analyses have also been hypothesis driven, that is, the investigator hypothesizes and then attempts to confirm which variables have the greatest impact on well-being. Studies that ask the respondents themselves what they think accounts for their current well-being are much less frequently encountered. (Recent studies that do take this approach include Bearon, 1989; Mukherjee, 1989; Ryff, 1989b; and Wood & Johnson, 1989.)

Researchers have also expressed concern that the lack of correlation with variables assumed to affect well-being could be due to unmeasured and/or extraneous factors. For example, it has been suggested that the critical variable is internal to the individual— that is, that a person's worldview or enduring aspects of personality, such as an optimistic or pessimistic disposition, determine evaluations of his or her current state of well-being. An emphasis on these types of variables is characteristic of the "top-down" view of well-being—the view that well-being is a global state that influences how one feels about particular aspects of one's life (see, for example, Costa et al., 1987; Diener, 1984; Krause, 1991; Lance et al., 1989; Neapolitan, 1988; Sagy, Antonovsky, & Adler, 1990). Thus a person with a pessimistic disposition would presumably be more likely to indicate dissatisfaction with health or housing than a person with an optimistic one, regardless of objective circumstances, and a person who found meaning in suffering would be likely to respond to reverses of fortune differently than someone who did not. Extraneous factors affecting both validity and reliability could also include such uncontrollables as period effects or the quality of the interaction between the interviewer and the interviewee.

Quantitative Versus Qualitative Approaches

The second issue of great concern to gerontologists has been the relative utility of quantitative and qualitative approaches to measuring well-being (Reinharz & Rowles, 1988; Ryff, 1989a; Thomas & Chambers, 1989a, 1989b; Wood & Johnson, 1989). Quantitative studies emphasize the collection of easily measured (quantifiable) data, employ primarily fixed-choice formats containing choices deemed relevant by the investigator, are administered impersonally by interviewers who do not expect to have subsequent contact with the interviewee and who try to minimize the impact of their own personalities or interests on the interview process (the impersonal aspect is, of course, most extreme in the case of telephone

interviews or surveys conducted by mail), involve study populations of several hundred or several thousand people, and decon-
textualize the data by reducing them to discrete variables that can
be compared across persons. In contrast, qualitative studies frequently collect data that cannot be easily quantified, such as life
stories or other narratives, contain many if not mostly open-ended
questions to allow the speaker to contribute to the development of
a range of population-relevant choices, are carried out by one or a
few interviewers who generally expect to have a sustained relationship with the interviewee and who regard themselves as part of the
research instrumentation—that is, who are acutely aware of the fact
that their own personal style and interests will have an impact on
the nature of the data collected—involve small populations ranging from fewer than 10 to about 200 people, and emphasize the
importance of context in understanding the significance of any
particular datum.

Although the above depiction of the two approaches emphasizes
their differences, two facts should be kept in mind. The first is that
any given study, including of course our own, is likely to use some
blend of both approaches; the second is that the choice of whether
to emphasize quantitative or qualitative approaches is largely based
on the objectives of the study. Testing hypotheses regarding relationships among variables, particularly when multivariate analysis is
planned, requires a large sample, the precise size varying with the
number of variables involved in the hypothesis and the heterogeneity of the study population. When study populations become
large, multiple interviewers must be employed, and interviewer
effects must be kept to a minimum to avoid confounding of the
data. Similarly, a predominantly fixed-choice format also restricts
the range of variation in answers that might otherwise occur because of diverse interviewer styles and interests. If, however, the
goal of the study is to explore the meaning of a concept or set of
related concepts to a particular population, qualitative methods are
more appropriate.

Neglected Issues

Although, as indicated above, gerontologists have used a number of ingenious analytical techniques in their efforts to uncover the

possible sources of variation in individual well-being, what is striking to those of us engaged in cross-cultural research is the relative lack of attention paid to more global sources of variation, such as historical change (manifested as cohort effects), period effects, and cultural factors. The importance of these global variables is not, however, limited to cross-cultural studies of well-being; they are equally important in understanding differences among age groups and ethnic groups within a single society.

Cohort Effects

One point on which social gerontologists seem to agree is that subjective well-being is a product of expectations and experience (Bearon, 1989; Campbell, 1981; George et al., 1985; Nydegger, 1980; Whitbourne, 1985). People develop a notion of desirable and possible conditions and, on the basis of their own and others' experiences in terms of these optimal conditions, conclude that they are doing well or poorly. The significance of this phenomenon in terms of the production of specific cohort-centric worldviews is potentially enormous.

When a society undergoes rapid change, particularly when, for example, the standard of living rises precipitously, younger and older people will inevitably have very different ideas of what constitutes an acceptable standard of living. The elderly, recalling that their parents or grandparents had no indoor plumbing or no financial resources in old age beyond those provided by immediate kin, are likely to be favorably impressed by such basics as running water and indoor toilets or by state welfare provisions for the aged, however modest. Young people, though, are more likely to take such provisions for granted and often to have more information via modern media about other ways of life that they perceive as even more desirable. Older persons in Clifden, for example, remembered when a visit to the doctor meant braving winter storms in a tiny curragh (wood and canvas rowboat). Home medical visits and a pension were remarkable improvements over the lives of their own parents, to say nothing of their grandparents. "Why, they even pay me for being old!" as one old man explained to us. Similarly, older people whose young adult lives were disrupted by war or civil unrest along with unemployment or famine—experiences of many elders in Hong Kong—are likely to view social and political stability favorably even if the stratification system is less than ideal and the political system undemocratic. Younger people are more likely to view this same stability as stagnation and to be distressed by the unequal opportunities they face. By emphasizing analyses of the relationships among synchronic variables, researchers have essentially ignored the role of historical factors in establishing the baseline expectations against which different cohorts measure their current status. In order to understand age differences in subjective well-being, it is critical to consider the historical context in which individuals developed their definitions of the good life.

Period Effects

The significance of period effects has also by and large been ignored in research on well-being. (Campbell's work is a conspicuous exception; see Campbell, 1981; Campbell et al., 1976.) Period effects refer to specific events or circumstances ongoing at the time of the study that can be expected to influence people's evaluations of their lives. Depending on the nature of the particular period effect, the evaluations of the entire population or only those of certain segments of the population might be affected. In Hong Kong, for example, most of the interviewing was conducted in the first half of 1983, during a period of high inflation, high unemployment, depressed property values, and an unstable Hong Kong dollar. In addition, at the same time, Hong Kong residents were gloomily awaiting the outcome of official Sino-British talks on the future political status of Hong Kong, an outcome that they anticipated could exacerbate an already unfavorable economic climate. Similarly, interviews with the !Kung and the Herero in 1988 took place in the midst of a long-term drought that had devastating effects on crops and livestock. It would be reasonable to expect that such severe economic conditions would be reflected in assessments of well-being, and this is clearly the case in our data. Period effects can be expected to express themselves primarily in terms of domain salience and secondarily in their impact on the life satisfaction of those individuals who are most directly affected by the particular events or circumstances.

Cultural Factors

When conducting research on well-being in societies other than their own, researchers must not only be concerned with all of the issues referred to above but also be alert to the impact of culture per se on people's answers. Two key questions must be addressed: (a) Are there unique cultural styles of interaction that tend to suppress or inflate the evaluations people are likely to make? and (b) Are there unique cultural definitions of the good life? Here we will discuss only the first question because the second is the primary topic of the remainder of this chapter. The impact of cultural values on response styles has already been commented on by Shanas et al. (1968) and by Thomas and Chambers (1989b) with reference to the English. In both studies the researchers were surprised that an individual's scores did not seem a valid reflection of actual quality of life and attributed this lack of correspondence to the high value the English put on stoicism or on keeping "a stiff upper lip." Thus, despite their own indications elsewhere in the interview that they were clearly dissatisfied with their lives, the English men in the Thomas and Chambers study could not bring themselves to complain about their situations by assigning themselves low life satisfaction scores. Similarly, but with directionality reversed, Rubinstein (1989) comments on the possible impact of cultural styles of expressive behavior on the response patterns of Jewish elderly.

Our Project AGE files also reveal effects of cultural response styles. Among the !Kung and Herero, for example, a complaint style is highly legitimate. Emphasizing one's terrible plight is a culturally acceptable way of attempting to elicit help from another—the interviewer or onlookers as the case may be. Furthermore, to express high levels of satisfaction, particularly with one's material circumstances, in a public arena such as the interview setting is to risk exposing oneself to requests for assistance from others. Thus both the !Kung and the Herero might well lament their circumstances for reasons other than those of theoretical interest to the researcher. Among the Chinese, on the other hand, there is a tremendous emphasis on avoiding excess emotions—there is a widely held belief that too much joy or too much sorrow unbalances one and can lead to poor health and clouded judgment.

Indeed, this emphasis on moderation contributed to a propensity among the Chinese to avoid strong statements and to place themselves "in the middle." Even when the interviewer attempted to insist that on a 6-point scale the respondent had to settle on a score of 3 or 4, the respondent frequently remained adamant and was ultimately allowed a score of 3.5! Given the potential impact of such differences in suppressing or inflating self-ratings, it is clear that simply comparing societies on the basis of their average well-being scores would reveal little useful information.

Methodology

Data Collection

Because the goal of this study was to learn how people think about and evaluate their experiences of aging, we sought to maximize opportunities for free expression through the use of many open-ended questions. We consequently favored subjective measures and qualitative approaches. We defined well-being as assessment of one's own life compared to one's definitions of the best life possible. Our primary measure was a modified version of the Cantril Self-Anchoring Ladder (Cantril, 1965). The modifications included a reduction in the number of steps in the original ladder (from 10 to 6 steps in five sites where most respondents were literate, and from 10 to 5 steps in two sites where many people were not literate), as well as the replacement of the ladder by a flight of stairs in Hong Kong and by the five fingers of the interviewer's hand among the !Kung and Herero. We selected a self-rated and self-anchoring measure so that our participants could specify the domains of greatest personal significance for their own well-being. The discovery of these domains is, of course, central to a research endeavor that includes the goal of evaluating the influence of cultural context on subjective well-being.

In order to learn the bases on which respondents assigned themselves a score, we asked them several questions intended to tap the domains of greatest personal salience. Depending on the particular site, these questions included asking respondents to specify the nature of the "best possible life" and the "worst possible life" in the community, the reasons for assigning their current lives a particular score, what it would take for them to assign the highest or lowest possible score, what score they would have given their lives 5 years ago and for what reasons, and what score they anticipated assigning to their lives 5 years from the time of the interview and for what reasons. Among the !Kung and the Herero no past and future well-being scores as such were sought; instead, the informants were asked simply whether their past life (10 years ago) was better or worse than their present, and the Herero were also asked about their expectations of life (better or worse) in the future.

These responses could then be compared with responses made to other parts of the interview, such as those dealing with the individual's perceptions and evaluations of the stages of life, including the stage to which they actually belonged. In addition we were able to gain a more concrete sense of the comparative basis for self-ranking by examining the examples provided earlier in the interview of older individuals personally known who were living the good life or the bad life. Thus we could situate people's direct statements about the status of their own well-being in the larger context of their beliefs about characteristics of people in the same stage of life and, in the case of the elderly, in the context of their concrete knowledge of what was actually possible for older people in the community. Although most of the numeric analyses presented below are derived from the participants' direct statements about why they rated their own well-being as they did, we were able to verify the salience of the themes used through examination of their responses to these less directly personal questions.

Findings

Evaluations of Well-Being

We begin with a summary of the numeric scores people assigned themselves on our ladder and comment on the patterns visible across and within the research locations (see Table 5.1). However, these numeric patterns acquire their full meaning only when joined with the text-based analysis that follows.

TABLE 5.1 Mean Well-Being Scores by Site

Score	!Kung (N = 102)	Herero (N = 186)	Clifden (N = 129)	Bless. (N = 170)	Mom. (N = 207)	Swarth. (N = 201)	H.K. (N = 192)
				Site			
1.0			1	3	1	1	4
1.2		38					
1.5	20						
2.0			3	3	3	4	13
2.4		56					
3.0	33		10	16	21	11	68
3.5							18
3.6		64					
4.0			30	51	66	40	49
4.5	8						2
4.8		19					
5.0			56	58	73	86	26
5.5	1						
6.0	41	9	29	39	43	59	11
Means	4.0	3.1	4.7	4.6	4.6	4.9	3.7

NOTE: The !Kung self-ratings have been converted from a 5-point scale, on which the lowest rating was not allowed, to a 6-point scale. This omission of the lowest possible rating on the scale leads to an upward skewing of the scores. The Herero self-ratings have also been converted from a 5-point scale to a 6. In this and all subsequent tables the means are based on the converted scores.

The mean self-ratings range from a low of 3.1 among the Herero to a high of 4.9 in Swarthmore and cluster in two groupings: the low self-raters (!Kung, Herero, and Hong Kong Chinese) and the high self-raters (the Irish and U.S. populations). As indicated above in the section on cultural factors, we believe that to some extent these differences are a function of response patterns: In the two African societies with an ethic of broad kinship-based sharing of resources, a strategy of playing up one's needs and playing down one's resources is, from the personal point of view, a maximizing one, and in the case of the Chinese, ideational factors valuing moderation in all things contribute to a concentration of responses about the midpoint of the scale.

Differences in scores may also reflect differences in the composition of the various samples. As indicated elsewhere in this volume,

Swarthmore elderly who were even mildly impaired physically were likely to disappear from the community when they could no longer maintain themselves in their own homes. The feelings of very frail individuals therefore had little influence on average well-being scores for that community. In Blessington frail elderly were likely to be in the community but not to participate in our interviews. In the Botswana and Clifden sites even severely impaired people remained in the community and did take part in our research. Given that in most sites the elderly are deliberately over-represented, their scores exert a disproportionate influence on the means. Scores could also, of course, reflect real differences in objective circumstances and/or real differences in people's perceptions of their circumstances—issues that will be dealt with more fully below.

The impacts of sex and age on well-being scores are displayed in Tables 5.2 and 5.3. Average scores vary only slightly with sex in any of the sites, and this variation is not significant statistically. In five of the sites, women give themselves slightly higher ratings than men, whereas in Blessington and among the Herero, men give themselves slightly higher ratings than women.

Each researcher was asked to divide the study population into three age ranges, broadly defined as young, middle-aged, and old. Variations by age were greater than those by sex, and the pattern of age differences also varied across the research sites. In Blessington and in both the U.S. communities, older respondents were more *positive* about their lives than younger ones; among the !Kung and Herero and in Hong Kong, this was reversed so that the old were more *negative* about their lives than the young. (In Clifden there was scarcely any difference in well-being scores by age at all.)

Because health status is generally assumed to have a major impact on life satisfaction (and even, perhaps, to be the mechanism underlying variation by age—especially when life satisfaction declines with age), we looked separately at the relationship between subjective health and well-being. (See Chapter 8 for a full description of the health-related aspects of the seven populations.) As can be seen from the means in Table 5.4, this relationship is the clearest one so far—in every community those in the poorest health have the lowest mean scores, and each improvement in health status is accompanied by an improvement in well-being.

TABLE 5.2 Mean Well-Being Scores by Site and Sex

Sex				Site			
	!Kung	*Herero*	*Clifden*	*Bless.*	*Mom.*	*Swarth.*	*H.K.*
Males	3.8	3.2	4.6	4.7	4.6	4.7	3.6
	(n = 51)	(n = 66)	(n = 61)	(n = 80)	(n = 94)	(n = 82)	(n = 99)
Females	4.3	3.0	4.8	4.6	4.7	5.0	3.8
	(n = 51)	(n = 112)	(n = 69)	(n = 90)	(n = 113)	(n = 119)	(n = 93)
Totals	(n = 102)	(n = 178)	(n = 130)	(n = 170)	(n = 207)	(n = 201)	(n = 192)

TABLE 5.3 Mean Well-Being Scores by Site and Age

Age Category				Site			
	!Kung	*Herero*	*Clifden*	*Bless.*	*Mom.*	*Swarth.*	*H.K.*
Young	4.1	3.7	4.8	4.2	4.2	4.5	3.9
	(n = 21)	(n = 47)	(n = 23)	(n = 57)	(n = 53)	(n = 50)	(n = 54)
Middle-Aged	4.3	3.1	4.7	4.7	4.8	4.9	3.6
	(n = 50)	(n = 78)	(n = 47)	(n = 53)	(n = 62)	(n = 79)	(n = 107)
Old	3.6	2.3	4.7	4.9	4.7	5.1	3.5
	(n = 31)	(n = 53)	(n = 59)	(n = 60)	(n = 91)	(n = 72)	(n = 31)

NOTE: For site-specific reasons the chronological ages defining the boundaries of these ranges vary slightly. Among the !Kung, Herero, and Chinese the ranges are under 30, 30-59, and 60 or older. In Clifden they are under 36, 36-64, and 65 or older. In the case of Blessington and Swarthmore the ranges are under 40, 40-64, and 65 or older, and in Momence they are under 35, 35-59, and 60 or older.

TABLE 5.4 Mean Well-Being Scores by Site and Health Status

Health Status				Site			
	!Kung	*Herero*	*Clifden*	*Bless.*	*Mom.*	*Swarth.*	*H.K.*
Poor/Fair	NA	2.2	4.4	4.3	4.2	4.4	3.4
		(n = 50)	(n = 39)	(n = 32)	(n = 40)	(n = 17)	(n = 16)
Aver./Good	NA	3.2	4.8	4.5	4.6	4.7	3.4
		(n = 55)	(n = 59)	(n = 80)	(n = 90)	(n = 74)	(n = 81)
Excellent	NA	3.7	5.0	4.9	4.8	4.9	4.0
		(n = 69)	(n = 31)	(n = 58)	(n = 77)	(n = 109)	(n = 95)

NOTE: In four sites a 4-point scale was used, and in three sites a 5-point scale was used. The actual labels used to describe the points on the scale varied somewhat from site to site.

In five of the sites the respondents were asked to rate how they viewed their lives of 5 years ago and in three to rate how they expected their lives to be 5 years hence. In the cases of the !Kung and the Herero, informants were asked only whether life in the past (10 years ago) was worse than, the same as, or better than now. The !Kung were not asked to speculate on the future, but the Herero and Irish were asked whether they expected their situations to deteriorate, remain the same, or improve. In terms of mean scores the Irish saw the least amount of change, and among those who did see change the Irish were almost equally divided between those whose lives had improved and those whose lives had deteriorated. The modal responses in Swarthmore and Momence also indicate stability, but the majority of Americans felt their lives had changed—improving in Swarthmore but getting a bit worse in Momence. Hong Kong informants generally felt their lives had improved over the past 5 years, whereas most !Kung and especially the Herero felt life had gotten worse. These two African populations had the least stability in well-being of all those in the study, a fact that can probably be attributed to the severe drought that directly threatened their resource bases of gardens and cattle.

Excluding the !Kung, for whom no data are available, and temporarily setting aside the Herero, who maintain a bleak view of the future, we were at first impressed with the optimism expressed by the inhabitants of the other five sites. Whereas in three of the sites the modal response was that things would stay the same, in Clifden and Hong Kong over 56% of the respondents expected things to get better, and in Blessington and the U.S. sites, among those anticipating change, 2.2 to 3.3 times as many expected things to improve as those who expected things to deteriorate. A closer examination, however, revealed a disquieting pattern—in every site the number of people willing to express views about the future was substantially less than the number willing to discuss the past or present. These are the same results that Cantril (1965) found in his study of 15 samples from around the world. Not surprisingly, our experience has been that those who fear a continued decline, a downturn, or their own death are the least likely to want to express a view about their future. Indeed, 14 people from Clifden stated simply that they would be dead in the future, and the Herero, who were the most negative overall, had the highest number of nonresponses. Even among the generally optimistic Swarthmoreans, several older people answered requests for their view of future well-being with black humor: "Where will I be in 5 or 10 years? Pushing up daisies!" "Where would I put myself in 5 or 10 years? Ten feet under!"

Interpretations of Well-Being

In order to understand the bases on which people evaluate their well-being, we needed to integrate the numeric with the textual information. Here we interpret patterns in both the evaluations and the reasons for them in terms of cohort, period, and cultural factors, first within each study site and then in an overall comparison across the sites.

Patterns of Well-Being Within the Study Sites

!Kung

> My life is not good. I don't know what will give me a life. I don't have a job, and I don't have a way of helping myself. I wish to be a rich man and have goats and cattle. [Male, under 30. Score = 2, lowest possible]

> Life is with me. I can take care of myself. I can cook and sew, and I still have strength. [Female, about 50. Score = 4]

> Because I have no sickness. Sahxali, a Bantu medicine man, told me that I had been witched by a Zhun/wa. I went to the Maun Hospital and got better. I got several injections that gave me life. [Female, about 40. Score = 5]

!Kung responses to the well-being questions appear to be influenced both by age and by the overall economic circumstances of the population. Young people generally feel that things have gotten better for them and relate this to their growing competency. Ten years ago, for example, many of them were regarded as children with little or no role in the community. The older people, however, rate their past life as much better largely on the grounds of better functionality or better material circumstances. Overall, those who think their current life is better are those with income-generating activities or those whose health has improved since the reference time of 10 years ago when they personally might have been under treatment for TB or been suffering from malaria.

Although age differences in comparisons of present and past lives are in the same direction for men and women, the magnitude of the difference is greater for women. Younger women are more positive about their present circumstances as compared to the past than younger men, whereas older women are more negative about their present circumstances in comparison to the past than are older men. Although these findings for young people are consistent with current well-being scores for young men and women—that is, young women score themselves substantially higher than young men—those for old people are not—that is, old women rate their current lives higher than old men do. Although one cannot resolve this puzzle with a cross-sectional data set, it is interesting to speculate that if the older women in the study also experienced a relatively pleasant youth, they might well feel now that they had fallen relatively further than men. In many cases it is clear that when asked to compare the past with the present, !Kung do not think back precisely to the "5 or 10 years ago" reference point, but rather to some particularly significant event or period of the past that contrasts with the present. Thus older women might think, "Those were the days! I was strong and could go out and bring back bush foods," whereas older men might think, "It was a struggle then, and it is a struggle now."

Herero

The only things I have in this world are two chickens, two goats, a cow, a calf, and a dog. I had a cat, but I had to give her away because I had no food to give her. Life used to be better because my father and my uncle were rich, but today I have nothing. [Female, age 48. Score = 2]

I am a 2 because I have only one cow yet the government still makes me pay taxes. If I had cattle in my kraal and melons in my garden, then my life would be better, but as things are, it is pretty bad. Even

so, it is better than it was ten years ago because then I was young and foolish and knew nothing while today I am mature.
[Male, age 57. Score = 2]

I have a few fields and some cattle, and my husband looks after me. I am also able to look after myself. [Female, age 57. Score = 4]

I have a job and my father has a job. Our cattle are in pretty good shape. [Male, age 22. Score = 5]

Compared to the other sites, the overwhelming predominance of Herero references to the material aspects of life is striking. Whether young or old, low in well-being or high, in poor or excellent health, the Herero uniformly give priority to economic concerns. The preoccupation with cattle and with the loss of cattle revealed in the individual statements made by Herero respondents reflects in part the 8 years of drought that the region had suffered. Many of the Herero had lost over half their cattle, and a few had lost all of them. Cattle densities around the Okavango Delta had declined by more than half by the end of the drought in 1988.

The interesting features of Herero ratings of their own well-being are the low average values they give themselves, the decline of these self-ratings with age, and the preoccupation with material security. Part of the explanation for these features is certainly that self-denigration and telling others that one is needy are routine conversational themes in this society and modulate the flow of resources and attention among people in daily life. Even so, it is striking that very few people mentioned personal concerns or mental states in their answers. In ordinary conversations with Herero the researcher knew well, well-being themes focused on relations with family members or loneliness were very common. Yet these themes hardly appear in the interview responses tabulated here. It is possible that links to kin are assumed as the medium of human existence and therefore mentioned only when lacking in the extreme. Their absence may also reflect the existence of different sets of conversational standards for formal and informal situations. Although psychologizing may be the stuff of everyday public conversations and discourse in the United States, it is not among the Herero. The interview format of much of the study may consequently have excluded many aspects of the sources of well-being in this society.

Clifden

I've no life at all. I'd rather be dead. [Male, age 68. Score = 1]

Don't complain. We're stretched financially, and two of the kids and myself aren't too well, but we make the best of it.
[Female, age 41. Score = 4]

Great, I've a job and am happy with my life, but I'll have to give more attention to my daughter. [Female, age 30. Score = 5]

You just have to put up with what you have. [Male, age 93. Score = 6]

What is remarkable about the Clifden data is the amazing uniformity and stability of well-being scores. Clifden has the least variation by age or over time of any of the sites. Furthermore, from the investigator's point of view it was initially surprising that given the hard lives of a substantial proportion of the Clifden population, scores were nearly as high as in Swarthmore. The explanation for the relatively high well-being evaluations overall, but especially those from older individuals, is complicated and multifaceted.

First, the social welfare system, which provides pensions for older people and unemployment compensation and a child allowance for younger people, ensures a low but dependable income for inhabitants of the area. Second, low-cost, personal, and available health care provides an important level of security for all people in the area. Third, cohort effects are evident in the high ratings provided by the elderly. Older participants continually compared their current lives not only with the way things were 50 or 60 years ago but, perhaps more importantly, to the conditions experienced directly by their own parents and grandparents when they became old. Sixty years ago conditions in Clifden and especially on the islands off the coast, which were inhabited at that time and on which many of the older respondents were born, were much different. There were no shops, no electricity, no doctor, and no nurses on the islands. Fuel had to be brought to the islands by small boat. Even in Clifden, 60 or 70 years ago, conditions for the elderly were very different. There were no pensions, no visiting nurse program, no free medicines, no tourism, and no comprehensive social welfare system. Comparatively speaking, older people today are much better off than the elders they knew earlier in their lives.

A fourth factor that may act to equalize and inflate self-ratings is a specifically cultural one. A glance at the reasons Clifden residents provide as explanations for their well-being reveals the "stiff upper lip" attitude mentioned earlier in connection with the English. How else is one to interpret a rating of 4 that comes with the comment, "Not much you can do about life—you have to take what comes" or a rating of 6 that comes with the comment, "Just have to put up with what you have"? These are hardly strong positive statements, but they may accurately reflect the ethos of the stoic Irish countryman.

Blessington

There are a lot of things we want to do. My husband was unemployed for a while, and we're just getting on our feet.
[Female, age 29. Score = 1]

I'm halfway through my life. I have my family and am beginning to emerge in my career. [Female, age 34. Score = 3]

I'm living at home with my parents. I'm working, own a car, have good relations with friends, and am living comfortably.
[Male, age 22. Score = 4]

We have no worries. All is running smoothly, children and ourselves in good health. Hopefully we'll get a holiday this year.
[Female, age 37. Score = 5]

Despite the heterogeneity of the population, Blessington residents appear to share a remarkably similar perception of both the life course and the sources of their well-being. Residents appear to divide the life course along two axes, one marking a domestic developmental cycle and the other broader social responsibilities.

When individuals evaluate their own well-being, they think about not only their current state of being but also the extent to which their behavior is consistent with community definitions of the life course.

In Blessington, people view life as a struggle to get established in work, marriage, and family. It is during the early and middle years of life that people spend most of their time trying to achieve these goals. Old age, however, is viewed as a time when one can enjoy the fruits of a lifetime of effort. It is time to retire, travel, and enjoy friends and family. It is likely that older people give themselves higher well-being scores because they feel that the main struggles of life are over. That this is not the whole story, however, is made clear by the counterexample of Hong Kong. Residents of Hong Kong share a very similar view of the life course—indeed, many Hong Kong residents describe the best part of being old as being "done with the struggle"—yet Hong Kong elderly give themselves lower, not higher, scores than the young. A major reason for this is the lack in Hong Kong of much cushion protecting the elderly from the same economic vicissitudes as those that affect other age groups. In Blessington, in contrast with Hong Kong but similar to Clifden, the elderly are relatively protected from material insecurities. The significance of this buffering is obvious from Table 5.7, which shows that the Irish elderly are much less likely than either the Irish young and middle-aged or the elderly in any other site to mention material concerns as factors in their well-being.

Momence

I'm unemployed, and the bills get bigger and bigger. I'm making it, but there's no job in sight. [Male, age 23. Score = 3]

I've raised a family and got a house. Good health. Kids turned out good. [Male, age 60. Score = 5]

I've learned to cope with living alone. God lives with me. I keep my bills paid. I'm a widow, but I've learned to cope and would never care to remarry. [Female, age 67. Score = 6]

In Momence the young give themselves lower well-being scores than the aged and focus much more on material issues. The young are worse off primarily because of the number of single-parent families and the difficulty in obtaining work. Those with the greatest employment opportunities tend to go elsewhere, and those who cannot make it elsewhere remain in or return to Momence. This has been a historical pattern, but at the time of the research Momence was experiencing an economic downturn that intensified the pattern. The elderly are more insulated from economic ups and downs by pensions, Social Security benefits, and paid-off mortgages.

Swarthmore

On my scale of things, because I'm still in school, not earning money, can't buy new furniture. [Male, age 26. Score = 3]

I don't like being single. Everything else is wonderful.
[Male, age 42. Score = 4]

We have good children. My husband and I are both working and have our health. We have no problem with money or aged parent. We're living where we want to be; we're active. [Female, age 39. Score = 5]

I hate to leave Swarthmore. [Female, age 84. Score = 5]

Lack of companionship is the only factor, but I'm probably the best person to be widowed because I'm very independent, and I still have my health so I can be independent. [Female, age 62. Score = 6]

Swarthmore has the highest mean well-being score of all the sites, a fact that at the simplest comparative level can probably be attributed to its wealth. The lack of salience of material issues also suggests the level of resources required to purchase a home in the town and the degree of financial security many residents of Swarthmore enjoy. When talking about the reasons for their well-being, Swarthmore respondents more than those of any other site mention social concerns, marriage and family, work relations, friends, and the community itself.

Which of these more specific areas of social relations they describe and what they say about them differ by age and sex, but only the variation by age has significance statistically. Distinctive life stage perspectives on well-being are apparent, and the distinction between men's and women's views is greater for the older people. There was little difference among people with different appraisals of their own health, and from respondents with different levels of well-being we heard descriptions of similar aspects of social life—but with a different valence. Although most respondents talk about marriage, for example, those with lower evaluations of their well-being describe marital problems or the pain of bereavement.

Both younger women and men talk about social sources of well-being primarily in terms of family—either enjoyment of family or wishes to have a family or to spend more time with family—and achievements in the world of work, either as goals or as accomplishments. Perceptions of family and work as clearly separate domains are revealed in comments about the difficulty of balancing their demands on one's time and energy. When middle-aged men and women are compared, family and work appear again but with different nuances. For example, several middle-aged women specifically ascribe their well-being to the fact that their parents or older relatives are still in good health and do not need care. People over 65, both men and women, talk most about their families and, in particular, their marital situations as parameters for their well-being. Men more often describe the quality of their marriages. Women more often either express their good fortune in still having a husband or describe, usually positively, the activities and friendships that have led to satisfaction with their lives as widows.

There are also age and sex differences in the way Swarthmore residents talk about physical or health issues. First, women in the middle-aged category talk relatively more about physical issues than those in the oldest age category, whereas for men the pattern is reversed. This reflects the fact that older men have lower health and functionality than older women, which in turn reflects the much greater likelihood that men have spouses to care for them. Older women are more likely to be widowed and to be concerned about possibly having to leave the community because of actual or anticipated frailty. The frailest older women are probably no longer in the community to give their responses, and the older women still in Swarthmore are under some pressure to minimize health problems that might push them to leave. Second, women more often refer to the health of *others*, usually their husband and/or children, as sources of their own well-being. When older men talk about well-being in terms of health and functionality, it is typically their own.

Hong Kong

My salary is not much and I have many children.
[Male, age 40. Score = 3]

Everybody has work, stable environment. It's not too bad.
[Female, age 23. Score = 3.5]

I have my son to rear me. [Male, age 70. Score = 4]

Because there is no such thing as saying the best [i.e., a score of 6]. It is the best if one is contented. Nothing difficult cannot be solved nor is there anything that irritates me—therefore it is good. I guess that there are many people who have difficulties which cannot be solved. Thus this makes them unhappy. [Female, age 29. Score = 5]

Every aspect is quite good. [Following is what she tells us when her mother-in-law leaves the room.] The most defective thing is to live with an aged person. We are different in terms of thinking, living habits. It is very difficult to live together. I have been living with her for more than 30 years. [Female, age 58. Score = 5]

In the aggregate, Hong Kong residents overwhelmingly stress the importance of the material conditions of life for their well-being. More than two-thirds of the respondents (70%) mentioned such specifics as financial security, standard of living, or employment opportunities as factors in their well-being. The other three thematic categories were mentioned by much smaller fractions of respondents: 29% referenced social themes, 21% personal themes, and 15% physical status themes. This high salience of the material domain was true of all categories of Hong Kong residents regardless of their age, sex, health status, or well-being score. As indicated earlier, these data were collected during the first phase of Project AGE in 1983, a time of exceptional economic insecurity in Hong Kong characterized by high (for Hong Kong) unemployment, inflation, drastic falls in real estate prices and the stock market, and an unstable Hong Kong dollar. Undoubtedly these contemporaneous facts at least partially shaped the nature of the responses we received; they are not, however, the whole story. Hong Kong residents have long been famous both locally and internationally for their materialistic orientation; even in the best of times it is probable that the material domain would be the most salient.

Once one moves beyond the material domain, however, there is greater variation in how people of different ages, states of health, and well-being scores interpret the causes of their well-being. When the Hong Kong population is divided into three age categories, a pattern of age-specific or life-stage-specific concerns emerges. Young people 18 to 29, who are locally viewed as "just starting out" or "just entering society," are substantially more likely to reference the personal domain—that is, states of mind or plans for the future—than are other age groups. Those 30 to 59, usually conceptualized as those shouldering the responsibilities of "family burdens," are far more likely than the other age groups to reference the social domain—that is, various aspects of family life. Those 60 or older, at the time of life when one is "done with the struggle," are nearly three to four times as likely to mention physical status as a factor in their well-being. These findings clearly support those researchers who have argued that different life stages are characterized by their own set of concerns.

There are few differences by sex in the frequency with which particular domains are cited; at a finer level, however, there are some differences within the domains. As in Swarthmore, women are more likely than men to mention another person's health or the qualities of their children as factors in their well-being, whereas men are more likely than women to mention goals and achievements. When health status is controlled, material concerns continue to predominate and even to intensify with poor health. The increased concern with the material domain reflects fears of medical expenses combined with a lack of independent income; that is, those in poor health are disproportionately elderly and lacking pensions. In addition, as one might predict, the poorer one's health, the greater the frequency of references to the physical status domain.

Comparison of Well-Being
Patterns Across the Study Sites

Most participants gave us two or fewer reasons for their current well-being. The numbers in the following tables (Tables 5.5, 5.6, 5.7, and 5.8) represent the percentage of individuals in each site who described their well-being in terms of a particular domain. Domains were only counted once: If a person mentioned two themes within a single category, such as quality of children and loss of friends, both of which fall into the social category, only one social reference was recorded. On the other hand, some compact responses such as "My children never give me any money" were recorded as falling into two domains—in this example, into both the material and the social. Because the purpose of this analysis was to discover what people saw as sources of well-being, general answers that did not refer to any specific sphere of life, such as "I'm better than some, worse than some," "I'm fine," and "I'm OK," are not presented in these tables.

From Table 5.5 we can see that there are two distinctive patterns of domain salience. The !Kung, Herero, and Chinese populations are overwhelmingly concerned with material issues—worrying about livestock, earning a living, and financial security:

!Kung: Because I can still do for myself. I can cook, sew, get water and food.
 I can get up and do the things I need to do.
 [Female, about 40. Score = 3]

Herero: I have no stock and no job, and I am blind. I am useless, and I can't
 help anyone. If I had my sight, then my life would be better.
 [Male, age 69. Score = 1]

Hong Kong: I have no money and do not have a job. But my condition is
 not the worst, therefore it is average. [Female, age 18. Score = 3.5]

Hong Kong: I have only a son in Hong Kong. He does not earn much, and
 I can't earn. The income is insufficient, the expenditure is great.
 Luckily, I have old age allowance. [Male, age 73. Score = 2]

The second most salient domain for both the !Kung and the Herero is the physical—probably reflecting the fact that in both populations physical strength and endurance are essential to success in subsistence activities. In Hong Kong, however, the next most

TABLE 5.5 Domains of Well-Being Mentioned, by Site (Percentages)

	Site						
Reason	*!Kung* *(N = 93)*	*Herero* *(N = 168)*	*Clifden* *(N = 125)*	*Bless.* *(N = 169)*	*Mom.* *(N = 208)*	*Swarth.* *(N = 109)*	*H.K.* *(N = 183)*
Physical	39	24	22	20	35	43	15
Material	67	91	21	41	49	44	70
Social	17	19	39	37	31	49	29
Personal	6	0	10	21	27	31	21

$p = .000$.

salient domain is the social, which in this case usually means the family as a unit. In the U.S. sites and Blessington, what is distinctive is the lack of any overwhelming preponderance of references to any particular domain. Although the rank order of the categories varies in these three sites, all four categories appear in the responses of at least 20% of the respondents in each of the sites, and no category is mentioned by a majority of the respondents. Clifden falls between these two patterns: In terms of variation within Clifden the social domain is relatively prominent, but not nearly so prominent as the material domain among the Africans and Chinese.

Within sites sex differences in domains of well-being mentioned are not particularly remarkable (see Table 5.6). The fewest sex differences are found in Swarthmore and Hong Kong, with increasing contrast among !Kung men and women, more in the two Irish sites, and most in Momence and among the Herero. When considered across sites, however, distinctive though not large sex differences appear. The most notable is the greater propensity of women to provide social, primarily family-related, reasons for their well-being—a characteristic of all seven sites, though by the barest margin among the !Kung and in Swarthmore:

- !Kung

  My father helps me. [She is unmarried, has 3 young children, and lives with her father.] [Female, age 20. Score = 4]

  Because I can still support myself and my husband helps me. [Female, age 47. Score = 3]

- Herero

  The cattle are dead and my husband is blind.
  [Female, age 54. Score = 2]

  I am married. My husband looks after me. [Female, age 71. Score = 4]

- Clifden

  My family are all around and all are good to me.
  [Female, age 62. Score = 6]

  Pretty good, I guess. My children are well. [Female, age 44. Score = 4]

- Blessington

  I'm happy. I have two healthy kids and a wonderful husband. We
  enjoy ourselves. [Female, age 27. Score = 6]

  We have a lot of problems, but they are surmountable. We have a
  good marriage and great kids. [Female, age 42. Score = 5]

- Momence

  Because my marriage is good. If my health was better I'd be a 6.
  [Female, age 50. Score = 4]

  Life was beautiful until my husband died. That caused the step
  down. We had a beautiful marriage. [Female, age 62. Score = 5]

- Swarthmore

  Because I'm generally very satisfied with what I'm doing, with my
  family. The primary challenge is caring for my mother, yet I prefer
  it to the alternatives. [Female, age 50. Score = 5]

  My needs are all satisfied. I have children who are loving and
  caring, coming and going. They include me in their lives. Grandchildren call. Children, grandchildren make me feel I can help
  make a decision. [Female, age 74. Score = 6]

- Hong Kong

  The economy is not very good. I have no property. My husband is
  not very healthy. I have to depend on my children to help us. I can
  earn, but not much and not enough. [Female, age 46. Score = 3]

TABLE 5.6 Domains of Well-Being Mentioned, by Site and Sex
(Percentages)

				Site			
Domain	!Kung (M = 48) (F = 45)	Herero (M = 66) (F = 102)	Clifden (M = 57) (F = 68)	Bless. (M = 83) (F = 86)	Mom. (M = 95) (F = 113)	Swarth. (M = 75) (F = 115)	H.K. (M = 90) (F = 93)
Physical[a]	39	24	22	20	35	43	15
Male	40	32	18	18	39	45	16
Female	38	19	25	21	31	41	14
Material[b]	67	91	21	41	49	44	70
Male	71	94	23	46	56	48	69
Female	62	89	19	37	42	42	71
Social[c]	17	19	39	37	31	49	29
Male	17	5	28	29	24	49	26
Female	18	30	49	44	36	50	32
Personal[d]	6	0	10	21	27	31	21
Male	10	0	11	18	31	32	23
Female	2	0	9	23	25	30	18

a. $p = .72$.
b. $p = .28$.
c. $p = .03$.
d. $p = .37$.

I am not worse off than others. But I am not the best off. Now I do not work. My children give money to me. [Female, age 65. Score = 3]

Second is the greater propensity of men to reference the material domain, primarily subsistence activities and employment, a characteristic of all sites except Hong Kong, where women reference it marginally more than men. Similarly, men are more likely to give personal reasons, such as attainment of goals or actualization of ideals, than women—true of all sites except Blessington, though the magnitude of the sex difference is small.

• !Kung

Because I can feed myself and do things. I can get a lot done. I can support myself. [!Kung male, over 50. Score = 5]

I am working in drought relief, getting money and working with Herero. [Male, under 30. Score = 5]

- Herero

  I have work. My father has work. The cattle are OK.
  [Male, age 22. Score = 5]

- Clifden

  I'm all right. No complaints. I have a job. [Male, age 22. Score = 5]

- Blessington

  I have a good job, health, children. The mortgage is manageable.
  [Male, age 44. Score = 4]

  I've achieved a lot in my life. [Male, age 65. Score = 4]

- Momence

  I'm unemployed, and the bills get bigger and bigger. I'm making
  it, but there's no job in sight. [Male, age 23. Score = 3]

  I have career ambitions that I haven't met yet. I feel I have an image
  to go before realizing goals, to be superintendent of schools.
  [Male, age 38. Score = 4]

- Swarthmore

  I still haven't achieved all my career goals. All work takes away
  from my personal life. [Male, age 19. Score = 4]

  I get personal satisfaction from work, being right on the edge of
  exciting things. [Male, age 47. Score = 5]

- Hong Kong

  Because I have just come out to work. There is pressure.
  [Male, age 22. Score = 3]

  Because I can still earn a living. [Male, age 61. Score = 4]

Table 5.7 shows the frequency with which people of different
ages mentioned the major domains of life as they described their
well-being. The clearest pattern across the study sites is the significance of the physical domain for the elderly. In every population
except the !Kung, among whom the middle-aged actually make the

TABLE 5.7 Domains of Well-Being Mentioned, by Site and Age (Percentages)

Domain		Site					
	!Kung (Y = 24) (MA = 31) (O = 30)	Herero (Y = 44) (MA = 50) (O = 6)	Clifden (Y = 39) (MA = 55) (O = 31)	Bless. (Y = 31) (MA = 81) (O = 57)	Mom. (Y = 40) (MA = 91) (O = 77)	Swarth. (Y = 23) (MA = 60) (O = 107)	H.K. (Y = 17) (MA = 138) (O = 27)
Physical[a]	36	24	22	20	35	43	15
Young	23	17	15	2	15	35	9
Mid. Aged	46	17	15	2	15	35	9
Old	37	30	31	30	52	48	37
Material[b]	68	91	21	41	49	44	70
Young	73	91	45	53	68	52	70
Mid. Aged	67	89	28	44	59	47	69
Old	58	94	7	28	32	36	74
Social[c]	17	20	39	37	31	49	29
Young	18	13	45	26	30	59	21
Mid. Aged	15	22	36	56	38	48	34
Old	21	22	40	30	27	45	25
Personal[d]	6	0	10	21	27	31	21
Young	5	0	0	25	40	39	34
Mid. Aged	10	0	9	17	31	30	11
Old	0	0	14	20	17	30	31

a. $p = .000$.
b. $p = .036$.
c. $p = .09$.
d. $p = .004$.

most references to health and functionality, there is a direct relationship between age and salience of the physical domain. Second is the fact that in five sites the young are more concerned with material issues than the middle-aged or old. On the one hand, this pattern reflects the difficulties young people encounter in "getting started"—acquiring the resources to support a growing family— and on the other the security provided to the elderly either through their own efforts, as in affluent societies such as Swarthmore, or through government-funded programs, as in Ireland. In the two aberrant cases, the Herero and the Chinese, in which the old are more likely to mention material issues than the young, the age differences are, in fact, minimal. These are also the two populations in which material concerns loom large for everyone.

There is little obvious patterning by age of references to the remaining domains other than a slight tendency of the middle-aged to mention the social domain more than the other age groups, and in the four most differentiated societies (Blessington, Momence, Swarthmore, and Hong Kong) a tendency of the young to reference the personal domain. A large part of this latter tendency is related to youthful concerns with goals and achievements and, in some cases, shows the influence of a "life plan." In both Swarthmore and Hong Kong a substantial minority of informants explicitly viewed the ladder (or stairs) as something that one climbs up in the course of one's life, reaching one's peak if not the actual top at midlife. Because they had not yet achieved their goals, they necessarily felt they could not place themselves on the highest level. On the other hand, a few successful but modest individuals declined to give themselves the highest rating because they didn't want to be viewed as "boasting."

A common misperception among elderly Hong Kong residents was that the scale was intended to measure how well they could climb stairs, though fortunately most interviewers caught on to this problem right away. When Charlotte Ikels later used the stairs model to assess the well-being of urban elderly in China, some informants thought they were being asked to choose the floor they would most like to live on—the interviews were conducted in 1991, a time when many people were being reassigned to newly built housing and were routinely asked to express floor preferences. As these examples illustrate, using even the most concrete and familiar objects to stimulate thinking about well-being can be a high-risk procedure. Using less culturally familiar objects, such as some of the mental health scales commonly employed in the United States, is probably an even riskier procedure.

Table 5.8 allows us to evaluate the extent to which domain salience varies with well-being rating. The relationship between these two variables is most apparent in the case of the material domain, where low scorers and, to a lesser extent, middle-range scorers predominate over high scorers. There is also a tendency for low and middle scorers compared to high scorers to emphasize physical reasons for their well-being. In Blessington and the U.S. sites, references to the social domain increase steadily with increases in scores:

TABLE 5.8 Domains of Well-Being Mentioned, by Well-Being Scores and Site (Percentages)

				Site			
	!Kung	Herero	Clifden	Bless.	Mom.	Swarth.	H.K.
	(L = 19)	(L = 80)	(L = 5)	(L = 19)	(L = 25)	(L = 14)	(L = 15)
	(M = 34)	(M = 60)	(M = 37)	(M = 54)	(M = 66)	(M = 37)	(M = 124)
Domain	(H = 40)	(H = 28)	(H = 83)	(H = 96)	(H = 115)	(H = 138)	(H = 38)
Physical[a]	39	24	22	20	35	43	14
Low	58	19	60	26	32	50	13
Middle	24	27	30	17	38	49	15
High	43	32	16	20	34	41	11
Material[a]	67	91	21	41	49	44	70
Low	79	99	20	47	56	50	61
Middle	79	90	16	46	39	35	75
High	50	71	23	38	52	46	55
Social[a]	17	20	39	37	31	49	29
Low	16	25	40	32	24	43	53
Middle	26	13	43	33	24	46	23
High	10	18	37	40	36	51	37
Personal[b]	6	0	10	21	28	31	21
Low	5	0	0	21	28	29	20
Middle	6	0	8	24	33	30	15
High	8	0	11	19	24	31	42

a. $p = .000$.
b. $p = .09$.

- Blessington

  I've been fortunate. Good health, happy marriage, and a happy family. [Male, age 56. Score = 5]

  I have so much going for me—my health and my family. [Female, age 77. Score = 6]

- Momence

  Basically I'm a happy, satisfied person. Happy with marriage, happy with kids. If not for the economy, satisfied with my job. [Male, age 42. Score = 5]

  I've got my health, wonderful family. Got a good place to live, comfortable financially, got a car, friends. [Female, age 72. Score = 5]

- Swarthmore

  I've got a wife. I enjoy working in the yard, working for a few organizations. I have children who are a joy—three grandchildren who are coming along. I like reading—read two newspapers a day. I have some good friends and the money to spend part of the year in Swarthmore and to travel and have some part-time help in the house. [Male, age 71. Score = 6]

In Hong Kong and among the Herero, however, social references occur most frequently among the low scorers, suggesting that failures and losses in social relationships make more of an impression than successes.

- Herero

  My stock are dead, I've got no husband to feed me.
  [Female, age 65. Score = 2]

- Hong Kong

  I'm living in Hong Kong alone. My family is in the place of origin. I am an employee, I have to work. I have to support the family. [Male, age 33. Score = 2]

  I still have to work now. The children are not grown. It can't be considered the best. If I am doing good, I will be the best when I am old in the future. Now I am the average, I can manage. [Female, age 37. Score = 3]

Table 5.9 allows us to evaluate the relationship of health status to the salience of various reasons used to account for well-being. Not surprisingly, in all sites people in the poorest health are more likely to mention health issues than those in better health. Less anticipated is the finding that in the African sites and Swarthmore, those in the best health are almost as likely to give health-related reasons for their well-being. We believe that this unlikely cluster occurs because in Swarthmore loss of health, or fears of that loss, undermine social participation in this community as dramatically as frailty impedes physical participation in the subsistence activities of the Hereo and !Kung in Kalahari.

TABLE 5.9 Domains of Well-Being Mentioned, by Health Status and Site (Percentages)

Domain	!Kung (P = 24) (A = 31) (E = 30)	Herero (P = 44) (A = 50) (E = 68)	Clifden (P = 39) (A = 55) (E = 31)	Bless. (P = 31) (A = 81) (E = 57)	Mom. (P = 40) (A = 91) (E = 77)	Swarth. (P = 23) (A = 60) (E = 107)	H.K. (P = 17) (A = 138) (E = 27)
Physical[a]	39	24	22	20	35	43	15
Poor/Fair	50	27	36	32	65	52	29
Average/ Good	32	18	13	20	30	33	14
Excellent	37	26	19	12	25	46	11
Material[a]	68	91	21	41	49	44	70
Poor/Fair	63	95	10	45	35	43	82
Average/ Good	77	96	18	44	51	40	72
Excellent	63	85	39	35	53	47	56
Social[a]	16	19	39	37	31	49	29
Poor/Fair	25	20	38	23	20	43	35
Average/ Good	10	20	35	47	32	55	26
Excellent	16	18	48	30	34	48	41
Personal[b]	6	0	10	21	27	31	20
Poor/Fair	8	0	10	13	10	30	6
Average/ Good	3	0	13	21	20	38	21
Excellent	7	0	3	25	35	26	26

a. $p = .000$.
b. $p = .001$.

- Herero

  I can still support myself. [Male, age 31. Health = Excellent]

  I can support myself. [Female, age 37. Health = Excellent]

- Swarthmore

  I'm able to do pretty much what I've been doing. No physical or financial worries. Some worries with wife's health. [Male, age 72. Health = Excellent]

My family and my health. We're intelligent, self-supporting, engaged in work we find fulfilling. [Female, age 62. Health = Excellent]

Discussion

In this final section we address two questions. The first concerns the issue of validity. How convinced are we that we have, in fact, identified the sources of well-being that are relevant to the populations in the study? The second concerns the contributions of this study to the theoretical debate about the nature of sources of well-being. What has the consideration of the sources of well-being in this broad range of societies taught us about the phenomenon of well-being itself?

Validity

Certainly the first thing we can say with confidence is that the interview situation itself is a culturally defined context that may be sociolinguistically awkward per se, as for !Kung, or in which some topics are not appropriately discussed, as we saw among the Herero. Further, interview participants are constrained to couch satisfactions and dissatisfactions in such a way as to bring as little discredit to themselves as possible and to maximize opportunities for gain, material or emotional, by providing reasonable answers to the researcher—thus, for example, stoicism in Clifden and socially sanctioned manipulation among the !Kung and the Herero. In addition, even the most comfortable and best-intentioned respondent may not be given full scope for self-expression by the typical questionnaire or interview schedule. Consider, for example, the 45-year-old Hong Kong man who frankly gave himself a rating of 1 and confessed that many "difficulties [were] puzzling" him and that this was "the worst stage of [his] life." Without considerable probing or access to other information from the interview, the researcher would still be uncertain as to the precise nature of these difficulties. In fact, this man had recently seen his second marriage collapse. Although he had initially retained custody of his children because his mother was available to look after them, he had recently lost custody because several months before the interview his mother suffered a paralyzing stroke. Although at the time of the interview she was in an infirmary, health care provider expectations in Hong Kong are that a family member will be available to provide most of the personal care. Consequently this man spent much of his time looking after and even bathing his mother. As a self-employed broker, he was unable to attend to his business. He was understandably puzzled and thought that his mother would be better off dead. All of this information was made available to us in the "warm-up" chat before we even started the interview—in some research designs such important data might be considered mere noise and be lost.

Another Hong Kong informant, a well-to-do 32-year-old woman, placed herself on the midpoint of the scale (the improbable 3.5) and explained her rating with the stereotypical comment that "some are better off [than I], and some are worse off." When pressed to explain how others were better or worse off, she limited herself to half-heartedly listing how people were worse off—laborious lives, disappointing marriages, and financial or health problems. Yet from her own affect during the interview as well as her responses to questions in other parts of the interview, it became clear that she was seriously depressed. When asked which age group she would most like to be in, she said none, actually, as it was better never to have been born. Similarly, she thought long and hard when asked whether she had any health problems (mental health problems are very stigmatizing in Hong Kong), sought clarification of the meaning of "health problem," and finally admitted to thinking depressing thoughts, having insomnia, and lacking both the energy and the motivation to perform at work.

As the two examples above illustrate, uncovering the sources of well-being is not easily carried out using a single scale or even a single open-ended question. Rather, the interview as a whole must be considered the resource for discovering the sources of each individual's well-being. Because our interpretations are grounded in the whole interview and not simply the tabulations of domain salience, we believe that we have gotten as close as one is likely —short of a psychiatric interview—to the real thing.

Furthermore, in our view the entire enterprise of Project AGE has confirmed that subjective and qualitative data are essential for an understanding of the cultural significance of well-being. Despite the various methodological difficulties discussed above, we are convinced that without in-depth discussion in both formal and informal settings with members of the population being studied, researchers are vulnerable to being hostages of their own hypotheses. That is, by framing well-being in their own terms, researchers will ask only questions—and hear only answers—that fit within this framework. Proper attention to context is also required to avoid misreading cohort and period effects for age effects.

Contributions to Theory

The findings from Project AGE encourage us to address three questions that have long been of theoretical concern to researchers in the area of well-being—whether there are differences in the sources of well-being among subpopulations, whether well-being is a bottom-up, top-down, or bidirectional phenomenon, and finally whether there is a pan-human hierarchy of needs such that as one need is met, the next emerges.

We believe that our results indicate that there are indeed predictable differences by life stage in sources of well-being. The problem is that these regularities do not readily reveal themselves except where two conditions are met. The first is that regular and distinctive life stages are the general experience of the population under study. When life is so unpredictable that, for example, poor health, withdrawal from subsistence activities, and widowhood occur at any time in the life course, it is unlikely that people will see much in the way of stages in their lives. The categorical and scheduled division of labor characteristic of industrialized nation-state economies also promotes a "staged" view of life. (These points are discussed in detail in Chapter 6 on the life course.) The second condition is that some minimal standard of living be attained such that people can be freed from constantly focusing on where their next meal is coming from. It should be no surprise that the sites in which the investigators note life stage differences in sources of well-being are those that meet these two conditions (Blessington, Momence,

Swarthmore, and the higher-income neighborhoods of Hong Kong).

With regard to the second question—the directionality of well-being—it is, of course, safest to take the middle ground and assume bidirectionality but then to ask whether one direction might be a little more influential than the other. The evidence from our own work suggests, first, that cultural or individual factors set the appropriate level (high, middle, or low) from which people gauge their well-being, and second, that satisfaction in fundamental do-mains contributes more to overall well-being than a generalized sense of well-being influences evaluation of these specific domains of life. This can be seen by the tremendous influence of the material and health domains on personal assessments. If there are problems in these arenas, they are strongly reflected in well-being scores. Even people with optimistic dispositions are laid low by material and health problems.

Consistent with this, people with high scores are, by and large, people without problems (or with the perception they have no prob-lems). Further evidence for this interpretation is provided by the distribution of responses falling into the general (i.e., non-domain-specific) category—data not presented here. In every site people with high well-being scores are more likely—usually much more likely—to know things are going right for them but to have diffi-culty saying why. People who know things are not going right for them have no difficulty spelling out precisely what is bothering them. The pessimistic interpretation of this finding is that for many people high well-being is a null state—that is, its chief characteristic is the absence of problems.

It should be obvious from our comments so far that the answer to the final question—whether there is a pan-human hierarchy of needs—is affirmative, at least for the most basic needs of economic and physical security. Just as Cantril (1965) reported in his study of 15 nations, which had only one society (the United States) in common with our study, we found that people at the lower end of the well-being ladder are especially concerned with economic mat-ters. Similarly, people in poor health are the most likely to reference health matters and to give themselves low well-being ratings. Not until material and physical issues can be put in the background do people relax enough to contemplate the affective as opposed to the instrumental dimensions of their personal relationships or to speculate on the likelihood of attaining a desirable mental state or realizing their personal goals.

6

Age and the Life Course

*A*lthough the life course perspective has become close to a paradigm for research in gerontology (Baltes & Nesselroade, 1979; Campbell, Abolafia, & Maddox, 1985; Featherman, 1981; Hagestad, 1990; Neugarten, 1968; Neugarten & Datan, 1973; Riley, Johnson, & Foner, 1972), few researchers have posed direct questions to people anywhere about how they view the life course (exceptions are Neugarten & Peterson, 1957, and Fry, 1976, for U.S. populations). Rarest of all are investigations that have included direct questions about the life course in other parts of the world. Much of the cross-cultural data available comes from secondary analysis of ethnographic reports. Our Project AGE team members are among the first to systematically explore the life course in a variety of

AUTHOR'S NOTE: This chapter was written by Christine L. Fry, based on information provided by other members of the Project AGE team. Portions of the Conclusion appeared previously in "Perceptions of the Adult Life Course: A Cross-Cultural Analysis" by C. Ikels et al., 1992, *Ageing and Society, 12*, pp. 49-84.

cultural contexts (Fry, 1990; Ikels et al., 1992). The life course is a central part of our research design.

At the core of the usual conceptualizations of the life course is an assumption about how the life course is constructed—that as individuals pass through life, they enter and exit discrete stages. Stages are a deeply familiar part of our thinking about age, both literary and everyday, and long before Shakespeare, Europeans pondered the "ages of man" (Covey, 1989). In formulating our research instruments, we too assumed that the adult life course could be partitioned into stages. After all, in clarifying the very terminology anthropology uses to study age, Radcliffe-Brown (1929) defined "age grades" as the *divisions* of life from infancy to old age (in contrast to "age sets," which are groups of persons who pass through the grades). For our own ethnography of age, a major goal was to examine the variation in numbers and markers of age grades and their meanings across our far-flung sites.

In this chapter we present the research strategy used to collect comparable data about the life course from the seven ethnographic sites and the results that have led us to question the universality of a staged life course. First, we look at our research instrument, the "Age Game," with its promise and problems. Second, we examine what we learned about the life course in each of our seven research settings in terms of our major questions about structure and meaning of life stages. The special challenge of presenting what we learned about the life course is that it requires a mix of data and critique because some of our most important findings appeared through analysis of flaws in our original assumptions and the methodology based upon them.

The Age Game Card Sort: Promises and Problems

The research protocol we created to elicit perceptions of the life course we originally called the Age Game. The first part of the protocol was the most game-like, in that respondents read and sorted cards containing descriptions of hypothetical but fairly realistic people who might live in their community. As respondents made judgments about similarity and differences in age and life stage, they placed cards in piles that we labeled with the respondent's own terms ("young adult," "middle-aged," "over the hill"). Respondents were then interviewed about different aspects of these age groups, including the transitions between them, the best and hardest things about them, the major concerns of persons in them, and information about actual individuals the speakers knew in the later life stages they defined. (See Appendix, p. 338 for an example of this Age Game for one of the U.S. sites.) As our project moved into its second phase, in Botswana and Ireland, we realized that the game metaphor for our sorting task was confusing, and in Clifden even alienating. We consequently reduced our use of this label.

The underlying premises of the card sort are derived from a long line of cultural research known as ethnosemantics and developed in the late 1950s. Using language as the code to culture, ethnosemantics analyzes the components of meaning and the semantic boundaries of cultural categories to arrive at a cultural grammar that contains the rules participants in a culture need to follow in order to generate appropriate behavior (Colby, 1975; Fry, 1986). The portability of elicitation frames has been assumed to be a strength of such strategies. Sorting tasks, triad tests, and other frames appear to have reasonable cultural neutrality; if people can make decisions about similarity and differences, they should be able to group or to sort things. In theory, all the anthropologist has to do is to devise the appropriate sorting task and culturally appropriate items, in our case "people," to be sorted.

We also needed an instrument that would permit us to transcend chronology. Identification of age with chronology was an obstacle for us in two ways. First, in at least one location, among the !Kung in the Kalahari, we knew that people did not use numbers, so that questions about chronological age would be meaningless. Second, in the sites where age and chronology were most tightly linked, we were likely to miss deeper meanings of age if we could not probe beyond a numerical response.

Did the Age Game live up to our expectations? In some respects yes, in that we did learn a great deal about the life course within each community. In other respects no, because we encountered difficulties in using the instrument and interpreting the results. In no site was the card sort an easy task, although it worked better in some than in others. In our first phase, in Momence, Swarthmore, and Hong Kong, some problems were encountered, but for the most part it worked. However, during our second phase, in Ireland and Botswana, the problems mounted. Only Blessington respondents responded with the relative ease of people in the first phase. Among the !Kung and in Clifden, problems were prominent because age as a basis of categorization appears to be little used by people in these settings. Herero, on the other hand, promptly placed our imaginary people in categories demarcated by sex and age, but in the end the results of their sorting are very difficult to interpret. Herero use age categories to some extent, but these have low cultural salience in comparison, for example, to kinship, in terms of which they are usually subsumed, giving age categories salience as relative rather than absolute social identities.

This chapter presents our research into the life course in two voices. One relates the construction of the card sort and the results we obtained from the respondents who were comfortable using it. The other gives a counterpoint of what we learned from the ways this method and its assumptions were inappropriate for some individuals and for some entire cultural contexts.

Structure of the Life Course

Markers of Age

The first step in constructing the card sort was to discover in each setting the attributes by which age was perceived and indicated so we could create imaginary but plausible "people" for our cards. Key individuals, representing a range of social locations in each research site (male, female, different ages, different occupations, different duration of residence), were interviewed about the types of people present in the setting.

These interviews began in the most open-ended way possible, asking about what different kinds of people lived in the neighborhood, village, or town. We often phrased this in terms of wanting to be sure that during our research we talked with people in all the different categories that were meaningful in that setting. If age or life stage were not mentioned spontaneously, the interviewer introduced them, but only later in the encounter.

For Momence and Swarthmore a variant of the familiar parlor game of Twenty Questions was used to elicit the information people needed in order to guess an unknown person's age. This strategy did not work well elsewhere. For instance, in Ireland games were viewed as childish, and among the !Kung direct questions and answers are not the usual style of discourse.

From these broad interviews we derived a preliminary list of attributes that appeared to be used to define life stages. Once we had created this preliminary set of characteristics, our respondents were asked to judge the appropriateness and believability of various combinations. We then asked these key participants to critique our "grammar" in terms of (a) the appropriateness of the attributes marking age and (b) the believability of how they were combined to make a person. Another check we asked them to make was to attempt to describe *themselves* using the set of attributes, which revealed any information not available in our inventory of age markers.

Site-Specific Criteria

Some criteria are used in all sites: marital status, children's status, grandchildren's status, household composition, housing arrangements, and work. However, the attributes used in reference to certain statuses vary. In the societies with universal education, for example, children and grandchildren are typically described in terms of their level in school. Elsewhere offspring are described by size, age, or only in terms of total number. Work activities, of course, also vary widely. For Herero, the number of cattle in a herd is a work-related attribute of life stages. In Swarthmore career ladders of promotion and achievement contrast with the shift from commuting to establishing a small business that marks a life stage transition in Momence.

Other criteria are site-specific. For instance, migration is a theme that is relevant only in Ireland. Community activity is salient as an indicator of age or life stage only in Blessington, Swarthmore, and Momence, where the community-wide organizations are age graded. Status of parents (alive or dead, health and functionality, working or not, place of residence) is a criterion most differentiated in Swarthmore and relevant to some extent in Clifden and among the Herero. In those communities a life stage for adult children is distinguished by responsibilities for parents.

On the other hand, other criteria are absent in some sites. Great-grandchildren are not referenced in the Botswana sites because great-grandchildren are still very rare. The same is true of education because among the !Kung and Herero education beyond the primary grades can be obtained only in regional centers. There is also variation across the sites in the extent to which the life stage criteria used are differentiated. Four domains receive considerable differentiation within all seven communities, most notably (a) domestic aspects of marital status, status of children and grandchildren, and living arrangements, and (b) subsistence activities. For other domains, finer distinctions are made in some sites than in others: For example, grandchildren's education and marital status are differentiated in all sites except in Botswana, and household arrangements are finely differentiated only by Herero.

The Sorting Task

Forty-eight descriptions (24 females and 24 males) constituted the sorting task in Blessington, Momence, Swarthmore, and Hong Kong. Thirty "people" (15 females and 15 males) were used for Clifden, Herero, and !Kung. (See Figure 6.1 for examples of descriptions from each site.)

Ideally the items in a sorting task are presented in a format that allows respondents to handle them, group them, and review them. Three-by-five cards with descriptions typed on them were used in all but two of our sites. The !Kung have no written language, and thus writing could not be used. Pat Draper, with the assistance of a !Kung artist, developed icons to represent age markers. These were pictures of such things as hunting or gardening (aspects of physical vigor and work); couples holding hands (marriage); large and small children; and sitting by a hut (no longer able to work). Although the Herero have a written language, initial work indicated that reading skills were not very proficient. Henry Harpending adopted the strategy used in the sites where despite near-universal literacy we encountered an occasional person who had difficulty reading. In these circumstances, and for Herero, we read the de-

!KUNG
A woman who is married, has older children, does vigorous work, gardens, husband works for Herero.
A man who is married, has younger children, hunts and gardens.

HERERO
A woman is married as a senior wife, has five small children, has 10 cows given by her father, has a nice, well-built hut nicely maintained.
A man who has married two wives, his child is away at job, he has a village, he has 150 cattle.

CLIFDEN
A woman who is married, has two children in secondary school with others working, she works, her husband's mother lives with them.
A man who has never married, oldest child in college, lives outside of town, needs help to bring in fuel.

BLESSINGTON
A woman who is single, has no children, lives with parents, works in a local business.
A man who is married, oldest child in college, lives with his wife, owns his home, is a professional in Dublin.

MOMENCE
A woman who is divorced, has elementary school children, paying mortgage on home, is a high school graduate, working for a business in Momence.
A man who is married, has great-grandchildren, lives in a nursing home, is a high school graduate, is retired.

SWARTHMORE
A woman who is widowed and not remarried, her youngest grandchild is in college, she lives alone in a Swarthmore apartment, she is retired.
A man who is married, has elementary and high school children, lives with wife and children, his parents are retired, works full time in a local corporation.

HONG KONG
A woman who is married, has children in middle school, living with parents-in-law, has temporary/part-time work.
A man who is married, has his first grandchild, lives with a married child, and has temporary/part-time work.

Figure 6.1. Examples of Card Sort Descriptions From Each Site

scriptions to the respondent, who then indicated the life stage within which each seemed to be.

Dimensions of the Life Course

Previous research in Lafayette, Indiana (Fry, 1976), revealed tremendous variation in the number of divisions of the life course perceived by members of the same society or residents of the same town. Indeed, across all of our Project AGE sites the range of variation is from zero ("it is all one flow") to 11 age groups, with an average of around 5.

We asked each participant to sort the descriptions into piles, grouping together those that seemed to be of about the same age or life stage. We gave each person first the set of cards describing imaginary individuals of his or her own sex and then the set for the opposite sex. Once participants had sorted the descriptions, we asked them for a term or label they would normally use to refer to people in each group (pile). From then on, we used their own term as we asked further questions about the content of the different stages and the transitions between them.

As described in the Introduction, respondents from Blessington, Herero, Momence, Swarthmore, and Hong Kong for the most part carried out these requests quite comfortably. Recent arrivals to Clifden, typically of younger age and higher occupational status than locals as well, also participated in the sorting task with little hesitation. In sharp contrast, Clifden residents of local origin, as well as our !Kung respondents, were very uncomfortable with this method. In Clifden, many simply did not do the card sort. The !Kung, characteristically eager to be helpful to members of our team, tried to take part but clearly found it a puzzling and frustrating enterprise (Draper & Glascock, n.d.).

The following excerpts from field journals give a flavor of the conversations about the card sort in Clifden and with !Kung.

Pat Draper with !Kung:

PD: So, you say that for women you would use four age terms. You mentioned the young women, the middle-aged women, the elder women, and the aged women. Let's talk about these. For example, let's start with the young women. What is it about the young women that makes them alike? What do they have in common?

!Kung: What do you mean alike? They're nothing alike! I've already told you that. Some of them are hard workers, others are lazy, some of them have children, others have no children. What makes you think they are alike? They're all different.

Tony Glascock in Clifden:

AG: What do people in this grouping have in common?

Resp: What do you mean?

AG: What is it about these people that made you put them together in the same category?

Resp: [After a long pause] Well, it's hard to say.

AG: You know, why do you think that they are about the same age?

Resp: Ah, the same age. Well, maybe they aren't the same age. It's really hard to say.

AG: Do these people have anything in common? [The "people" in the grouping were all middle-aged married men.]

Resp: Maybe they don't really fit here. You know, this man really shouldn't be with the others. He should be here. [This card was then placed by itself, and it was clear that the respondent was not at all satisfied with the grouping he had created and really wanted to separate the cards.]

In the presentation of results that follow, data from the card sort include responses from the 60 Clifden residents who completed it. The !Kung data are from interviews about stages of life that did not include a physical sorting activity. The concluding sections of the chapter will differentiate the !Kung and Clifden sites from the others and discuss the characteristics we believe account for their distinctive response to the sorting task. Each respondent who did the card sort worked out his or her own approach to the sorting. Some used chronology in intervals of 10, 15, or 20 years. Others systematized life stages such as "young families" or "the retired." One older man in Swarthmore refused to place any unmarried person beyond the phase of youth because he felt they had never taken on adult roles. Many used combinations of age and life stage. The result is variation that presents great challenges to interpretation and parsimonious display of results because the units of analysis (the age groups or life stages) are specific to each participant.

Standardized Age Groups

Knowing that variation would present difficulties as well as insights, we enlisted the help of the respondents themselves to define a standard framework for comparison. At the conclusion of each card sort, we asked the person who did it to review his or her categorizations one more time. If the person had four or more age groups we asked him or her to group these into three divisions for the purposes of comparison. Once this was completed, further questions were asked about chronological boundaries and names of the groups. These more comprehensive groupings are used in our analysis to examine the more qualitative aspects of the life course, such as transitions between groups and the evaluation of life stages.

Underlying Dimensions of the Life Course

For our interpretation of the card sort responses, we turned to two techniques frequently used for data with noted variability and data that are based on individual judgments about differences and similarity. These are Multidimensional Scaling (Kruskal & Wish, 1978; Shepard, Romney, & Nerlove, 1972) and Cluster Analysis (Aldenderfer & Blashfeld, 1984). Both of these techniques are designed to display the structure of the data in geometric representations (see Endnote 1).

Multidimensional Scaling Solutions

Two principles guided our selection of multidimensional scaling (MDS) solutions. The first was a program-generated metric called *stress*. This is a measure of the goodness of fit, which ranges from 0.0 to 5.0. The best fits are closest to zero. Higher stress measures indicate that regardless of iterations, there is a lack of fit. The acceptable level of stress is between 2.0 and 3.0, with an occasional solution over 3.0 being published depending on the interest in the solution. All of our MDS solutions are well within the acceptable stress levels, with the highest at 0.17 for the !Kung in two dimensions (3.7 in one dimension). Most are closer to 0.03, indicating an excellent goodness of fit.

Our second guideline was interpretability. For judgments about the meaning of these visual displays of our data, we turned to each fieldworker with a series of questions. Does the resulting plot of the card descriptions make sense? Is there sufficient order in the data, reflected in the fact that "people" with similar characteristics are close to one another? Can the X and Y axes be given meaning—labeled in ways that make sense in a particular site? In all sites, with the exception of the !Kung and Herero, the interpretability is excellent. Linearity is the primary theme. When reduced to one dimension, the "people" are ordered by increasing age. In reading the one-dimensional solutions, the ordering of the "people" from left to right on the X axis is one of increased means and modes for chronological age and higher-numbered age groups. Remarkably, for the five sites, the stress measure is low (below 0.1), indicating that age is the primary dimension.

Graphed in two dimensions, objects that can be arranged in a linear scale produce a picture of a horseshoe. Because the linear scale bends in a horseshoe, the challenge for interpretation is to assign meaning to the X and Y axes that produce the bend. The card descriptions sorted in Hong Kong, the United States, and Ireland, when represented in two dimensions, produce variations on the horseshoe image, exactly what we would expect if our respondents ordered the description in terms of a linear model of successive life stages. In Figure 6.2 we see this image clearly in the two-dimensional plot of card sort responses from Swarthmore. The "people" are clearly ordered. An arrow is superimposed on the plot of the MDS solution to show the arrangement of "people" by age. At the base of the arrow are the young, and at the head are the old. The three not encompassed by the arrow are the intentionally ambiguous descriptions that included a mix of attributes usually associated with different life stages. Because they required more thinking about placement, these descriptions were very useful in prompting participants to think out loud and articulate explicitly their reasons for placing the card in one category or another. These cards could be, and were, placed in nearly any age group. They are proximate to each other because their ageless qualities make them similar.

This image contrasts starkly with the MDS solution for the Herero in two dimensions. Here (Figure 6.3) the image is more of a random scatter. A few clusters can be interpreted, but there are more questions about the groupings than resolutions. Even super-imposition of a cluster diagram did not reveal an order. Thus despite a good stress score, the interpretability is low.

An interesting variant of the horseshoe image is found for both of the Irish sites. In one dimension, increasing age is the scale.

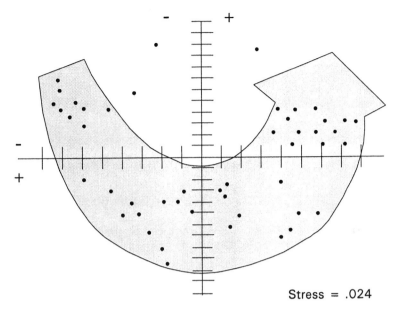

Stress = .024

Figure 6.2. Two-Dimensional Representation of Swarthmore Card Sort

However, in two dimensions, two horseshoes appear as the image: one for descriptions of males and one for descriptions of females. Figure 6.4 is the two-dimensional solution from Blessington with the double horseshoe. A near carbon copy appears in the image from Clifden for those who completed the sorting task. Technically this is explained by the fact that 8 to 10% of the sorts were either completed for only one sex or had different groupings for male and female descriptions. When these respondents are removed from the analysis, the image became the single horseshoe similar to that representing the responses from Swarthmore. What the graphics reflect is the greater sex differentiation of the life course in Ireland.

What are the meanings of the X and the Y axes that bend the otherwise linear representation of age? To answer this question, we returned to the attributes that define the imaginary people that were sorted (see Endnote 2). Each researcher reviewed the descriptions on the cards that fell in each quadrant of the two-dimensional solutions, looking for the commonalities in attributes. The meanings of the two dimensions defining the quadrants were then compared across our sites. The most striking aspect of this com-

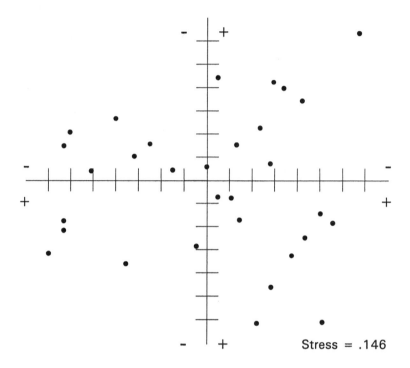

Figure 6.3. Two-Dimensional Representation of Herero Card Sort

parison is the prevalence of domestic status as the meaning of the X axis or the first dimension. On the other hand, the second dimension or the Y axis is less obvious in its definition, other than that it is indicative of something beyond the family.

Domestic status has considerable parallelism across all sites, including the !Kung and Herero. The reason for this parallelism centers on the universality of reproduction: Marriage, children, and residence are issues all societies must resolve, although they do so in diverse ways. Although the details are specific for each community, the core of domestic status consists of marital situation, children's status (inclusive of grandchildren and great-grandchildren), and household composition. A major difference is that the status of children in Hong Kong, Ireland, and the United States (as discussed above) is indicated by level in school, then by adult statuses (job or

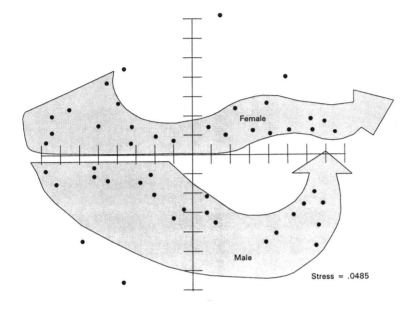

Figure 6.4. Two-Dimensional Representation of Blessington Card Sort

marriage), then by level of school for grandchildren. For the Botswana societies, this is not the case. Rather, people refer primarily to the number of children and their relative size (large or small). There are other differences. Status of parents is an important criterion in Swarthmore, in that 86% of the descriptions include this information (it is lacking for the very old). Descriptions on the cards used in Clifden and with Herero only occasionally reference the status of children. In the Botswana sites, ownership of a village for Herero or, for the !Kung, working for a Herero is important. In the working-class sites of Momence and Blessington, renting, buying houses, and paying off home mortgages are markers of age.

Across sites, the second dimension does not have the same consistency that we see in domestic statuses. In Blessington and Momence, this dimension is interpreted as engaging in or getting established in life and particularly life in the community. Responsibility, especially for family, is the second dimension in Hong Kong, whereas in Swarthmore it is most directly seen as work status. In Clifden the second dimension is difficult to interpret, probably because of the very high levels of unemployment there. Broadly viewed across our sites, subsistence activity or work is at the core of this dimension.

Cluster Analysis

Cluster analysis permits a somewhat more refined analysis of similarity groupings in a data set because relations between clusters are drawn in the form of a tree diagram in which short branches indicate the least distance or the most similarity. Conversely, the longer branches reflect the most distance or dissimilarity. For instance, in Figure 6.5 we see the dendrogram of the Hong Kong card sorts. In this picture, there are clearly three main clusters that could be identified as young, middle, and old. All clusters are "tight" in that the branches are short and are linked with other major clusters only at the greatest distance (15 or higher). Analysis of the attributes reveals that Clusters 1 and 2 are young, 3 is middle, and 4 and 5 are old.

- Young: For Hong Kong our main cluster is the youngest, consisting of three subclusters. The first, identified as "Just Getting Started," is made up of "people" who are not yet married, who are living with parents, and who are either students or not working. The next cluster is the "Getting Established" stage. Here children are no older than elementary school and work is increasingly stable. Exceptions are the two persons who join this group late. The cluster joining the latest is distinguished by children who are predominantly in middle school or postsecondary school, and by work that is regular and steady.
- Middle: Linked to the young cluster is a middle cluster that is relatively undifferentiated. "People" here are described as "Established" (Cluster 3). Children are more mature, pursuing postsecondary education, or are employed and married. The group of four to join this cluster late are even having their first grandchild. Work is regular and steady, and women are returning to work.
- Old: At the greatest distance, the oldest cluster joins the first two. Like the youngest, it is divided into two distinct groupings. The first (Cluster 4) is the "Responsibilities Completed" group. Here grandchildren are common, and no one is employed. In the last cluster (5), the defining feature is the presence of great-grandchildren.

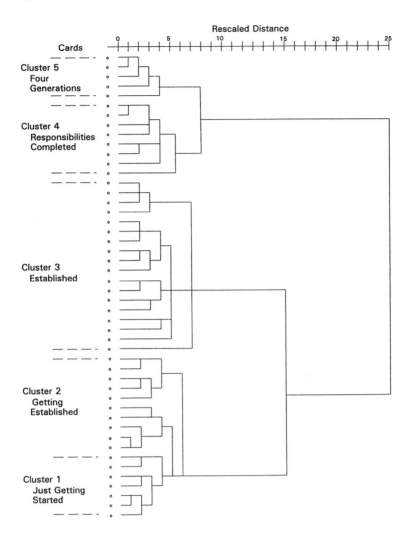

Figure 6.5. Cluster Analysis of Hong Kong Card Sort

Dendrograms of the card sorts were created (see Endnote 3) for each site and then interpreted by the researchers using site specific terms to describe the meaning of each cluster. The results of these analyses are presented in Figure 6.6. !Kung and Herero dendro-grams were not as "tight" as the one we see from Hong Kong and again present interpretability problems. With the exception of

!KUNG
Not Interpretable

HERERO
Not Interpretable

CLIFDEN
Singles
Young Families
Older Families
Grandparents

BLESSINGTON
Single Adults
Getting Established
Married/Older Children
Grandparents
Older Grandparents

MOMENCE
Preparing
Young Families
Older Families
Maturing Families
Retired

SWARTHMORE
Singles
Starting Families
Established Families
Grandparents
Frail Great-Grandparents

HONG KONG
Just Getting Started
Getting Established
Established
Responsibilities Completed
Four Generations

Figure 6.6. Life Stages Indicated in Cluster Analyses, by Site

Clifden, the interpretations of the dendrograms concluded with five clusters. The most striking feature is the prevalence of the family cycle (domestic status). Intertwined with this is getting established, setting goals, making decisions, and preparing for an adult life of family, work, and, where possible, careers.

With the prevalence of a domestic cycle in all sites, why did the results of the Herero sorting not reveal some structure by domestic status? Two factors best explain this. First, school attendance is a relatively recent phenomenon. In addition, children must leave the villages to attend school and live with relatives in regional centers during the school week. So a more likely categorization may be in school or not, rather than which grade the child is in. Children are grouped by size and number, features that only vaguely mark the passage of time. Second, a high fertility rate further obscures whatever calibration the status of children may give to the social clock. With a low fertility rate, the generational separation between parents and children is evident. But conditions of high fertility such as experienced by the Herero blur this separation because a household may have children ranging from infancy to young adults in their early 20s. Consequently developmental stages of households are spread out, and change is gradual in that a household expands with the addition of children and then very slowly contracts when children establish households of their own. In the case of the Herero, this blurring is further increased by polygynous households and by women who remain unmarried at their natal homestead but have a higher fertility rate than their married counterparts. Yet another factor is the prevalence of fostering children from their birth household to another, often that of an older female relative. When Herero responded to interviewers' questions about kin and household, they made no distinction between fostered children and birth children. Consequently a woman might refer to a son who had been fostered to her by a niece and was therefore of the biological generation of her grandchildren.

Transitions

In a life course that is linear and divided into stages, there are entrances and exits to denote passage from one to the next. Respondents in all sites were asked either about the transitions into the age groups they had created or about their own transitions or both. Analysis of the responses revealed nine themes, which can be further grouped into (a) processes of time and (b) social processes. Processes of time are perceived to "just happen," in contrast to social processes, which involve transitions in roles. The results are presented in Figure 6.7.

Processes of Time

The following themes share the inevitability that separates these types of life transitions from those marked by changes in role.

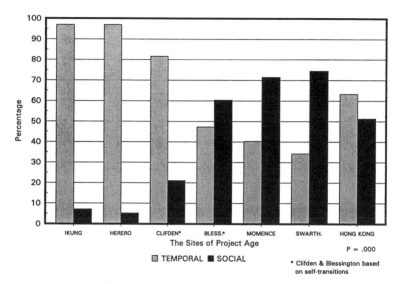

Figure 6.7. Temporal and Social Life Stage Transitions by Site (Percentage of Total Number of Age Groups Created by Respondents for Which Transitions Are Mentioned)

At the core is a theme we identified as *natural*. Such responses as "God does it," "the passage of time," or general references to age make up this theme.

Chronological age, the second theme in this group, refers to passage of time as calibrated by calendar years. For the !Kung and Herero, chronological age had little meaning because no one knew his or her age in years. Herero have a system of named years (for example, the year of the death of an important man, or the year the anthropologist asked questions). All Herero knew the name of the year in which they were born. Because these named years were linked to historically recorded events, they could be translated into chronology. However, for the Herero, they indicated only relative age (younger or older) and were not translated into exact ages.

In all other sites, nearly everyone knew his or her age because it was part of the culture through record keeping (birth certificates) and eligibility for state-granted rights and duties—military service, voting, driving, drinking, working, and Social Security. Here many answers to our questions were expressed in terms of years. Chronological age as a marker of transitions was mentioned with highest frequency in Clifden (45% of the total number of age groups created by respondents) and lowest frequency in Swarthmore (9%). Blessington and Momence were at 20% and 22%, respectively, and Hong Kong at 33%.

Finally, *physical changes* to the body may be seen as indicators of life stage. The beginning of menstruation, menopause, and signs of physical decline such as wrinkles, loss of strength, and increase of chronic problems make up this theme.

The most striking comparison shown in the transition data in Figure 6.7 is the nearly linear decline of references to processes of time as the sites increase in societal scale or complexity. Conversely, we see a near-linear increase in social themes. Temporal transitions predominate precisely in the communities where we had problems with the card sort either in administration or in interpretation (!Kung, Herero, and Clifden). A mix of social and temporal transitions is found in the other communities, where the sorting was carried out with relatively few difficulties.

This pattern reflects the effects of the role differentiation that is part of increasing societal scale. Blessington, Momence, Swarthmore, and Hong Kong are fully part of an industrial economy and linked to various institutions of a nation-state, including schools. Accordingly, these institutional statuses of work and education mark the passage from one stage to another.

Social Processes

Differentiation within the domain of social processes is most prominent in the responses from the U.S. sites and Hong Kong. Four roles or configurations of roles punctuate the life course: work roles, domestic cycles, state institutions, and indicators of social maturity. Figures 6.8 through 6.11 display in percentages the frequency with which these four themes respectively were mentioned for age groups created by respondents in each of the three sites, when these groups were reclassified within the broad categories of "young," "middle," and "old" life stages.

Subsistence Activities

For the three sites under consideration, subsistence activities mean engaging in or disengaging from wage labor. As is apparent

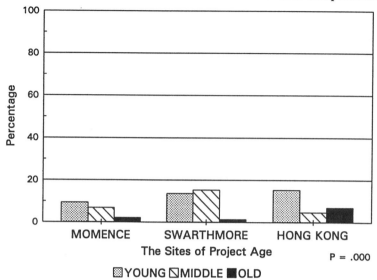

Figure 6.8. Life Stage Transitions Involving Subsistence Activity, by Life Stage and Site (Percentage of "Young," "Middle," and "Old" Age Groups Created by Respondents for Which Transitions Are Mentioned)

from Figure 6.8, work roles do not stand out as a major transition that calibrates the life course. This is a reminder that few people work in jobs that have career ladders whose levels are articulated or available enough to become major life stages. No more than 15% of the transitions in any life stage category were described in terms of career levels in this way. (Achievements as gauged by career advancement were more often present—or absent—in people's evaluation of different life stages. For example, in Swarthmore a phrase often used to describe the hardest aspect of late middle age was "knowing that you will never be vice president of the company.")

Domestic Roles

Because of the prevalence of the domestic cycle in both the MDS solutions and the cluster analysis, we expected domestic changes also to be significant transitions across the life course. Indeed, Figure 6.9 reflects exactly that, especially for the middle age category, in which between 45% and 49% of the age groups created by respondents were characterized by changes in domestic status as markers of transition into them. Domestic transitions are age graded,

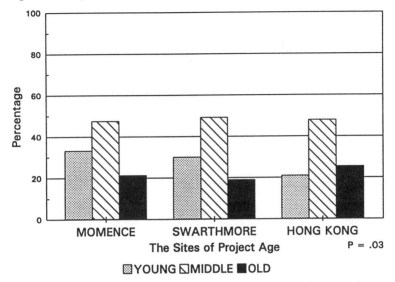

Figure 6.9. Life Stage Transitions Involving Domestic Roles, by Life Stage and Site (Percentage of "Young," "Middle," and "Old" Age Groups Created by Respondents for Which Transitions Are Mentioned)

beginning with courtship and proceeding in most cases through marriage, then to children, who range in turn from infants to adults, and then to grandchildren. It is during midlife that domestic changes most frequently mark life transitions.

State Institutions

In managing the welfare of their populations, nation-states have devised age-graded institutions. Universal education prepares people for the labor force; pensions support them once they have withdrawn from it.

In Figure 6.10, transitions within state institutions are displayed by life stage for the three sites. In Hong Kong, we find these transitions inconsequential except for the youngest age groups. In 40% of the "young" age groups created by respondents in Momence and Swarthmore, life stage transitions were described with reference to state institutions. Analysis of the specific transitions involving the state is even more striking. For the young stage, over 90% of these transitions are the completion of one's education. This is also the one transition in which a state institution is referred to in Hong Kong. For the middle stage, over 75% of these transitions

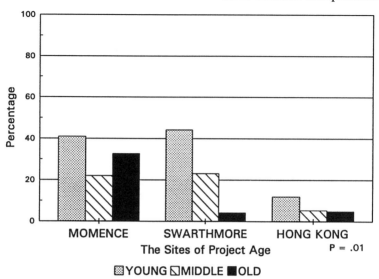

Figure 6.10. Life Stage Transitions Involving State Institutions, by Life Stage and Site (Percentage of "Young," "Middle," and "Old" Age Groups Created by Respondents for Which Transitions Are Mentioned)

are the status of one's children as marked by progression through the finely graded educational system (preschool, elementary, high school, college). Retirement is the transition into old age, with over 80% mentioning it specifically.

State-mandated universal education places individuals in a series of levels graded by chronological age beginning at age 5 or 6 and ending around 16 at the earliest. All children must attend a school unless the school itself expels the child from the system. Because parents must oversee their children's participation in school, the finely tuned age grading indirectly reflects their age. The categories here are not grades but major divisions in the school system, from elementary school on to college. This indirect transition is of lower salience than one's own educational status and is complementary to domestic roles (see Endnote 4).

State-managed tax transfer programs establish an age threshold for eligibility and an age to withdraw from the labor force. Retirement and the pensionable age consequently become a major transition into the oldest groups in the U.S. communities. In Hong Kong, by contrast, there is no general transition into a status of being retired. Because pensions are minimal for most older persons, they "retire"

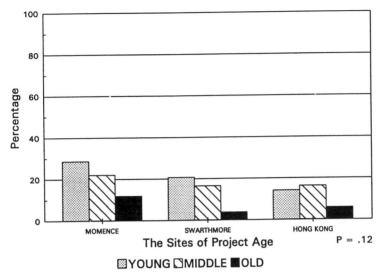

Figure 6.11. Life Stage Transitions Involving Social Maturation, by Life Stage and Site (Percentage of "Young," "Middle," and "Old" Age Groups Created by Respondents for Which Transitions Are Mentioned)

when they no longer have steady work or any work at all, and then must rely on a son and daughter-in-law for housing and support.

Social Maturity

Perceptions of social maturation are more complicated than those about entering and exiting roles. Maturity is a configuration of roles and implies a definite sense that there is a trajectory to the life course. "Setting your goals," "getting started," getting established," "getting settled," and "accomplishing something" are all statements that assume there is an order to life and a plan to be put together in order to participate fully. As Figure 6.11 shows, this theme characterizes transitions primarily for the "young" life stage, especially in Momence, where it was mentioned for 28.6% of the age groups created by respondents, and to a lesser extent in Swarthmore, where it was mentioned for 20.7% of the age groups created by respondents.

Transitions from one stage to the next reflect the political and economic contexts of each community. In the Botswana sites and in Clifden, passage through the life course is predominantly the passing of time. For communities where vital statistics are a feature

of political life, with birth certificates and death certificates, chronological age calibrates time. Social processes complement these more
natural processes in the settings in which participation in the
political economy of industry is most extensive. Calibration is not
exact, but given a low fertility rate, the most notable transitions are
changes in domestic roles, along with completion of education and
eligibility for old age pensions.

Concerns and Expectations Across the Life Course

Perceptions of a life course encompass content as well as structure. We therefore asked participants in our study to evaluate each
life stage by telling us good things about that life stage as well as
difficult things about being in each stage. Some responses were broadly
and sharply evaluative, for example, "Nothing is hard." These responses were given for "young" and occasionally "middle" age
groups primarily in Hong Kong and Clifden and among the !Kung.
On the other hand, "Nothing is good about this time" is a response
reserved for old age (stated in connection with 15% to 23% of the "old"
age groups created by respondents) in all our sites except Blessington
and Momence. Most responses are not so sharply polarized, and
analysis discloses that concerns are expected to change with age and
are linked to community context in interesting ways. Six issues are
discussed in this section: physical concerns, material issues, social
maturity, family and kinship, loneliness and bereavement, and
freedom. Figures 6.12 through 6.21 display in percentages the
frequency with which each issue was mentioned for age groups created
by respondents in each location, when these groups were reclassified
under the broad categories of "young," "middle," and "old" stages of
life. Examples of what we heard as people told us what is good or
what is difficult about life at different ages are also presented below.

Physical Issues

Health, functionality, vitality, and being able to work are the core
physical issues our respondents discussed. In Figures 6.12 and 6.13
it is apparent that physical issues are more often mentioned negatively than positively, especially in reference to old age. For the

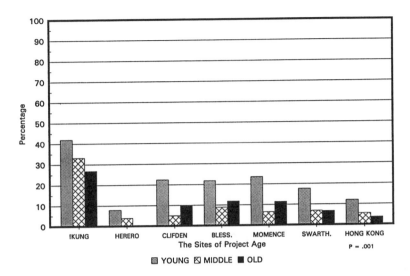

Figure 6.12. Positive Mentions of Physical Issues, by Life Stage and Site (Percentage of "Young," "Middle," and "Old" Age Groups Created by Respondents in Which These Mentions Appear)

!Kung, positive physical references are to strength, the absence of sickness, and the ability to do physical labor.

> What makes them happy is when they are good, strong, of good temperament and keep each other well and live well together.
> [!Kung man, late middle-aged, about a middle-aged group]

> No sickness, nothing bad, just growing up. Your flesh is still good. Nothing makes you sick.
> [!Kung woman, late middle-aged, about young age group]

In Ireland and the United States, positive comments about physical aspects of different life stages center less on the ability to do hard work than on vitality and good functionality.

> Still feel young and can do what you want.
> [Clifden woman, age 31, about a younger age group]

> They have youth and vitality, and they should be able to face the future with hope and optimism.
> [Blessington man, age 56, about his youngest age group]

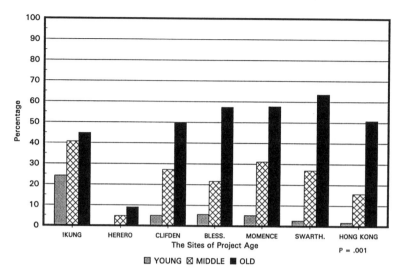

Figure 6.13. Negative Mentions of Physical Issues, by Life Stage and Site (Percentage of "Young," "Middle," and "Old" Age Groups Created by Respondents in Which These Mentions Appear)

> Strength of your youth: ability to do three or four things at the same time.
> [Momence woman, age 41, about her youngest age group]

> You're young! Don't get up with an ache here, a pain there.
> [Swarthmore woman, age 67, about her youngest age group]

In Hong Kong, positive physical concerns are linked to the absence of deterioration, aging, and illness.

> The good point is that one does not have the scent of aging yet. One is not yet 40.
> [Hong Kong woman, age 70, about the youngest age group she defined]

> At that time one is still in the youthful period, does not have so much illness. When one has come to 40, he will have much illness. One is healthier when one is young.
> [Hong Kong woman, age 39, about her youngest age group]

As good things, health and functionality are primarily mentioned about youth, but in fairly low frequency (in connection with about

10% to 20% of the "young" age groups created by respondents). Our exception is the !Kung, who mention them about twice as frequently (40%). Physical strength is obviously very important to !Kung, given their lack of labor-saving devices and their continued reliance on some foraging to supplement the meager results of their herding and gardening. Herero, too, mention strength as well as physical attractiveness in order to attract the attention of the opposite sex. In Ireland, the United States, and Hong Kong, vitality and energy as well as health are the themes that appear when positive comments are made about physical ability, usually in reference to youth. For older groups, when health comes up, it is in the form of a qualifier—"*If.*"

> You've survived. You can still enjoy various aspects of the world, *if* you have your health.
> [Swarthmore man, age 47, about his oldest age group]

A very different picture appears when one is looking at negative comments about physical issues for different life stages. First, they are more prominent for nearly every site. Second, they are primarily associated with old age and to a far lesser extent with middle age. In Figures 6.12 and 6.13 the exceptions are the !Kung and Herero. For the !Kung, physical issues are decidedly difficult across the entire life course, although more so in middle and old age.

> These people think, I am getting old. I have gone far and have killed lots of meat. My bones are hurting me and I am almost old.
> [!Kung man, young, about a middle-aged group]

> They are old and don't know how they are going to feed themselves.
> [!Kung man, early middle age, about a middle-aged group]

The Herero are quite anomalous with comparatively few references to physical issues, either positive or negative. Strength is important, but the specific ability to work that brings wealth is what Herero comment on more frequently. As for the !Kung, physical decline has consequences in terms of getting food and the quality of daily life. However, with greater wealth than the !Kung and with homesteads full of kin, many of whom are children, Herero can compensate for physical declines through interdependency with kin.

> Crying for food and sleeping in shit because too weak to go to bush.
> [Herero woman, age 47, about her oldest age group]

> Body becomes bad and can't look after village.
> [Herero woman, age 24, about her oldest age group]

Frustration with decreased mobility and doing things are the troublesome aspects in Ireland and the United States.

> Your body starts not letting you do what you want to.
> [Clifden man, age 48, about an older age group]

> Ill health makes it hard to get around.
> [Blessington woman, age 68, about her oldest age group]

> More ailments to cope with.
> [Momence woman, age 80, about her oldest age group]

In the United States, respondents commented about the potential length of incapacity and positive aspects of death.

> Sick all the time; minds are slipping; imminent death which might be a relief.
> [Momence man, age 40, about his oldest age group]

> For some it is a sentence and not a stage of life. They become incapable of doing anything. They just vegetate and feel sorry for themselves.
> [Swarthmore man, age 30, about his oldest age group]

For some Hong Kong Chinese, it is living with and supporting an incapacitated older person that is the focal aspect of physical difficulty in later life. As we saw in the previous chapter, interpersonal relationships are central to the views Chinese in Hong Kong express about many aspects of life.

> It is clumsy, everything has to be served by others. Everybody loathes them if they have to be served for a long time. Those who say that they like the oldest people are telling lies.
> [Hong Kong woman, age 35, about her oldest age group]

It is rather ironic that people in complex societies where medical technology is the most developed view physical problems as al-

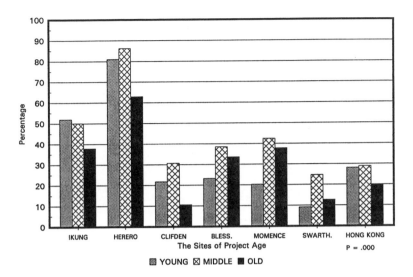

Figure 6.14. Positive Mentions of Material Issues, by Life Stage and Site (Percentage of "Young," "Middle," and "Old" Age Groups Created by Respondents in Which These Mentions Appear)

most the single hardest thing about old age. Between 50% and 65% of the "old" age groups created by respondents in these settings were described in terms of declines in health and functionality. This exceeds even the !Kung, for whom deterioration in strength is a matter of life and death. It is in these technologically advanced societies that people can survive despite their infirmities, and chronic ailments can make old age a fearful time:

> Health deteriorating and not going to last forever;
> may not see grandchildren. Fear of living long, but incapacitated.
> [Swarthmore woman, age 62, about an older age group]

Material Issues

What we labeled material issues are about the economy and making a living. Across the Project AGE sites, these issues refer to security in terms of subsistence and finances as well as to jobs and education. Material issues can be both negative and positive (Figures 6.14 and 6.15) and are comparatively salient across all sites,

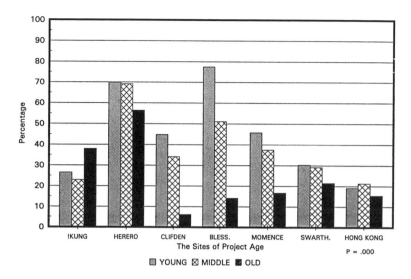

Figure 6.15. Negative Mentions of Material Issues, by Life Stage and Site (Percentage of "Young," "Middle," and "Old" Age Groups Created by Respondents in Which These Mentions Appear)

but more so for the !Kung and especially the Herero. Because of very different economic systems and bases of subsistence, the material concerns are markedly different between the two groups in Botswana and those in the technologically more developed societies. In the Botswana sites our respondents discussed food and the means of getting it by hunting, gardening, cattle herding, and crafts.

> He is happy when he is eating a lot of food. Over his life that is the only thing that makes him feel good. Having a lot to eat is the most important thing.
> [!Kung man, early middle age, about a middle-aged group]

> Collecting bush food and looking after your village to avoid hunger.
> [!Kung man, over age 60, about his oldest age group]

> Cattle, wealth, many foods, tobacco, and tea.
> [Herero man, age 71, about his oldest age group]

Having your own village, riding, hunting, milking cattle, shaking the calabash, making butter, and sewing. [Herero woman, age 26, about a middle aged group]

The penetration of the market economy is very clear in Ireland, the United States, and Hong Kong. Here people are talking about jobs and money.

Should have enough money to afford the things you want.
[Clifden man, age 49, about a middle-aged group]

They have their own home and probably they have a secure job.
[Blessington man, age 28, about a middle-aged group]

Financial stability, learned to live within means, have the mortgage paid.
[Momence woman, age 28, about an older age group]

Can begin to see some economic relief; begin to balance your income versus expenses better; become more content with where you are.
[Swarthmore man, age 56, about a middle-aged group]

Your career is exciting, and the sky's the limit if you got that good education.
[Swarthmore woman, age 67, about a younger group]

They have a little foundation in their economy. Their standard of living is quite high.
[Hong Kong woman, age 36, about a middle-aged group]

As a good thing, material issues are associated with middle age and, surprisingly, old age for the Herero and !Kung as well as residents in Blessington and Momence. Working-class people directly feel the effects of economic cycles. Older groups in Blessington and Momence are seen to be insulated from these ups and downs because of pensions and Social Security. In a different way, the old among the !Kung and Herero are also shielded from tough times and starvation through interdependency with kin. The work of the young provides food, tobacco, and tea not only for themselves but also for their village, in particular their elder kin.

Material difficulties are seen as issues primarily for the young and slightly less so for the middle-aged groups. This is especially true in Blessington, Clifden, and Momence, due in part to high rates of unemployment at the time of research. For the Herero, material concerns are prevalent at all stages of life. Only among the !Kung and Herero was meeting subsistence requirements seen as a hard thing for the oldest groups.

> Your heart is bad all the time because you don't know what you are going to eat.
> [!Kung man, over age 60, about his oldest age group]

> He cries to God, saying, now I am too old. Who would help me and give me food to eat? He thinks about his sons and daughters who are not present.
> [!Kung man, early middle age, about his oldest age group]

> No cattle, no horse, no rifle, and lazy parents who leave them nothing.
> [Herero woman, age 69, about his youngest age group]

> Crying for food, having no food or cattle.
> [Herero man, age 73, about his oldest age group]

In Clifden, Blessington, and Momence, the main difficulty for the young is considered to be that of getting jobs, given an economic downturn and high rates of unemployment. Money gives one access to the market and the ability to consume. Stable jobs and predictable incomes provide a margin of security. However, in the market economy it is the young who are viewed as experiencing the most financial stresses in finding these good jobs with good incomes.

> No money to provide for them as you would like.
> [Clifden woman, age 72, about a middle-aged group]

> You might not have a job or money.
> [Clifden woman, age 44, about a younger group]

> Trying to make ends meet and to keep the house going.
> [Blessington woman, age 48, about a middle-aged group]

Not enough work for the educated work force. Having to immigrate.
[Blessington man, age 28, about his youngest age group]

Not being financially set or having all the material things you want.
Not having security in your job.
[Momence man, age 23, about his youngest age group]

You've already tasted money and you know you can't do without it.
[Swarthmore woman, age 28, about a younger age group]

It is very tiresome to earn money.
[Hong Kong man, age 33, about his youngest age group]

Finally, the effects of the policies of the welfare state can be seen for Ireland, the United States, and to some extent Hong Kong. As a difficult thing for old age, material worries are comparatively minor. In Ireland and the United States, state pensions and Social Security programs provide a financial floor. As observed by a woman from Momence about her older age group, they are "retired and probably have enough money to do what they want." In Hong Kong the state provides health benefits for all. Also for people in Hong Kong and to some extent in Ireland, the present is materially far more secure than the past.

Social Maturation

Maturation implies a life trajectory that is forward looking and involves the idea that one must take certain actions to engage in the life course: decisions about a career, forming a family, and accumulating enough wealth to purchase a house and to launch oneself on a life path. Life trajectory themes are somewhat more positive than negative, and clearly they are salient in descriptions of youth and to a lesser extent of middle age (see Figures 6.16 and 6.17). On the positive side are control, flexibility, and having made the decisions and finally getting started.

Life in front of you and a say in how it'll work.
[Clifden man, age 24, about his youngest age group]

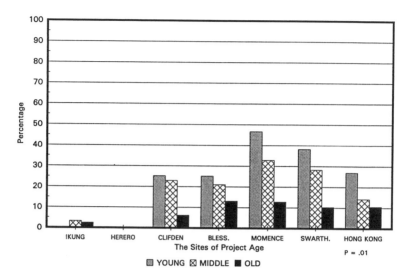

Figure 6.16. Positive Mentions of Social Maturation, by Life Stage and Site (Percentage of "Young," "Middle," and "Old" Age Groups Created by Respondents in Which These Mentions Appear)

All settled—decisions made about career and family.
[Clifden woman, age 24, about a middle-aged group]

You're settled—have your own home.
[Blessington woman, age 82, about her youngest age group]

Have decided or it has been decided for you what you are going to do for the rest of your life—where to live and what to do professionally.
[Momence man, age 21, about a middle-aged group]

Probably more opportunities to structure your life in the way you want to. You have flexibility at this age. To relocate is harder later. You have more control over what you're going to do.
[Swarthmore man, age 39, about his youngest age group]

On the difficult side are societal pressures, the uncertainty about the future, a seemingly endless array of choices, and then an end to flexibility as one is locked on course.

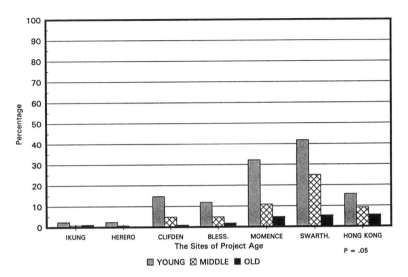

Figure 6.17. Negative Mentions of Social Maturation, by Life Stage and Site (Percentage of "Young," "Middle," and "Old" Age Groups Created by Respondents in Which These Mentions Appear)

Being pressured by other people, finding out where you are and what your values are.
[Momence woman, age 31, about her youngest group]

Some have just stepped into the society. It is a time of hesitation and not knowing which way to go. It is a period of unstable foundation. Easy to be tempted, if you don't have firmer mind. They don't have sufficient experience.
[Hong Kong woman, age 28, about her youngest age group]

The multiplicities of choices careerwise and a lack of boundaries in their sexual choices. I think it is hard. There is too much freedom. Hard to confront your idealism with the world the way it is.
[Swarthmore woman, age 59, about her youngest age group]

Decisions are made; their flexibility is curtailed.
[Blessington man, age 37, about a middle-aged group]

Their social status is almost settled. If they want to make changes, they will have fewer chances to do so. If good, they will be contented.

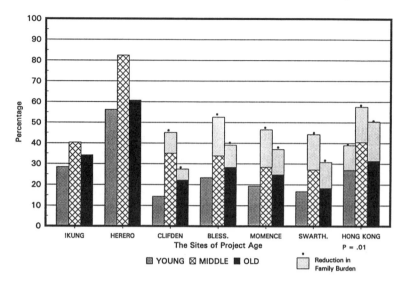

Figure 6.18. Positive Mentions of Kinship, by Life Stage and Site (Percentage of "Young," "Middle," and "Old" Age Groups Created by Respondents in Which These Mentions Appear)

If not, they will have neither interest nor feelings.
[Hong Kong woman, age 33, about a middle-aged group]

Interestingly, social maturation themes are restricted to sites with industrial economies. In the Kalahari, life is centered on family units, with an occasional trip to Maun to market cattle and to purchase tobacco or other supplies. Life in Ireland, the United States, and Hong Kong is less centered on families. Individuals engage in a balancing act between family and the world of jobs and money. Children are launched from families to find their way in this world of corporations, markets, and voluntary associations. Social maturation themes are primarily those of engagement in the world beyond the family as well as of forming one's own family unit.

Kinship

Marriage, family, children, and grandchildren are all included in the theme we labeled kinship. As shown in Figures 6.18 and 6.19, families are a central concern with both positive and negative

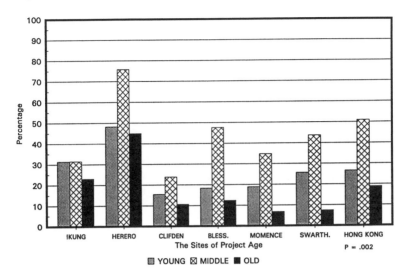

Figure 6.19. Negative Mentions of Kinship, by Life Stage and Site (Percentage of "Young," "Middle," and "Old" Age Groups Created by Respondents in Which These Mentions Appear)

valence for people in all our sites, and most emphatically for the Herero. The pattern of nearly identical frequency of positive and negative mentions holds for the "young," "middle," and "old" age groups created by respondents and also for all our sites. In all sites, kinship is most salient in descriptions of middle age, which mention kinship relations both up and down the generations.

Family organization differs considerably across the Project AGE sites, and one important axis of this variation has to do with the economic organization of domestic units. In the statements made about kin being a good aspect of a life stage, we find two related themes. The first deals with the relationships between relatives, and the second is concerned with the responsibilities for children. Combined, these themes reveal marked differences in kinship ideologies.

Relationships With Relatives

!Kung and Herero families operate within the framework of a domestic division of labor and a domestic economy. Family members work with and for each other. Interdependency with family members is vital. This is revealed clearly in their statements about relatives as positive things across the life course. It is considered good for the young to care for their elders, for the middle-aged to work together to support both the old and young, and finally for the old to benefit from the work of the young and middle-aged.

> If they have a mother, they love her. They love to be with and take care of their relatives. If you can help yourself, that is good.
> [!Kung woman, over 60, about her youngest group]

> He wishes to marry a wife so that they can help each other.
> [!Kung man, under 30, about a middle-aged group]

> You can feed yourself and feed your elders who birthed you. You can get things for yourself and give yourself life.
> [!Kung man, over 60, about a middle-aged group]

> Many children work for you, keep sacred fire, kill mice in your house, daughters work for you.
> [Herero woman, age 26, about a middle-aged group]

> What is good is if they have someone to help such as a wife or a husband or a child to bring them things and help them out.
> [!Kung—about an old group]

> Commanding children to milk cattle, bring food, tobacco, and tea.
> [Herero man, age 54, about his oldest age group]

In contrast, the statements from Ireland and the United States are not reflective of interdependency with a larger unit beyond a nuclear family. Instead, families are enjoyable and are very rewarding socially. In descriptions of the youngest age groups, the focus is on development of relationships with a partner and young children. This is followed by the development of family and growth of children. In old age the good side of kinship is enjoyment of adult children and grandchildren.

Marriage and getting settled.
[Blessington man, age 21, about his youngest age group]

Doing things with children, going out, close family ties.
[Momence woman, age 75, about her youngest age group]

Becoming a parent; feel [you] belong to a unit.
[Swarthmore woman, age 79, about a younger age group]

Rearing family, kids are great fun.
[Clifden man, age 40, about a middle-aged group]

Family is together growing up.
[Blessington woman, age 41, about a middle-aged group]

Really enjoy kids as young adults; have a great time together; develop some of their own interests and abilities.
[Momence man, age 59, about a middle-aged group]

Children unfolding; differences in talents; thrilling to watch them grow up. [Swarthmore woman, age 78, about a middle-aged group]

Having family around you.
[Clifden man, age 88, about his oldest age group]

Enjoy grandchildren without being responsible for them.
[Blessington woman, age 28, about her oldest age group]

Most have family, get most enjoyment from family getting together.
[Momence man, age 28, about his oldest age group]

Seeing both sides of each family; enjoy grandchildren more than your own. [Swarthmore man, age 45, about his oldest age group]

In Hong Kong we also see the rewards of the "family warmth," but the stem family relies on the family economy to provide for their members, especially the old.

Marriage is a turning point; have a family; change from having no
worries to having a sense of responsibilities.
[Hong Kong woman, age 35, about a younger age group]

Have second generation; more people talk; it is fellowship.
[Hong Kong woman, age 70, about a middle-aged group]

If family environment is good, there are people who support them.
[Hong Kong man, age 62, about his oldest age group]

Responsibility for Children

Clearly !Kung and Herero parents want children and want them
to stay near them and work together. In the other sites, responses are
more complex. Although there is great pleasure expressed in closeness
to children, there are also frequent references to finding joy in their
increasing independence and the corresponding decrease of responsibility for them, what in Hong Kong is eloquently referred to as
relief from the "family burden." An interesting difference in emphasis
on the consequences of decreasing responsibilities for children is that
in Ireland and the United States we heard explicit positive references
to the newfound freedom of parents whose children are grown.

Kids gone, go back to do your own thing and enjoy them.
[Clifden woman, age 32, about a middle-aged group]

Children are grown up and parents are a bit more relieved of their
responsibility.
[Blessington woman, age 66, about a middle-aged group]

Like a honeymoon with the children gone—enjoy children—go off
and enjoy each other.
[Momence woman, age 70, about a middle-aged group]

Kids coming into bloom; look forward to kids being more responsible
for themselves.
[Swarthmore woman, age 37, about a middle-aged group]

Have their children to support them; they need not support their kids
anymore.
[Hong Kong woman, age 27, about a middle-aged group]

In many respects kinship as a hard thing is the mirror image of the good things. !Kung and Herero complain about the lack of cooperation or the unavailability of kin to help them out.

When your elders don't give you things and don't take care of you.
[!Kung woman, late middle age, about her youngest age group]

Neglect of parents.
[Herero man, age 67, about his youngest age group]

Having her daughter refuse to work for her.
[!Kung woman, under 30, about a middle-aged group]

If you don't have a child you are in pain.
[!Kung woman, late middle age, about her oldest age group]

No children to give you care.
[Herero man, age 74, about his oldest age group]

In Ireland and the United States, problems in a marriage or children having problems or being difficult tend to be the main negatives about kin relations.

Relations with family such as feelings of rebellion.
[Swarthmore woman, age 24, about her youngest group]

Realizing marriage requires work.
[Blessington woman, age 69, about her youngest age group]

Marriage; if on the rocks or not; get tired of each other; if do get divorced, how will it affect the kids?
[Momence woman, age 23, about a middle-aged group]

You are so wrapped up with children that you lose contact with the outside world.
[Blessington woman, age 46, about a younger group]

Worries of what kids will do after school.
[Clifden man, age 55, about a middle-aged group]

Not seeing your kids and grandchildren often enough.
[Clifden man, age 55, about an older group]

Learning to live without children; learning to live just with spouse.
[Blessington woman, age 20, about an older age group]

The children not wanting you around.
[Momence woman, age 65, about her oldest age group]

For Hong Kong Chinese it is the family burden and the potential problems that arise when children are not filially obedient and fail to meet their obligations to their parents.

The most laborious, have small children to take care of, have father-in-law to serve.
[Hong Kong woman, age 32, about her youngest age group]

Bear the burden of family expenses. Besides working, they have to take care of their children. They lack the time in enjoying them-selves—to stay alone, be not disturbed, and have a good time.
[Hong Kong man, age 23, about a middle-aged group]

If children bad to one, drive him away from home. One has to be a beggar. Those who are the most out of line leave them in the hospital and do not attend to them.
[Hong Kong man, age 21, about his oldest age group]

Subsistence economies and industrial economies alike shape the economic roles of families. In the Botswana sites the family is both a unit of production and a unit of consumption. Family members cooperate to produce their subsistence and whatever wealth they can accumulate. By comparison, in industrial economies with extensive divisions of labor, families become primarily consumption units. Individuals leave their families to find work and to produce in the labor market. Consequently families are eager to place their children well, which typically requires their leaving home. There are also differences of orientation among the industrial societies, along both temporal and individual versus collective dimensions. Whereas the American families view the child's future role in the productive system from the point of view of the quality of the child's own future life, in Hong Kong the emphasis is on the child's position as a gauge of the future well-being of the parents.

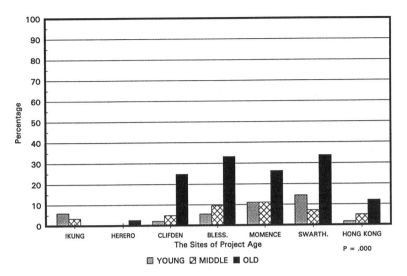

Figure 6.20. Negative Mentions of Loneliness and Bereavement, by Life Stage and Site (Percentage of "Young," "Middle," and "Old" Age Groups Created by Respondents in Which These Mentions Appear)

Loneliness and Bereavement

One surprise for us in the responses to difficult things about a life stage is the low frequency of references to widowhood and loneliness. At most, when combined (Figure 6.20), references to the two are made for between 25 and 33% of the "old" age groups created by respondents. These highest frequencies appear in the Irish and U.S. sites. The restriction of references to bereavement and potential loneliness primarily to our sites in Ireland and the United States reflects family organization and household composition. Households in these societies are usually neolocal—that is, the norm is that each couple sets up an independent household, so that each family is residentially separated from kin (although in Ireland several related families may live very close to each other and share meals). With the death of a spouse, widows or widowers usually remain as long as possible in their own homes, living alone. In the Botswana sites and Hong Kong, family groups are not residentially distinct, and questions about loneliness or living alone produced not negative evaluation but puzzlement.

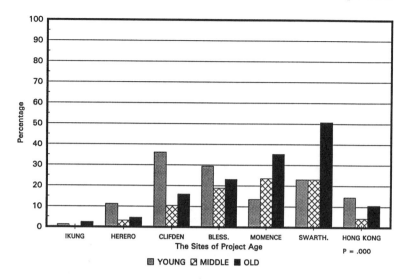

Figure 6.21. Positive Mentions of Freedom, by Life Stage and Site (Percentage of "Young," "Middle," and "Old" Age Groups Created by Respondents in Which These Mentions Appear)

Freedom

Freedom from responsibilities is seen only as a good thing and seldom as a difficulty. Like loneliness and bereavement, it is a theme prevalent in Ireland and the United States (Figure 6.21). In Ireland the freedom of youth is the most prominent. However, from Clifden to Swarthmore we see a near-linear increase in references to freedom as one of the good things about old age. These references to freedom from responsibilities are more than a reduction in the family burden. They also include freedom from the obligations of a job and freedom from having to earn an income—Social Security, pensions, and savings take care of material needs.

> No longer so much pressure. Probably the nicest age for people with reasonable security. Children are not directly dependent. This is the most stable point in your life. [Swarthmore woman, age 36, about an older age group]

> Don't have to get up and go to work if retired. Can develop latent talents you never had time to do. Have time to enjoy things. [Swarthmore woman, age 72, about an older age group]

Freedom. No more setting alarm clocks. Can do as you please.
[Momence woman, age 66, about her oldest age group]

Don't have to answer to anybody; pretty much on their own; no
tie-downs.
[Momence woman, age 22, about an older age group]

Conclusion

From listening to what people had to say as they did, or did not
do, our card sort it is apparent that the life course has widely
different forms and rhythms in our different cultural settings. In
addition, there are vast differences in the salience of the concept of
a life course and its choreography. Our interpretation of our entire
set of information, including both the direct results of the sorting
task and the indirect data derived from its failures, adds support
for one familiar hypothesis and also introduces others.

A number of authors (e.g., Mayer, 1986; Mayer & Muller, 1986)
have argued that it is the state, especially the welfare state, that
accounts for increased age grading of life. Our research clearly
shows the powerful influence of state organization, as well as its
characteristic industrial organization of work, on the shape and
salience of the life course. We also discovered other influences,
however, many of which help to explain the mechanisms through
which the state exerts its effect on definitions of the life course and
consequently on individual lives.

Sources of Variation
in Salience of the Life Course

We believe that important sources of variation in the salience of
a staged life course are: (a) characteristics of the social field, (b)
education, (c) predictability of life events, and (d) variability in
timing of normative social or work roles.

The Social Field

The single most important characteristic of the social field appears to be the extent to which the people one interacts with are

familiar or unfamiliar individuals. Familiar individuals are those with a known history even if one has never before encountered them. The social field is small enough so that in the case of the !Kung, for example, one may not actually recognize someone, but nevertheless have heard enough about him from others so that on hearing the name, one can immediately call to mind such facts as that she was once attacked by a leopard, that her child died in a jeep accident, that she lost all her livestock in the drought, or that she is related to so-and-so in the following way. One *knows* this person already, and there is no need to make assumptions about her based on age or any other impersonal characteristic. In Clifden, the people who had lived in the community the longest or for the greatest part of their lives and consequently knew or knew of most residents very well were the least prepared or willing to do the card sort. One does not have to think about people as members of abstract categories when one already has a great deal of information about them. In short, one thinks in particularistic and not universalistic terms.

Size of the social field may also explain at least in part the fact that some older persons, even in the communities that overall had a high rate of participation in the sorting task, had difficulty with it. Although nominally members of large-scale societies, we suspect that these elderly individuals were *de facto* members of small-scale societies. Specifically, we would argue that those people who had difficulty conceptualizing age categories were accustomed to functioning in small social fields in which all (or nearly all) of the participants were personally known to them. In other words, older people, whether because of long-term residence in the community, impairments that restricted their involvement in community activities, or personal inclinations to "keep to themselves," had no need to categorize their familiars on the basis of age because, like the local people of Clifden, the Herero, and the !Kung, they interacted almost exclusively with people long known to them as individuals.

Residential mobility probably plays a role here also. If there is little change in community personnel over one's lifetime, there is little inclination to resort to categories. On the other hand, in communities with high rates of migration (in or out), categorization immediately becomes useful. At a minimum one wants to be able to distinguish between "us" and "them." Here we see some interesting confirmation from Ireland and Swarthmore. In Clifden the locals categorized outsiders (not necessarily with reference to age) but not locals. Alternatively, in Swarthmore it was the elderly in-movers who struggled desperately to extricate themselves from the faceless category of "old people." They quickly joined community organizations so that they could come to be known as individuals.

Hong Kong offers an illustration of how the influence of both size and permanence of social field affects categorization of others, in particular by age. Most of the older people in Hong Kong grew up in the Canton Delta region in relatively large rural villages containing several hundred to several thousand households. Women who married into these patrilineal villages were unlikely to know everyone personally, yet they were expected to interact with them as if they were relatives of their husband's families: that is, to address them as if they were relatives. Traditional Chinese address terms are largely (but not exclusively) kinship based. Where a North American might address a stranger as "Sir" or "Ma'am," a resident of Hong Kong, especially one with little education, would be likely to use "Uncle" or "Aunt" (or, if only slightly younger, "Big Brother" or "Big Sister"). Indeed, we had a confusing time eliciting names of age groups because the expression we used to do so ("What do you call people in this age group?") was as likely to elicit address terms as reference terms. People did think in terms of generational categories even though these categories were not organized, functional collectivities like age sets.

Size of social field may act as an intervening variable transmitting the influence of participation in an industrial state into the rhythm of individual lives. Higher education, military service, and wage labor all exert centrifugal pressure on small communities, drawing their members into larger social fields.

Education

Education in the sense of formal schooling seems to facilitate the ability and/or the willingness to make generalizations on the basis of scant data. In the case of Hong Kong, for example, education was the only independent variable to have a significant effect on the number of age categories identified and described. In addition, less educated informants were more likely to use their own life experience as the basis for discussing the life course in general—that is, they remained concrete rather than abstract in their approach to the questions. In Momence educational attainment differentiated between those who could and could not play the Age Game; it was also a possible confounding variable in Clifden. Universal systems of education are, of course, a prominent common feature of industrial states.

Predictability of Life Events

Predictability of life events seems to have a major impact on the willingness of informants to generalize on the basis of age. People in Swarthmore and Momence feel they are being reasonable in expecting to remain in good health for much of midlife and to avoid widowhood, if not divorce, until at least their 50s. Therefore they can describe the older age categories as the time when health fails and widowhood arrives. Similarly, given the comparatively stable nature of the U.S. economy, most Americans can plan career trajectories with the reasonable expectation that their progress will be steady and reverses few. The !Kung, the Herero, and the current cohort of elderly in Hong Kong, however, do not see these events as characteristic of the later stages of the life course. Nor do they see progress in the material domain as necessarily correlated with age; anyone can lose all his livestock in an epidemic, and anyone can be unemployed in a recession. In the case of the !Kung and the Herero, due to the prevalence of infectious diseases and the absence of medical care (and in the case of Hong Kong elderly—who spent most of their lives in China—prolonged and intermittent civil disorder), poor health and mortality are not uniquely associated with old age but are viewed as events that can occur at any time. Consequently the !Kung, for example, resisted efforts to categorize by saying, "If you are healthy, it [any and every given age stage] is good. If you are not, it is bad." Hong Kong Chinese, who are very sensitive to downturns in the economy, given the absence of any "security net" for the unemployed, resisted categorization by saying, "If you have money, it [any and every given stage] is good."

As a possible intervening variable between the industrial state and the lives of individuals, predictability of life events seems most likely to be promoted by the welfare state. However, the case of Clifden illustrates that this does not hold true when there is *only* welfare but no work.

Variability in Timing of
Normative Social and Work Roles

Entrance into certain statuses such as widowhood is dependent on factors beyond the individual's control. Due to environmental factors, such as famines and epidemics, widowhood may be randomly distributed throughout the life course or concentrated in the later stages. Only in the latter case is it possible even to conceive of widowhood as being "on" or "off" time and to discuss the implications of an "off-time" occurrence for the adaptation of the affected individual. That childbearing in the West and in Hong Kong is concentrated in the 20s and early 30s is due not to state setting of age limits on parenthood but to other factors such as reduced infant mortality rate, greater opportunity costs of children in more industrialized societies, and a standard of living high enough to permit the accumulation of resources other than children for support in old age. Now that the conventional wisdom has changed with advances in medical technology, later childbearing is making a comeback in the United States, with increasing numbers of "career" women having their first, and possibly only, child in their late 30s or even early 40s. Thus in the near future knowing that someone has preschool children will be less helpful in predicting their age and vice versa. Indeed, among the Herero, who practice both polygyny and child fostering, the presence of children of any age in a household is of little value in predicting the age of the parent. Thus it should not be surprising to learn that the Herero did not mention children's status when describing the characteristics of the stages of the life course.

Variability in timing of normative social and work roles is an issue that has been addressed by many socilogists of age and age stratification. Much of the research in western industrial societies has focused on the roles of the state and industry in imposing age limits on individuals by specifying minimum ages of entry or exit from particular roles.

The Life Course as Waged and Staged

The one factor that has received most attention as an influence on definition and salience of life course is the state. After all, it is the state that controls or monitors entrances and exits: birth, education, marriage, work, Social Security benefits, and death. From this point of view the life course in industrial economies is a product of the social organization of work. Life courses are work courses. People are mobilized from their domestic units as individuals to work in bureaucratically organized corporations. Kohli (1986b) argues that the institutionalization of the staged and waged life course is a structural response to four problems: rationalization, succession, social control, and integration. Chronology is a very impartial and effective strategy for accomplishing each of these. It is easily operationalized and does not involve complicated testing and examinations. Others have noted that at times its very simplicity makes chronological age unfair as a proxy for other variables (Neugarten, 1982). Regardless, bureaucracies use chronological age to rationalize succession, participation, and public transfers. Integration in small-scale societies such as those of the !Kung and the Herero is less problematic in that kinship provides sufficient social linkages to facilitate long-term and collective well-being. In a large-scale state, it is the life course that is the main regulator of atomized individuals (Kohli, 1986a). By engaging in the work course, one takes a longer-term perspective on life. Benefits from work such as health insurance, unemployment insurance, and pensions encourage a belief in long-term material security regardless of disruptions in health, economic conditions, and eventual withdrawal from the labor force.

Analysis of the life course in the seven communities of Project AGE reaffirms but also complements the historic record and the structural analysis of modern states. With data of a very different nature, we have been able to demonstrate ordering of the life course by the state in some of our research sites. We have also been able to illustrate mechanisms through which features of the state exert their influence. Although the four sources of life course structure and salience previously described may vary independently of the presence of the industrial state, they are also characteristic features of it, and in its context they exert their powerful combined effects on the life course. Likewise in those of our sites where the state has only marginally penetrated, we find that the life course is less structured and less salient.

One way to link our findings with the broad hypotheses about waging and staging is to consider variation in what is required for work, rather than in how it is recompensed. In our set of societies, subsistence pattern probably plays the most important role in people's conceptions of aging. The more one must depend directly on physical strength to be regarded as a fully participating member of society, the more one associates the coming of old age with declines in physical capacity and the earlier one perceives its onset. This relationship was also apparent in the more technologically advanced societies, where socioeconomic level frequently, and in the case of Hong Kong obviously, is associated with type of work. Those earning their livings by the sweat of their brow saw an earlier onset of old age than did those with white-collar or professional jobs. Among the Herero and the !Kung, physical exertion is a necessary part of getting through the day. Not only is the onset of old age earlier than in the other societies, but its effects are amplified by the absence of technological means of coping with them. No dentures, no analgesics, no waterbeds or air mattresses cushion their bodies from the aches and pains of old age.

The case of Clifden raises the question of effects of participation in work. For those who had no jobs or work history and who, because of little education, were not prepared for the labor market, the card sort and its questions were irrelevant. In contrast, for those in Clifden who were engaged in a work course, the instrument was reasonable. This posed for us the interesting issue of ethnic minorities in the United States who are blocked from participation in the labor force by discrimination. Would they be more like those in Clifden who were born there, not working and undereducated? One of the few African Americans interviewed in Momence read the "people" cards, looked the anthropologist in the eye, and said, "blacks are always retired, they have no life, they never get a chance to work."

Stratification and the effects of level of participation in blue-collar, pink-collar, or professional jobs can be seen in the comparisons of Swarthmore with Momence and Blessington. Swarthmoreans with professional jobs are more likely to see career ladders and careers. Working-class people in Momence and Blessington see work as a way to purchase homes, to get some security, and, in Momence, to get health insurance. For some there are many jobs across a working life, and for many there is self-employment in the trades (carpenters, plumbers, electricians, etc.) and managing a small business. Suggestions that differences in stratification shape the life course are found in the MDS solutions. Swarthmore data were arranged in a very clear and deep horseshoe. Momence data produced a horseshoe that was still clear but not as deep, and the Blessington shape was very shallow, with two horseshoes differentiated by sex. A plausible hypothesis is that occupational stratification is associated with clarity in definition of the life course. Professional and bureaucratic jobs result in a closer approximation to the staged and waged life course.

If the state and the structure of work define the life course, then variation in states and the policies regulating work should also alter the life course for people in these nations. All of the states in Project AGE have been touched by the British empire. Each state has distinctive policies on health and Social Security benefits, as we discuss more fully in Chapters 7 and 8 on political economy and on health and functionality. The United States, the Republic of Ireland, the Crown Colony of Hong Kong, and the Republic of Botswana are clearly a very small sample of the world's nation-states. Other nations in highly industrialized northern Europe, and in Asia, or developing nations in Central and South America, may reshape our knowledge about the defining parameters of the life course.

As an institution, the life course has defined parameters and timetables that permeate individual lives. The life course has become a principal cultural connection between individual lives and the larger society through an image not only of the good life but of the timetable according to which it should be achieved. The state and its industrial economy are generally believed to have led to greater standardization in the timing of life transitions for individuals. Thus Modell, Furstenberg, and Hershberg (1976) demonstrate how the transition into adulthood in Philadelphia, involving school exit, work role entry, leaving the parental household, marriage, and setting up one's own household, was compressed from 21.7 years in 1880 to 14.4 years in 1970. With greater standardization, age comes to be a more valid indicator of where a person stands in the life course and thus a useful tool for predicting other aspects of that person's life, such as marital and reproductive statuses as well as career placement. A real fear of many middle-class parents is the delayed and therefore potentially failed launch of their children. The definition of youth as a period of training for entry into adult economic roles is mirrored by the invention of retirement as the life stage following exit from those roles. Indeed, the early literature in social gerontology is rife with images of a "roleless role" for retirement. Actually, as our comparisons with the African communities show, the use of social criteria to define life stages, including retirement, opens a possibility of perceiving positive aspects of late life. The positive potential of retirement as a life stage is expressed by participants in our research from both Swarthmore and Momence. It is true that, as in our other sites, physical issues of health and functionality topped the list of negative things about the oldest life stages in the two U.S. communities. However, on the good side, large proportions of respondents described both release and renewal. Thirty-five percent of the people who talked to us in Momence and over 50% of those in Swarthmore viewed late life in terms of decreased family responsibility and increased personal freedom (Figure 6.21).

> This is what we're born for—not having the pressures of getting dressed and putting on makeup for your job. [Swarthmore woman, age 59, about an older age group]

> I think it's a wonderful age. Whole outlook on life changes. No pressures of making a living—can be relaxed and just enjoy things. [Swarthmore man, age 74, about his oldest age group]

The voices in this chapter—results of the card sort and critique of its failures—bring their story to a common conclusion. Like other aspects of age as a part of human lives or of human communicaties, the life course itself is universal in neither form nor salience and acquires meaning only in social, cultural, and environmental contexts. The view of later life as a potentially positive stage may be seen as a creation of the factors discussed above, especially when they exert combined influence through the context of the industrial state. As we will explore in the conclusion, however, this potential is not always realized, and the great challenge of aging in the future will be to discover ways to do so.

7

Political Economy and Age

It's very comfortable with the pension. . . . I was worse off financially in the past. Everyone was in the same situation. . . . Now you can go and buy whatever you want. It's great. It has gotten much easier especially since we got the pension. We don't have any financial worries now at all. Certainly finances were a major worry in the past. It eases things that much. I'm so used to making do with this, that, and the other that I still try to stretch things. The family laughs at me because I could go out and buy more of something. I can't see that we will ever have any financial troubles in the future. [Woman from Blessington, Ireland, age 83]

Of course the population of Blessington has grown a lot. Blessington is not the same to me any more. It has changed an awful lot as far as I am concerned. Too many blow-ins have moved in from Dublin. They think that they know everything. The blow-ins moving in has

AUTHOR'S NOTE: This chapter was written by Jeanette Dickerson-Putman based on information provided by all members of the research team.

been bad for the area. I see people mentioned in the newspaper that live in Blessington and I have never even heard of them. [Woman from Blessington, Ireland, age 81]

These two Irish women expressed to our interviewer pros and cons of social change that have been echoed by students of old age from many fields and over many decades. On the one hand, the increasing intervention of national government into local arenas and individual lives may bring benefits to categories of persons, such as the elderly, officially defined as vulnerable. The Irish national system of financial and medical support is an excellent example of the benefits that a welfare state can provide for older citizens.

On the other hand, the increasing scale of political integration also brings bureaucratic categorization on the basis of chronological age, which may obscure individuality and personhood for the elderly. In addition, it undermines the advantages of seniority in a local setting by introducing new bases of authority, resource control, and prestige and by expanding the horizons of younger people who become unwilling to "wait their turn" to reach the next rung on a local ladder of seniority.

Influences of economic roles and resource control on the well-being of older persons have been the focus of much of the comparative research on old age. Different approaches have emphasized cultural or social structural influences and, more recently, the melding of these two into the broader perspective of political economy. Control of information, including traditional skills, is a key feature of cultural interpretations (Amoss, 1981; Dowd, 1983; Maxwell & Silverman, 1970; Simmons, 1945). Structural variables such as scale, differentiation, and integration have been considered primarily in terms of change. Interest in how specific processes of change affect the resource control of the elderly developed out of more general considerations of the effects of change on older people (Cowgill, 1974; Cowgill & Holmes, 1972; Palmore & Manton, 1974). Increases in societal scale, for example, are associated with economic marginalization of the elderly (Halperin, 1984, 1987), and changing linkages between towns and cities is used by others to account for decreases in the community-based resources of older residents in rural areas (Cawley, 1979, 1980; Lewis, 1979; Paul, 1965a, 1965b; Smyth, 1970).

Political economists have proposed that broad changes in the political and economic organization of nation-states, such as the development of industrial capitalism or the introduction of bureaucratic management, have elicited the definition of age in chronological terms, promoting marginalization and dependency of the aged (Estes, 1979; Graebner, 1981; Guillemard, 1983; Myles, 1984, 1988; Olson, 1982; Phillipson, 1982; Phillipson & Walker, 1986; Quadagno, 1988; Townsend, 1981; Walker, 1983a, 1983b; Williamson, Evans, & Powell, 1982). However, among others, Johnson (1989) has criticized the political economy approach for too little empirical attention to either economic or subjective measures of dependency.

Both cultural and social structural features will appear as we discuss the economic situation of older persons in the AGE sites. We have used the integrative approach of political economy, with its attention to national system-level characteristics and their links to local units. However, we have also tried to respond to critics of the political economy perspective by grounding our descriptions of political economy in empirical and humanized information about the meanings of age in our specific social settings.

For this discussion we define *economics* as control of valued social, cultural, and material resources. Value is by definition in the eye of the beholder, and we expect that what is valued in different settings varies. Valuable resources in our selected sites include skills, knowledge, property, social relationships, community leadership, and medical benefits. Both cultural and social structural factors affect the control that elderly people have over these resources. Cultural ideas about appropriate roles for the elderly, norms of familial support, and notions of what are the requirements of full personhood all influence economic circumstances of old people. Resources available to them are also shaped by the political structure and scale of the settings in which they live. Of particular interest are the linkages or interrelationships between local-level, regional, and national institutions and the role that state-level organizations play in the lives of older people.

The seven sites of our project were chosen in part for their variation in political economy. Intervention by the nation-state into the local settings we observed ranged from minimal for the !Kung to maximal in Ireland. Most important for understanding the mechanisms through which state penetration exercises its effects, and the features of local experience that mediate those effects, is the variation across our research settings along other dimensions. Although Herero, for example, have considerable involvement with national systems of education and economic distribution, the chronological categorization of persons is only minimally developed. The genealogical idiom of Herero kinship also counters marginalization of the elderly through its emphasis on seniority and its corporate rather than individual focus in the familial domain. The Clifden community in Ireland reveals another way in which state bureaucracy, with its reliance on chronology, may not produce a category of marginalized elderly. Although chronological age is the basis of entitlement to income maintenance and health care, the actual benefits differ so little from those available to the entire population based on their employment status that the elderly are scarcely identifiable as a category, much less marginalized. If, in the Herero and Clifden cases, marginalized dependency predicted to follow from state intervention has at least not yet emerged, in other of our sites dependency appears to exist, but without the negative connotations clearly assumed by many political economists. The elderly in Hong Kong, for example, perceive dependency as an appropriate relationship of old to young and would, if anything, prefer greater dependency, if not on their own children then on the state.

Contrasts between paired sites within Botswana, Ireland, and the United States also account for important differences in the experiences of old people. Between the !Kung and the Herero the most significant contrasts from the point of view of political economy are those in the level of material resources and in the organization of kinship ties. The Herero are an excellent example of the circumstance, described in our introductory chapter, in which elderly benefit from the accumulation of material resources in the context of a kinship organization that emphasizes seniority and defines groups in which seniority gives rights to property. In Ireland, the impact of state policy is different in the contexts of Clifden and Blessington. The greater social differentiation of Blessington, with its "locals" and "blow-ins," has encouraged the definition of social categories and organization by chronological age. Between Momence and Swarthmore there is a similar contrast in emergence of age-graded organizations, in this case apparently due primarily to the contrast in residential stability between the two towns. The underlying structural parallel between the Irish and the U.S. cases appears to be that when there are countervailing commonalities, social, economic, or temporal, the state is less likely to impose a chronological categorization that leads to marginalization of the old.

Equally important are the ways the elderly view the cultural and structural changes that have taken place during their lifetimes. In other words, do the elderly view changes in state intervention and the basis of urban-rural integration in a positive or negative way? Like other scholars, we have observed, for example, that many elderly make judgments about their current conditions by comparing their current circumstances to their memories of what life was like in the past for themselves and/or their parents. Among our sites this mechanism is always apparent, although the valence of the consequent judgments varies widely, from usually positive comparison of present to past in Ireland and Botswana to more frequently negative contrasts in the United States and mixed responses in Hong Kong, where the elderly view economic circumstances as better than those they experienced in the past in China but view filial relations as worse.

In the following sections of this chapter the economic situation of older people in each of our research locations is described first in temporal perspective and then from the point of view of the elderly. The concluding section reassumes a comparative stance to interpret the influence of structural and cultural factors on economic well-being.

Botswana

The Republic of Botswana is a landlocked nation of 400,000 square miles (about the size of Texas) in southern Africa. Much of the country is sparsely populated Kalahari desert, and the 1.25 million people are concentrated in the southern and southeastern parts, where there is more rainfall and better soils. The northwestern corner of the country, where we carried out our research in the Ngamiland district, contains the famous Okavango Delta, an inland swamp fed by rivers from southern Angola.

Although there are archaeological remains of herding people from almost a millennium ago, most of Botswana was inhabited by Khoisan, relatively light-skinned and short people who practiced hunting and gathering and small stock keeping until the 19th century, when Bantu-speaking settlers who practiced agriculture and cattle and goat pastoralism moved into the region. One of these groups, the Batswana, penetrated as far as the Okavango Delta and established political hegemony over what is today the northwest corner of the country. In the late 19th century the Tswana became alarmed at the prospect of encroachment of Afrikaners from the south and Germans from Southwest Africa. They requested British protection, and the Bechuanaland Protectorate was established in 1886. British administration continued until independence was declared in 1966. Today Botswana is a relatively prosperous parliamentary democracy with an economy based in beef exports, tourism, and diamonds, copper, nickel, and other minerals. In 1991 total exports were worth approximately 2.7 billion U.S. dollars. There was little in the way of economic development before independence in 1966, but since independence development and government infrastructure have been growing at a dizzying pace.

The !Kung and Herero who were the subjects of our research live approximately 60 miles west of the Okavango Delta in the extreme northwestern corner of the country. This region was historically far from the political and administrative centers of either the Tswana chiefs or the British administrators. Indeed, the Herero lived far to the west, in what is today Namibia, until in 1904 their ancestors were the subjects of a genocidal war by the German administration. The people with whom we worked are descendants of refugees from the slaughter who were given land and employment by the Batswana and other people around the Okavango Delta. In this century the Herero have become prosperous cattle keepers widely envied for the size of the herds.

The !Kung, on the other hand, have occupied this region for many millennia. Most were full-time hunter-gatherers until the mid-1950s, when Herero from the Okavango Delta moved into the region. An economic and social symbiosis was established between many of the !Kung and the Bantu-speaking Herero newcomers. Thus the !Kung of this study have almost half a century's history of complex and varying contact and interaction with their Herero neighbors. Aside from the occasional veterinary or medical officer, there was little presence or influence of the central government in this region until after independence.

Soon after independence, government services began to appear in this part of the nation. Then in the 1970s a school and a clinic were established in !Angwa, the local administrative center. Today there are medical, educational, agricultural, veterinary, and social services available there. In the 1960s, when Pat Draper and Henry Harpending lived there as members of the Harvard Kalahari Project, there were perhaps four government vehicles per year on the track from the town of Nokaneng, on the Okavango Delta, to !Angwa. Today there are more than four per day.

Cattle Industry

The economy of the Herero depends directly on the production of cattle, and the economy of the !Kung is also indirectly dependent on cattle because of the economic ties between !Kung and their Herero employers. Within the last several decades a number of !Kung have established their own herds, so they are becoming more and more attached to the world economy through cattle.

Pennington and Harpending (1993) estimate Herero cattle ownership from several sources at several different time periods. All their estimates are nearly the same—Herero maintain herds of about 13 head of cattle per person, corresponding to perhaps 100 head per *onganda* or homestead.

All cattle marketing, except for the occasional head sold to local butchers in the larger towns, is through the Botswana Meat Commission (BMC). Established in 1966 as a processing and marketing agency, they maintain several abattoirs in the country. The abattoir at Maun, where the Herero cattle from Ngamiland are sold, has a capacity of 100 head per day. Farmers make appointments to bring their stock to the quarantine grounds for the abattoir and camp with their animals for at least 21 days until they are slaughtered.

Most of the cattle drives to Maun are made during the winter months, May to September, when the throughput of the Maun abattoir exceeds 2,000 head per month. The average cold-dressed weight per carcass at the Maun abattoir in 1991 was 231 kg, and it brought a price to the farmer of 603 Botswana pula, corresponding to 300 U.S. dollars (Botswana Meat Commission, 1991). The average Herero household, then, receives on the order of 1,500 to 2,000

U.S. dollars per year from its cattle. This is certainly the most important source of cash income, but a number of households have other economic enterprises such as selling small stock to local butchers and digging wells. Only a few !Kung participate directly in cattle marketing to the BMC, but their numbers are growing as a few entrepreneurial families establish and maintain their own herds.

Some of the beef is consumed within Botswana, but much of it is exported to South Africa and especially to the European Economic Community (EEC), with which Botswana enjoys very favorable terms of trade.

Services

The provision of basic health and educational services has been growing rapidly in Botswana since independence in 1966, especially since the development of a mining industry in the 1970s that provided government revenues to support social services. But because the population is young, most of these resources have been devoted to education and to maternal and child health. Only recently have social workers appeared in rural areas with a mandate to help the old and infirm.

The !Kung have been special beneficiaries of a direct government welfare program, "drought relief," that provided maize meal and occasionally cooking oil to poor rural peoples. A large government truck appears approximately once a month in the !Angwa region and dispenses this free food to !Kung who have registered for help. In the early 1990s there was debate in the press in Botswana about whether this program should be continued, with supporters claiming that the rural poor needed the food supplementation, and detractors (including many Herero) claiming that the program was fostering a welfare-dependent rural underclass.

From the point of view of political economy, our two sites in Botswana represent the most recent and least extensive intervention by a nation-state into local communities. Contrast between !Kung and Herero, especially in terms of material resources and organization of kinship, also illuminates ways in which consequences of state policy may vary depending on local circumstances.

!Kung

The !Kung of western Botswana are one of the few hunting and gathering peoples in southern Africa whose foraging lifestyle persisted into the 20th century, although today they no longer pursue full-time hunting and gathering. !Kung are in regular contact with Bantu-speaking Africans, chiefly of the Herero and Tswana tribes, who subsist primarily on their herds of cattle and goats. Although the Bantu presence has been felt in the western Kalahari for years, in recent decades their numbers and the numbers of their stock have increased sharply.

Changes in Political Economy

The shift to a sedentary lifestyle pervades the contemporary !Kung way of life. By the 1980s the !Kung lived in small villages located around sources of permanent water. These villages varied in the extent to which the !Kung were economically dependent upon the Bantu. Whereas before, !Kung who were attached to Bantu retained frequent connections with kin living in diverse groups in the bush, today all !Kung have settled down into sedentary villages. These villages are small discrete clusters of dwellings located within about a mile of permanent water.

The !Kung now derive their primary subsistence from a mixture of gardening, small stock keeping, government distribution of maize meal, craft sales, and sporadic hunting and gathering. Today hunting and gathering contribute little to subsistence. The !Kung find it necessary to remain closer to the home villages, where they have more material property, permanent housing, fences, gardens, and stock to supervise. All of these economic conditions bring with them a more complex set of subsistence practices and more careful attention to the scheduling of tasks.

The fact that the bush is minimally exploited today is significant for various reasons. In former times the bush constituted a reservoir of people and knowledge that represented an alternative economy to that of the cattle keepers who offered food and a degree of security to the !Kung in return for their clientship. In recent years mobile !Kung are no longer available for the purposes of finding mates, visiting, or engaging in trade. The closing of the bush means that the !Kung nowadays must either work for Bantu or support themselves as independent food producers.

The recent increase in the numbers of cattle-herding Bantu (Herero and Tswana) in the !Kung area has been a major impetus to the changes in the !Kung economic base. These pastoralists, with their different lifestyle and superior subsistence technology based on herding and gardening, have constituted a powerful magnet to the !Kung, drawing them away from the nomadic bush life and offering them an opportunity for another type of subsistence based on a more-or-less voluntary service to the cattle keepers.

Many !Kung now see the opportunities provided by the Bantu as a mixed blessing. At a certain level, cattle, goats, donkeys, and horses create serious ecological pressure on limited resources of water and vegetation. Hunting prospects are also weakened by the pastoralists, whose western expansion brought guns and the possibility of mounted hunting. Consequently, over time, it has been less and less possible for !Kung living in proximity to Bantu to maintain or even supplement their diet by hunting and gathering, for indigenous plants are either trampled on or eaten by herbivores. Regions of relatively unused bush are located at distances too great to allow !Kung to pursue their traditional economy while also working for Bantu.

Having opted for a settled, food-producing economy based largely on stock raising, !Kung are poorly equipped to compete with ethnic groups that are far wealthier in know-how, technology, and stock ownership. The accelerating pace of this contact with an economically superior people, together with an inability to retreat back into the bush, is a severe challenge to the ability of the !Kung to maintain themselves as an ethnically separate group. Most !Kung are poor in comparison to their Bantu neighbors. Few !Kung males own more than three or four cattle; many own no cattle. Other men have no cattle, goats, horses, or donkeys. The !Kung are at a distinct disadvantage because their herds are much smaller than those of their neighbors. Kung complain that when Bantu families move into an area, they exhaust the water supply and overgraze the land with their large numbers of animals so that the immediate area is ruined for grazing and it becomes impossible to gather bush foods nearby the settlements.

In the !Kung areas of Botswana, access to land is still based upon "use rights." There is no individual ownership of land, and people are entitled to take water from local wells for human use. As yet, none of the lands in these areas is fenced, and grazing is "open." However, the ability to water domestic stock from the wells requires some form of permission and must be received from the local Bantu headman.

These economic changes have produced new patterns of marriage and family organization that also affect the character of the domestic settings in which !Kung live. This has resulted from !Kung women both mating and marrying out to the Bantu. Some women have been permanently lost to the !Kung marriage pool because they have consorted only with Bantu men. Other women have remained in the !Kung community but as adult daughters in the villages of their parents, bearing children but often not marrying and bringing in a son-in-law.

The "state" in Botswana is definitely making itself felt in the lives of the !Kung, although more recently and to a lesser extent than in the case of Herero. In the 1980s, when a severe drought gripped central southern Africa, !Kung would have known real famine had not the Botswana government intervened with the distribution of drought relief foods. Some services offered by the central government have become available since the mid-1970s. For example, medical clinics, schools (through the seventh grade), and tribal headmen are available at three remote centers in the districts in which many !Kung live. Some !Kung actually inhabit these regional centers. For them there is easier access to schools and medical services. Most !Kung, however, live in small communities scattered at distances of 2 to 20 miles from these regional centers. Most !Kung children do not attend school, deterred not only by distance but also by their family's inability to pay entrance fees or purchase appropriate clothing. Likewise, few elderly !Kung can take advantage of medical services in centers such as !Angwa. Although clinic staff make valiant efforts to visit the scattered settlements, one or two people can give only limited coverage to a population spread over hundreds of square miles.

In the long run, the transition to settled life will probably be injurious to the elderly, as to other !Kung. Traditionally the !Kung were, in a certain sense, impoverished, in that they had no material wealth. However, they had the tools and know-how to maintain an independent subsistence as foragers. Today they are impoverished and also in an economically disadvantaged position in that they lack the ability to acquire sufficient cattle to become independent pastoralists and are only able to sell or trade their labor to Bantu in return for poor wages or food.

Economic Roles of the Elderly !Kung

Whether living as hunter-gatherers or as clients to pastoralists, the elderly !Kung were limited in their ability to provide security for their old age. As mobile foragers, !Kung did not accumulate durable property, and therefore older people could not accrue rights in property that gave them leverage and influence over younger kin. Foraging, with its requirements of frequent moves, put a premium on the individual's physical strength and endurance and acted as an additional leveling device that also worked against age stratification. Particular old people, for example those with admirable personal qualities and especially those with numerous surviving relatives, were well treated and respected. Other elders without kin and lacking an accumulation of social credits fared poorly. In times of dire necessity, old people who could not keep up on the march were eventually abandoned to die regardless of their social ties or personal characteristics. We heard poignant firsthand accounts of these events that made clear to us that families abandoned an old person only in extreme circumstances and did this with painful regret.

The rigors of the hunting-gathering life exacted their toll by middle age, and men felt the brunt of senescence more acutely than women because hunting and tracking were physically more rigorous than the gathering done by women. By their 40s and 50s, !Kung men began to rely increasingly on the hunting abilities of younger men due to their failing eyesight and physical vigor.

There is some independent evidence to support the assertions of older !Kung that, at least in the short run, old people are better off living in the sedentary villages. Demographic studies reveal that in 1967-1968 only 8% of the population was over 60 years of age and that in the late 1980s 14% of the population was over 60 years of age. Sedentism is in large part responsible for this increase. Older people don't have to walk as much and they have regular access to clean water. Older people also have a more nourishing, though less nutritionally varied, diet now that they are eating cornmeal, milk, and some meat.

Among the settled !Kung who live as servants to Bantu pastoralists, the physical demands of daily living have been reduced for older persons, but, like elders living in the foraging groups in previous times, they are not able to amass a material basis for high status that can be used to "control" the services of younger people. Settled !Kung who work for Bantu cannot accumulate sufficient wealth in the form of domestic stock to become independent food producers and to live without the patronage of the pastoral people. Thus, as among foragers, elderly settled !Kung are dependent upon their younger kin. Lacking control of economic resources, they cannot command respect or support from their juniors, but rely on good will and personal ties with their children. Age still reduces ability to perform subsistence tasks, especially for older !Kung men who are less able to do the physically demanding work required by their patrons such as stock watering, cattle driving, and fence construction.

The physical environment of the elderly !Kung does not make it possible for them to cushion themselves against the physical losses of aging. There are no amenities such as toilets, running water, electricity, dentures, hearing aids, or medicines. Many older !Kung also lack enough blankets to keep them warm at night. The differences between !Kung and their Bantu neighbors are evident with respect to the physical challenges of everyday life. Many Herero are much more affluent than even the most prosperous !Kung; they have more clothing, more blankets, and more substantial housing.

With the exception of the periodic government distribution of maize meal, !Kung work directly to feed themselves. The everyday work of village life is divided mainly along lines of sex, though in no very rigid manner and with an emergent but minimal differentiation by age. Unless they are quite decrepit, old men and women collect their own firewood and water, gather their own grasses for roof repairs, and collect bush food when it is available not too far from camp. It takes an older person longer to do these things, but, older people primarily provide only for themselves and their spouses. Their children are grown and, though typically living nearby, are no longer in a strict sense dependent on their parents. Therefore, in sedentary villages the economic contribution of older !Kung is potentially greater.

Older people can remain in the village as supervisors and managers while younger adults do other tasks. The settled food-producing life is more labor intensive and brings with it a more differentiated series of tasks: supervising children, receiving visitors, and making sure that wandering animals do not come into the villages and destroy stores of food. Some older women continue to gather, mostly during the rainy season when berries are available within easy walking distance. In general, there is no formal retirement from life's work. As an older person's physical stamina fails, he or she does less work and expects more and more help from younger people. This help is viewed in the context of a lifetime of interdependence and is not described by either givers or receivers with the imagery of dependence and "burden" that appeared insistently in our U.S. interviews.

As a consequence of these features of !Kung life—the minimal division of labor, the absence of hierarchy whereby seniors can obligate younger people to work for them, and the pervasive scarcity of material resources—aging !Kung cannot look forward to a life of leisure. Indeed, our older respondents accepted this state of affairs, but they stressed over and over again that two things contributed to a good quality of life for an older person. These were, first, keeping the physical stamina to get up and around and do for oneself, and second, having one or more adult children to provide food when one is too old or infirm to find food for oneself.

Until people are very old and nearly at the end of life, they are connected to many different people and in multiple ways. Not only is there no occupational retirement, but there is neither social retirement nor spatial retirement, in the sense that old people cannot choose to become less public and less accessible to the demands of others. Old people are not shielded by money or private housing from involvement in the affairs of others. Consequently they are immersed in the everyday wear and tear of living. These experiences are undoubtedly psychologically and physically exhausting at times and may well contribute to morbidity and death among the elderly. On the other hand, the high rates of compulsory participation keep old people socially motivated and challenged by frequent novel events.

Herero

The Herero are the only purely pastoralist Bantu-speaking group in Africa. Today they share southern Botswana with the !Kung, but prior to the 20th century they occupied the northern and western parts of Namibia. At this time the Herero were very mobile and lived off their herds and did not practice gardening. They lived in large settlements as a defensive strategy geared to the presence of chronic warfare with the Nama. After arriving in Botswana in flight from the genocidal war of 1904, the Herero undertook contract management of cattle for several tribal groups that lived around the Okavango Delta. By the 1930s the Herero had built up their own herds and achieved economic independence. Herero populations began to colonize remote valleys of northwestern Botswana in the 1950s because of outbreaks of tsetse fly and increased competition for land. These new areas could not support large groups, so the large Herero hamlets split, and a new, dispersed settlement pattern was initiated.

Changes in Herero Political Economy

The shift of the Herero into the northwestern valleys of Botswana brought them into contact with the !Kung. Today the Herero live in dispersed hamlets that contain 10 to 25 individuals. The hamlet is under the nominal control of a single "owner" who is the senior male of the family. Each hamlet is also associated with a herd of cattle and a herd of small stock including goats and sheep. There are two levels of hamlet organization: the *onganda* (homestead) and the *orapa* (hut cluster). The onganda is defined by the kraal and a herd of cattle and is under the control of a senior male. The orapa are the actual houses of the onganda and are female units, each under the control of an adult woman. The senior male never has a house of his own, but rather has as his main house the orapa of his senior wife. Of course, he also spends time in the orapa of his other wife or wives. Reflecting the matrilineal emphasis in Herero social life, a cluster of huts may be defined by parent-child or sibling relationships traced through women. For example, a woman's unmarried daughters and their young children may be part of her hut cluster. The orapa are the loci of all food processing, including that of milk and milk products, and of consumption, child care, and domestic work.

Old men control the herds of cattle in the sense that they manage them and are responsible for them. Sons remain with their father in his onganda rather than establish their own hamlet and herd. However, ownership of the cattle appears to be more complex than this would indicate. In the first place, women appear to own many cattle, conceivably as many as one-half of the total herds sampled during the research. Female owners control whether their cattle are sold and receive money from any sales. Furthermore, when women marry, their cattle tend to be left with their fathers, resulting in older men being responsible for animals belonging to their mothers, sisters, daughters, and so on. Thus controlling animals and owning them are two different things, meaning that a residential hamlet, or onganda, does not ordinarily correspond to an economic unit but encompasses several.

Domestic animals—cattle, sheep, and goats—along with wild game, purchased maize and maize meal, and occasional garden foods supply the food for hamlet members. Cattle will be eaten if they die but otherwise are killed only for ceremonial purposes. The Herero are especially secretive about food, and therefore it is difficult to know exactly how food is distributed within the orapa. It is not unusual to see a child, at almost any time of the day, duck into an orapa and reemerge with food all over its face. Each year less than 10% of the hamlet's herd is sold at a government agency located several hundred kilometers away. The money obtained at market is used to buy maize products for food as well as cloth, clothing, tack, tools, and other provisions from stores in town.

Although it can be argued that neither colonialism nor the penetration of the Botswana government has had a profound effect on the Herero, who are renowned for their conservatism, several changes have been brought about by the encroachment of the state. One of the first and most dramatic effects of state intervention was the introduction of antibiotics for the treatment of yaws in the 1960s. These antibiotics aimed at curing yaws had the side effect of reducing infection and infertility. As a result, between the 1960s and the late 1980s, the population of the Herero doubled. Without doubt, the lives of old people improved greatly as a result of this population increase because the relatively greater number of children available provided more care for the elderly.

In the 1970s the Botswana government introduced schools into the northwestern valleys, and schooling through elementary grades became universal for Herero children. Children attending school spend the week in the local administrative centers where the schools are located and return to family hamlets only on weekends. The weekday absence of children has made life more difficult for old people at the rural hamlets because the children cannot be called upon to perform chores. To some extent, this has changed the normal patterns in the hamlets, and this change is not viewed as positive by some older people. As one 67-year-old woman stated:

> Today's children go to school and have no time for marriage. A child should be taught by her mother, a male by his father, to work. They should want a village and village work to do. Today, a child learns to write, and when her mother tries to tell her something, she says, "No, I am educated." When we try to marry our daughters to men, we see men with no cattle and nothing in their names.

During the same time period that the Botswana government introduced schools into the northwest valley, medical clinics were opened at several administrative centers (see Chapter 8 for a discussion of their impact).

After independence in 1966, the Botswana government received favored status as a beef exporter to EEC countries. Under this agreement an agency of the Botswana government purchases cattle from the Herero and sells the beef to EEC countries. This marketing program is extremely important to the financial well-being of the Herero, increasing the value of their cattle and making many Herero wealthy. Without this marketing arrangement, the Herero would be much poorer than they are. The development of the government cattle-marketing program has had the unexpected consequence of diminishing the number of stores in the northwest valleys. Individuals established stores in the Herero territory as early as the middle of the 19th century. However, most of them functioned as cattle-buying stations, buying from the Herero and reselling at larger centers, rather than trying to make a profit by selling goods. With the establishment of the government's marketing program, several such stores have gone out of business, and most of the Herero in western Nagamiland are not within 60 miles of a store.

The Economic Roles of Elderly Herero

The more sedentary lifestyle of the contemporary Herero has undoubtedly made life easier for the elderly. However, the greatest influences on the well-being of older Herero are the control of resources—in particular, cattle—and the lineal organization of kinship ties. It is through cattle that older people can ensure care, food, and respect. As stated previously, sons stay in their father's onganda until the father's death. At this time, a man's herd is normally divided among his kin. Occasionally some Herero perform a kind of formal or ceremonial retirement. In this context an old person formally hands over the family property to others. Older women, through the control of animals, also can ensure care from their kin. It is not uncommon for elderly men and women to give cattle to others for milking. In this way, the older person obtains milk, and after the death of the older person, the younger person inherits the cattle. The elderly who are in good physical condition can also play very important roles in community affairs and property management. The perception of kinship as shared descent (rather than simply a network radiating from a particular individual) emphasizes seniority as a basis of respect and influence and provides every individual a mutually valued link to others in any local community.

Children are an especially important resource for older people because they act as caregivers for the elderly. In many ways, the presence of children, who perform daily tasks such as fetching water, fetching firewood, and cooking, is *the* key to successful aging among the Herero. The care of the elderly is viewed by Herero of all ages as a responsibility rather than a burden. There is some economic benefit afforded younger individuals who care for the elderly, but overall the Herero view this care as simply normal and not deserving of special reward. A common response from Herero in their 20s to our request for a description of the "best possible life" was a reference to being able to take care of one's parents. The newer dispersed settlement pattern, along with the impact of schooling for younger Herero, has reduced the number of children available to care for the elderly. As a result, fosterage, as a way to provide care for older persons, has increased. Fosterage (widespread in sub-Saharan Africa) among the Herero is especially important because it provides support for elderly individuals who were childless because of pathological infertility. Because there is a very large proportion of such childlessness in the cohort of people now around 70 years of age, fosterage is an important feature of Herero society from the point of view of care for the elderly. It is also a further instance of the Herero perception of family relations, for it is children who are seen as more interchangeable and the elderly who are viewed as the individualized focus of family responsibility, and of pride in fulfillment of that responsibility. The American researchers were struck by the contrast to many families in the United States whose young children are the focus of family energies and resources and whose elderly, especially widowed women, are more typically the "circuit-riders" among the households of their adult children.

The Republic of Ireland

Prior to the early 1900s older people in Ireland either supported themselves or relied on the support of friends and relatives. However, especially since the end of World War II, the development of the Irish welfare system has brought about a dramatic change in this traditional pattern as the state has had an increasing impact on the resources and lifestyle of the elderly (Myles, 1988). Although the Irish welfare state provides a smaller proportion of its programs for income maintenance to the elderly than, for example, is the case in the United States—47% of the Irish income maintenance programs go to the elderly versus 73% in the United States—the importance of government programs to the well-being of the elderly cannot be overemphasized. The Irish have developed a comprehensive system of social welfare, income maintenance, health care, and community care that affects both individual older people and the structure, organization, and integration of the communities in which the Irish grow old. The penetration of state programs is by far the most extensive in Ireland among our Project AGE sites.

To understand the importance of the role played by the Irish government in the lives of the elderly in general and in Clifden and Blessington in particular, it is necessary to answer three main questions: (a) how did the system develop; (b) what role does it play in the lives of the elderly today; and (c) what impact will it have on the lives of the elderly in the future as the burden on the state enlarges because of increased unemployment, the expansion of the elderly population, and spiraling urbanization?

The History of Income
Maintenance for the Elderly

The British established public provision for the care of the elderly and poor beginning in the 18th century, but the vast majority of the elderly remained either self-supporting or cared for by family (Guinnane, 1991). After 1922 the new Irish state began to create its own programs for the elderly that were grounded on a belief in the need to maintain and care for the elderly in their homes and communities. Nevertheless, the Irish government, and the British before it, recognized that some form of income maintenance for the elderly was necessary.

Thus in 1908 the British established a noncontributory pension, based on a means test and available to persons 70 and over. The Irish government expanded the program by reducing the age requirement to 65 during the period of 1973 to 1977, which greatly increased the number of old who could apply for this benefit. A contributory old age pension was created in 1960 that was payable at age 66 and did not require means testing. However, recipients had to have both established a work record and accrued a given amount of social insurance. In 1970 an additional retirement pension, payable at 65, was created for insured persons who had fulfilled certain earning requirements.

Over the years the Irish government expanded the income maintenance program by adding other cash benefits for certain categories of the elderly based on household status, income, and degree of disability. These include a Fuel Allowance (1942 and 1980), a Rent Allowance (1982), a Comfort Allowance, an Elderly Single Woman's

Allowance, a Living Alone Allowance, and some tax benefits. Numerous noncash benefits are also available to qualified elderly in the Republic: free electricity, free bottled gas, a free TV license, free phone rental, and a butter subsidy. All elderly also receive free travel on public transportation (National Council of the Aged, 1984).

Current Income Maintenance
Programs and the Income of the Elderly

Three state departments coordinate community care efforts for the elderly: the Department of Health (discussed fully in Chapter 8) oversees the efforts of the eight regional health boards that dispense medical care at the community level; the Department of Social Welfare regulates income maintenance schemes and public assistance for the elderly; and the Department of Local Government concerns itself with matters of housing, amenities, and the operation of community-based medical clinics.

The Department of Social Welfare oversees the operation of social welfare income maintenance services, including social insurance and social assistance. Social insurance encompasses unemployment insurance, contributory pensions, and occupational pensions, and social assistance incorporates noncontributory pensions and various cash and noncash benefits. The three types of social welfare pensions—noncontributory, contributory, and insured—significantly affect income maintenance for Irish elderly. In 1982, 56% of the elderly in the Republic received noncontributory pensions, 30% contributory pensions, and 13% insured pensions. However, it is important to note that these social welfare pensions are not the major source of income for most older people in the Republic. When combined, the three types of pension make up only about 44% of the income of elderly persons. The rest of the income of the elderly is derived from employment and/or personal assets including cash, investment income, and homes. For example, 49% of the income of elderly households in rural areas comes from self-employment, which is usually farming. The main personal asset for the elderly is their own home. A full 68% of the elderly own their own home, but unfortunately, many of the homes lack basic amenities (Powers, 1980; Whelan & Vaughan, 1982). Savings, although important for many elderly, are not a significant resource for most older people. It is also important to keep in mind that there is considerable income differentiation among elderly households. The incomes of the oldest elderly (80+), the pension-dependent elderly, and the oldest old living alone are generally lower than those of other elderly households.

The Department of Local Government oversees efforts to provide safe and adequate housing for the elderly. About 10% of local authority (low-income) housing is supposed to be targeted for the elderly, and most of the Republic's 26 counties have been able to adhere to this 1960s mandate (National Economic and Social Council, 1987). Local government councils work with the health boards in running local clinics and also implement grants made available through the Essential Repairs Scheme to repair the homes of the elderly.

As an adjunct to the various programs administered by the national government, several voluntary organizations and church-related groups provide community care for the elderly. The major areas of assistance provided by these groups include (a) providing contexts for social contact among the elderly in the form of visits, parties, and trips; (b) providing material assistance in the form of fuel, laundry, and transportation; and (c) organizing and providing such paramedical services as chiropody. Generally, voluntary organizations in urban areas are more actively involved in providing care for the elderly than in smaller and more rural communities (National Council of the Aged, 1983).

The Future of Income Maintenance

The current Irish income maintenance system is under pressure from three sources. First, continued high unemployment (19% during the research period and staying at this level for much of the last 5 years) strains the ability of the Irish government to maintain the health care, pensions, and other benefit programs that provide for the elderly within the country. Ireland is not the only industrial country to be faced with the decision of how to allocate resources between entitlements and economic development, but the high Irish unemployment rate makes this decision extremely difficult. Second, Ireland, compared to the rest of Europe, has a relatively small elderly population. This will change over the next three decades, resulting in ever-escalating costs of maintaining current levels of benefits and programs as the number of older people increases.

Third, many Irish rural communities like Blessington are being gradually absorbed into larger urban structures, creating urban fringe communities with an entirely different set of economic and social characteristics (Cawley, 1979, 1980). This polarization and segregation within urban fringe communities leads to the loss of cohesion or integration that characterized them in the past. This decline in community cohesion based on kinship, residence, and interaction could decrease the respect, security, power, and, perhaps most importantly, support given to the elderly by family, friends, and community. Thus this could result in additional costs to the government as the welfare system is required to provide the support that previously was furnished by the community.

The economic and political changes experienced in Ireland during the 20th century have affected the lives of older persons differently in the types of communities represented by the AGE sites of Clifden and Blessington. Although the elderly in both communities have access to the national Irish system of benefits and care, Blessington's location in the eastern half of the country and its proximity to Dublin mean that its residents have experienced more effects of state intervention and economic development. In addition, the different age and class structures of the two communities resulting from their distinctive histories of in-migration and out-migration have shaped the lives of their older members and channeled the impact of national programs in contrasting ways.

Clifden

Before John D'Arcy inherited the estates of Kylemore, Sillery, and Ardbear in 1804, there was no major seaport or town in western Connemara, only scattered communities of fishermen and mountain farmers. In 1812 D'Arcy proposed establishing a port and commercial center at Ardbear, and in 1815 he built Clifden Castle, about 2 miles from the proposed town. Between 1822 and 1834 a quay, port facilities, roads, and a pier were constructed. The Irish famine of the 1840s left much of Connemara deserted, and "some townlands had only one tenth of the population it had before the famine" (Villiers-Tuthill, 1986, p. 20). Emigration to United States became the major hope of many people living in and around Clifden, and landlords encouraged the exodus by offering financial inducements. Many merchants and business people in Clifden suffered financial loss, and numerous shopkeepers and their families left the area.

Changes in Clifden's Political Economy

Little changed in the overall conditions of the Clifden area until the end of the 19th century, when two events altered the economic climate of the area. First, the creation of the Congested Districts Board by the British government in 1891 paved the way for the resale of land holdings to tenants. Although it was a slow process, by the outbreak of World War I much land in western Connemara had been purchased by former tenants. The second event was the opening of the Galway/Clifden railroad in 1895. The railroad brought a modicum of prosperity to Clifden town and western Connemara, but even with the railroad and tenant ownership of land, economic recovery was slow.

The postponement of Home Rule because of the outbreak of the First World War brought increasing trouble to western Connemara and Clifden, and an active contingent of the Irish Republican Army operated in and around the town. There were several incidents of violence during the years 1917 to 1921 that pitted local inhabitants against the dreaded British "Black and Tans." The truce between England and the provisional government of Ireland in 1921 resulted in the establishment of the Irish Free State, but the control of Clifden and western Connemara switched many times between the Republicans and Nationalists during the Civil War of 1922 to 1923. The end of the Civil War did not bring about economic prosperity to Clifden; a "change of Government or political attitude could not . . . convert rocks and bogs of Connemara into fertile fields" (Villiers-Tuthill, 1986, p. 159).

Thus emigration continued to play a major role in the economic life of Clifden from the 1920s through the 1950s (see Chapter 2 for more detail on population decline), with the population of the town and surrounding townlands decreasing at each census. Although various economic development schemes were generated during the 1950s and 1960s, Clifden's remoteness from the rest of the country kept even small-scale industry from moving into the area. In 1970 only one industry was located in Clifden, Millar's tweed mills, employing a handful of local people. The economy of the area remained based upon small-scale farming, livestock raising, and fishing (see Chapter 2 for more detail). The number of unemployed people increased steadily during the 1970s and 1980s, despite the general increase in tourism in the Western Connemara area.

Tourism began in earnest during the 1970s as people from the rest of Ireland, the United States, England, and even the Continent discovered the beauty and tranquility of western Connemara. For a while it appeared that tourism would provide the economic stimulus that Clifden needed to provide employment to its youth and to stop the drain of emigration. The Irish government, as it did throughout the country, provided grants to local residents to establish bed and breakfast facilities; many local people took advantage of these funds, and B&Bs sprang up in the town and surrounding townlands throughout the 1970s and early 1980s. However, despite the fact that shops, restaurants, and pubs catering to tourists were opened and many local people employed, the work was seasonal—only during the 3 months of summer—and low paying, and offered almost no advancement. Local publicans, grocers, B&B and restaurant proprietors, and musicians did increase their incomes, but much of the benefit of tourism went to outsiders. These entrepreneurs, some from as far away as Germany, purchased local businesses or opened new attractions aimed at tourists. As an additional attempt to profit from tourism, traditional institutions, such as the yearly Pony Show, were enhanced in order to draw more people to the area, and new endeavors, such as the Arts Festival, were created to extend the tourist season. Nevertheless, overall economic development did not occur, and by the late 1980s emigration and unemployment were as high as ever before. This is reflected in our hearing from 60% of our respondents that unemployment was the biggest problem in Clifden during the research period. When asked if this problem affected different age groups differently, all but three replied that young people were the most affected.

The most dependable source of income for both younger and older residents of Clifden is the Irish social welfare system. Thus many residents of the Clifden DED are dependent on the Irish government for their livelihood, and as a result, the survival of Clifden itself depends on the extensive nature of the Irish social welfare system. This dependence, however, is accompanied by a marked independence of attitude that approaches enmity to authority of all types and particularly to the government and its minions. In many ways this demeanor is reminiscent of the attitude of the traditional "sea people" who occupied the western coasts of Ireland in the 18th and 19th centuries. It is not so much a disrespect for the government as it is an indifference to all rules, regulations, and authority. This attitude is also noticeable in the large number of people who are on the dole and yet are working "part time." This and other behaviors can be classified under the rubric of "fiddling," which is raised to an art form in and around Clifden.

Economic Roles of the Elderly in Clifden

The circumstances of older people in Clifden are affected by several major economic and political factors. First, because of its isolated geographical location, Clifden residents have limited access to infrastructure and facilities that can be important to the elderly and their families, such as long-term care facilities and adult day care centers.

The Republic continues to emphasize the development of the eastern half of the country, where more employment opportunities are available to communities such as Blessington than to those like Clifden, located in the west. One consequence of this for older persons is that in Clifden retirement is not a major life transition. Only three respondents, none of them elderly, listed retirement as an indicator of old age. Few people in Clifden have what could be called "jobs" from which to retire. Those who do work are either self-employed—as owners of pubs or shops—or work in agriculture and fishing, from which people never really retire. For many people there is little difference between receiving the dole and receiving the pension, except for the day of the week one must go to the post office to collect it.

Second, the proportion of the elderly in Clifden is very high compared to the Republic as a whole and to our other research location, Blessington, in particular. Over 16% of the total population and over 25% of the adult population in Clifden is over 65. In addition, the dependency ratio, even without including the approximately 35% of the work-age males who are officially unemployed, is an astounding 0.98:1. The Clifden DED (District Electoral Division) is largely a community of children and old people, and given the continued hard economic times in the west of Ireland, the pattern of emigration of young adults is likely to continue. Therefore the tendency for the elderly to be dependent on the income maintenance schemes and other benefits provided by the state can only increase in the future.

Third, although Clifden could not by any stretch of the imagination be considered an urban fringe community, it is undergoing some of the effects experienced by these communities because of the impact of tourism. Middle-class people have moved to Clifden to take advantage of the business opportunities offered by the growth of tourism and perhaps even to experience a more meaningful community life. Their numbers are not large, but their presence in the community has had an effect. They are not part of the existing prestige structure and do not easily fit into the local hierarchy, which is based upon name, longevity in the community, and family background. Their goals for the community center mainly on expanding its tourist potential, and they are not supportive of the local social structures that maintain security and social participation for the elderly.

Fourth, somewhat surprisingly, despite the large number of elderly people in the Clifden DED, the community has no senior citizens' committee and, except for a small chapter of St. Vincent de Paul, is devoid of formal organizations aimed at helping old people. This is not a reflection of noncaring, but rather an indication of the strong role of family within Clifden. Older people rely on relatives, often quite distantly related, for help with a wide variety of tasks. In addition, the availability of nationally insured health care that is accessible, affordable, and hands-on provides security for the elderly and enhances the ability of family members to provide their other needs.

Finally, older respondents in Clifden expressed general contentment with their lives and with Clifden as a community in which to live. The reasons for this attitude are complex and multidimensional, but in general three reasons predominate: the ability to age in context, in a familiar environment, surrounded by relatives, friends, and neighbors whom one has known for a lifetime; the Irish social welfare system and hands-on health care system, which truly provide a safety net for older people; and the fact that life is better today than it was for parents and grandparents of today's elderly. When combined, these factors appear to result for the old people of Clifden in satisfaction with their lives, their community, and their expectations for the future, even without many of the programs and services taken for granted in the United States and other parts of the industrial world.

Blessington

The Manor of Blessington was created in 1669 by Charles II, and throughout the 1700s and 1800s Blessington, like other estate towns, acted as a commercial center for the surrounding area (Daly, 1981; Sadler, 1928). Turnpike roads linked Blessington to Dublin and other Wicklow towns, and coaches provided public transportation and mail delivery. Weekly markets, as well as three fairs a year, brought both local and nonlocal persons into the area. Even though in the late 19th century tenants were provided with loans to purchase their holdings, Blessington remained a small market village serving the needs of its surrounding rural population (Daly, 1981). Even the establishment in 1895 of the Dublin-Blessington Tramway did not change the nature of Blessington (Foyle & Newham, 1963).

Although contemporary elderly portray Blessington during the early decades of this century as undifferentiated and integrated by ties of kinship and intermarriage, there appear to have been several lines of demarcation within the community. One particularly important distinction was between the prosperous Protestant dairy farmers in the lowlands and the less prosperous Catholic sheep farmers in the hills. A second source of social differentiation was family reputation or family history. Families with the longest period of continued residence in Blessington tended to be viewed as "core families." Descent from one of these families and residence in the area gave individuals greater status than people and families who had been in the area for a shorter period of time. Finally, although denied by most local residents, religion (Catholic vs.

Protestant) has differentiated residents in Blessington since the founding of the community in the 17th century.

Older people controlled various resources during this early period. The male head of each family controlled the inheritance of resources, which were passed on undivided to one son, usually the youngest (Aalen, Gilmore, & Williams, 1967; Hannan, 1979). Parents remained in their homes and were supported by the designated heir, while noninheriting sons often found work as laborers on other farms in the area. Great respect was displayed for the elderly within both the family and the community; they wielded considerable economic control within the family and exerted extensive power in community decision making.

Changes in Blessington:
Political Economy

The decision in 1935 by the Electricity and Supply Board (ESB) and the Dublin Corporation to create the Poulaphuca Reservoir and Power Station on the Liffey-Kings River Valley directly adjacent to Blessington town brought dramatic changes to the entire area. The dam and power station, first proposed in 1921 (Griffith, Jeffcott, & Griffith, 1921), were designed to meet the future power and water needs of rapidly growing Dublin, and although the outbreak of World War II delayed the project, it was completed in 1943.

The building of the dam and the creation of the 7-square-mile "Blessington Lakes" reshaped the Blessington region in several ways. First, because there was insufficient local labor to fulfill construction needs, many workers migrated into the area. Some of these workers settled permanently in the area when two tracts of Local Authority housing were created in the late 1940s. Workers at the Roadstones Quarry, established just outside of Blessington town to meet the demands of construction, also took advantage of this low-income housing. This was the first significant in-migration to the Blessington area, and it had a long-term impact on the community. Second, the plan for the dam and resulting reservoir had the consequence of flooding a valley, Ballianahown, which was the home to about 100 families. These families were offered financial compensation for their loss, and most used this money to purchase farms outside the Blessington area. The eviction of the

Ballianahown families also had a devastating effect on the Church of Ireland's (Protestant) population. As a result of the eviction, the church lost 50% of its congregation and Protestantism became for the first time the minority religion in the area.

The penetration of the state in the form of the reservoir also resulted in considerable resentment on the part of residents of the area. Many older people in the Blessington area, to this day, believe that Ballianahown residents were not treated fairly by the state. This attitude was expressed to us by an older resident of the area in 1988:

> The ESB and the Dublin Corporation treated the area badly. They came in and took us over. Dublin people get their water from our Lake while our water rates keep going up. The ESB won't even let us fish in the lake. The ESB got away with murder. Everything changed after they made the lakes. There was an atmosphere about the place before they flooded Ballianahown. Everyone was a neighbor. Farmers and shopkeepers like myself all worked together. You knew everyone and you could stop and have a chat. The lakes also made a boundary between people. Before the lakes the shops in Blessington served the whole area. Now people on the other side of the lake have their own shops. Now they say they are separate from Blessington.

Finally, the creation of the lakes inaugurated tourism in the Blessington area. Use of the lakes and surrounding lands for summer recreation was enhanced in the 1950s with the establishment of regular bus service between Dublin and Blessington. In addition, the establishment of the Downshire Hotel in the early 1960s meant that English tourists could also enjoy the beauty of the lakes.

The dam, the reservoir, and tourism were harbingers of Blessington's boom period of the late 1960s and 1970s. A local development organization called the West Wicklow Development Association (WWDA) marketed Blessington in local and national newspapers as an El Dorado waiting to be discovered. The WWDA convinced the Local Government Council to establish an industrial estate on the edge of town. Between 1970 and 1975, 16 small industries became established there, resulting in the creation of 400 new jobs (Social Studies Course, 1982). In fact, these industries came to replace Roadstones Quarry as the major employer in the area. Large tracts of low-income housing were constructed to provide housing for incoming workers and young couples raised elsewhere in West Wicklow who moved into Blessington to take advantage of the newly available housing and employment opportunities.

In-migration reached a peak in the late 1970s, when middle-class Dubliners decided to build their dream homes near the lakes and private tract condominiums were built for less affluent middle-class households. The Blessington area as a whole experienced a population increase of 45% between 1971 and 1979 (Social Studies Course, 1982). The economic development and immigration of commuters into the Blessington area reached a plateau in the early 1980s.

Economic Roles of the Elderly in Blessington

Because of local cultural norms that prevented specific questions about money and income, it is impossible to present a detailed analysis of either the amount or sources of income of older people in Blessington. However, a general overview of their income can be presented. Most elderly in Blessington, like those elsewhere in Ireland, are affected in some fashion by state income maintenance schemes. Fifty percent of the elderly in Blessington are retired and thus receive one of the three types of pensions available. More than half (55%) of the elderly respondents stated that state pensions, as well as state-supported fuel, telephone, health, and transportation schemes, contributed to their well-being. Certainly, the myriad of available benefits are especially critical to the well-being of the 40% of the Blessington elderly who live alone. Of those respondents who work full time, 70% are farmers, and therefore it is very difficult to even estimate their income. Many of those individuals who are employed part time also receive some benefits from the state. The fact that all elderly respondents in Blessington owned their own homes confirms the pattern of home ownership being the most important tangible asset for the elderly in Ireland. As reported in more detail in Chapter 8, state-supported health and community care are crucial resources for the elderly in Blessington.

This reliance by older people in Blessington on income maintenance and benefit programs could appear to make them dependent on the state. Undoubtedly, the state does control significant resources that are closely related to the well-being of many elderly residents of the Blessington area. However, two extremely important resources are not controlled by the state and are really almost ignored by the Irish government: family caregivers and voluntary organizations. The vast majority of care for older people in Blessington is given by family members or other relatives, and there is no provision in any of the government's programs to compensate or support these efforts. Similarly, the efforts of the local Senior Citizens Committee have also gone far beyond the support provided by the state.

When compared to previous generations, government programs, along with family and the work of voluntary organizations, provide a relatively secure old age for most individuals in the Blessington area. This security is abetted by the healthy economic environment of the region. Over 30 businesses and 49 organizations serve the needs of the local community. In fact, only 7.3% of the residents (aged 15-65) are unemployed. Almost 57% of the sampled population are employed locally, 36% commute to jobs in Dublin, and 15% of the local population are employed in agriculture. Although there has been a gradual decline in agricultural employment since the 1960s and the bloom of economic development has faded to some extent, Blessington has a much lower unemployment rate than the Republic as a whole (19%) and, more particularly, Clifden.

Several forms of social differentiation define life in contemporary Blessington, but the distinction between nonlocals and locals is the most important. Locals were born and raised in Blessington, whereas nonlocals, or blow-ins, were born outside the area. There are two categories of blow-ins: lower-income manual laborers and college-educated commuters. Although these differences could be seen as class distinctions, local residents view them in terms of residence and interaction. It is the second category of blow-ins, the college-educated commuters, that is particularly disturbing to the local population because they, in the minds of many locals, have changed the dynamics of community life.

The following description given by a local man in his 70s is representative of how many elderly people view these more affluent newcomers, whose single homes are locally called bungalows:

> The lakes attracted people from Dublin. They built bungalows everywhere. I almost consider myself a stranger in town. I have no interest in the people that live in the bungalows. They don't have anything

common with me. They aren't really a part of the area because they never spend any time or money in town. Yet they always try to change things. They want to build this or develop that. Local people resent this. I never get involved. They don't know our ways, so they shouldn't try to change things. Local people also don't want to fix up their shops or develop the area around the lake to attract day trippers from the city because we've had enough of Dublin already.

The image that many elderly have of Blessington is that of the town as it was before the creation of the lakes in the early 1940s. They view the creation of the lakes as the beginning of a pattern of development imposed from outside the community. Many local elderly extend this generalization to all government programs, which are seen as forms of interference rather than opportunity. The immigration of blow-ins is considered by many older locals as a continuation of Dublin's efforts to control local affairs. Therefore many locals will not support any new ideas and activities for the community if they are proposed by blow-ins. Although in the minority, local people control most of the shops and own much of the land in the area, and thus their lack of participation has retarded community development.

United States

As in Ireland, changes in the U.S. political economy have had dramatic effects on the lives of older people. However, differences in governmental policies, as well as in the social and cultural context into which they were introduced, have resulted in different current circumstances for older people. In the United States many of the changes in political economy have weakened local bases of affiliation, and social relationships at the local level have become more transient and less personalized. The proportion of women in the workforce has increased steadily during the 20th century and dramatically since 1940. Suburbanization has increased the inter-dependence of nonurban areas with cities and promoted mergers of formerly independent institutions in various domains, including transportation, schools, and planning. Increases in size and complexity of corporate businesses have reverberated on more local levels as employees are transferred among offices and formerly independent local businesses become branches of national or regional companies. Momence and Swarthmore have experienced such changes to lesser and greater degrees, which, as we describe below, in turn affect the consequences of national programs for the elderly in each community.

The U.S. government, as in all postwar democracies, has assumed much of the responsibility for the maintenance of the elderly. However, the specific policies that have emerged over the last six decades differentiate the American model from those found in many of the other industrial democracies. In the United States a benefit program developed that was largely based upon the principles of universality and wage replacement. These policies have resulted in 73% of expenditure on income maintenance in the United States being directed toward the elderly, a much higher figure than is found in other industrial countries. These policies have led some researchers to label the United States as a Social Security welfare state (Myles, 1984; Schultz & Myles, 1990). Thus to comprehend the importance of the state in the lives of elderly Americans in general, and of the elderly in Momence and Swarthmore in particular, it is necessary to understand how the system developed, the impact it has on the elderly today, and what the future may be as the country continues to age.

The History of Income Maintenance for the Elderly

The poverty of the Depression era, decline in productivity, and a stagnating labor force led to the development of the Social Security Act in 1935. In its early years Social Security covered only about 60% of the workforce because only certain occupations were included (Hendricks & Calasanti, 1986). The act was amended several times to include more occupations, and cost-contributing formulas were added after World War II. Disability benefits were added in 1956, but the Social Security system embodied American values of individualism, self-reliance, and productivity throughout its first three decades.

The needs of the elderly gained wide recognition during the 1960s and 1970s as benefits became tied to the consumer price index and began to approach "income security" levels (Schultz & Myles, 1990). In 1974 the original old age assistance program was replaced with a supplemental security income (SSI), which made eligibility dependent on age and residency and was for the first time means-tested. Old Age Survivors and Disability Insurance, better known as Social Security, continued as an income maintenance program of the "entitlement" type, in which participation was based on work experience and age.

The creation of community-based social services for the elderly began with the introduction of the Older Americans' Act in 1965. This act stimulated development of a coordinated service delivery system in that federal funds channeled through Area Agencies on Aging supported programs such as transportation, senior centers, meals, and home health care, usually on a sliding scale system of payment. Although this service intervention approach has been criticized as forcing the elderly to accommodate to the system rather than modifying the system to meet the true needs of the elderly, it has provided many services that were previously lacking (Estes, 1979; Olson, 1982).

The U.S. government began to subsidize the health costs of the elderly in 1965, with the creation of Medicare. There are two parts of the health system for the old (see Chapter 8 for details). Medicare, the American medical insurance program, is linked to the Social Security system, and therefore to previous work experience, and provides primary health care for the elderly. Medicaid is a means-tested program that pays for the health care of needy Americans, including poor elderly. Medicare itself includes two programs: Part A covers hospitalization costs and Part B covers outpatient care. Medicare insurance was shaped by the orientation of American medicine toward specialized, high-technology health care delivered within institutional settings and focused on curable, acute conditions rather than on chronic problems. The common American perception of individuals, rather than groups such as families, as the appropriate recipients of social benefits also appears in Medicare policy.

Current Income Maintenance
Programs and the Income of the Elderly

Thus in the United States a tripartite system of income maintenance developed: (a) Social Security as a universal income benefit program; (b) Medicare/Medicaid as a universal health insurance program; and (c) services provided through local Area Agencies on Aging. Although the benefits of this system are numerous and the general economic status of the elderly in the United States today is dramatically improved from the period before Social Security in the 1930s or even prior to Medicare in the 1960s, this is not a system without critics.

Although the per capita income of the elderly in the United States increased by 30% between 1970 and 1986, there remains wide variability in the economic well-being of the old. In particular, the incomes of the oldest old, elderly women, and minorities are below those of the "young old," older white males, and younger populations, and even in the late 1980s a full 25% of the elderly in the United States could be defined as poor (Smeeding, 1990). A second critique of the U.S. income maintenance programs is that class differences among the elderly are maintained and in some cases exacerbated because programs and policies for the elderly are largely based on one's preretirement income and working history (Estes, Swan, & Gerard, 1984; Hendricks & Calasanti, 1986). Thus a major differentiation of the elderly emerges on the basis of the ability of the individual to have access to retirement income in addition to Social Security and Medicare. In the United States "one must be both a citizen and employed in a job providing access to employer-sponsored pension plans to achieve adequate retirement income" (Schultz & Myles, 1990, p. 233). Without this supplemental retirement income, many elderly, especially those who were employed in low-paying occupations, have meager resources on which to rely during old age.

Even with the growing number of federal, state, and local programs for the elderly, there remain many unmet needs, and this has resulted in the development of an extensive "aging enterprise" in the United States. Specialized residential and health care settings, Medigap insurance programs, professionally credentialed service providers, and a multitude of specialized products are directed to senior consumers—which as a group have the highest discretionary income of any population segment in the United States. However, the ability of the elderly individual to take advantage of these services and merchandise is largely based upon the level of retirement income. In addition, the "aging enterprise" system surrounds older Americans with messages that their age places them in a distinct social category whose members are assumed to have more in common with each other than with those of other age groups.

Thus many critics conclude that the income maintenance program in the United States (a) treats the elderly as a distinct, homogeneous, and dependent class; (b) creates welfare programs that have increased the isolation, dependence, and state control of the elderly; and (c) results in a complex bureaucracy of age-segregated programs, services, and institutions (the aging enterprise) to serve the needs of this isolated and dependent class (Estes, 1979; Estes et al., 1984; Minkler, 1984).

The Future of Income Maintenance

Over the last 60 years Social Security, Medicare/Medicaid, and the wide variety of programs and services for the elderly channeled through local Area Agencies on Aging have dramatically changed the relationship between the state and the elderly population. Another important question, therefore, is, what about the future?

The United States, as is the case in all industrial countries, is faced with an aging population that will result in the elderly proportion of the population increasing from approximately 12% today to over 15% by 2025. Perhaps even more important, the over-85 age group is growing at six times the rate of the rest of the population of the United States, a trend that will result in its doubling over the next 75 years. Although the majority of older Americans are vigorous and active well into advanced age, the growing older population will eventually strain the income maintenance system that is currently in place. As the baby boom generation moves into retirement age, a nation faced with huge federal budget deficits, a declining industrial base, and ever-increasing health care costs appears poised on a demographic precipice.

Already programs directed toward the elderly, including Social Security and Medicare, make up the largest segment of the federal budget, and there is no doubt that this proportion will continue to increase. How the nation chooses to allocate tax dollars as the nation ages will have continued consequences on the well-being of the elderly throughout the nation. Even as the many detractors of the existing system criticize its bureaucratic, segregating nature, many elderly insist on the continuation and expansion of the system and its programs.

The positive and negative aspects of the U.S. income maintenance system are illustrated well by the experiences of older people in the AGE sites of Momence, Illinois, and Swarthmore, Pennsylvania. Although the elderly in both communities have access to the system's benefits, geographic, economic, and cultural factors greatly influence the nature of the relationship between the state and the elderly in the two communities. The most salient features in the contrast between Momence and Swarthmore are residential stability—in particular its effects on seniority and proximity of kin—financial resources, and social class.

Momence

In the early 1800s northeastern Illinois was populated by Potowatomi and other Native American groups who were continually being pushed westward by the expansion of European settlement along major waterways. By the mid-1800s treaties with a number of the Indian populations opened up the Momence area for European settlement, and agriculture, focused on the production of corn, soybeans, and grain, became the main industry of the area. Retail business developed in the town of Momence initially to service the surrounding farms, and the town settled into a pattern common to hundreds of small agricultural communities throughout the Midwest. Because of its location on the Kankakee River, Momence, unlike most other farm communities, had, in addition, a natural resource to attract tourists. The island at Momence was developed as a tourist center, and individuals fleeing the heat of Chicago have eagerly traveled to the area for relief for almost 100 years.

One characteristic of such small American rural communities is the importance of kinship, and Momence is no different; kinship was and still is at the core of social life in Momence. Although many children were forced to emigrate out of the town in order to find work, at least one child in most families settled locally, giving continuity to the population. Kinship networks were, and are, not only active for family celebrations and crises but a critical basis for daily interaction. In addition, family and kin provide support and security for older adults in Momence and throughout its environs.

Changes in the Political Economy of Momence

Economically, Momence experienced alternate expansion and decline as the nation's economy boomed and busted. Population growth and development of transportation diversified the economy and linked the local economy into a national network, with the result that Momence became the major redistribution center for the eastern part of Kankakee County. The opening of the "Dixie Highway" in the 1920s allowed local firms to distribute their products on both a regional and national level. This hard road also paved the way for the immigration of commuters who traveled northward to jobs in Chicago and Gary, Indiana. The Great Depression brought hard times and economic stagnation to the area.

Following the end of World War II, Momence was increasingly incorporated into the regional and national economy. Local industries such as the dairy and bakery were closed, and national brands replaced the local products. Factories were built in Momence by corporations in other states, and they produced for national markets. Perhaps more important to the character of the community than any of the other changes, agribusiness replaced agriculture. Most small-scale farmers were either driven out of business or forced to farm only part time. The local economy received a boost when Sears Roebuck and other corporations made Kankakee a production center, but the nature of the work for people employed with these companies was much different.

Prior to the Great Depression differentiation among residents of Momence was based largely on land ownership, importance of family, reputation, and social skill. To a certain extent, the Depression acted as a leveling mechanism in this local system of stratification, and it was not until after World War II that the basis of local stratification changed. Blue-collar workers were attracted to the area by the increase in job opportunities, and although wage labor had been long established in Momence, the changing economy of delocalized control altered the opportunity structure and the life chances of those who stayed to work in the area. More people were now working as blue-collar laborers rather than in agriculture or retail establishments.

The 1980s brought a major recession. Factories closed as the tax policies passed during the administration of President Carter made it advantageous for many companies to relocate to the South, where nonunionized labor was cheaper. These developments led to increased emigration of local young people, and local business suffered to the extent that storefronts in the downtown area were increasingly vacant. However, by the end of the 1980s the regional economy began to reverse itself. The creation of a local mall drew national chain stores and opportunities for employment, although another consequence was the closing of yet more downtown businesses. The possibility that a third Chicago airport could be built in Kankakee also stimulated the local economy, and recent rises in taxes and the cost of local property may be the first signals of an increase in local suburbanization.

Economic Roles of the Elderly in Momence

The economic roles of the elderly, like the economy of Momence itself, have undergone dramatic change over the last three decades. The cohort whose members were young during the Great Depression and the Second World War was shaped by an era when farming and small retail shops dominated the Momence economy. Many of these individuals are members of the former local elite and still view Momence as a small farming community with its small town values and interrelationships. The younger cohorts have been shaped by a different economic environment. Many of these individuals participated directly in the changing economy by working in blue-collar jobs. Their values are different, and their view of Momence is much different from that of the oldest residents of the area.

Overall, regardless of age, older people in Momence consider themselves "pretty well off." Individual conditions, of course, vary depending upon the amount of Social Security benefits available and whether individuals have private pensions. Medicare has also made the lives of older people more affordable. This is not to say that Medicare is without problems. The elderly in Momence are aware of increasing health costs and the necessity to have coverage (Medigap insurance) as a supplement to Medicare. An older man who had major surgery complained:

> In Chicago they said that it would all be covered by Medicare. When I got the bill it was over $100,000, and Medicare only covered half of it. At my age I don't want to mortgage the house again!

The presence of family, friends, and neighbors provides an informal front-line safety net for the elderly and augments the government programs.

The main problems that the elderly face have to do primarily with the high costs of long-term care. The available long-term care facilities in and around Momence (the first nursing home was also established in Momence in the 1960s) are private for-profit institutions, and therefore many elderly are faced with a difficult choice: If they move into one of these facilities, they will greatly diminish the inheritance available to their children; if they are cared for by their children they run the risk of strained relationships and being regarded as burdensome. The privatization of long-term care, increased health costs, and the limited coverage of Medicare result in a degree of apprehension on the part of many elderly as they think about the future.

Welfare benefits are widely used in Momence, but not by older people. The elderly are most likely to use such benefits as the visiting nurse or home help aide after a period of hospitalization. Even though retirement is not common for most of the oldest old in Momence because few of these individuals worked as wage laborers outside of the town, Social Security is becoming increasingly important for the next-youngest cohort who have worked in covered occupations and therefore now receive a monthly check. Although this benefit is viewed in a very positive way, it is not seen as the sole source of economic support. Most older residents of Momence have various sources of income, including investments, pensions, real estate, and insurance. As one older man stated:

I couldn't make it without Social Security. My pension and the interest from my investments would not be enough to live on. With Social Security, I am living fairly comfortably.

Services for the elderly continue to expand in the Momence area. In the 1980s the local nursing home was enlarged and upgraded to a skilled care facility. A bed and board home, which helps a small number of older people to meet their daily needs, came into existence in the mid-1980s, and a business, "We Care," which offers older people support services such as cooking and cleaning, was also launched. The Area Agency on Aging also provides a series of services and benefits to elderly individuals. It, along with the Catholic charities, functions as the major agency delivering services to the elderly, including Meals on Wheels and household help. These services are very underutilized, and there seems to be little public awareness of the various programs that are available. Even with its large elderly population, Momence does not have a Senior Center.

In general, older people in Momence are highly regarded. This is especially true if they were descended from original settler families. Older persons who are involved and visible in community life and who possess social skills and physical vigor are admired and often very powerful. The leaders of many community organizations and clubs are in their 60s and 70s. The prominent participation of the elderly in the annual Gladiolus Festival reaffirms the role played by older people in the development of the community and the maintenance of its traditions. Most elderly residents still have kin living in and around Momence and have frequent interaction with them. When family members are not present to offer companionship and care, friends and neighbors are quick to help out. One woman who experienced a serious fall exclaimed:

When I came home from the hospital, I had more food in the house than I could eat. I finally had to tell them, let me do it myself or I will never get well.

Swarthmore

Older Swarthmoreans are part of the first American cohorts to be affected by elder-focused income maintenance and health care programs and to experience mandatory retirement. For them, chronology rather than functional and idiosyncratic considerations marked a person's entrance into the social categories of "retirement" and "old age." A life stage defined by retirement was also encouraged by the creation of Social Security. Of the 73 Swarthmoreans we interviewed in the over-65 age category, only 6 persons were working full time. Older Swarthmoreans, however, do not expect Social Security to provide all income after retirement. Individual savings and investments, along with pensions from private employers, are expected to be sources of supplementary income.

Changes in Political Economy in Swarthmore

Definition of older persons as a distinct social category has increased in the town's organizations during the lives of many of our study participants. Several groups that once included members of a wide age range, such as the Swarthmore Women's Club, had by the time of our study become almost exclusively associations of older persons. One consequence of increased age differentiation across the community's organizational structure, rather than within each group, has been to weaken seniority as a basis of influence or prestige.

Swarthmoreans view retirement as a life stage with distinctive expectations and behaviors. Positive aspects of retirement as a life stage after work, but before frailty, were eloquently described. For example, one 76-year-old man said that during retirement "you can do what you want." A 59-year-old woman from Swarthmore said that retirement brought "freedom to pursue your interests, enjoying your grandchildren if you have any, freedom to travel if health permits, and an absence of a lot of pressures."

American systems for delivery and financing of health care also introduced important changes into the circumstances of older persons in the Swarthmore community. The fundamental decision of whether to live in Swarthmore was often made by older persons on the basis of actual or anticipated needs for medical care. One recognizable category of older residents included short-term residents who had moved into town to be near a child, usually a daughter. They seldom shared a home with their child, because all concerned preferred, and could afford, to maintain independent households. The parent often moved into a rental or condominium apartment. These units were in many cases purchased by the child, while the parents paid the monthly fees. Most of these apartments were in buildings with a large enough older population to offer possibilities for peer socialization and support. Although concern about eventual frailty was the reason most older people moved *into* Swarthmore to be nearer a younger relative, when the need for care actually arrived, or was viewed as a more immediate threat, the old person usually made another move *out* of town, into housing that offered some level of supportive services and health care.

Similar feelings of responsibility to plan for their own eventual medical needs and a fervent desire to escape the threat of ending up in a nursing home were shared by longer-term residents of Swarthmore. The obstacles they saw to remaining in town were mainly, but not only, the lack of affordable, long-term care at home and the unavailability of domestic help and of local transportation. One 72-year-old woman, who 6 months before had moved with her husband from Swarthmore to a continuing care retirement community 15 miles away, said:

> I think that we would have remained home, and I think everybody we know that I've ever talked to about this would consider it if one could be assured of more adequate care than is possible now—if there was a set-up where there was an agency like Meals on Wheels, but Nurses on Wheels and Doctors on Wheels, that could be counted on to be available on a regular basis if you need it. But that doesn't exist.

We could not help noticing that the much less well-to-do residents of Clifden enjoyed these very services and that, as our Swarthmore speaker surmised, these supports did permit the elderly of Clifden to remain in their homes and in their community.

Notable increases in societal scale have occurred in various domains of the lives of older Swarthmoreans. Although the town has always had many commuters, by the 1980s the destinations had become more diverse, and the links to Philadelphia in particular were less reciprocal than was true in the past. Before World War II, as now the Swarthmoreans went to Philadelphia for work, but the Philadelphians then also came to Swarthmore for summer and winter recreation.

Long-term residents of Swarthmore were able to describe various changes in the business district of the town. As they described the successive uses of each building, we could visualize a shift away from economic self-sufficiency. Several formerly independent local businesses in fields such as real estate, insurance, and banking had become branches of regional and national organizations. Many essential services, such as the grocery store and the pharmacy, which are now offered by one enterprise, were once available in two or three establishments. At the time of our research, several other needs especially essential to older persons could no longer be met in the borough at all. For example, there was no optometrist and no local taxi service.

Many Swarthmoreans attributed the decreasing local availability of goods and services to increasing availability of personal automobiles, which gave easy access to the nearby shopping malls. Dependence on the car, however, created new challenges for older persons. If they could not drive, they had to depend on other people for rides, and because there was no local taxi service, that dependence had personal rather than simply financial implications.

Increasing scale in American corporate organization also affected Swarthmore. Work transfers both drew people in and sent them out of the town. According to one 72-year-old woman, the town became markedly more transient beginning in the 1960s. She said that "it was formerly much more stable. Everybody knew one another. We called houses by the names of former owners. But now there is much more turnover." Work transfers and the high level of mobility in and out of Swarthmore had two important results for the elderly. First, older and younger generations of the same family were often separated by great distances. And second, the importance of seniority as a basis for prestige and community influence declined. In many cases senior residents of the community lost control of commercial assets. Younger in-movers to the town could not know and respect the history of long-term residents, and the older persons who moved into the town could not transfer their own personal histories to Swarthmore. "Nobody knows who I was" was the lament of many widows who were shocked to find that as newcomers their own identities in Swarthmore were only "old lady" and "Harriet's mother."

Increased social scale also affected the nature of community interaction. Older residents of the town also reminisced about the more intimate and personalized social relations in past years. One Swarthmore woman born in the town in 1916 told us:

> When I was little, the town was so small that everybody worried about everyone else's children. Every storekeeper knew whose child you were. We had one taxi, and of course, Jimmy knew all the kids in town. If it was pouring rain or something and he saw you, he'd stop the car and say, "Come on . . . get in the car. I'm going to take you home. It's too wet." And he would just take you home.

Feelings of intimacy and ease were also, according to older people, promoted by the relative homogeneity of Swarthmore residents before World War II. The racial and economic differences that did exist in earlier years were the basis of tighter social compartmentalization. The railroad tracks served as the classic demarcation of the higher and lower sides of town in social as well as geographic terms. More separation of college and village life, along with a generally less academic atmosphere, were also mentioned as changes over the last 50 years in Swarthmore. The student body of the college has become more diverse and the faculty have become more mobile. Long-time residents also commented on the declining visibility of Quakers and Quakerism in the town.

Another particularly painful shift toward greater dependence on the wider society was the 1982 merger of Swarthmore High School into a larger institution in a neighboring town. Loss of school autonomy weakened the voices of older Swarthmoreans as property owners, especially as regarded property taxation, because Swarthmore's voice on the school board in general was weakened. People of various ages no longer mixed in the stands of the games on the high school fields, and the band no longer marched through town on Saturdays when games were played.

Development of the Swarthmore Community Center was another less direct, organizational response to the loss of Swarthmore High School that has had more positive consequences for older people. Activities at the center were organized for two distinct groups—teenagers and senior citizens. There were three ways in which participation in the center provided a potential resource for older people in Swarthmore. First, the needs of older persons *as a community concern* received legitimacy through allocation of funds by the Borough Council to the center and by articulation and consideration of older people's interests in design of furniture and access to the building. Second, although at first participation in the senior activities was mostly by older people who had recently moved to Swarthmore, there was gradually more attendance by longer-term residents. Third, the center became the locus for the kind of creative and beneficial peer relationships that have been reported in groups of older persons.

Economic Roles of the Elderly in Swarthmore

Resources of older persons in Swarthmore have been affected in many ways by the changes in political economy described above. Some benefits have required costly trade-offs, and some resources, although still controlled by older persons, are more vulnerable than formerly to external influences. Moves into a continuing care community could have important consequences for intergenerational transfers of assets. In many continuing care contracts, older people purchased lifetime occupancy and care, but not equity, so that the estate available for inheritance by children was substantially reduced. On the other hand, as the old people frequently pointed out to us, their children would never have to take care of them. (Many adult children gratefully acknowledge this fact as well.)

Public financing for medical care of the elderly affected inheritance patterns within families in another way. Because of the high costs of nursing home care and the Medicare restrictions on reimbursement for custodial care, many people who enter these institutions as paying patients must shift to Medicaid when their expenses are no longer eligible for Medicare reimbursement. Because there are strict limits on assets that may be owned by anyone receiving Medicaid, some families make efforts to transfer the elder's assets *before* nursing home placement is needed in order to avoid the "spend-down."

Income and health insurance from the national Social Security and Medicare programs increased financial security and at the same time promoted definitions of retirement as a life stage and old age as a social category that placed some constraints on older people in Swarthmore. The increased financial security made possible by private pension plans as well as Social Security also permitted older people in Swarthmore the option of living independently from their children. Given the institutional and acute care foci of American medical financing, older Swarthmore residents who wanted to maximize their chances for independent residence and access to long-term care often decided to enter continuing care facilities. Emergence of this pattern created an "elder drain" away from the town.

The peer groups found in some residential and organizational settings offered some insulation from age stereotypes and had, in the case of the Community Center, been used as a leverage to obtain some minimal community resources. However, old age is far from being a significant base for political participation in Swarthmore. Not only has seniority as a principle been undermined, but locally based social rankings have become less salient in general, and external sources of prestige have become more numerous and more diverse.

Statements about lack of tangible political and economic resource control by older persons seem contradictory to the ceremonial roles of old residents on July Fourth or Memorial Day and to the comments one hears about the charm of Swarthmore's eccentric old persons and the attractiveness of Swarthmore as a location for the later years. The presence of many old people seems to give younger people the sense of living in an established small town, which is an image they prefer to that of the transient suburb. Two distinctions about resource control are needed to understand the position of older people in this town. First, the distinction between symbolic and tangible resources separates participation in images and ceremonies from more concrete assets such as homes or votes. Second, the distinction between being a symbolic resource and controlling symbolic resources emphasizes the fact that older persons may have great symbolic importance for the image Swarthmoreans wish to have of their community, but they may not be aware of this or be able to manipulate it to their advantage. In addition, the pressure on older people to leave the town to find social and especially physical security continuously undermines the possibility that a stable critical mass of elders might successfully press for change.

Hong Kong

In terms of political economy, Hong Kong provides contrasts to the other Project AGE sites both in the extent and form of government policy and in the historical, cultural milieu to which it is directed. Most significant are Hong Kong's status as a colony, the rural Chinese cultural context in which its older residents came of age, and the recent history of political and economic instability they have experienced.

Prior to 1841 the land that was eventually to become the British Crown Colony of Hong Kong was sparsely settled. In 1841 Hong Kong was taken over by the British to serve as a base for their trade with China, and from that time until the beginning of World War II, commerce dominated the local economy. The population grew rapidly from 1850 to 1931 as young and middle-aged laborers from Mainland China migrated to Hong Kong to find work. When no longer able to continue employment, these men returned to their home communities, expecting to be looked after by their children who had been supported by the remittances sent back from Hong Kong.

Regardless of their financial success, traditionally Chinese elderly were not only entitled to be but expected to be dependent upon the economic support of their sons. Ideally a family in a Chinese village would support itself on its own land. Land was owned and managed by the senior male of the household on behalf of his descendants, and as his sons came of age, they were entitled to work their father's land. A man's sons were supposed to marry and remain in the parental household, functioning as a single economic unit of production and consumption, whereas his daughters married into other households and had no economic responsibilities to their parents. At the time of the father's death, property was supposed to be divided up equally among the sons, though frequently a slightly larger share was given to the eldest son to provide him with the extra income needed to carry out his ritual responsibilities such as honoring his parents through "ancestor worship." Economically speaking, sons were the key to survival for the elderly.

Reality for families in Guangdong was somewhat different from the ideal. First, there was a very dense population that could not possibly earn a living from the small plots of land that would have been available had all land been distributed on an equal per capita basis. Consequently some families owned more land than they could manage, whereas others owned only a little or none at all. Second, Guangdong had a highly commercial economy even traditionally, so many people engaged in petty trade. Third, Guangdong was a high exporter of labor not only to Hong Kong but also to Southeast Asia and the United States. Thus, depending on the type and amount of a family's resources, the elder's options were severely circumscribed. The landed elder came closest to the ideal. If he had enough land so that all his sons could work together and pool their money under his management, his authority, prestige, and power remained high.

However, most families did not have much land, and interpersonal family dynamics (among the brothers and their wives) easily led to perceptions of inequity and pressure on the father to divide up the property as soon as all the sons were married, if not sooner. When a household "divided," the brothers had to stipulate how they would apportion responsibility for care of their parents. Size of share in the property and the nature of filial responsibility were explicitly linked. In most families the land or the petty trading enterprise was insufficient to support a single household with several adults. As the sons came of age they would sheer off, so to speak, and try to make it economically on their own, though one of them would normally be expected to remain behind to work the parent's land or run the small shop. Parents would attempt to find their sons jobs through their personal networks, but such networks were in many cases the only resource they could manipulate on behalf of their sons. Absentee sons, whether in Hong Kong or the United States, were expected to send remittances back to China to support their parents. It was also a parent's obligation to provide the funds necessary for his son to marry and to provide space in the parental home for the new couple. Because older workers returned to China, the elderly were a numerically insignificant segment of the local population, and thus Hong Kong itself did not have to develop any special policies or programs for them.

Changes in Hong Kong Political Economy

Hong Kong fell to the Japanese in December 1941. Because of major food shortages, the Japanese encouraged the people to return to China if at all possible. By the end of World War II only 600,000 people remained in Hong Kong. The immediate postwar period was also characterized by tremendous population movements. China was engulfed in civil war, and hundreds of thousands of political refugees entered the colony along with those simply looking for work.

In pre-Communist China social stratification was based on a combination of political, cultural, and economic factors. The rural areas were dominated by the gentry, an elite class made up largely of landlord families whose male members were versed in the Confucian classics and ready to serve as scholars and government officials. Their role as exemplars of Confucian values was fully as important as their economic role. Entry into this class was open to anyone who could attain success in the imperial examination system and/or convert wealth obtained by other means, such as commerce, into land.

In Hong Kong, however, the cultural basis of this traditional class system was eliminated. Stratification came to be defined almost entirely in economic terms (Lau & Kuan, 1988). Anyone who could amass a fortune could become a member of the new elite. Unlike wealth in China, this wealth was invested not in land but in expanding one's commercial and, later, industrial operations. Because Hong Kong was a colony, Chinese economic power could not be translated directly into political power. Furthermore, the British had no interest in the perpetuation of Confucian values, and the historical link between the political, cultural, and economic spheres was consequently severed. In this context, influence within the Hong Kong Chinese community came to be defined almost entirely in terms of wealth. As one 87-year-old man remarked, "If you have money, you can talk. If you don't have money, you can't talk" (that is, if you don't have money, you don't have a voice). The moral status of this group was shaky, and they had no sense of cultural or moral mission. The dominance of this amoral elite, together with the shunning of the moralizing role by the colonial government, meant that there was no powerful group or institution to safeguard tradition and Confucian virtues.

In the late 1940s and the early 1950s many capitalists from large cities on the mainland fled to Hong Kong, bringing their industrial plants with them or starting them from scratch. As one older Hong Kong man related:

> We have to thank the Communists for making Hong Kong into a prosperous and important city in the world. Due to the Communists, all the rich people, the learned, the cleverest, the best rushed to Hong Kong. It was the Shanghai people who started textile factories and everything in Hong Kong. All the brilliant and clever people gathered in Hong Kong to make it into a prosperous and developed city.

Manufacturing quickly replaced trade with China as the primary source of the colony's wealth (Roberts, 1990).

The Communist takeover of China also brought to an end the prewar labor migration pattern. The refugees of the late 1940s and the early 1950s had no intention of returning to China. Although many did send remittances back to their home communities, most young people married and settled locally. Most older workers also chose to remain in Hong Kong. Consequently the elderly population of Hong Kong began to grow, expanding from 4.9% in 1961 to 11.5% in 1986 (Central Committee on Services for the Elderly, 1988, p. 11).

When exploring the role that the state has played in the lives of the elderly, one must remember that neither the government nor the people of Hong Kong think of Hong Kong as a welfare state. Instead, the government welfare policy is to play as small a role as possible, and more is spent on education, housing, and health than on what the government describes as social welfare. Making political use of the cultural expectation that children *should* take care of their parents, government policy concerning the elderly is based on the assumption that children *will* take care of their parents. Only a limited amount of government support for the elderly is available, and these funds are aimed at the elderly with no families. One elderly Hong Kong resident summarized this policy:

> We support them when they are small, and they support us when we are old. This remains very clear in their minds. It is only if the children do not support one that one would have to continue working or have to apply to the government for public assistance.

The government's main social welfare programs include a public assistance program for the destitute and various special needs allowances. The government, however, does not support an unemployment insurance scheme or a health insurance program for noncivil servants. Only about 19% of those persons 65 and over are actively employed. Most nonworkers do not receive pensions but at the time of retirement are given a modest lump sum based on length of service and rate of pay. Unlike most welfare states, which draw their revenues from taxation, the Hong Kong government gets only 43% of its revenue from direct taxation.

Prior to 1948, social welfare activities in Hong Kong were the province of private, charitable organizations. Except with respect to those in homes for the aged, the elderly were not viewed as a group with needs different from those of the general community. Official government involvement in social welfare activities began in 1948 with the establishment of a Social Welfare Office within the Secretariat for Chinese Affairs. In 1958, the Social Welfare Office became an independent department that gradually expanded its services. By 1978 this office operated through six divisions. The Elderly Division was specifically dedicated to developing services and facilities for older persons, especially those with no family.

By the early 1970s the elderly had gained recognition as a specifically vulnerable group. Attention had been drawn to their needs by the spectacular expansion in the 1960s of homes for the aged. In 1955 there had been only 3 homes for the aged, and by 1973 the number had grown to 21. Various interdepartmental committees were formed to consider the direction that policy and planning should take to best serve the needs of the elderly. One basic conclusion was that services should allow the elderly to remain in the community rather than urge them to enter institutions (Ikels, 1983). This concept of "care in the community" for most elderly, equivalent to family care, became the social welfare theme of the Hong Kong government throughout the 1980s, and therefore throughout the period of field research.

Social security is a noncontributory program that provides financial assistance to various categories of recipients. The programs of particular importance to the elderly are the Public Assistance Scheme and the Special Needs Allowance Scheme. Public financial assistance, although available to a very small proportion of the population, is of such great importance because the private sector seldom provides much in the way of retirement income. A survey of the elderly (including people 55+) found that only 7.1% were receiving any retirement benefits (Chi & Lee, 1989). The most frequently cited source of financial support was the family (68%).

In 1971 the government set up a Public Assistance Scheme to provide cash assistance to families and individuals whose incomes fell below a prescribed minimum. This Assistance Scheme is means-tested and requires a minimum period of residence. In 1989 when $1.00 U.S. = $7.80 H.K., the base allowance for a single person was $HK620 per month, only 12% of the monthly salary received by workers. At the end of 1989, only 66,000 persons were considered public assistance cases, the majority were the elderly, the disabled, and single-parent families. The Special Needs Allowance Scheme provides flat-rate allowances for the severly disabled and elderly. The old age allowance was $HK355 a month in the late 1980s and available to those 70 years or older regardless of income or family status. At the end of 1989, 401,300 were receiving the disability or old age allowance.

In addition to providing funding, the Social Welfare Department also supports a number of services and facilities in the community at large and also in public housing estates. Approximately 50% of the Hong Kong population live in public housing with highly subsidized rents. In several of the older housing estates, the elderly account for more than 20% of the residents. The government also contributes to the support of home help teams, social centers, multiservice centers, and seven day care centers. Social centers are mainly recreational, informational centers for the elderly that are located in areas with high densities of older people. Multiservice centers for the elderly provide such services as meals, laundry, and home helpers. All three types of centers are in short supply. The elderly also have a wide variety of inexpensive health services available to them (see Chapter 8 for details).

Economic Roles of the Elderly in Hong Kong

Most of the elderly in Hong Kong do not have great financial resources to assist their offspring or to put great pressure on them. Most young people have more education than their parents and expect to work in very different types of occupations. A substantial proportion of the elderly do, however, control one valued resource, namely housing, either as owners or, more likely, as chief tenants. Most young people cannot afford to rent independent housing when they are first married, whereas their parents often live in subsidized public housing where the adult children may remain living with the parent. Another important resource that parents can provide is babysitting.

Older people expect and look forward to being supported by their children in their old age. Unfortunately, younger and older people do not always share the same values. One younger woman eloquently summarized this dilemma:

> People's attitudes towards old age and the elderly will be heavily conditioned by the fact of their age. The mentality of the generations is very different. People 50 and older tend to have pretty traditional views. They see nothing wrong with dependency, and they expect their children will take responsibility for them. People in their 40s have a mixed view, but people in their 30s are quite Westernized, and people in their 20s are very Westernized. Younger people do not think that dependency is a good thing.

The major fear of elderly in Hong Kong is that when children are of an age to contribute to the household they will move away. As we saw in the discussion of well-being, both young and old view an old person's best strategy for a satisfying life as being tolerant and easy to get along with, thus improving chances of care from children.

Most older residents of Hong Kong have a very positive attitude about the social welfare benefits available to them and only wish the government would do more. Like the elderly in Clifden, older Chinese in Hong Kong view their present lives positively in contrast to conditions remembered from the past. The Hong Kong elderly, being migrants from China, tend to compare life in contemporary Hong Kong with life in China several decades ago. From this perspective, Hong Kong is a great place to live. First, Hong Kong abounds in consumer goods, including such fundamentals as food and clothing. Most older Chinese remember severe food shortages, rationing, and a general scarcity of consumer items in China. They are ecstatic when describing the variety and quality of goods they can so readily acquire in Hong Kong. Second, most older Chinese experienced the Japanese invasion of China as well as the Chinese civil war and, less directly, the various mobilization campaigns of the Communist government. They do not take political stability lightly and are grateful that there are no similar political mobilization campaigns in Hong Kong. Third, older people are heartened by the wide availability of employment alternatives in Hong Kong. Although most are themselves out of the labor force, they are very concerned about the employment prospects of their descendants. Many older people left their home communities precisely because of the scarcity of employment opportunities, and they are relieved that few of their children will have to do the same.

Perhaps the most important factor to keep in mind about Hong Kong is that it is a British colony, founded to enhance Britain's trading position in the Far East. From the very beginning the primary aim of the Hong Kong government has been to keep expenses down and minimize the development of any legislation that might hamper business profits: "the primary role of the government is to provide the necessary infrastructure and a sound legal and administrative framework conducive to economic growth and prosperity" (Roberts, 1990, p. 61). The Hong Kong government makes no pretense of being a democracy. The governor, always a nonlocal person, and appointed from Great Britain, has the final word on legislation. If he does not assent to it, then it doesn't become law. The government is relatively insulated from public opinion. To a certain extent the people of Hong Kong tacitly accept the basic line that the less government the better.

Old people know that given the scarcity of pensions and of long-term care facilities, they have no choice but to rely on their families once they are no longer able to care for themselves. In this respect they are not much different from old people in prewar China. Perhaps the major difference is that the overall standard of living is higher and that there is a minimal type of publicly funded safety net. Given their financial dependence and the educational gap that separates most of them from the younger generation, it should not be surprising that the typical elderly Hong Kong resident does not play a leadership role in the affairs of either the family or the community.

Cross-Site Comparison and Conclusion

Variation in political economy was an important basis for our choice of research locations. However, the additional social and cultural variation within and across our research sites complicates the pattern, and the assumed negative influences of categorization and dependency predicted from the perspective of political economy were not always apparent in the lives of the elderly we encountered.

Intersections of individual lives and various political and economic aspects of a nation-state are most frequent and influential in Ireland and the United States, minimal for the !Kung and the Herero, and moderate for Hong Kong, which remains a colony until 1997. The results of our comparisons do include some of the broad patterns described in the literature of political economy. Old persons are placed in a bureaucratic category bounded by chronological age in all the nations except Botswana, and dependency upon the government as a source of financial and medical support is greatest for old people in the two most comprehensive welfare states, Ireland and the United States. However, social and cultural influence intervene in important ways in the relationship between state integration and the lives of individual old people. The structures and values defining kinship, the requirements of full personhood, the evaluation of dependency, and the stability or mobility of population in a community all deflect and reshape the influences of political economy in various ways. In addition, the temporal comparisons perceived by older people have important consequences for their own subjective view of life in a changed society.

As a recently independent nation, Botswana is in the early stages of state development. Basic amenities such as electricity and running water have not yet been extended into the hinterland, and there are no government-sponsored programs or benefits specifically for the elderly. The central government has begun to establish medical clinics and schools in central areas and has stepped in to provide drought relief. Few !Kung children attend school, and getting to the clinic is often impossible for elderly who are frail or ill. As of the late 1980s the !Kung area had not been the object of specific development plans.

The clearest effect of development on the elderly !Kung has been sedentism. Both the government, mainly through provision of wells, and the in-migration of pastoral peoples have contributed to this shift. Today most !Kung live in sedentary villages. The foraging way of life, with its emphasis on physical strength and endurance, did not provide security in old age, but sedentism, as well as a more varied diet and decreased emphasis on mobility, has led to an increase in the number of older people. Sedentism has changed, and to a certain extent increased, the roles of older people, in that contemporary elderly now play important roles as child minders and as protectors of village stores. As more frail old people survive, there are demands on younger people to assist them with obtaining food and perhaps moving about. However, these supports appear to be viewed by young and old alike within the lifetime experience of interdependency shared by all !Kung and do not evoke notions of dependency.

The Botswana government has indirectly affected the lives of older Herero in several ways. High prices paid by the government for cattle have increased the value of the key resources controlled by elderly men. The government eradication of yaws resulted in the birth and survival of more children and hence more caretakers for older people. However, the recent establishment of government schools means that such help from children is available only on weekends. Although distances are great and travel strenuous, Herero, because they own donkeys, are more capable than !Kung of reaching centers such as !Angwa where health care is available.

Of all the Project AGE sites, Hong Kong ranks highest in terms of social scale and industrial development. Its placement as a British colony, however, means that as yet there has been no development of an independent state in control of its political economy. The British government from the start has developed Hong Kong as an income-generating entity. Its efforts are focused on providing the infrastructure necessary for sustained economic growth. Very little government money is spent on social welfare for anyone, including the elderly. The limited public assistance funds directed to the elderly are available only to those without families. However, the government has provided inexpensive health care for all.

Traditionally, it was expected that children in Hong Kong would take care of their parents, and parents looked forward to being dependent upon their children in old age. The colonial government policy that emphasizes the community care of the elderly is based on the assumption that children will take care of parents. Government expectation that families will care for their old is reflected in its failure to develop adequate long-term care institutions and in-home help. Unfortunately, contemporary value differences between generations sometimes affect the willingness of children to provide expected care. Whereas elderly perceive dependence on their children as highly appropriate, some younger adults feel it as onerous.

Although the state is only marginally involved in the lives of the elderly, most older residents of Hong Kong have a very positive attitude toward the notion of government support and would like to see the minimal benefits available to them greatly expanded. Images and memories of the hard life they experienced and remembered in China make the elderly view Hong Kong as a favorable place to live.

Welfare state development profoundly affects the lives of the elderly in Ireland and the United States. Since 1922 state level machinery in the Republic of Ireland has included a comprehensive system of social welfare and community health care. The resulting programs place great emphasis on community care, which in Ireland is but another word for family care. Although families continue to provide the bulk of the care to the old, the existence of the national health service facilitates this in important ways. Most notable of these is that medical care delivered to old people at home and paid for by the national insurance means that the elderly can remain close to the family members, who can then fulfill Irish cultural norms of family support in both sentimental and practical forms. The important contrast with Hong Kong is that in Ireland care from public and family sources weaves a complementary net, whereas in Hong Kong, publicly financed care is intended for those without family.

State penetration and urbanization have also affected the lives of the elderly quite differently depending on where in Ireland they live. Because the eastern part of the country has been the focus of most state development, better employment opportunities and greater access to services are available for the old in Blessington. Decades of unemployment and restricted access to services have created a different environment for the elderly in Clifden. The old in both communities, however, view government services and benefits positively, largely because the elderly remember the very hard times of the past.

The United States was the last liberal democracy and welfare state to provide economic maintenance for its elderly. The scope of these welfare benefits is less comprehensive and more bureaucratic than those in the Republic of Ireland. As in Ireland, one's experience of aging and access to benefits in the United States are determined by class, sex, and work history. One of the greatest differences between the welfare states of the Republic of Ireland and the United States is the nature of health care for the elderly. The community-based and noninstitutional nature of health care in the Republic provides a major contrast with the acute-care, institutional orientation of the aging enterprise in the United States. As we will discuss further in Chapter 8, the lack of community-based care in the United States offers old people and their families a starker choice between family provision of extensive care and acceptance of the alienating institutional requirements of care provided by the government.

State-supported health care in the United States was shaped by the orientation of American medicine toward specialized high-technology health care delivered within institutional settings and focused on curable acute conditions rather than chronic problems. The American cultural emphasis on self-reliance and independence means that unlike elderly Chinese, elderly Americans are often reluctant to admit their needs for care to kin and that unlike their counterparts in Ireland, American families who do provide care for chronic illnesses receive little recognition or government support.

Elderly in both the blue-collar small town of Momence and the white-collar suburb of Swarthmore have been categorized through the development both of retirement and of an increasingly bureaucratic and complex aging enterprise. However, the stability of the Momence population has protected older people there from the social and political marginalization experienced in more mobile communities like Swarthmore. The development of high-cost and technologically sophisticated health care means that elderly residents in both communities are faced with difficult decisions. In Momence these more often involve whether to "spend down" in order to be eligible for Medicaid. In Swarthmore, where typically financial resources are greater and kin resources more scarce, the choice is usually perceived as whether to remain in the community. Both the lower extent of involvement in the national system of finance and status and the greater stability of Momence also protect the public role of older people, who benefit from a seniority principle not available to those in Swarthmore.

Although the Project AGE sites reflect a wide range of diversity, some common themes have emerged from this exploration of the effects of state penetration on the lives of the elderly. Sociocultural influences have channeled the impact of state development and the political economy differently in the different research settings. In both Hong Kong and Ireland, government support for the elderly was based on the recognition that cultural values assured participation of families in the care of the elderly. However, the Irish policy, with its community focus, reinforces and facilitates family care, whereas the Hong Kong policy views family care as a substitute for support from the government. The future availability of caregivers in both of these areas will be affected by future patterns of labor force participation and emigration. Dissonance between the cultural values and expectations of different generations may also affect the availability of care, as is clearest in Hong Kong. The development of health care is also affected by cultural patterns in the United States. The value association made by many Americans between independence and full personhood and our tendency to view the individual as the relevant unit for social policy, combined with an acute care model of medicine, have had a major impact on the development of health care programs for the elderly that are neither community based nor focused on the family.

Cultural images and remembrances of the past can affect the ways in which the old perceive the effects of state penetration. Culture also affects what political economists have termed the dependency of the elderly. It is often assumed that state development has a negative impact on the old because it makes them economically and structurally dependent. However, in Hong Kong, for example, older people see dependence as an important value and as an aspect of traditional Chinese culture. The elderly feel it is appropriate to their stage of life to be dependent on their children. In !Kung communities, interdependence is a lifelong and community-wide way of life, so that need for care is not clouded by fears that dependency will threaten personhood. Images of hardship in the past also mitigate the so-called economic dependence and marginalization of the elderly in both Hong Kong and Ireland. In Hong Kong and Ireland the elderly view the availability of benefits and services in a positive light because they remember the hardship of the past. Past cultural traditions can also affect the ways in which the elderly adapt to change. In Blessington, many elderly have difficulty adapting to contemporary town dynamics and what they view as the interference by the state in local affairs because they long for the kind of town life and cultural interaction that they remember existed in "the good old days."

This review from the perspective of political economy shows in broad strokes the way in which the effects of state structures and policies on the elderly are mediated by cultural values and behaviors. In the following chapter we will take a closer view of the interrelations of state policy, cultural values, and family organization by focusing on the ways these factors shape the impact of health and functionality on the lives of older people.

8

Age, Health, and
Functionality

*P*erhaps even more than wealth, people of all ages in the United States wish for good health. This is especially true as Americans age because our obsession with independence drives us to remain healthy and functional and most of all not to become a burden on others. Of course, the increasing high cost of health care in the United States reinforces this desire to remain healthy and functional. One of the main goals of Project AGE was to ascertain whether this same preoccupation with health, functionality, and independence was to be found in other cultures. In addition, it was our goal to determine to what degree these factors contributed to the well-being of the elderly in the different sites.

Although it is easy to see why health and functionality should be included in a study such as ours, their prominence in the lives

AUTHOR'S NOTE: This chapter was written by Anthony P. Glascock based on material provided by all members of the research team.

of older people makes a simple consideration difficult. In addition, health and functionality are complex concepts in and of themselves. Accordingly, an understanding of what is culturally meant by good health, poor health, disease, disability, functionality, and so on in each of these seven sites is as important as, or more important than, a mere listing of illness episodes and treatment patterns or answers compiled from a series of ADL/IADL (Activities of Daily Living/Instrumental Activities of Daily Living) scales. Thus in this chapter, we aim to accomplish three main objectives: first, through the use of short descriptive narratives, to convey the variation in scope, availability, sophistication, and utilization of health care in the seven sites; second, to examine the morbidity and disability characteristics of the inhabitants of the sites; and third, to explore the relationship between culturally relevant functionality and the well-being of the elderly in the communities, including compensatory behavior that mediates the experience of age-associated disability.

However, two caveats are necessary before the discussion can begin. First, none of the seven researchers is a trained physician, and no clinical assessments were undertaken in the field. Therefore no epidemiological data were collected, and all health data are from self-assessments by the respondents in the communities. Respondents were asked a series of questions concerning their health status, current and past illnesses and other "health problems," and health care utilization; but other than observations during the interviews, no check on these statements was possible. Second, once again, data on the functionality of the respondents in the seven communities are derived from self-assessment. No instruments were used to measure grip strength, hearing, sight, mobility, or the ability of respondents to carry out tasks. Of course, the interviewers were able to judge some of these functions, such as hearing and sight, during the interview. Nevertheless, the data on functionality are based largely on the answers to questions rather than clinical measurements and direct observations.

Health Care

Because the seven sites included in Project AGE were selected for differences along several dimensions, it is not surprising that there is tremendous disparity in the scope, availability, sophistication, and utilization of health care in the communities. Understanding this variation is crucial for discerning the way health and functionality contribute to the well-being of the elderly. For example, as we shall endeavor to show, the sophistication of the health care available in the different communities contributes in important ways to the definitions of such basic concepts as disability, impairment, good health, and illness. Thus these short descriptive narratives will provide the framework from which the more analytical discussion will flow.

!Kung

The provision of Western-style health care to the !Kung has improved markedly in the last 15 years. In 1976 a health clinic was established in !Angwa, the administrative center of the region in which the !Kung and Herero studies were conducted. Considerably expanded over its original two-room, thatched-roof, rectangular building, the !Angwa clinic now consists of three buildings, including a maternity ward. Stationed at the !Angwa clinic are three nurses, one of whom is a head nurse whose training appears to be roughly comparable to that of a pediatric nurse practitioner and midwife in the United States. In more recent years additional clinic stations have been located at /Ai/ai, 30 miles from !Angwa, and at N!aun!au, 100 miles from !Angwa. Basic medical care of good quality is provided at these clinics. Although women are encouraged to come to the clinics to give birth, few !Kung take advantage of the maternity services. However, women whose pregnancies have been troubled, or who have experienced difficult births in the past, are beginning to use the prenatal services offered by the clinic and to agree to giving birth at the clinic. The clinics offer a well baby program, and this service, unlike the hospital birth service, is much appreciated by local people. Mothers are encouraged to bring their newborn infants to the clinics for evaluation, weighing, eye drops, and registration. At appropriate intervals registered babies are given a standard battery of immunizations against polio, diphtheria, and pertussis. In 1987-1988, as an added inducement, mothers who brought their infants in for an initial examination and monthly visits were provided with 12 kilograms of food supplementation.

Because during this period the country was in the grip of a 7-year drought, this inducement persuasively encouraged clinic visits.

The clinic personnel treat a variety of complaints on a first-come, first-serve basis, and it is usual to find 10 to 15 people sitting in a relaxed manner in the waiting area of the clinic. Even though most adult !Kung are nonliterate, they understand that they are to bring the clinic cards for each patient who expects to be seen. On a typical day about one-half of the patients will be mothers with children, with the remainder being adults with various complaints. The clinic is equipped with a good supply of familiar medicines—standard antibiotics, birth control pills, and antimalarials.

Many !Kung have tuberculosis. These individuals are originally diagnosed and treated in the rural area clinics, but those who are in an acute stage of the disease receive more intensive treatment at Maun, the closest fully equipped hospital in the region, approximately 200 miles away. Under the best conditions, the drive to Maun can take 12 hours and can take as much as 24 hours if water or heavy sand interferes. Emergency patients, such as TB patients in an acute crisis or accident victims, are driven to the Maun hospital in the four-wheel drive vehicle belonging to the clinic. This service, as well as the basic medical care, is provided free by the government of Botswana.

Two features of the medical care cause difficulties for the !Kung: language and the long distances that separate remote villages from the clinics. Typically, the medical personnel come from the eastern part of Botswana, where the institutions of higher learning are located. These people are likely to speak Setswana and English, only occasionally speak Ojitherero, and rarely have any knowledge of the !Kung language. !Kung women and children usually have little command of the Bantu languages, such as Setswana and Ojitherero, that are known to clinic personnel; men, who from early ages work for Herero, can speak Ojitherero but have little opportunity to learn Setswana. Lacking a common language with the clinic personnel creates some difficulties for !Kung patients, which they try to solve by bringing with them friends or relatives who can provide translation. !Kung coming from more remote villages will try to find a multilingual acquaintance who lives at !Angwa to accompany them to the clinic. In addition, there is substantial turnover among the nurses, who regard !Angwa as a hardship post, and this has created difficulties for the !Kung in dealing with clinic personnel.

Perhaps even more important, medical care is often too far away to be of use to a patient who is seriously ill. Even though the Botswana government has placed clinics at three regional centers, most inhabitants live in small hamlets—30 or 40 people—10 to 15 miles away, a distance too great to be walked by sick people. In recognition of the problem of serving a geographically dispersed population, the government has instituted a mobile clinic service. On a rotational basis two of the nurses and a driver make visits to the more remote hamlets in the clinic's four-wheel drive vehicle. They spend a half-day or more at each settlement, sometimes conducting the clinics in the shade of a tree from the back of the clinic truck, sometimes moving into a thatched mud rondavel built specially for this purpose. The larger of the more remote hamlets are visited in this manner once every month. The !Kung recognize that this monthly visit is better than nothing, but they told us that it is common for people to fall ill in between visits. When an emergency arises, a nurse and driver will come from !Angwa to the patient's home and transport him or her back to the clinic. However, someone from the patient's family must first walk or ride on donkeyback to !Angwa to alert the staff about the emergency.

The health care available in Ngamiland would have to be described as low-tech. The !Angwa clinic is not set up for surgery and has no capability of administering anesthesia. However, conditions are much better than they were even 20 years ago and are certainly not "primitive." The clinic buildings are "modern," built of cement block, roofed with sheet metal, and equipped with glass-paned windows. The police station (a single rondavel and two policemen) operates a radio link with Maun, and clinic personnel use this radio to communicate with the hospital in Maun about emergency conditions. !Angwa, /Ai/ai, and N!aun!au have grass landing strips for small airplanes, and in 1987-1988 a team of two flying doctors made monthly visits. The water at !Angwa comes from a deep bore hole and is therefore of good drinking quality. The clinic has running water, and the clinic, police station, and school at !Angwa are equipped with outdoor latrines. However, because there is no electricity at !Angwa there is no possibility of sterilizing instruments except by boiling them in water.

The remaining obstacles to the ability of !Kung to receive good medical care are cultural and psychological. Not surprisingly, the !Kung have not acquired Western attitudes about medical care. Whereas Westerners are probably over-ready to seek medical treatment and overconfident that all ailments can be "fixed," !Kung are slow to apply for help from the clinic and not confident that they will be cured. This is particularly true of the attitude of adults and old people about their own ailments. The !Kung have not had Western medicine for very long, and many people have the attitude that sickness is something to be borne and waited out. When an old person is sick it is seen as part of being old and not thought of as a remediable condition. The elderly seem to concur. Though old people are full of complaints on a variety of subjects, one never hears of their blaming younger kin for failing to help them receive medical care. On the other hand, when children are sick, people respond with more alacrity and will go to great lengths to take sick children to !Angwa.

Herero

The Herero live in widely scattered homesteads over approximately 15,000 square miles of western Ngamiland. These homesteads are served by the same clinics described above for the !Kung. Among Herero there is a great deal of praise and very few complaints from people about the clinics. The staff members are respected and well liked, and people appreciate their dedication. Relations between the Herero and the clinic are informal and personal rather than formal and bureaucratic; for example, the clinic vehicle provides lifts to relatives of sick people whenever there is room to accommodate them.

Although perhaps 100 Herero live less than a mile from the !Angwa clinic, many live at homesteads up to 20 miles away. As for the !Kung, for Herero to make a trip to the clinic means a long ride on a donkey or a long walk on foot, and for the decrepit elderly this is impossible. Consequently these individuals do not receive medical care, whereas more mobile elderly can and do visit the clinic regularly. Although it is rare for !Kung to have access to a donkey, many Herero do. Herero in their 70s do not hesitate to jump on a donkey to visit !Angwa when they have medical problems. Herero, in contrast to !Kung, are eager to use Western medicine, including for care of the elderly. Families of decrepit old people will occasionally arrange for them to live in the settlement of !Angwa itself so that they can be taken care of by the clinic. For example, one old person with open ulcers over his lower body was moved to the settlement, where he was visited in his hut every day by the clinic staff and given fresh dressings.

Clifden

By American standards, the health care available in Clifden is extremely limited. There are only general practitioners in the area, and in 1987-1988 the local hospital lacked an operating theater, X-ray facilities, and an obstetrical unit. Thus all but the most basic health care required a trip to the Regional Hospital in Galway, a round trip of over 100 miles. This included eye exams, many laboratory tests, and all consultations with specialists, in addition to hospitalization. However, this did not mean that health care was lacking in the area; quite the contrary, health care was available and, from the inhabitants' point of view, of high quality.

Two full-time general practitioners resided in Clifden at the time of the research, and they, along with a third, semiretired physician, provided the everyday health care for the people of the DED. Each of the two full-time resident general practitioners had surgery hours 5 days a week, including Saturdays, and each made house calls every day. The fact that each of the physicians made house calls whenever requested, along with the fact that the physicians were very willing to admit older people to the Clifden hospital, indicates that very personal and dependable health care is provided to the area's residents.

A second important component of health care was the visiting nurse program, which provided a wide range of free health services to medical card holders. In 1987-1988 there were three full-time district nurses, who were responsible for an area extending approximately 25 miles from north to south and 12 miles from east to west. Patients were referred to the district nurses by the primary care physicians, and although the service was provided officially 5 days a week, visiting nurses regularly made home visits on weekends and at night. The services provided included general health maintenance, administering medication and injections, postnatal care, and changing dressings. Perhaps of even more importance, because the visiting nurses were continually in peoples' homes, they provided a constant monitoring of the general well-being of people that included more than just health. The nurses made sure people had fuel, that houses were warm, that people had food and were eating, that people were not forgetting things and were not confused. If things were not right, the nurses had the ability to take action. They could, and did, recommend that the person be hospitalized, either in Clifden or in Galway; through the community welfare officer, they could obtain fuel and even emergency funds; they could refer individuals for medical tests, eye exams, dental work; and they could, and often did, contact relatives to suggest additional care or help.

Finally, the 40-bed Clifden hospital, even with its limited medical facilities, was of immense importance to the health care of older people. It had a full nursing staff, and the local physicians made rounds on a daily basis. For most of the year all the beds were filled by older people. During the height of the winter rains and winds, the hospital capacity was stretched to overflowing as 43 elderly individuals were admitted. The hospital was utilized as a refuge for older people who were having difficulty caring for themselves because of illness or chronic problems, because they lived alone, or just because of the severity of the winter. Although officially a patient was not to remain in the hospital for more than 6 weeks, exceptions were made on a regular basis. Thus the hospital was crucial to the well-being of the elderly in Clifden because it allowed people to remain in their own homes and in the community. If the hospital were not available to provide both medical care and housing, many older people would have had to move in with, or at least become completely dependent upon, relatives, and some older people currently living in the community would have had to leave.

Hence, between the local physicians, the visiting nurses, and the hospital, older people in the Clifden DED had daily access to primary health care. This hands-on type of health care, although largely devoid of the sophisticated medical technology found in the United States, gave great security to people in the area.

Blessington

There are no local hospitals in Blessington, and the closest acute care hospital is in Naas, a 20-minute drive by automobile. In 1987-1988, many local residents utilized the services of various Dublin hospitals, the closest being St. James', approximately 30 miles from Blessington, which offered some specialized care for older persons through 296 extended care geriatric beds, 60 assessment beds, and 57 rehabilitation beds. St. James' also offered day hospital services to older people.

Older persons could also receive specialized care at Baltinglass District Hospital, 45 minutes from Blessington by automobile. Since 1974 this institution had specialized in geriatric care offering the following types of services: (a) acute care, nursing care, and assessment; (b) care of the ambulatory old; and (c) two independent group homes. Doctors visited the acute care patients daily, and the rest of the patients were seen once a week. X-rays and related services were offered only three times a week in 1987-1988 as a result of budgetary cuts. Through a program that allowed individuals to leave their older relatives for up to a period of 2 weeks, Baltinglass Hospital also offered respite to caregivers.

In 1983 a day care center for the aged was opened at Baltinglass Hospital. Fifty percent of the funding for the center came from the Eastern Health Board and the rest from donations from various West Wicklow communities. Day care was offered five times a week, with people from a different part of West Wicklow being transported by minibus to the center each day. Day care was also available in Naas, but people in Blessington could not utilize this service because they did not live in County Kildare. Patients were referred to day care by their doctor, the district nurse, the community health officer, or the psychiatric nurse, and were offered chiropody, physical therapy, baths, laundry service, hairdressing, medical attention, and, probably most importantly, opportunities for socializing. People who attended day care were asked for a donation, and most usually gave 2 pounds. During the research period in 1987-1988, 10 people from the Blessington area attended day care. Three old women in the sample attended day care—two on a monthly basis and one more than once a month.

Some health services were available to Blessington area residents at the Eastern Health Board Clinic located in Blessington. A new clinic was opened in 1983 offering immunization of infants, a monthly eye clinic, and monthly psychiatric counseling. One general practitioner resided on the grounds and treated both medical card holders and private patients, and other health practitioners operated out of the clinic's building. The clinic doctor made house calls, and two other local physicians treated people in the area. A district nurse who treated patients of all ages within the Blessington area was especially concerned with older people living alone and visited them once a week in winter and monthly in the summer. A psychiatric nurse ran a monthly clinic and visited the area weekly, delivering both medication and advice to patients. A social worker, specializing in children, was available at the clinic one day a week, as was a community welfare officer who assisted people in applying for medical benefits and helped older people make out their wills. A locally organized mother/toddler group and a women's health group used the clinic facilities once a week for meetings.

A very active Senior Citizens Committee further extended community care to the older residents of the Blessington area. In 1987-1988, there were 11 members on the committee who monitored the approximately 200 older individuals in the area. Each committee member was responsible for a number of older people, and five committee members were specifically charged with helping older people in the study area. Various members of the committee also visited the elderly residents in the Baltinglass Hospital. The committee organized and partially subsidized a local chiropody clinic when the health board cut this service. Only five Blessington residents received home help. There were no local nursing homes and no Meals on Wheels service within the Blessington study area.

Momence

Momence is too small to have a local hospital, but it does have some medical services. In 1983-1984, four physicians, one podiatrist, one chiropractor, and two dentists had offices/clinics in the center of town. All the physicians specialized in family practice and had linkages to Kankakee through its hospital facilities. In 1988 a new skilled care wing of 50 beds was added to Momence's 78-bed intermediate care nursing home. This enabled individuals requiring skilled care to remain in Momence rather than enter one of several nursing homes in Kankakee. In addition, the nursing home had an active outreach program.

More specialized health care required a 13-mile trip to Kankakee, where a full range of specialists and two hospitals were available. Even here the medical services were not equivalent to those in more urban and wealthier areas. Some of the most specialized physicians maintained branch offices in Kankakee, but they were really based in south suburban Chicago. The two hospitals were major competitors in the local health care market, and the competition had resulted in redundant facilities. As was true of most American hospitals, an increasing amount of care was in the form of outpatient services. Both hospitals had nursing home facilities, and one had announced plans to build a retirement facility with 95 beds for residential use and another 45 beds for assisted care. The use of these hospitals by residents of Momence is revealed by an analysis of obituaries, which indicated that nearly 70% of Momence residents died in a hospital. In an emergency, the only way for Momence people to reach the medical facilities was to be driven by a relative or friend or to call the ambulance.

Medical care in Momence was expensive. For those who were working, some form of medical insurance defrayed cost, although many people in this community had no insurance. Medicare was available for those over the age of 65 who had work histories involving contributions to Social Security, but both Part A (Hospital Insurance) and Part B (Medical Insurance) involved deductibles. In 1985, for the first 2 months of hospitalization, Medicare coverage excluded $400 of total cost. As the length of the hospital stay became longer, the costs increased until, at the end of 150 days, all costs were assumed by the patient. Home health care coverage under Medicare B involved an initial $75 deductible plus 20% of the approved costs. If costs exceeded the approved rate, the patient paid the difference. Home health care as medically necessary was also covered by Medicare B. For posthospital care in a skilled nursing home, Medicare A completely covered costs for the first 20 days. From the 21st until the 100th day, the patient paid $50 per day, after which the patient was responsible for the full cost. Medicaid was an option for Momence residents only after Medicare was expended and the patient's assets were exhausted. Funding for this state-administered program came from a combination of federal and state money. Increased costs during the early 1980s had produced shortages resulting in providers being left unpaid. Consequently, in Momence Medicaid patients were not favored.

Home health care for older people was available primarily through providers in Kankakee. Although 10% of the over-65 population in the county resided in the two townships that made up the study area, there were no formal local providers in Momence. An exception was the Meals on Wheels program run by the local nursing home, which had a very low utilization rate of between two and four participants. When a medical crisis necessitated home help, it was the Catholic charities that located and provided help, usually funded by Medicare.

Informal help provided by relatives, neighbors, and church members was less visible but was the most prevalent form of care for older people. The vast majority of this help was voluntary and unpaid. If the medical crisis became a chronic situation, an informal support system of local women could be mobilized. This included hairdressers or "cleaning ladies" who took older persons shopping, neighbors who tended to household chores, and friends who prepared a main meal. At an extreme, if families were wealthy enough, three women could be hired to provide 24-hour care for an older person in the home. One woman had organized an informal group of women into a home care service for older people. She advertised at the two senior groups and charged, in 1988, $6.00 per hour.

Swarthmore

The highest levels of medical technology and specialization were available in or near Swarthmore. There were eight general hospitals in Delaware County, four of them within a 15-minute drive of Swarthmore, and five medical schools with their associated hospitals 12 miles away in Philadelphia. Within a 15-minute drive of town there were four diagnostic imaging centers, two of them with magnetic resonance imaging (MRI) equipment. There were four nursing homes within a 15-minute drive. Over 700 physicians were listed in the Yellow Pages for the suburban area within an approximately 15-mile radius of Swarthmore. There were two medical buildings within the town itself and several physicians and dentists who practiced from home offices. Although physicians did not customarily make house calls, both not-for-profit and proprietary home health organizations did offer services, including visiting nurses, for a fee, which under certain conditions could be partly paid by Medicare.

Consistent with the abundant availability of medical practitioners and facilities in the area, almost every older person in our sample said that their medical needs were met in or near the community. Only one respondent over 60 voiced anything other than satisfaction with medical facilities, by regretting the recent retirement of the family physician and her hopes that more good doctors would move into town. Several people mentioned the lack of an optician, but one has opened a practice since the study ended. He chose Swarthmore in part because he believed that the large older population offered many potential clients.

However, security was not the pervasive attitude about health issues among older residents of Swarthmore. Concern about the possibility of eventually becoming too frail to stay in one's own home was widespread. Many people actually did leave the town for a retirement community or to live nearer an adult child. According to the obituaries printed in the town newspaper during the study period, 12% of those over 65 died in a retirement community, all but one in the Swarthmore area (within about an hour's drive). In addition, of those who died outside the Swarthmore area (n = 49), 31% had died near the residence of at least one child.

Those older people who stayed in Swarthmore perceived their choice as "risky" because they feared that if they did become too frail to stay home, they would have to enter an institution. The reasons for this, discussed at length in Draper and Keith (1992), included the widely shared value emphasis on independence and the dispersal of adult children out of their household of origin.

Hong Kong

Given its status as a British colony, Hong Kong modeled its medical and health care services along British lines and provided its residents with a wide range of inexpensive services. In 1983 patients in general beds (in large wards) in government and government-assisted hospitals were charged a single daily fee of HK$10—about US$1.28. This all-inclusive fee covered everything from diet to X-ray examinations, laboratory tests, drugs, surgery, and any other necessary treatments. In case of hardship this fee could be waived. Alternatively, patients for whom money was not a consideration could elect to stay in private wards or go to private hospitals. Hong Kong had a total of 22,935 hospital beds in 1983—a ratio of 4.3 beds per thousand. Of these just under 12% were in the private sector. At the beginning of 1990, though the total number of beds had increased to 25,059, the ratio remained at 4.3. In 1983 more than 639,000 inpatients had been treated at the 13 government and 19 government-assisted hospitals, and overcrowding was severe.

Because income, employment status, and age had little impact on one's access to hospital care (although, as indicated above, higher income did increase one's options), few Hong Kong residents worried about the direct financial costs of major medical procedures. On the other hand, the indirect costs had to be considered. Until the mid-1970s, much maintenance care of patients was provided by unskilled or semiskilled *amahs*, "servants" who, though technically employees of the hospital, usually required tipping by the patient's family before they would fully attend to his or her needs. In the mid-1970s this practice was deemed "corrupt" and outlawed; yet at the time of the study most people with hospitalized relatives feared that the maintenance care was inadequate and considered it necessary to delegate a family member to stand by and be sure the care was carried out or do it themselves.

In 1983 4,385 physicians and 935 dentists were on the medical register, as were more than 13,000 registered nurses and more than 4,000 enrolled nurses. These figures represent only a portion of the people actually practicing medicine in Hong Kong. First, there was a substantial number of uncertified doctors who were trained in "Western medicine" in China but who, because of language problems or inadequate training, could not be registered in Hong Kong. Second, there was a large number of practitioners of "Chinese medicine," largely herbalists, whose credentials were unknown but who, like the unregistered doctors, nevertheless could and did practice medicine—all they usually required was a business license to set up their pharmacies. In order to prevent iatrogenic disasters, however, the government had restricted their use of X-ray machines and certain poisonous substances. Most neighborhoods had a Chinese pharmacy with a traditional Chinese practitioner seated at the back who took pulses and prescribed a mix of dried medicines to be boiled down at home. Although they were relatively expensive, they seldom had waiting lines and were readily accessible. Furthermore, there were certain ailments, such as bone injuries and joint troubles, that many Hong Kong residents, especially the elderly, believed to be best treated by traditional *tit da* doctors who massaged the affected parts with special medicated oils. Unlike the Chinese government, the Hong Kong government had made almost no attempt to combine Western and Chinese medical traditions under the same roof, and only Western medicine was subsidized.

Although emergency care was readily available, routine outpatient care was not. Long lines formed early in the morning at the doors to the outpatient clinics, and specialty clinics requiring appointments, such as for routine eye exams, had as much as a 6-month wait. The total attendance figure, in 1983, at government outpatient clinics was 15.1 million. Charges were low; in 1983 the charge for a consultation at a general outpatient clinic was HK$5 and at a specialty clinic HK$6. This fee included medicine as well as x-ray examinations and laboratory tests. Additional fees were charged for injections or dressing changes—HK$2 in 1983. Long-term care is in seriously short supply. There is a waiting list of several years for "public care and attention homes," and in 1983 the unmet demand for long-term care resulted in scores of unlicensed private care facilities operating with no supervision.

Summary

The above descriptions graphically illustrate the diversity in the availability and sophistication of health care in the seven research areas. Ranging from the extremes of high-tech and readily available in the upper-middle-class suburb of Swarthmore to low-tech and sporadically available in the more isolated areas inhabited by the !Kung, not only does the type of health care vary, but the expectations of the inhabitants differ significantly. Perhaps it is not surprising that many !Kung, although realizing its benefits, do not have the almost religious view of health care found among many people in the industrialized world. However, it is perhaps a bit more unexpected that people in Clifden are so pleased with the relatively low-tech, person-to-person medicine available, and that individuals in Hong Kong rely on herbalists in addition to Western-trained physicians. These differences account for much of the variation that is present in the views of the inhabitants of the seven sites about the effectiveness of health care and the limitations placed on their behavior by chronic health problems.

Morbidity and Disability Characteristics

The variation in the availability, sophistication, and utilization of health care in the seven sites depicted above, when combined with their general environmental and geographical characteristics, places the following discussion of morbidity and disability in proper context. It is impossible to discuss, even in the most general terms, illness, disease, frailty, and disability without considering the cultural context in which the terms are applied. The effects of this cultural influence are not restricted to nonindustrial societies but, as the following example shows, are present even in the United States. There has been an increase, over the last several decades, in the prevalence rates of specific fatal and nonfatal diseases in the United States. Although a decline in mortality accounts for some of these increases, it alone does not explain the magnitude of the changes. Verbrugge (1989) suggests that changes in the cultural context in which these diseases occur explain most of the appearance of "worsening" health among the elderly in the United States.

> People are now more aware of their chronic diseases than before due to improved diagnostic techniques, more frequent visits to physicians . . . and more candor from physicians toward patients. This greater awareness leads to higher reporting in surveys, and thus higher prevalence rates. . . . Also, people are more willing and able to adopt the sick role, both for short periods and long ones, than several decades ago. There are ampler social supports for disability, and public attitudes about long-term disability have become more gracious. Thus, increase in disease prevalence and disability rates can

reflect these factors, as well as lowered mortality. (Verbrugge, 1989, p. 30)

Therefore, even though the following definitions, by necessity, are couched in largely standard terms, one should not lose sight of the fact that it is the cultural context in which the concepts are applied that gives meaning, affords the most valuable comparative analysis, and is the focus of the pertinent discussion.

First, parameters need to be established and positions clearly staked out. Aging is not a disease, but a normal process. However, "while a change may represent 'normal aging' inasmuch as it is present in the entire population and cannot be avoided, one should not assume that this 'normal' change is necessarily harmless" (Minaker & Rowe, 1985, p. 332). Aging increases the risk for certain diseases and health problems, and disability is positively correlated with age (Bould, Sanborn, & Reif, 1989; Haynes & Feinlaub, 1980; Heikkinen, Waters, & Brzezinski, 1983; Ikels, 1991). Thus as one ages, the likelihood of remaining disease-free lessens—disease being defined as "any process that results in clearly adverse clinical sequelae measured as either morbidity or mortality" (Minaker & Rowe, 1985, p. 332). The onset of morbidity has a limited number of consequences: (a) illness from which recovery is relatively quick and long-term repercussions are negligible; (b) the appearance of chronic disease, but without impairment; (c) the appearance of chronic disease with impairment; or (d) death (Manton & Soldo, 1985). Although the consequences of morbidity are limited, the analysis of morbidity in a cross-cultural study such as Project AGE is not simple. The sick role varies from one of the seven cultures to another because of the ability of the social group to support the ill individual; the same chronic disease may produce impairment in one cultural context but not in another, and although death would appear to be fairly clear-cut, even it is subject to cultural variation (Glascock, 1982a).

Nevertheless, some standard definitions of these important terms and concepts must be presented in order for fruitful comparison to be undertaken. Following the lead of the World Health Organization (1980, 1982, 1985), we distinguish between four basic health statuses: (a) disease-free; (b) experiencing an acute illness; (c) experiencing a chronic disease, but without impairment; and (d) experiencing a chronic disease with disability. However, even these distinctions, for a study such as Project AGE, require fine tuning. Once again following the lead of the World Health Organization, we have differentiated between impairment, disability, and handicap.

> An impairment is defined as "any loss or abnormality of psychological, physiological, or anatomical structure or function." A disability "is any restriction or lack (resulting from an impairment) of ability to perform an activity in the manner or within the range considered normal for a human being." A handicap "is a disadvantage for a given individual, resulting from an impairment or a disability, that limits or prevents the fulfillment of a role that is normal (depending on age, sex and social and cultural factors) for that individual." (Ikels, 1991, p. 652)

Thus these concepts form a progressive sequence from an impairment without restrictions on activity, through disability where restrictions exist but no disadvantage is present, to handicap in which the fulfillment of the "normal" role within the particular cultural context for the particular individual is impossible. As will be demonstrated shortly, the timing and nature of this progressive sequence vary from one site to another, with the result being significant impact on both older individuals and the cultural context of the site.

General Health

Every respondent in each of the seven sites was asked to rate his or her health on a scale of 1 to 4, with 4 being excellent, 3 being good, 2 being fair, and 1 being poor. Table 8.1 displays the mean scores for males and females for three age groupings[1] for each of the seven sites. The overall pattern that emerges from these figures is one of a decline in the self-assessment of health with age. The decline varies from the steepest among the Herero to the most shallow in Swarthmore but is evident in each setting and for both sexes. This result was expected and conforms to other research; what was not anticipated was the variation in the findings for males and for females. In most studies of the subjective evaluation of health, males, at all ages, rate their health higher than females (Verbrugge, 1988). The findings depicted in Table 8.1 show a much more varied

TABLE 8.1 Mean Health Scores by Site, Age, and Sex

	Age Group								
	Young			Middle-Aged			Old		
Site	Total	M	F	Total	M	F	Total	M	F
!Kung	3.22	3.14	3.31	2.93	2.99	2.90	2.40	2.48	2.28
Herero	3.06	3.04	3.07	2.68	2.90	2.55	1.86	1.81	1.90
Clifden	3.39	3.45	3.33	3.04	3.09	3.00	2.50	2.37	2.61
Blessington	3.37	3.17	3.40	3.17	3.04	3.25	2.80	3.00	2.70
Momence	3.59	3.75	3.45	3.23	3.12	3.35	2.85	2.90	2.81
Swarthmore	3.68	3.75	3.59	3.58	3.50	3.63	3.12	3.00	3.20
Hong Kong	2.76	2.94	2.50	2.67	2.85	2.37	2.13	2.30	1.95

pattern. Only Hong Kong conforms to the standard model, and only in Hong Kong is the pattern consistent—that is, the same sex in all three age groupings evaluated their health higher. For all the other sites there is variation from one age grouping to another. There is no readily apparent explanation for the overall pattern, although interpretation on a site-by-site basis is possible. For example, in Swarthmore older men evaluate their health more negatively than older women for several reasons. First, most older men in Swarthmore are married and consequently have a spouse available to provide care. This means that men who become frail face fewer obstacles to remaining at home and in town than do women, who are more likely to be widowed and alone. In addition, the average age of older women in Swarthmore is 5 years more than the average age of older men. When old women evaluate their own health and functional capacity, they may be using an older reference group of peers. Older women may also face some pressure to emphasize the positive aspects of their physical condition because of their perception that frailty implies leaving the community.

Illness Episodes

Reports of illness episodes from respondents in each of the settings suggest, somewhat obviously, that the main reason for the decline in the self-assessment of health with age is that older people, in general, are more frequently ill than younger people, that their illnesses are more serious, and that they experience many more episodes, and more serious continuing health problems, than younger people. Although older respondents were not found to be ill more often than younger respondents in every site, the illnesses experienced by older respondents were more serious and required more care.

Although a slightly higher percentage of younger and middle-aged !Kung respondents (37.5% versus 35%) reported being ill in the 12 months prior to the research period than older respondents, the illnesses that older !Kung experienced were more serious and resulted in longer breaks in their daily routines. Among the Herero a higher percentage of respondents over the age of 60 reported illness episodes within the last 24 months than younger people. Like the !Kung, older Herero reported more life-threatening illnesses than did younger respondents. In addition, all but one of the respondents who stated that they had never had an illness that interrupted their daily routine were under the age of 60.

In Clifden 68% of the elderly individuals interviewed reported that within the last year they had their daily routine broken by illness. This contrasted with only 31% of people under the age of 65 reporting such an episode of illness. In addition, respondents 65 and older were eight times more likely to be admitted to the local hospital for their illnesses than younger people (16 older people versus 2 younger), whereas the numbers being admitted to the regional hospital were almost equal (16 versus 18). However, if one eliminates the younger people who were admitted to the regional hospital for childbirth and injury, the numbers become more telling: Only six younger people were sent to the hospital for an illness, whereas illness was the reason for admittance for all 16 older people. A final contrast between young and old people is in the length of time the illness disrupted the person's daily routine. Older people are almost twice as likely to have had their illness last for 2 weeks or longer than younger people. In contrast, in Blessington the incidence of a break in one's daily routine caused by illness within the last year was slightly higher for younger people (36%) than older people (33%). Nevertheless, for 35% of the older respondents this illness required hospitalization, and 61% of these individuals stayed in the hospital for a period of one fortnight to one month.

In Momence there is little variation in the frequency of illness episodes by age. Approximately the same percentage (60%) of respondents under and over 60 years of age stated that their last illness occurred over a year ago or that they were never ill. However, men reported more frequently than women that they were never ill or that their illness was not in the recent past. Duration of these illnesses shows considerable variation, ranging from a day to several months. Fifty-six percent report a short illness of a week or less, but 23% report their illness lasted more than a month. As age increases, the duration of an illness increases, and for those 75 and above, 65% reported illness lasting a month or more in comparison with only 23% of those under 50 reporting a similar situation. A larger proportion of Swarthmoreans under 65 than over that age actually reported an episode of illness that interfered with their daily routine within the last 24 months: 50% versus 35%. In both age categories, almost one of five (19%) said they had never experienced such an illness. Similar to older respondents in Momence, people over the age of 65 reported that their illnesses lasted longer and required more treatment than illnesses of younger respondents. People over 65 who had one of these illness episodes within the last 24 months reported that the flu or a virual infection were the most common ailments.

A total of 57 (of 200) people in Hong Kong indicated that they had had a health problem within the past year that had interfered with their daily routine. Nearly one third of these people (17 of 57) had experienced an episode of cold, flu, or fever; 5 had suffered a fall or injury; and 5 each had experienced digestive problems, surgery, or severe blood pressure problems. Approximately one third of people 60 or older had experienced a health problem (usually of an acute nature), compared with about one quarter of younger people.

Chronic Health Problems

The frequency and severity of continuing health problems for five of the seven sites are portrayed in Table 8.2.[2] The data are, once again, depicted for the three general age groups—young, middle, old—and are in three categories: no continuing health problems; continuing health problems that do not restrict the behavior of the respondent (impairment); and continuing health problems that restrict culturally relevant behavior (handicap). It is readily apparent from Table 8.2 that wide variation exists in the number of individuals both reporting continuing health problems and indi-

TABLE 8.2 Frequency and Severity of Chronic Health Problems by Site and Age

Site	Age Group	No Chronic Problem		Problem Does Not Restrict Behavior		Problem Restricts Behavior	
		n	*%*	*n*	*%*	*n*	*%*
!Kung	Old	NA	NA	NA	NA	NA	NA
	Middle	NA	NA	NA	NA	NA	NA
	Young	NA	NA	NA	NA	NA	NA
Herero	Old	NA	NA	NA	NA	NA	NA
	Middle	NA	NA	NA	NA	NA	NA
	Young	NA	NA	NA	NA	NA	NA
Clifden	Old	22	37	5	8	33	55
	Middle	38	81	6	13	3	6
	Young	21	92	1	4	1	4
Blessington	Old	24	40	16	27	20	33
	Middle	38	73	5	10	9	17
	Young	52	90	1	2	5	8
Momence	Old	28	31	29	33	32	36
	Middle	34	56	17	28	10	16
	Young	40	76	5	9	8	15
Swarthmore	Old	34	47	28	38	11	15
	Middle	55	70	15	19	9	11
	Young	39	78	5	10	6	12
Hong Kong	Old	14	35	9	22	17	43
	Middle	70	65	17	16	20	19
	Young	35	65	15	28	4	7

cating either an impairment or a handicap. Although the material on the young and middle age categories is presented to provide a comparative framework, the elderly are the focus of the following discussion.

Older people in all five sites represented in Table 8.2 both report more continuing health problems than young and middle-aged respondents (Clifden 63%, Blessington 60%, Momence 69%, Swarthmore 43%, Hong Kong 65%) and report that these problems result in a restriction of some type of culturally relevant behavior (Clifden 55%, Blessington 33%, Momence 36%, Swarthmore 15%, Hong Kong 43%). Of the older !Kung respondents who answered questions concerning continuing health problems, a full 75% of the women and 68% of the men reported that they experienced a chronic problem that restricted their behavior. Among the Herero, 90% of older respondents reported that they had some continuing health problem, but unfortunately, no determination of whether the problems restricted behavior was made. It is customary for Herero to claim health problems at a very high rate, and therefore the 90% figure should be viewed with caution.

The overall direction of the findings depicted in Table 8.2 is as expected, but the relatively large variation in the number of older people reporting a handicap—from a high of 55% in Clifden to a low of 15% in Swarthmore—needs to be examined. The variation is not, as one could initially think, the result exclusively of a contrast in the health care availability in the different sites or differences in the definitions of impairment and handicap. Rather the nature of the older population in the various settings contributes significantly to the differences. In contrast to Swarthmore, in which many frail older people had left the community and entered care facilities and thus were not in the sample, in Clifden the elderly remained in their homes even when the health problem became extremely serious. The Irish welfare and medical systems, along with the availability of relatives to provide care, allowed frail older people to stay in Clifden, to be included in the study, and to have their handicaps reported. The second highest percentage of handicapped elderly is found in Hong Kong, and two reasons appear to account for this finding: In lower-income households the expense of long-term care prevented many frail elderly from leaving their households; in higher-income households the availability of servants and nurses allowed the elderly to be cared for in their homes. The percentage of handicapped elderly in Momence is much higher than in Swarthmore, primarily because of the availability of relatives in the closer knit midwestern population to care for the frail elderly in their homes and because of the lower income levels in Momence, which put care outside the home beyond the means of many respondents in the sample. In Blessington the reluctance of several frail older people to participate in the study reduced the percentage of the handicapped elderly, which otherwise, it is assumed, would have approached the figure in Clifden.

The importance of chronic health problems, their connection to functionality and to well-being, necessitates a further discussion on a site-by-site basis. Neither the !Kung nor the Herero respondents were familiar with Western, industrial categorization of health problems. This was particularly true for older respondents and therefore especially affected the nature of the data collected concerning the chronic health problems and their impact on behavior. Although it was not possible to collect data to "fit" into neat categories, it was possible for us to discuss their problems with our respondents and then to apply comparative concepts to what we heard.

Utilizing this approach, we found that muscular-skeletal problems predominate among both the !Kung (70% of females and 50% of males report such problems) and the Herero. These problems range from minor backaches, pains in the finger joints, and stiffness in the knees and hips to more clearly serious arthritic conditions and perhaps rheumatism. These muscular-skeletal problems among the !Kung elderly make a hard life even harder—they make just getting around difficult and restrict the older person's ability to carry out daily tasks. Likewise, these muscular-skeletal problems prevent older Herero from accomplishing many of the harder, more labor-intensive tasks referred to earlier, such as drawing water for their cattle, carrying firewood, and riding donkeys long distances to visit relatives. In addition to muscular-skeletal problems, many elderly !Kung are afflicted with respiratory problems that make breathing difficult and result in deep incapacitating coughs, made worse by smoking tobacco. Many Herero and a few older !Kung are also afflicted with tuberculosis, which not only restricts behavior but is life threatening and requires Western medical treatment.

The most frequently reported health problem in Clifden was arthritis, followed by heart and blood pressure difficulties and diabetes. People older than age 80, especially females, reported multiple problems that usually combined circulatory or respiratory difficulties with arthritis. The majority of older respondents reported that their problem(s) made "getting around" difficult. In most cases this referred to the ability to walk to town and shop on their own, but in a few cases individuals reported difficulties in moving about their own homes. Five individuals, all males with multiple problems, reported that they were housebound, and two older females stated that they were confined to bed. Six of these seven individuals were older than 80 at the time of the interview.

In Blessington 59% of older people interviewed versus 20% of people younger than 65 reported that they had continuing health problems, and interestingly, men reported twice as high an incidence of health problems as women. The most frequently reported problem was arthritis, followed by high blood pressure, heart problems, and asthma. Five older people reported multiple problems. The majority of older respondents reported that their problems made "getting around" difficult. Most often problems in getting around referred to situations of mobility, such as the inability to walk to town or ride a bike, but three older persons (one male, two females) were housebound.

Age among the respondents in Momence was clearly linked to the presence of chronic problems, for nearly 65% of those younger than 50 reported no chronic health problems at all, whereas only 3% of those older than 75 were free of such problems. Sixty-six percent of those who had three or more problems were older than 65. Sex differences were also present, with males reporting fewer problems—54% of the males reported no problems versus 45% of the females. Also 72% of those having more than two chronic problems were female. The most frequent problems were cardio-vascular—high blood pressure and heart problems—and muscu-lar-skeletal—arthritis. About one half of those reporting a chronic problem stated that it interfered with their daily routine, generally in that it restricted mobility and the capacity to work.

Few older people in Swarthmore had chronic problems that interfered with their daily activities. Just more than one half (53%) of them said they had at least one continuing health problem, but only 15% of Swarthmoreans older than 65 said they had a chronic problem that interfered with their daily routine. (This is 28% of those who stated they had a chronic problem.) The most common chronic problems, accounting for more than one half of those mentioned by Swarthmoreans older than 65, were heart diseases, arthritis, and diabetes. About one in four younger residents (26%) said they had a continuing health problem, but a smaller proportion (9%) stated that the problem interfered with their daily routine. The problems mentioned by younger persons were more diverse, including allergies, high blood pressure, and back trouble.

When respondents in Hong Kong were asked about long-term health problems, 82 indicated that they had such a problem, and of these, 49 (or 60% of those reporting a problem) said that it interfered with their daily routine. In actuality, some who said they were unaffected by their health problem *were* affected by it but had accommodated their lives to their health problems for so long that these accommodations were now viewed as a part of the daily routine rather than as a disruption of it. This was particularly true of older people. The most common long-term health problems of those 60 or older were circulatory diseases, aches and pains ("rheumatism"), and respiratory diseases. Younger people were more likely to mention digestive, circulatory, and skin disorders as well as aches and pains. Three young people had epilepsy. The prevalence of what are frequently assumed to be tension-related illnesses in people under 60 was striking. These 57 respondents mentioned a total of 62 ailments, including four mentions of mental health problems, two of lack of (psychological) energy, and two of insomnia. In addition, many of those with chronic digestive or skin disorders attributed them directly to tension, especially to problems with work or economic issues and less frequently to family issues. These health data give some insight into why Hong Kong respondents mention that one of the best things about old age is its freedom from worries and responsibilities.

Health Care Utilization and Caregiving

The care of the elderly when ill or affected by a chronic health problem is best examined by depicting both the formal and informal systems that exist in the seven sites. As is apparent from the previous discussion, the formal care systems vary dramatically from Hong Kong and Swarthmore to the Kalahari. However, in each of the seven sites, some formal health care is present, and the way it integrates with the more informal system represented by relatives, neighbors, and friends plays an important role in the way older people view their lives.

Few older !Kung (less than 10% in the year prior to the research period) rely on the Western health care provided either at the stationary clinics or by the mobile health clinics operated by the Botswana government. Most elderly !Kung live in the more isolated hamlets far from the clinics, and even when the mobile clinics operate in or near these hamlets few older individuals visit them. A combination of a formal health care system that places emphasis on the inoculation of infants and pre- and postnatal care and an almost fatalistic attitude on the part of older !Kung is the main reason for this lack of reliance on Western medicine. Elderly !Kung also utilize traditional healers when ill. These healers are most often residents of the same hamlet and will enter a trance state in their attempt to provide relief to the older individual. Whether using Western or traditional health care, the elderly ill rely primarily on the care provided by relatives who live in their own hamlets: Two thirds of the elderly respondents who received care said that they received it from an individual living in the same hamlet.

In contrast to the !Kung, older Herero when ill make frequent use of Western health care. It is almost universal for older Herero of both sexes to move to villages in which clinics are located, or at least to a nearby village, in order to make use of the available Western health care. Because Herero move quite frequently and often have houses in various villages in widely scattered locations, this movement to villages in which health clinics are located is not unusual. Many older Herero also visit traditional healers for treatment of various ailments, including witchcraft. This treatment may involve moving to the location of a traditional Herero healer or to a Herero village located near a healer of another tribal grouping. In either case, the seeking of treatment from a traditional healer is viewed as similar to that from a government health clinic.

Providing for an older individual who is ill is regarded by the Herero as a given; the only question is which relative or relatives will provide the care. The kinsmen who provided care to Herero respondents during the research period ranged from daughters and daughters-in-law to distant relatives by marriage. In several cases, a child was fostered to an older individual specifically in order to provide the required care. There appeared to be no resentment by those providing care, and younger Herero frequently boasted of the care they were providing to older relatives who were ill or incapacitated by a chronic health problem.

As one would expect, older people in Clifden make frequent use of available health care. Over 90% of the respondents 65 and older utilized some health services during the year prior to the interviews.

Almost 50% had seen the doctor during that year, 20% had been visited by the district nurse, and 25% had spent some period as an inpatient in the Clifden hospital. Over 70% of the older people interviewed had utilized more than one health service during the year, and almost the same percentage had used the same service more than once. Older females were more than twice as likely to be hospitalized as were older males, and males were more frequently visited by the doctor in their homes. Not surprisingly, the older old, those over the age of 80, made more frequent use of health services and were hospitalized more often than the younger old (ages 65-79). Also as expected, older people called upon health services much more frequently during the winter months than during the summer, and hospital admissions of older females reached the highest point during January and February. Finally, three older people (5%), made the trip to the outpatient clinics in Galway during the year prior to the interviews, whereas 25% of the older people had spent some time as an inpatient at the Galway regional hospital during the same period of time.

Informal caregiving was equally important to older people as the formal health care system. Exactly one half of the elderly individuals interviewed stated that a member of their own household cared for them when they were ill. However, 10% stated that they had no one to care for them when they were ill, and the remaining 40% responded by listing a series of other nonhousehold members who provided care: other relatives, 20%; neighbors, 5%; and the doctor and/or nurse, 15%. This lack of any caregiver and the reliance on nonhousehold members and nonrelatives to provide care are the result of two main factors. First, the continual emigration of young people out of the Clifden area, as discussed earlier, frequently results in the children of older people being scattered around the world. Second, almost 30% of older people interviewed lived alone. Ten of these individuals were widowed females, most of whose children had emigrated, and three of the seven males had never married. Because a sizable number of men in Clifden never marry, many males do not have a spouse or children to provide care when they are old. Forty-four percent of the older males interviewed had never married, and almost 30% of men between the ages of 40 and 65 were unmarried. Thus it should not be surprising that a large portion (30%) of the elderly population in Clifden had no one to rely on for care or had to rely on people other than household members and relatives for the provision of care when ill.

About 80% of the older people in Blessington utilized some health service during the year prior to interviewing. Of those who utilized services, 57% had seen the doctor during the year and 37% stayed for a time in a regional hospital. About 24% of the older people utilized more than one health service. More women than men utilized health services—26 women versus 19 men. Not surprisingly, the oldest old more often than the younger old found it necessary to use health services in the year prior to interviewing.

The question of who cares for older people is both an individual and a community concern in Blessington. Fifteen percent of the older people interviewed claimed that they lacked any potential caregiver; 39% of the older people said that a household member would care for them; 45% said other relatives would care for them; and 16% said that nonrelatives would care for them. Although the provision of care by relatives outside the household is high, it must be remembered that most older people in the Blessington area have relatives living close by and see them often. Most older Blessington residents prefer living independently from, but maintaining regular contact with, their relatives. In fact, 42% of elderly Blessington residents live alone. The recent increase in emigration may change this caregiving pattern.

When people are ill in Momence, most use physicians and hospital facilities in Kankakee. The offices of the family physicians in Momence are satellites from their main base of operations in Kankakee and are consequently open only 2 days a week. Phone contact with a physician or his or her answering service is comparatively easy. When illness is severe, the picture changes significantly. The patient seeks higher technology and more specialized medical expertise, either out of frustration or in response to the urging of family and friends. Also, local physicians recognize their own limitations and make referrals to larger-scale medical facilities in Urbana or Chicago. Those who can afford it regularly check in at the Mayo Clinic in Minnesota.

Who avoids the available medical facilities? The answer is those who cannot afford them—that is, people who have no medical insurance. One consequence of the need for health insurance is that individuals sacrifice the autonomy of running their own business for jobs that have medical insurance as a benefit. Also, families make decisions about older members that prevent entry into the medical system. These decisions often hasten the death of the individuals involved. They result from inability or unwillingness to pay high medical costs and, in particular, the wish to avoid the erosion of inheritable capital through the Medicaid "spend-down." The level of Medicare coverage during the 1980s has resulted in more and more people avoiding the medical system unless they know they are protected from the costs.

Long-term care and the final exit are medicalized, as elsewhere in the United States. Families try to keep the affected individual at home for as long as possible. If there are sufficient funds, families hire local women to care for their older members in their own home. This may mean hiring three women for around the clock care of 8-hour shifts or having women move in with the affected person for several days of the week. As a last resort, those who can no longer live at home enter a nursing home. (In the local nursing home the majority of patients are not from Momence but from an extensive catchment area.)

The overwhelming response to our question about who cared for older respondents when they were ill in Momence was a relative (nearly 56%). The source of help does not vary by age, but sex differences are apparent, with males either requiring no help or being more likely to use paid help. The age of helper reflects age homogeneity, suggesting that most of these helpers are spouses.

Statistics from Delaware County, Pennsylvania, in which Swarthmore is located, indicate that older persons use both hospital and physician services in greater proportion than younger persons. Discharge statistics for the eight general acute care hospitals in Delaware County show that persons 65 and over accounted for 36% of the discharges in 1988. The average length of stay was also greater for the older users: 10.7 days for those 65 and older compared to 6.2 days for those under 65. In the United States as a whole, during our study period, among people with average family incomes comparable to those in Swarthmore ($35,000 and up), 12.5% of those over 65 had a stay in an acute care hospital during 1983, 7.3% of those aged 45 to 64, and 7.1% of those aged 18 to 44. Older persons were also twice as likely as the middle-aged to have more than one stay during the year.

During the same year, older persons also reported greater contact with physicians. The average annual percent of persons with 10 or more contacts with a physician during 1983 was 15.5% for those 65 and over, 10.8% for those 45 to 64, and 8.8% for those 18 to 44. When these figures are examined for those who evaluated their health as better or worse, there is almost no difference in physician contact among those who say their health is "poor" or "fair" (lowest two scores on a 5-point scale). However, among those who evaluate their health as "good" to "excellent" (highest three levels on a 5-point scale), 9% of the older people report 10 or more physician contacts during the year, compared to 5.8% of those 45 to 64 and 7.6% of those 18 to 44.

A clue to the reasons older Swarthmoreans have concerns about health care appears in their responses about help during illness. Of those who named an illness episode during the previous 24 months (older than 65, $n = 26$; younger than 65, $n = 65$), one half of the Swarthmoreans older than 65 said they had help from someone: 70% of the men, but only 38% of the women, said they had a helper. The sex difference among the responses from younger people is less dramatic: 62% of the men and 50% of the women younger than 65 said they had a helper. Overall, 55% of the younger respondents had help. Most of the helpers for older people were relatives who lived in the household, most often spouses or daughters.

Important aspects of access to health care that are not obvious in the numerical data are organization and transportation. Although medical care is available in extraordinary amount and quality, access to it is, with a few exceptions, not possible on foot. Emergency ambulance service was provided through a neighboring fire company during the study period for a nominal annual contribution ($15 per household). However, transportation for more routine medical care was problematic. Many people who expressed satisfaction with various services in Swarthmore noted that their satisfaction depended on their being able to drive. A common service offered to frailer elderly by more active older persons, or by younger relatives, is driving; in a suburban community, rides to doctors and shopping centers are lifelines for people unable to drive. A countywide transportation service for the elderly, managed by a nonprofit corporation, offered low-fare rides ($9 for 10 trips) to senior centers, to doctors, and to shopping centers. However, these needed to be arranged at least a week in advance once a book of tickets had been purchased by mail.

Management of this type of transportation, as well as of other services available from various profit and not-for-profit organizations, is a second important service usually provided by younger relatives, sometimes from a long distance. Older persons in Swarthmore are not usually linked to a network of service providers, as an old person receiving social assistance for income or medical care might be. It requires considerable energy, time, and persistence to organize the various supportive services available from different businesses and public agencies. The old people in Swarthmore most likely to be informed about services such as the transportation tickets are those who participate in the senior activities at the Community Center.

In Hong Kong the vast majority of health care is obtained at public outpatient clinics, necessitating long waits in line. One goes early in the morning to line up, but it is possible for the elderly (and possibly others by now) to obtain a number so that they have some idea of when their turn is likely to come up. However, it is usually too much trouble to leave and come back, so they wait at the clinic anyway. A visit to a specialty clinic (dental, eye, ear) for routine (as opposed to emergency) care is arranged by appointments made 6 months in advance. Those with money to pay the higher fees of the private sector may go to physicians at private hospitals, clinics, or group practices who also practice Western medicine. However, there are some ailments that will be taken to practitioners of Chinese medicine, either after Western medicine has failed to improve the situation, in tandem with Western treatment (thought to treat the acute manifestations but not the underlying systemic imbalance), or as a first choice by reason of convenience or belief in superior effectiveness. Although such treatment is paid for completely by the patient (or his or her family), it is readily available. Chinese herbalists are highly accessible at the back of their medicine shops; there is seldom any wait. They will read the pulse and diagnose a sore throat, cold, or other minor acute problem and write up a prescription that they themselves or their assistants fill. Similarly, elderly people with bone or muscle aches, sprains, or minor fractures will normally go to a "bone-setter," who will manually knead the bones or muscles with oils and ointments. Such treatments may extend over several weeks or even months, and the injured person will pay a visit every few days. Finally, there is much over-the-counter self-treatment using both standard patent Western medicines and traditional herbal medicines. These types of health care utilization do not find their way into government health statistics. However, a number of studies have suggested that the vast majority of visits are to public outpatient clinics. When people are asked how they would respond if they had such and such an ailment, they almost always say they will go to a Western-trained physician and not a Chinese-style one. The elderly are the only exception to this rule, and only for uncomplicated bone and joint conditions. Ironically, given its reputation in the West, acupuncture is very seldom sought.

There is a definite sequencing to caregivers, depending on both the nature of the ailment and the composition of the household. Because most disabling conditions are experienced by the late middle-aged or elderly, disabled people usually have children. The caregiving order seems to be, in the case of women, children, including daughters-in-law in the household; grandchildren in the household; daughters from outside the household; other relatives from outside the household; and friends/neighbors. Even when disabled women have coresident husbands, the men are rarely if ever mentioned as caregivers. In most cases the husbands are long dead. For men with disabling conditions, the caregiving order is essentially the same except that a spouse precedes everyone else. The vast majority of primary caregivers are people living in the same household. In such multigenerational households it is sometimes impractical to speak of a primary caregiver. Whoever is around when the impaired person has a particular need will usually meet it. People with no one in the household or no one young enough to be helpful just struggle along until they collapse. At that point they will probably be moved into a child's home if there is one in Hong Kong. Otherwise, they will be admitted to a hospital, perhaps a chronic hospital, and ultimately be sent back to their home with occasional visits by a community nurse. If it is clear that there is no possibility of their being looked after by children and they have no money, they may jump the wait list for sheltered living situations or a care and attention place. If they have no children but have money, they have the option of hiring someone to live in and look after them or to come in for part of the day or even of going to a private nursing home, although most of these leave a great deal to be desired, are expensive, and are in short supply. The well-to-do frequently already have servants in the household, and if someone becomes ill or disabled, caregiving is simply added to their job description. Probably 80% of the elderly, however, fall into the category of having children but not a lot of money. By having children they have almost no chance of nursing home placement in government-subsidized establishments (virtually free for residents). On the other hand, having children does not necessarily mean they can afford either private nursing home placement or the hiring of a domestic servant. Thus caregiving is a family affair, and if the family can barely carry on, that is just how it is.

Summary

To recap, older respondents in all seven sites rate their health lower than young and middle-aged individuals; are afflicted with more serious and longer lasting illnesses; are affected by chronic health problems that restrict the culturally appropriate behavior of a large percentage of older people in every site other than Swarthmore; utilize the available health care system to a greater degree than younger people (except among the !Kung) and rely on close kin and relatives for care and support when ill or afflicted with chronic health problems. Although the overall nature of these findings is not startling, there is interesting and important variation in the details from each of the sites. This variation raises a series of questions concerning the fundamental differences extant in the perception of impairment and handicap, the definition of physical capacity, the compensatory strategies employed to overcome impairment, and the relationship of health and functionality to the well-being of the elderly in each of the settings.

Physical Loss and Functionality

Although it is possible simply to conclude that the variation in illness prevalence, chronic disease, and the impact of health problems on the elderly discussed in the last section results from tremendous contrast in the scale and environmental setting of the sites, it appears that other factors influence these differences.[3] In particular, the variation appears to be largely the result of differences in the nature of the tasks undertaken by older people, the way physical capacity is defined in the various settings, and the nature of the compensatory supports available. In order to determine the relative impact of these variables on the functionality and physical capacity of the elderly and in turn to measure the overall influence of functional capacity on well-being, a more detailed examination, utilizing principal component analysis, was undertaken. Through the application of this statistical procedure, the most salient functional tasks or capabilities should emerge in each of the study areas.

In each of the seven sites investigators asked respondents to rate their own abilities and difficulties on a series of physical attributes and on their capacities to carry out routine tasks. Many of the items were the same across sites, but others were quite different because of issues of meaning and appropriateness. Examples of items that were asked in every site include vision, memory, ability to carry things, and ability to walk. Other questions were rather site-specific. For example, it turned out to be quite inappropriate to ask !Kung and Herero about whether their appetite was satisfactory because in these cultures the tenet is that everyone is hungry, that there is never enough food. How could a person ever not want to eat? Doing yard work had little meaning for the !Kung and for most respondents in Hong Kong, but had meaning in Swarthmore and Momence, whereas lifting water for cattle was a daily task only among the Herero. Nevertheless, both yard work and lifting water are energy-intensive outdoor tasks, and there is some basis for comparison. The specific functional capabilities or tasks the respondents were asked about can be seen in Tables 8.3 through 8.9.

Covariance matrices among responses to self-ratings on sets of items were computed, and the weights or "loadings" of the items on the leading principal component are shown in Tables 8.3 through 8.9. Covariance was computed rather than correlation matrices because it was important to avoid forcing all items to bear the same weight in the computations. If some item hardly ever varied at a site, we retained that information by using covariances. For example, if one person in 100 had difficulty with vision, and 40 in 100

TABLE 8.3 Loadings on Leading Principal Component of Functionality for !Kung

	Loading		
Sex	*High*	*Intermediate*	*Low*
Males	Hunt	Digest	Vision
	Get bush food	Get wood	Visit
	Get water	Sit and stand	Walk
	Pick up things	Joints	Memory
	Ride donkey	Cook	Hear
	Reach	Sew	
Females	Ride donkey	Vision	Memory
	Get bush food	Visit	Hear
	Sew	Joints	Digest
	Get water	Sit and stand	Reach
	Get wood	Walk	Pick up things
		Cook	

with climbing stairs, it was important to conclude that variation in ability to climb stairs was a more salient consequence of aging in the particular site than was difficulty with vision. The simplest and least controversial view of principal components analysis is that it provides an optimum (in the least-squares sense) summary or condensation of multivariate data into a reduced number of dimen-

TABLE 8.4 Loadings on Leading Principal Component of Functionality for Herero

	Loading		
Sex	*High*	*Intermediate*	*Low*
Males	Lift water	Ride donkey	Vision
	Get water	Cook	Walk
	Sew	Travel	Count money
	Build	Get firewood	Chew
		Carry things	Hear
Females	Get firewood	Build	Count money
	Lift water	Travel	Chew
	Ride donkey	Carry things	Vision
	Get water	Walk	Hear
		Sew	
		Cook	

TABLE 8.5 Loadings on Leading Principal Component of Functionality for Clifden

| Sex | Loading | | |
	High	Intermediate	Low
Males	Do yard	Clean house	Hear
	Walk to town	Get a meal	Appetite
	Get water	Walk up steps	Memory
	Bring fuel	Balance	Vision
	Do laundry	Teeth	Get dressed
	Carry groceries		
Females	Get water	Carry groceries	Appetite
	Bring fuel	Hear	Do laundry
	Do yard	Balance	Clean house
	Walk to town	Teeth	Get a meal
	Walk up steps	Memory	Get dressed
	Vision		

sions. Loadings are presented on the leading components from our various sites in just this exploratory spirit. Although a numerical procedure to summarize numerical ratings is used, caution must be observed in order not to suggest a level of precision that is not present. To undertake the analysis, it is necessary to assume, for

TABLE 8.6 Loadings on Leading Principal Component of Functionality for Blessington

| Sex | Loading | | |
	High	Intermediate	Low
Males	Walk up steps	Drive a car	Get fuel
	Teeth	Memory	Do yard
	Balance	Carry groceries	Get dressed
	Ride bike	Hear	Clean house
	Walk to town	Appetite	Make tea
	Vision	Do laundry	Get a meal
Females	Walk up steps	Vision	Appetite
	Teeth	Carry groceries	Get a meal
	Ride bike	Walk to town	Make tea
	Drive a car	Clean house	Hear
	Do yard	Balance	Get dressed
	Get fuel	Do laundry	Memory

TABLE 8.7 Loadings on Leading Principal Component of Functionality for Momence

| Sex | Loading | | |
	High	Intermediate	Low
Males	Stairs	Home maintenance	Drive
	Yardwork	Memory	Hear
	Repairs	Clean	Vision
	Balance	Reach	Appetite
	Walk	Live alone	Manage time
	Cook	Get around	Manage finances
	Hold		
Females	Yardwork	Repairs	Vision
	Stairs	Live alone	Manage finances
	Get around	Clean	Appetite
	Drive	Balance	Hear
	Walk	Memory	Cook
	Reach	Home maintenance	Manage time
	Hold		

example, that a rating of 3 on a scale of 5 on "carrying groceries" is somehow equivalent to a 3 on "vision." We also have to assume that the difference between a 1 and a 2 on a 5-point scale is equivalent to the difference between a 4 and a 5 on the same scale.

TABLE 8.8 Loadings on Leading Principal Component of Functionality for Swarthmore

| Sex | Loading | | |
	High	Intermediate	Low
Males	Home maintenance	Walk	Reach
	Repairs	Stairs	Get around
	Cook	Vision	Manage time
	Yardwork	Clean	Hear
	Live alone	Hold	Drive
		Memory	
		Manage finances	
Females	Yardwork	Walk	Hold
	Stairs	Stairs	Manage finances
	Get around	Clean	Memory
	Drive	Get around	Cook
	Walk	Vision	Hear
	Reach	Reach	Manage time
	Hold	Live alone	

TABLE 8.9 Loadings on Leading Principal Component of Functionality for Hong Kong

	Loading		
Sex	High	Intermediate	Low
Males	Write	Stairs	Cook
	Manage finances	Memory	Clean
	Read	Hold	Balance
	Get Around	Vision	Appetite
	Walk	Reach	Hear
Females	Write	Clean	Balance
	Read	Walk	Reach
	Manage finances	Cook	Vision
	Get around	Memory	Hear
	Stairs	Hold	Appetite

Even though these assumptions suggest caution, it is still possible to proceed with the analysis and to use the leading principal component as the natural answer to the question of what abilities are the most salient markers of differences in functionality between people in each of the seven sites. A marker that varies considerably in the sample and is highly correlated with other markers that decline with age will have a high "loading" on the leading component, whereas a marker that does not vary in step with others or that does not vary much at all will not have a high loading.

The traits are, somewhat arbitrarily, divided into thirds—those with high, intermediate, and low loadings. Within each category, traits are listed in order of their magnitude. Given the nature of the data, error analysis and significance testing have no place here, but some idea of the stability or instability of differences among settings can be obtained by comparing ratings for men and women at the same site. Similarly, reliable sex differences in the salience of markers of aging, if there are any, should show up in several of the sites.

As indicated in Figure 8.1, there is a clear pattern of decline with age of the mean principal component scores across all seven sites. A pattern of sex difference is also apparent; women, in general, rate themselves lower on functionality than do comparably aged men.

However, there is a discernible difference in the nature of this overall pattern of decline. In Clifden and among the Herero and !Kung, the ratings that respondents gave themselves on questions about functionality decline steadily with age. In contrast, in the higher-scale settings of Blessington, Swarthmore, and Momence, there is not a uniform downward trend; instead, middle-aged and elderly respondents in many, but not in all, measures reported high levels of satisfaction with their abilities to perform necessary tasks and did not appear to attach a great deal of significance to their declines in physical capacity. The pattern in Hong Kong is in outward appearance similar to that for the !Kung, the Herero, and the residents of Clifden, but an analysis of the actual tasks and capabilities that compose the principal component leads to a different conclusion.

Thus three related questions become important: Why the difference in the patterns, what are their relationships to general health, and how does the pattern relate to the well-being of the elderly? To answer these questions each site is discussed individually, beginning with the three that show the most consistent decline over the life course.

Among the !Kung, people were asked to rate their abilities to hear, see, sit, and stand, and other abilities indicated by the labels in Table 8.3, but several of these require explanation. Water is brought to the camp in containers, usually 3-gallon buckets or jerry cans, from wells or water holes that are one half to one mile distant. "Getting water" refers to the ability to walk to the well and to carry back several gallons of water. "Visiting" may involve walking within a small radius to neighboring household or several kilometers to a more distant village. "Getting wood" refers to the ability to collect and carry back bundles of firewood from a distance of about two thirds of a mile to 2 miles from the village.

As shown in Table 8.3, getting water, getting wood, getting bush food, and riding a donkey have the greatest weights on the first principal component. In addition, hunting ability or its loss is a major perceived marker of senescence for !Kung men (women do not hunt), and difficulty with sewing and beadwork is of comparable significance for women. These are the abilities that best

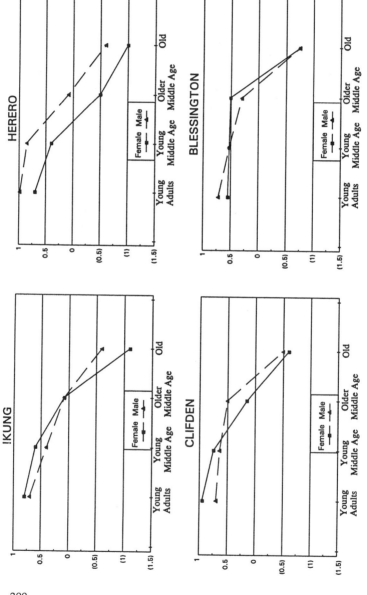

Figure 8.1. Covariance Matrices for Functionality by Site and Sex and Age

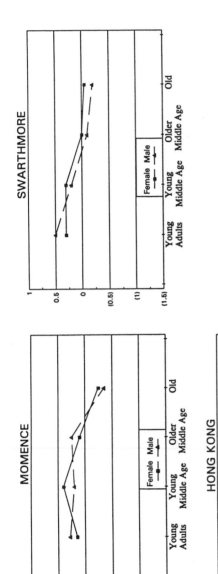

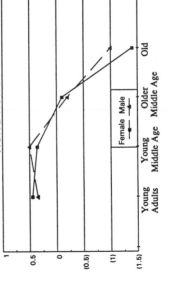

Figure 8.1. Continued

301

differentiate people with high levels of retained functionality from those not doing well. Walking, sitting and standing, vision, cooking, and ability to visit have intermediate weight, and memory, hearing, and digestion are of little significance for either sex.

Women seem to be more concerned with loss of vision than are men. This sex difference is probably related to the relatively recent demand for beadwork and other craft products. These sewn items are mostly produced by women, and the work demands fine muscle coordination and good close vision. Further, among the very oldest people there were a number of blind women and women with very impaired sight. This part of the sample probably accounts for the higher weight that vision is given by !Kung women.

Among the Herero, the main axis of variation among people has to do with abilities to water cattle, ride a donkey, fetch water and firewood, and travel. For males, sewing is a salient dimension, whereas building is for women. Some explanation of these tasks is in order. During the dry season, the cattle have to be watered every day from wells dug out of the limestone bedrock. The water level may be 6 to 10 feet below ground level, so that one must stand in the well, scoop buckets of water, lift them up, and pour the water into a hollowed tree trunk that serves as a watering trough. It is hard work that goes on for hours every morning. Fetching water and firewood are less difficult, but both involve carrying heavy loads over distances of one to several kilometers. Traveling ordinarily involves riding a donkey or a horse, and Herero visits extend over hundreds of kilometers. A better gloss for "sewing" in the context of male activities is leatherwork. This involves the manufacture and maintenance of tack, of footwear, and of leather chaps to protect horsemen in the thornbush. Men are apparently highly aware of the loss of this ability with age.

Herero houses are built by women, although men are often seen helping. Villages with young women can be discerned by the presence of beautifully built, well-decorated houses, and the quality of construction is a source of great pride among women. Older women say that the work is too difficult for them. It is very difficult labor, involving cutting down several dozen trees to make posts and roof framing, collecting many bundles of thatching grass, and collecting termite earth and cow dung to make the plaster that is applied to the walls.

On the other hand, hearing, vision, and chewing ability vary much less among individuals and contribute little to the first component of variation. As self-perceived markers of senescence, these basic biological functions are not particularly salient to Herero.

In Clifden the major source of variation among subjects is dominated by tasks requiring mobility and muscular effort—walking to town, climbing stairs, and carrying things. Other fundamental biological abilities such as seeing, remembering, having an appetite, and hearing are not heavily represented in the dominant principal component. Routine daily tasks like cooking, making tea, and getting dressed seem not to be troublesome, especially for females.

Some explanation for the tasks that were ranked highly is necessary. Few of the elderly in Clifden are able to rely on the labor-saving devices that are so prevalent in the United States. Central heating is rare in Clifden, and fuel—coal, peat, bottled gas—must be carried into the house. Peat is usually stored in a "turf pile" anywhere from a few feet to 50 yards from the house, coal is purchased in 100-pound bags, and a container of bottled gas weighs at least 50 pounds. Consequently, the older person in Clifden must expend considerable muscular energy just to bring fuel into the house, and it is not surprising that over one-half of the individuals 65 and older who were interviewed could not carry fuel into their own homes. This was particularly true of older women, of whom almost 60% could not accomplish this task.

The other highly ranked tasks also require considerable physical effort. Walking to town, or for that matter just walking around the town in the rain and wind, can be difficult for younger people, let alone for older people. Of older people interviewed, 30% said that they could not get to or around town on their own, and slightly more said that they could not carry their groceries and had difficulty walking up and down stairs. Almost one half of the people living outside of town could not accomplish these tasks, and this reflects the distances, up to 2.5 miles, that some of them lived from the town of Clifden. Because most older people do not own cars and public transportation is nonexistent, the ability to walk is very important to the normal functioning of people within the community.

In Blessington, people perceive decline in their functional ability as they age, but unlike the declines perceived in the three previous sites, this decline does not begin until late middle age. Although males record a slight decline before late middle age, both sexes perceive a rapid and sharp decline in their abilities late in life. One explanation for this difference is that men may see a clearer decline in their functionality as a result of their work roles. Until 15 years ago, most men worked in manual labor and farming, and a functional decline in one's abilities may have been more obvious in these contexts.

As in Clifden, the major source of variation among Blessington subjects is tasks requiring muscular effort and mobility such as walking up stairs, riding a bike, walking into town, and carrying shopping. People in Blessington must spend a considerable amount of time meeting their basic needs such as the provisioning of fuel. Many older people walk or ride their bikes to town to do their local shopping and to attend Mass. Although most older people live in single story homes, their difficulty with stairs may be related to their difficulty stepping up to enter the local buses. Sight was the only fundamental biological ability that was strongly represented in the principal component. This is logical because one's sight has a profound impact on one's mobility.

Teeth also ranked high in the principal component. Two aspects of Blessington culture help to explain this. First, the Irish consume many sweets (candy, cakes) throughout their lives, and thus most people experience problems with their teeth. Second, the quality of dental care available in the Blessington area does not appear to be high. Blessington, in fact, has no resident dentist. A traveling dentist provides care to residents once a week. Older people with tooth and denture problems constantly complain about the quality and availability of dental care.

In Momence there is not as sharp a decline in functional ability as in the sites outside the United States, and the deepest decline is in the oldest category. However, the decline is not nearly as steep as that present in the four previous settings. In fact, the pattern for respondents in Momence is at the midpoint between Swarthmore and the lower-scale sites.

The decline in functionality in Momence means quite different things than in the non-U.S. sites. Because of technological buffers the consequences of functional decline are not as catastrophic as in the other settings. Undoubtedly, there is the retreat into the living room and kitchen on the first floor; the sofa becomes the bed and TV the main contact with the outside world; family, neighbors, friends, and church members launch a major effort to assist; groceries or food are brought in; pets are cared for; houses are cleaned; repairs are made. Even when the medical problems involve such issues as respiration, oxygen concentrators are installed and the affected individual is tethered to the device. Self-medication is instructed so the individual can remain at home and out of the expensive hospital or nursing home.

The image of the decline in functionality is of minor crossovers. Cross-sectionally, the sex difference is minimal. For the youngest group, women have slightly reduced functionality due to reproductive issues. After the early reproductive years, they exceed men in their estimations of functional capacities and then decline slightly in the oldest grouping. For men there is little variation until the oldest group, where a decline is observed that is in all likelihood work related. For males in physically demanding blue-collar jobs, the alternative is to seek local employment that does not make such physical demands. Reduction of commuting and physical demands improves perception of one's own functionality.

The variables that produce the most variance are those associated with mobility and strenuous physical performance—stairs, yard work, and walking. These are important activities in that they permit one to utilize one's entire residence, keep up the external appearance, and be visible in the community. The variables that produce the least variance are hearing, appetite, and the ability to manage finances and time. Hearing difficulties are resolved by hearing aids. In a complex, literate society the management of finances and schedules is a minimal skill for all or can be resolved by tax accountants. Notably, there are sex differences, with males having low variance on repairs and driving and higher variability on cooking (a skill for which they are dependent on women). Females, on the other hand, report high variability on driving (a male skill) and lower variability on cooking (a female skill). Thus we find sex differentiation in social roles and functional capacities required to fulfill those roles.

Declines with age in self-evaluation about the functionality indicators are gradual in Swarthmore, and the lowest levels do not reach the depths reported on other settings. This pattern reflects two important characteristics of this community, which have somewhat contradictory effects on the overall functionality level of its members.

First, as residents of a well-to-do town in a modern, industrial nation, people in Swarthmore have access to many technological buffers for frailty. Eyeglasses, dentures, hip replacements, cataract removal, and other "hi-tech" procedures and prostheses are all available to compensate for physical weaknesses. The existence of automobiles, telephones, television, radio, and commercially pre-pared foods makes possible mobility, communication, and subsis-tence even for the physically frail.

Second, and somewhat paradoxically, residents of this suburban community share a view of the life course that includes decisions about leaving the town based on fears about eventual frailty and dependence. Because many older individuals do leave Swarth-more in search of greater security in case of physical decline, overall functionality ratings for the town are higher. The dispersal of younger kin characteristic of a middle-class suburb, the high value placed on individual autonomy and independence, the perception of the individual as the unit of life course transition and decision, a lifelong experience of spatial mobility as a concomitant of life course transition, and the specter of institutionalization in a nurs-ing home combine to define a decision point at which older resi-dents weigh the costs and benefits of staying in Swarthmore. A decision to stay in town is perceived as "risky" because *if* the individual becomes too frail to maintain an independent house-hold, then institutionalization is seen as a grim possibility. Other older people, for the same reasons, move into Swarthmore to be near children. These in-movers usually live in condominium or rental apartment buildings with a high proportion of older resi-dents. However, if these individuals become, or fear becoming, very frail, they will move again, usually into a specialized setting such as a retirement community, continuing care community, or nursing home. The influence of residential instability on the func-tionality patterns in Swarthmore is highlighted in contrast to those displayed in the table for Momence. The greater residential stability there is associated with a steeper and deeper decline in functional-ity by age. Availability of kin and a lifelong experience of greater residential stability combine with a lower level of economic resources to keep more older, and potentially frailer, individuals in the community.

Within the relatively narrow overall range of variation in functionality, the functionality indicators that vary most within the Swarthmore population are those linked to maintaining an independent residence. For both men and women these include household repairs, working in the yard, and cleaning the house. For men, cooking and the social state of living alone are also highly variable. The greater variability among women of ability to move around inside and outside the home is also understandable in terms of the greater average age of women in Swarthmore and the fact that older women are likely to be living on their own. For them, the abilities to function in a two- or three-story residence and to get to stores on foot or by car are perceived as requisite to remaining in the town. Men are more likely to have a younger spouse to provide help if needed. The low to moderate loadings for memory do not indicate lack of salience, but lack of variability. Many respondents described fear of memory loss and its assumed sequel of further cognitive decline.

The scores reported for Hong Kong are not at all surprising: That reading, writing, and finance loom so large is due to a cohort phenomenon. Older people are far less educated, hence less often literate, and are consequently holders (or former holders) of jobs that drew primarily on their physical rather than their intellectual strengths. These cohort differences in literacy are especially marked for females. Once out of the labor force, they seldom have pensions and must rely on their adult children for financial support. The type and range of occupations available to younger people draw more on their intellectual than on their physical strengths. Getting around and climbing stairs are relatively salient variables because many people live in high-rise buildings without elevators or up on hills, and problems with these motor activities severely compromise one's ability to go to work, to do the marketing, or to go visiting. Because cleaning and cooking are primarily female tasks in Hong Kong, they contribute to more variation in functionality among females than among males. The low loadings on most of the sensory variables reflect their relative lack of salience to the informants as well as, possibly, little actual variation. Poor vision, after all, is often corrected in Hong Kong by glasses.

Summary

Although the site-by-site explanations account for the intrasite patterns, there still remains the question of why such clear differences exist in the intersite patterns in the principal components between the !Kung, the Herero, and Clifden, on the one hand, and Blessington, Momence, and Swarthmore on the other. In addition, it is still necessary to explain why, even though the pattern for Hong Kong is similar to the first three sites, the reasons for the resulting configuration are quite different. There appear to be three main reasons for the differences in the patterns: the nature of the social structures in the seven sites; the age structure of the various populations; and the variation in the cultural definitions of meaningful tasks and capabilities, along with the compensatory supports available.

First, the inhabitants of Clifden, and the !Kung and the Herero share certain common social structural characteristics as well as a pattern of common responses to the questions asked about physical capability and functional capacity. Although the three populations differ markedly linguistically, economically, and in terms of social institutions, they nevertheless share certain structural similarities. In each case the local communities are small in size and characterized by both stability and multiple linkages among people by ties of kinship and marriage. (Note that although Herero move geographically, they often move as a group.) Though relatively similar in the number of inhabitants, Swarthmore and Blessington are less face-to-face communities in which the inhabitants are linked by generations of interaction and intermarriage. Momence, because of its stability, shares more of these characteristics with the Botswana villages and Clifden. (Tables 8.10 through 8.13 summarize the availability of spouses and children to the older people in our seven sites.)

Swarthmore is dominated by population movement associated with an upper-middle-class American suburb, and although Momence has the stable population lacking in Swarthmore, the scale of the community and its integration in the larger society are much different from those of the more self-contained sites. Even Blessington, so similar to Clifden in population and culture, has been strongly affected by in-migration and a split between "blow ins" and "natives" and differences in religion and social class. In addition, Clifden, the

TABLE 8.10 Old People Who Never Married, by Site

Site	Women	Men
!Kung	0% (0/33)	0% (0/39)
Herero	6% (7/124)	11% (7/66)
Clifden	9% (3/33)	44% (12/27)
Blessington	6% (2/36)	12% (4/33)
Momence	3% (1/34)	4% (1/25)
Swarthmore	6% (4/62)	10% (3/31)
Hong Kong	0% (0/20)	0% (0/20)

"Old" = 60+ for all sites except Clifden, where "old" = 65+.

!Kung, and the Herero are located far from centers of urban influence. In contrast, Swarthmore and Blessington, although this is denied by many of their respective residents, are suburbs of very

TABLE 8.11 Old People Who Were Married at Time of Interview, by Site

Site	Women	Men
!Kung	65% (28/44)	80% (36/45)
Herero	24% (30/124)	68% (45/66)
Clifden	27% (9/33)	30% (8/27)
Blessington	33% (12/36)	52% (17/33)
Momence	41% (14/34)	60% (15/25)
Swarthmore	50% (31/62)	84% (26/31)
Hong Kong	60% (12/20)	95% (19/20)

"Old" = 60+ for all sites except Clifden, where "old" = 65+.

TABLE 8.12 Old People Who Have No Surviving Children, by Site

Site	Women	Men
!Kung	36%	31%
	(16/44)	(14/45)
Herero	21%	16%
	(27/124)	(11/67)
Clifden	12%	63%
	(4/33)	(17/27)
Blessington	22%	36%
	(8/36)	(12/33)
Momence	11%	12%
	(4/35)	(3/25)
Swarthmore	18%	10%
	(11/62)	(3/31)
Hong Kong	0%	0%
	(0/20)	(0/20)

"Old" = 60+ for all sites except Clifden, where "old" = 65+.

large urban areas. Similarly, even though Momence is much more of a rural community, it is linked to larger neighboring communities and Chicago in ways unimaginable in the other three sites.

TABLE 8.13 Proximity of Children to Old People, by Site

Site	Women	Men
!Kung	77%	84%
	(30/39)	(30/36)
Herero	85%	85%
	(79/93)	(47/55)
Clifden	83%	90%
	(24/29)	(9/10)
Blessington	93%	86%
	(26/28)	(18/21)
Momence	74%	54%
	(25/34)	(13/24)
Swarthmore	61%	61%
	(31/51)	(17/28)
Hong Kong	80%	85%
	(16/20)	(17/20)

NOTE: Proximity = one or more children within 1-hour walk (!Kung, Herero, Clifden) or 1-hour drive (Blessington, Momence, Swarthmore, Hong Kong). "Old" = 60+ for all sites except Clifden, where "old" = 65+.

Second, the visibility of elderly, their functionality and consequent community knowledge about their functionality also differ across the sites. In Clifden and among the !Kung and Herero, the elderly are highly visible to others in the community, and there is a "full range" of older people within the sites. Among the !Kung and Herero, the old people who are in the worst shape are still living in the community. As in most underdeveloped countries of the Third World, there are no government or private institutions for the care of the aged. Further, !Kung and Herero live in open, domestic compounds, most of everyday life takes place out of doors, and there is no belief that an interviewer should not intrude into the heart of the family space. In this way, old people are completely visible, and no one shields them from being interviewed or from taking part in general conversation.

The elderly are also highly visible in Clifden—this despite the fact that the living conditions in the west of Ireland are quite different from those of the !Kung and Herero. Although the weather in winter and the crush of tourists in summer limit the amount of outdoor activity, older people are quite noticeable in Clifden throughout the year and unless they are extremely frail or bedridden are actively present in the community. Even older people with failing health have the support of relatives, friends, and neighbors, as well as the extensive Irish social welfare system, which enables them to remain in their own homes. Moreover, unlike Swarthmore, in which many frail older people had left the community, or Blessington, in which many frail elderly were reluctant to be interviewed, in Clifden even the two bedridden and five housebound elderly participated in our interviews.

These factors contribute significantly to the pattern of responses in Clifden and among the !Kung and Herero. In the first place, the high visibility of the elderly and the extent to which they are integrated into everyday life mean that knowledge of their physical condition is available to everyone. In the more diverse setting of Swarthmore, the elderly can maintain a pretense of high functionality because of the greater privacy and age segregation of daily life. (The greater mixing of ages in Momence and the greater visibility of the elderly made this kind of image management less possible.) This fact, coupled with the high cultural value placed on self-reliance and independence, can easily lead to inflated self-ratings by older respondents. In the more face-to-face, lower-scale communities, there are few secrets, at least regarding a person's physical health, and there appears to be no profit or loss in anyone rating his or her health higher than it really is.

Third, the variation in the cultural definitions of meaningful tasks and capabilities, along with the compensatory supports available in the seven sites, differentiates the !Kung, the Herero, and the inhabitants of Clifden from the inhabitants of Blessington, Momence, and Swarthmore. Two examples illustrate this difference. Among the !Kung, memory has little weight on the first principal component, while among the Herero it was not a culturally relevent indicator of functionality. These two sites are similar in terms of community organization. Both communities are small, homogeneous, face-to-face, kin-based settings, and in these circumstances lapses of memory are less significant because one spends one's days in familiar settings surrounded by familiar people. On the other hand, Clifden (for females), in Blessington (for males), Swarthmore (for males), and Momence greater weight is placed on memory. In the United States, individuals fear that forgetting things will lead to the loss of independence, and they especially associate memory loss with the dreaded onset of Alzheimer's disease.

Likewise, the fact that functionality levels decline more sharply for men than for women in Swarthmore and Momence compared to the pattern in Clifden and in Botswana reflects differences in cultural customs concerning marital relationships and demographic patterns. Older men in the two American communities, as in the United States more generally, are married, whereas most of the older women are widows. Thus men are likely to be able to stay in the community despite greater anticipated or actual frailty because they have spouses to care for them. Also, older women who are still in the American communities may evaluate their own functionality somewhat more positively both because they compare themselves to their larger, and older, peer group of other old women and because they are reluctant to acknowledge frailty that, especially for widows, implies, once again, a loss of independence. As has been discussed previously, there is no need in the lower-scale communities for people to hide or discount their frailty. Frail individuals of both sexes are visible within these communities, and therefore the decline for females, who also live longer than males in these settings, is steeper than for males.

Finally, what about Hong Kong? The pattern, depicted in Figure 8.1, of a steep decline in functionality starting in early middle age is clearly similar to that of the small, lower-scale, face-to-face settings, and yet Hong Kong is by far the highest-scale and the least stable of the seven sites. The explanation for this similarity is simply that although the pattern is analogous, the components that make up the patterns are significantly different. In Hong Kong the major components are writing, managing finances, and reading, quite unlike those for the !Kung and Herero and in Clifden, where tasks requiring physical dexterity predominate. The emphasis on the cognitive variables in Hong Kong thus reflects a cohort effect in that the younger generation possesses these important skills, whereas because of illiteracy and decrements associated with aging, the older generations do not.

Conclusion

So what can be said about the relationship among health, functionality, the aging process, and the well-being of the elderly? In Chapter 5 we discussed some of the more quantitative relationships between overall ratings of well-being and self-assessment of health status. However, these findings are somewhat superficial and even, to some degree, misleading. It is our view that the relationship between health status and well-being is really ameliorated by the functional status of the elderly individual. The self-assessment of health, although giving an overview of the individual's general health status, is actually interrelated with functional capacity to such a degree that it has little direct correlation with well-being. Thus in order to understand the impact of health/functionality on well-being, analysis must focus on the ability of the individual to undertake culturally relevant behavior within the context of a particular setting. This conclusion bolsters the findings of recent work by a number of gerontologists (Baltes, Wahl, & Schmid-Furstoss, 1990) who argue that the context in which the older person lives, acts, and copes is the key to understanding both the individual's functional capacity and its bearing on life satisfaction. In other words, the ability of an individual to operate at a given level of functioning in the "real world" is the key to understanding well-being.

The real world, to risk an understatement, is intricate, and understanding the effect of the real world on functional capacity is complex and involves the consideration of a wide range of factors, such as the social support system, the nature and accessibility of health care, availability of prostheses, and personality factors. Also, as people age, chronic disease, impairments, and handicaps increase and change the relationship between the individual and these factors. Material presented in the earlier sections of this chapter on the effects of chronic problems and physical capacity indicates the tremendous variation in, first, what constitutes culturally relevant behavior and, second, what compensatory supports are available in the seven sites. A few brief examples illustrate this variation and the importance of detailed analyses of the context in which people live, act, and age.

Chronic health problems that result in handicaps pose powerful threats to people in Swarthmore. If they remain in the community, serious frailty compromises their ability to participate as full members, and their very personhood, which is defined in part by independence. Either in anticipation of frailty, or when they actually become unable to maintain a house, manage finances, and/or remember things, elderly move or are moved out of the community. Thus the small number of older people in Swarthmore who report chronic health problems that result in handicap. Even with access to many compensatory supports, including a very technologically sophisticated health care system, an upper-middle-class lifestyle and, for many, family in fairly close proximity, the cultural context encourages independence to such a degree that frailty is an obstacle to remaining a member of the community.

In contrast, among the Herero the impact of chronic health problems on the elderly is entirely different. First, the nature of the culturally relevant behavior is dramatically dissimilar: Physically taxing tasks—watering cattle, gathering firewood, riding donkeys— predominate in the real world of the Herero. However, when impaired by a chronic health problem, older Herero do not leave the village. Instead, relatives provide the compensatory support necessary, or a young relative is fostered to the older person to proffer the needed labor. Independence in the sense found in Swarthmore is not a cultural value; it is just accepted that older people are cared for, and this caregiving is not regarded as a burden. Similarly in Clifden, frail older people remain in the community in their own houses, but instead of fosterage the compensatory supports available are a personal, low-tech health care system, the extensive social welfare system, and a close-knit community in which people "look out after" the elderly. Forgetfulness, although recognized both in Clifden and among the !Kung, is not, as it is in Swarthmore, a sign of incapacitation. The contexts are different, and therefore the consequences of the handicaps vary.

The key to understanding the influence of health and functionality on the aging process and well-being, therefore, is to study people in their own world, not through abstract scales or in artificial environments. The culturally relevant behavior must be discerned because it will vary, as will the compensatory supports available to the elderly individual and even the definitions of what constitutes a chronic problem, impairment, or handicap. Without this real world analysis, there is no way of actually understanding the influence of functional capacity on the aging process and the well-being of the elderly.

Notes

1. As discussed more fully in Chapter 1, the age groupings used in all the health and functionality tables are empirically determined for each of the seven sites. The chronological ranges for these groupings vary from one site to another, but the meanings are comparable. Thus "young" in Clifden is designated, for culturally appropriate reasons, as the ages 19 to 35, whereas in Swarthmore, also for culturally appropriate reasons, the "young" group comprises the ages 18 to 39.

2. Although some detailed data on continuing health problems were collected among the !Kung and Herero, quantitative data concerning the impact of the health problems were not systematically gathered. However, more general findings were reported and are used as the basis for the comparative discussion.

3. Researchers in the field of cross-cultural aging have often assumed that old people fare best in more traditional, small-scale societies (Cowgill, 1974; Cowgill & Holmes, 1972; Press & McKool, 1972). Here the quality of old people's lives and their value to the community are greatest when families remain together and share

resources, individual geographical mobility is low, and the pace of cultural and economic change is sufficiently slow so that the skills of old people are not rendered obsolete. On the other hand, rapid economic change, proximity to centers of modernization, and the great residential mobility associated with modern labor force organization have been shown to work to the disadvantage of older people. Families do not remain together or pool their resources, high rates of individual geographical mobility are the norm, and the skills of older people can be obsolescent even before they reach compulsory retirement age.

Although this view has come under attack from several directions (Finley, 1982; Glascock, 1987; Goldstein & Beall, 1981; Hendricks, 1982; Nydegger, 1983), the critiques are also based on inferences concerning the consequences of differing forms of social structure for the aging process. As such, they tend to emphasize the transitions in social roles experienced by people as they mature. The aging process, however, affects not only transitions in family and social and economic roles but also the physical capacity of the individual. From the point of view of age-related declines in physical capacity, one might predict that the elderly would be most advantaged in complex societies and most disadvantaged in simple societies. We might expect that in societies of simple technology and few labor-saving devices, people would feel most keenly the loss of general physical strength that comes with aging. In more complex, affluent, and bureaucratically organized societies, people might be less sensitive to signs of increasing frailty with age because of the many medical and technological features that buffer the loss of physical capacity.

Part Three

Conclusion

9

Conclusion

What have we learned from Project AGE? In the first chapter we admitted that we could not give a simple answer to the Shangri-La question, "Where is the best place to be old?" Our years of research have introduced too many varying and interrelated conditions to let us point to a simple geographic answer. However, specification of those conditions and variables can illuminate the ways in which cultures of different human communities shape lives in old age. In this chapter the results of our project are summarized to provide that specification. The review of our findings will in turn become the platform for the closest we can come to a map of Shangri-La— that is, the guidance our research gives about choices and changes that could improve the meanings of age for those of us who will become old in modern, complex societies.

AUTHOR'S NOTE: Some material in this chapter has appeared previously in "Old Age and Age Integration: An Anthropological Perspective" by J. Keith, in M. Riley, R. Kahn, and A. Foner, 1994, *Age and Structural Lag: Essays on Changing Work, Retirement and Other Structures* (pp. 197-218). New York: John Wiley.

The most succinct we can be in summarizing what we learned from Project AGE is to state a painful paradox. Social and cultural processes have moved some human groups away from exclusively physical meanings of age, partly through creation of subsistence technologies that are less directly dependent on physical vigor and partly through health technologies that compensate for physical decline. However, these same processes that have made possible at least potentially positive definitions of late life have undermined the sources of social support and personal identity that can be taken for granted in the groups where aging, because it is defined by physical decline, is by definition negative. At the heart of the paradox is the fact that in the social contexts in which positive social and personal meanings of age could potentially transcend physical decline, the sources of social integration and personal identity are not easily available to many older persons. The challenge we face for the future is to resolve the paradox, to find ways to incorporate positive meanings for age into highly differentiated and special-ized societies. Although the resolution will not be a simplistic re-creation of traditional lifeways, our comparative study reveals principles that could guide new ways to meet some enduring human needs.

To return to the core questions we articulated to organize our study, we will organize this concluding section as responses to them. We asked first about cultural and social influences on defi-nitions of well-being in old age. The responses we will review here were of two types: influences of context on the process of self-evaluation, and influences of context on the substance of reasons for those evaluations. Second, we posed for ourselves questions about the cultural and social mechanisms through which broad characteristics of our research settings, including societal scale, stability, and resource level, were channeled into influences on in-dividual lives. Finally, we wished to know how these mechanisms shaped the effects on individuals of changes in their health and functional abilities. The responses to these questions that we find in our data will be presented here in three clusters. First, we review the more abstract perceptions of the life course acquired through the card sort, and second, the actual behaviors from which we were able to map the social boundaries of age. Finally, we will review the mediating influences of both the cognitive and the social meanings of age on consequences of decline in health and function. The final section of this chapter will return to our metaquestion about what guidance Project AGE can provide for personal and societal decisions about aging in the future. As we present this summary, two themes will appear persistently: the inextricability of the aging experience from social and cultural context, and the necessity of preserving personhood in order to live a full life in old age.

Well-Being in Old Age

What people saw as a good life to begin with, as well as how they talked about it, was shaped by the setting in which they lived. Both economic and cultural features were evident in the ways people evaluated their lives and assigned themselves scores on our ladder of well-being. The clustering of Chinese responses about the statistical mean clearly reflects the philosophical mean of Confucian moderation. The low scores from wealthy Herero men reflect a cultural adaptation to scarcity and unpredictability of resources: Those who have must share. The rich and powerful Herero elders were following a prudent path of deemphasizing their relatively advantaged circumstances, which in their culture imply *noblesse oblige* responsibilities for the less fortunate.

There is also patterning in the *ways* in which responses vary or not among individuals within the different locations. Definitions of old age itself show their influence. Where age is defined by physical capacity, old age is associated with lower self-evaluation of well-being. Where social definitions of age open up other bases of evaluation, old people may evaluate their lives more positively than young, as is the case in the United States and in Blessington. Another factor in this particular pattern is that the template of a staged life course also shapes answers about well-being when such a template is available. Younger respondents in Swarthmore, for example, reserve higher scores for the later stages of their lives, when they assume they will have achieved more of their goals.

What was not said about reasons for well-being in some cases offered as much insight as what was, by revealing what people apparently took for granted and therefore did not mention or mentioned only when it was lacking in the extreme. Considering the responses from older persons, for example, it is in Ireland and the United States that references to social themes, in particular kinship, appear most frequently. Material and physical themes are mentioned more often when they are problematic, by people who evaluate their well-being at lower levels. Conversely, in Botswana and Hong Kong material and physical themes are most frequent. Social domains, especially kinship, are apparently taken for granted unless they are problematic, for these topics are more frequently mentioned by those who place themselves lower on the well-being ladder.

In addition, basic aspects of the different locations influenced the overall frequency of references to certain themes. The relative scarcity of resources for most people in Hong Kong and for everyone in the Kalahari, especially in a period of drought, appears in the high frequency of references to these issues by people of both sexes and all ages. What makes life bad is lack of resources, and what would make life better is adequate resources. The broad differences within this similarity of scarcity appear in the secondary themes. In Botswana people talked about their physical status, which for !Kung and Herero has direct consequences for their ability to obtain material resources. In Hong Kong people talked about family, mainly in terms of care provided—or not provided—by children for their aging parents. In Ireland and the United States these broad patterns were not apparent because there was more diversity of response—especially in Blessington and the two American towns—where almost equal proportions of the participants referred to each major theme. More variable, personalized views of the good life appear to be a luxury in themselves, available only when people can take their minds off the bare necessities of survival.

In all research sites, older people talked about physical health and function as a source of well-being more than any other age group except among the !Kung. It was also the case everywhere that the people who felt their own health was poorest most frequently talked about health issues as the reason for well-being. A less anticipated but substantial emphasis on health and functionality by people in very good health appeared in Swarthmore and among Herero. We saw this as an important reminder, first, that frailty can affect well-being not only as an actual condition but as a focus for fearful anticipation, and second, that loss of functionality undermines social participation in an American suburb almost as inexorably as it undermines participation in subsistence activities in the Kalahari.

Life stages appeared in two guises in our analysis of the ways people talked about their well-being. First, as a topic, life stages and their associated expectations were used as gauges for well-being in Blessington, Momence, Swarthmore, and the higher-income neighborhoods of Hong Kong. People in these places talked about how well they were doing in terms of what they thought they should have accomplished according to the norms of certain stages of life. Life stages also demarcated categories of response by different people in these same sites. Younger people, for example, talked more frequently about personal issues, often with explicit references to goals and achievements within a life plan. As we mentioned above, when contrasted with responses from the other research areas, these are a reminder that personal development and life plans scheduling personal achievements must be seen as luxuries in worldwide perspective. The fortunate fact that bereavement and widowhood had not yet occurred was also more likely to be given as a reason for well-being by older persons who perceived themselves to be in a life stage where such events usually arrived. Here the contrast with what was said in Africa highlights the relative predictability of lives in which losses through death are associated with only some stages instead of being risks faced at all times by people of all ages.

Perceptions of the Life Course

Links to broad characteristics of the sites such as societal scale, industrial production, welfare state policies, and stability are most direct for the cognitive maps of an abstract life course. These connections are mediated in more complex ways when we shift from cognitive to social mapping of age boundaries. In addition, of course, the cultural construction of a life course itself becomes an influential channel through which broad societal attributes reach into individual lives.

The card sort was our principal method for discovering perceptions about the life course. As we recounted in Chapter 6, this technique produced information about age in two ways. First, through the difficulties we encountered in using it in !Kung villages and in Clifden, the sorting task differentiated from the other sites these two communities in which neither chronological age, age categories, nor the concept of a structured life course had local, real-life salience. The people in these two places who did arrange our hypothetical persons into an abstract model of a life course were either recent arrivals (Clifden) or learned to do it as an artificial task to assist the interviewer (!Kung). In the other five of our seven locations, age was clearly a meaningful concept, and people also told us a great deal about how they perceived different phases of the life course.

Our comparisons of the characteristics of the two places where age and the life course were not salient, and of the attributes of individuals within the different sites who had difficulty participating in this part of the interview, highlighted several meanings of age associated with the nation-state, industrial organization of work, size of social field, predictability of life events, and variability in timing of the assumption of social roles. These are all rooted in the scale, resource base, and stability of the societies we studied.

Chronological age has been adopted as a criterion for the bureaucratic sorting of persons in every nation-state, although it is used with varying degrees of flexibility. Welfare states in particular have used chronological age to segment populations into various categories of beneficiary. The industrial organization of work differentiates workplace from household and introduces specialized institutions of education whose grading by age has become one of the most important calibrators of the life course for both those in school and their parents. Universal education is also a characteristic of industrial nation-states, and educational level appears to account for discomfort with the assumptions of the card sort for some individuals in Clifden, Momence, and Hong Kong as well as for almost all !Kung.

The !Kung are the clearest-cut case of the general association between the industrial nation-state and the salience of age and the life course because they experience virtually none of these. Clifden is a more nuanced example and reveals more clearly how the society-level characteristics we are discussing affect the lives of individuals. Ireland is, of course, an industrial nation and a welfare state. However, residents of Clifden do not participate fully in the system of wage labor, and the very high proportion of adults who receive the "dole" are not differentiated sharply from those who by virtue of their age receive the old-age pension. The Clifden residents for whom age and the structure of a life course *were* salient notions were most often non-locally-born individuals who had a substantially greater exposure to the national system of education. Clifden and the !Kung villages are also the smallest social fields in our study. The consequence of this for the salience of age as a basis of categorization has more to do with categories than with age. When other individuals are familiar, either through direct experience or through a shared history, it is not necessary to think about them as members of abstract categories. This tendency to give higher salience to particularistic than to universalistic characteristics is exactly what was revealed in the !Kung and Clifden interviews.

Unpredictability of life events also reduces the perceived reasonableness of a staged view of the life course. The sources of unpredictability may, of course, vary. For elderly Chinese in Hong Kong it resulted mainly from political disorder; for !Kung and Herero in Botswana it was correlated with vulnerability to drought and disease.

The second type of information about the life course came from the card sort interviews in the five other research sites, in which age and the life course were meaningful concepts. Perceptions about them shared some universal patterns and from other points of view varied widely. The numbers of life stages identified varied, but within a narrower range across the sites, if means are compared, than within them, if individual responses are compared. The greatest average number of stages was 5.1 in the suburban American community; the smallest average number was 3.9 among the Herero in Botswana. There was also greater consensus, as indicated by a smaller standard deviation, among the Herero and the least consensus in Swarthmore. Within the suburban American community, individual responses ranged from 1 to 11 stages within a life course. The markers of age boundaries were chronological everywhere except in Africa. (Herero life stages were bounded by generation, not age.) From a chronological point of view the earliest age, on average, at which participants in the interviews would use the label "old" was 60 in Hong Kong, and Momence, and 65 in

Ireland and Swarthmore. As the number of stages increased, the lower boundary of this oldest stage moved up. For example, in Swarthmore the shift was from an average entry age of 61 for people who saw three stages in the life course to 68 for those who saw five stages, to 71 for those who saw seven or more. Old age began to be subdivided when people defined five or more stages, and when old age was viewed as having two or more phases, entry into the first one remained chronological, but entry into the later one(s) was signaled by physical status.

The content that was assigned to various stages of life displayed some universal themes across our sites, and others that were distinctive to certain locations. Kinship, reproduction, and domestic living arrangements were sources of significant thresholds in the life course everywhere, as shown, for instance, in the first axis of our multidimensional scaling results. In the industrial sites, various experiences beyond family and household—education, careers, mortgage payments, roles in community organizations—were additional sources of differentiation in the life course.

Age as a Social Boundary

The meanings of age that we could observe in behavior were only partly isomorphic with the abstract stages and categories people described when they talked about the life course. Among the !Kung the parallelism was clearest. Age categorization was not culturally relevant, and channeling of social behavior by age was absent to the point that it was difficult ever to find a situation in which the participants were not of mixed ages. The visual image of !Kung villages that Jennie Keith recorded in the journal of her visit to Botswana was of a coral reef, because people of all ages worked, rested, played, ate together, and were in close and almost constant physical contact—standing close together, frequently touching and leaning on one another.

Among the Herero the social meanings of age visible in the villages also corresponded to the abstract view of the life course described in interviews. The stages of life that Herero talked about had a generational rather than a chronological base, with a significant emphasis on seniority defined by position in the lineage. The first view of a Herero village shows social categories of generation as well as of gender. Older women in imposing two-pointed turbans sit in the shade of trees near their round thatched houses, with clumps of children nearby. Men are less immediately apparent because they are tending cattle—adolescents usually outside the village driving animals to graze or to water, adults near the corral, smoking tobacco. Seniority is most apparent in the ritual role of the senior wife of the senior man who "owns" the village, as she tends the sacred flame of the ancestors that must burn continuously between her house and the corral. The authority brought by seniority is exercised most visibly by the older women who command the children, many of them "fostered," who carry water and wood, watch the cooking fires, shoo the flies, and push the churn suspended from an overhanging branch.

In Ireland the social differentiation was greater in Blessington than Clifden, as shown, for instance, by Blessington's Senior Citizens Committee and specialized housing for the elderly. This social differentiation was consistent with the greater participation of Blessington residents in our sorting task. The higher employment levels in Blessington contributed to the greater differentiation of daily life for people of different ages. In Clifden, the lack of age categorization that led local people to find our age interview puzzling was also apparent in the shops and streets of the town. Age channeled social participation only as it was associated with physical frailty great enough to restrict mobility, and even the housebound were routinely visited by relatives and neighbors as well as by representatives of the national health service.

The two American communities did not differ markedly from the point of view of abstract models of the life course. Likewise in both the small town and the suburb we observed fine age distinctions separating people who carried out different activities, often in separate spaces, for many hours a day. Schools, clubs, workplaces, even movie theaters, bars, and apartment complexes contained people of different categories defined by chronological age.

However, there were important differences in the social meaning of age in Momence and Swarthmore. The intervening factor was residential stability, which made possible a ladder of seniority *within* community organizations in Momence. In Swarthmore age differentiation extended across the community, rather than being contained within each organization, so that many groups had memberships mainly within one age range. Consequently there was little opportunity for a seniority principle to influence the position of older residents as it did in Momence. The lack of residential stability in Swarthmore also reduced the influence of the family as a remaining haven for intergenerational relationships. Swarthmore was the site in which younger people's most common answer to our question about usual relationships with elderly was "I see them on the street."

In Hong Kong another distinction appeared, between the closeness or separation of age categories in space and their social integration. One of the more striking responses we received to questions about the age categories in which people knew most and fewest individuals was from Hong Kong, where according to these interview data, social networks were predominately homogeneous by age. However, almost every person who answered in this way was at the time living in a multigenerational household, and that household shared a very small apartment. The intervening factor here was the extensive and rapid social change that separated the generations by lifestyle and values, regardless of how closely they might live together in space.

Political Economy

Our chapter on political economy examined directly the influence of intervention by the nation-state on the lives of the elderly. At the most abstract level, state intervention posed a paradox of its own. State intervention in local communities and individual lives brings benefits to older persons, but eligibility for those benefits is defined by chronological age. This introduction, or reinforcement, of chronology as a basis of social differentiation may have negative effects on the social integration of older persons unless it is counteracted by other features of the welfare system or by attributes of other social domains such as kinship. Even the powerful influence of state structures in education or health is mediated by cultural and social factors such as family organization, definitions of personhood, and values about dependency. The least state intervention is apparent in Botswana, although Herero experience more than !Kung, both in education and in health care. As we will discuss further, the availability of education is undermining the availability of children as helpers for elderly Herero. Among the other societies, Ireland and the United States are both welfare states, whereas colonial policy toward Hong Kong has emphasized income maintenance but not social welfare. What Ireland and Hong Kong share is an assumption of a role for kin in providing support for the elderly. The distinction is that policy in Hong Kong is built on the assumption that care from kin is a *substitute* for public resources, so that public funds are used primarily for elderly without families. In Ireland public resources are used to *support* care from kin. Many Irish people are able to offer care to kin because public health providers give affordable in-home care that allows the old person to remain near relatives. Younger relatives are also not faced with the all-or-nothing choice between institutionalizing an old person or providing extensive hands-on care themselves that commonly confronts their counterparts in the United States.

Between the United States and Ireland, two dimensions of comparison are especially important. The strong emphasis on individual responsibility in much of American culture appears in norms about "taking care of oneself" and wishes for independence. In both communities in Ireland, we heard and saw evidence of strong family ties that were manifested in care for elderly kin, in many cases extending beyond the nuclear family to uncles, aunts, and other relatives. American entrepreneurial values and emphasis on specialized, technological approaches to problems also appear in an organization of medical care that contrasts with the Irish national health system. The comparison among our sites also showed that the attitudes of older people toward support available from the state are shaped both by their cohort and by cultural values about independence and dependence. The earlier experiences shared by members of birth cohorts have marked effects on appreciation of support from the state in both Ireland and Hong Kong. Old people in both places warmly describe the positive contrast of publicly financed benefits available to them now with the "bad old days" when their own parents and grandparents were elderly. In our American communities, attitudes toward state support are ambivalent but consistently rooted in wishes to perceive oneself as independent. Health care and income maintenance provided by public resources are positive because they help avoid dependence on children but are negative if they carry any hint of "welfare."

Consequences of Age
Boundaries for the Lives of the Old

When the !Kung and the Clifden sites are contrasted with the other five, the impact of the differential salience of age and life stage boundaries on the lives of older people is clear. For !Kung and for Irish residents of Clifden, old age does not pose a threat to personhood or individuality. There is not a salient category of old person to be stereotyped or stigmatized, and there are no barriers to social participation except those of physical frailty.

Among the views of the life course that emerged from the card sort in the five places where most people participated in it, the variation with the clearest consequences for older people is the extent to which physical and social boundaries of old age are distinguished. In the more complex definitions of later life in which people identified many phases of old age, physical decline could be perceived as a stage people might *never* reach. In other words, the social and physical definitions of old age were seen as distinct. There are two important risks and one possible benefit associated with this distinction. The first risk is denial, manifested on either individual or societal levels, of the likelihood of experiencing frailty in old age and a consequent lack of planning for it. The second is generalization backward from the frailty associated with later stages of aging to the chronological number used to define entry into old age. This opens a vulnerability to stereotypes of decrepitude for people defined as old chronologically—a possibility that is nonexistent when age is defined only by physical status, as it is among !Kung. The possible benefit of the complex definition of age is that the notion of old age as a life stage with positive attributes becomes at least plausible, rather than the oxymoron that "good old age" appeared to be for the !Kung.

The paradox with which we began this chapter is that the increasing physical security that makes this positive definition at least possible is often not matched by maintenance of the true social security of continuing personal identity and social participation. The tensions between these positive and negative possibilities are played out especially clearly in the lives of older persons in both the Irish and the American communities. As we will review below, other aspects of the settings that exert the strongest pull toward the opposite poles defining these tensions are family structure and health care financing.

Family Structure

In both Momence and Herero communities, those in the older categories face fewer obstacles to maintaining—*simultaneously*—personal identity, channels for social participation, and access to care. In the suburban community of Swarthmore, older persons are required to make choices among these three very basic needs. People and lives are so different in Momence and Herero communities that the two important similarities that affect the lives of their elders stand out very clearly. In both places kinship and seniority are principles that promote full participation by older persons. Kinship among Herero is *lineal*. Affiliations perceived as kinship are traced in a line of descent from a common ancestor, either through males or through females or sometimes both, but separately. Lineal kinship defines corporate groups, lineages, within which property is owned, authority exercised, and responsibility for members shared. All Herero have a place in such a kin group, and because of the seniority principles, older Herero have a privileged place that includes entitlement to respect and to care. Because of the corporate or categorical nature of their kinship organization, these entitlements are "vested" and "portable" from village to village. Kinship is very important in the Momence community, but it is of a different type. Like most Americans of European descent, people in Momence trace their kinship *bilaterally*. This way of reckoning kinship starts with an individual, and relationships are traced outward in all directions through both mother and father. Bilateral kinship cannot form corporate groups without the addition of some other principle, such as "the relatives I like" or "the relatives that live nearby." For kin to share property or responsibility, individuals must choose to do that. Position in any ad hoc kin group like this is not transferable in the way it can be in a lineal system. In Momence kinship can play an important role in community life because residence in the town is very stable. Kin are available to provide care for older people, although this responsibility is viewed in more individual terms than among Herero. Residential stability is also the reason why seniority can be a basis of prestige and resource control in Momence. Because American society is not structured primarily by kinship, as among Herero, seniority within a family is not transferable into seniority in any community. The advantages of more years for accumulating information, experience, and social connections are relevant only locally and to the same cast of characters. Because residential stability in Momence makes seniority meaningful, there is a structural basis for interconnections between residents of different ages.

By contrast, residents of Swarthmore have many fewer kin nearby (mean of under one close relative compared to mean of 2.2 close relatives in Momence). The lack of residential stability undermines seniority as a principle. The most readily available groups within which personal identity and social participation can be maintained in this suburban setting are those whose members are all old—retirement communities, and senior organizations. For many Swarthmore residents, access to care, either from kin or in an institutional setting, requires a move away from town. Lack of residential stability and of seniority as a principle presents these older people with difficult trade-offs. Personhood is best preserved in age-homogeneous groups, but at the cost of connection to others in the community. Maintaining responsibility for oneself, a requirement for full personhood, requires planning for care, which requires moving into a new setting, which erases personhood, unless the setting is reserved for older people, in which case it cuts links to those of other ages.

Health and Functionality

Everywhere in the world of our study old people talked to us in worried ways about their health. In every research location old people viewed their health more negatively than younger persons, used health facilities more, described more chronic health problems, and more frequently said that these problems restricted their behavior. There were, however, substantial differences in both absolute and relative levels of these health problems. Also, in every place we worked there was a decline in functionality with increasing age, although the patterns of this decline were not identical. Most important from our point of view was the variation we observed in what effects these declines in health and functionality had on the quality of lives for old people in our different communities. The two most influential factors in explaining this variation were the requirements of full functionality in the different locations and the compensatory supports available.

The requirements of functionality were more directly linked to the societal attributes of resource level, stability, and subsistence technology. Physical capacity is more salient to subsistence activities in Botswana, while memory is more salient in Ireland and in the United States. In Hong Kong, the effects of rapid social change appear in the meaning of literacy as an indicator of functionality not accessible to most elders. Available supports are linked to societal features such as scale and stability but are also mediated by social and cultural mechanisms such as kinship structures and values about independence and dependence. In Botswana the buffer between frail elders and social participation is provided by kin. This is also true in Hong Kong, but the buffer is being weakened as generational consensus about kin obligations declines. In Ireland there is a double compensation for frailty because the national health system and the family complement each other in keeping old people in their communities. In the United States, the identification of personhood with independence can combine with the high-tech and institutional provision of health care to send old people away from the community once they become frail. In Momence, residential stability that maintains local kin networks, and lack of resources to purchase long-term institutional care, shields most elderly from this double jeopardy. However, in Swarthmore the pattern was as apparent to the older residents as it was to us. Because acknowledgment of frailty brings the threat of exile, old people either go to great lengths to conceal frailty or exert as much personal control as possible over the inevitable move by beginning at relatively young ages to create life plans that include it.

Planning Beyond the Paradox:
Project AGE as a Guide for Aging in the Future

What can our years of comparative study offer as guidance for better lives in old age? The guidance we have discovered was expressed in many voices and in the worldwide range of environments offered by our research locations. Some themes appear throughout our data; others are clearest in one site or another.

If we listen first to the messages that come consistently from all our sites, they are the ones that follow. Physical aspects of aging must be distinguished from social and cultural aspects. Amelioration of physical frailty must be accomplished without loss of social participation. Neither physical decline nor the interventions made to arrest it should be allowed to threaten personhood of the elderly. In the modern societies in which old age is no longer coterminous with decrepitude, older people must be freed from the ironic choice between physical and social well-being.

If we shift our attention to the guidance that comes most clearly from specific sites, we hear the following. In Botswana, most dramatically among the Herero, we are reminded that kinship is *not* solely a biological relationship. The fostering norm among Herero offers great flexibility in "family" provision of care for older people. For many Americans, the biological imagery through which we view kinship is a barrier to acceptance, much less support, of bonds not based in what we see as "blood" ties. The elderly widows who have difficulty remaining in Swarthmore, in part because they live alone in large houses, are prevented from dividing these houses and renting to students because borough zoning laws limit households to families. More than four "unrelated" persons may not form a household and share a residence. Here the cultural definitions that impede social creativity by older persons are not of age but of kinship and household. Meanwhile older residents continue to leave the town partly because they cannot alone maintain large, old houses that require standing on ladders to change light-bulbs, extensive yard work, and carrying groceries and luggage up flights of stairs. The Herero and their fostered children remind us that kinship and who shares a household are not exclusively based in biology anywhere. These are cultural definitions that, if reified into laws, may lag behind changes in demography and social needs.

The Irish sites offer their strongest advice to us in the area of health care. The Irish health care system gives priority to home care for all over widespread availability of the most sophisticated medical technology. This priority makes support from the national health system itself supportive of continued participation in communities and consequently of care from kin.

Older people in Swarthmore, hoping to avoid having to leave town in order to provide care for themselves, had begun during our research to work with an experiment in "Life Care Without Walls." However, key players in this group continued to drop out in response to *momenti mori* such as their own experience of an illness or injury, the death of a friend, a nudge from concerned and distant children, or a gentle threat from the director of a life care community about his lengthening waiting list. As the elder drain continued, the remaining older residents found it difficult to maintain the momentum to create locally based solutions to health care needs. They also began to question their own decision to stay in town, wondering if it was "too risky" or "too great a gamble."

From our research in Hong Kong, perhaps the clearest counsel is the importance of basing policy decisions on actual circumstances rather than on norms for behavior that no longer exert their former influence. The Hong Kong health care policies that assume only elderly without children require support from public sources are a cautionary tale.

From our two American communities, the sharpest message is about the consequences of residential stability. It is the stability of residence in Momence that makes possible the continuing influence of a seniority principle. This principle offers a basis for the continuing influence in community affairs of older people themselves, who participate as the senior members within organizations whose memberships encompass many life stages. The more age-specialized organizations of Swarthmore do not offer these opportunities.

How can we combine these findings into guidance for personal and societal decisions that will lead to better lives in old age? *First,* we must be vigilant to question age separation wherever it occurs, no matter how "natural" it seems. *Second,* we should be alert to what older people themselves are saying and doing. Rather than inventing new solutions, as social scientists and policymakers, we should work to reduce the age barriers that now impede the innovation and flexibility of older persons. Just as we needed to be careful to discover, not assume, the salience and meanings of age as we formed questions in fieldwork, we need to be careful to discover, not assume, the salience and meanings of age as we form social programs.

For example, health policy designed to improve the physical circumstances of older persons should not be allowed to create or maintain social barriers to community participation. We must be vigilant in the current revisions of health care financing. Access to medical care should reinforce rather than threaten local and personal networks of support, as it does in Ireland. What we observed in Swarthmore is a strong warning that although it may be for social and cultural reasons that the threat of frailty seems so overwhelming, individual and societal responses may be misguidedly focused exclusively on avoidance of physical decline. In fact more attention to decoupling the physical frailty from the negative effects on personhood and community participation would decrease the level of threat and perhaps permit more reasonable approaches to defining medical priorities on both individual and societal levels. If people were less afraid that physical decline would lead to exile from a community, they would be more likely to acknowledge deficits and seek care. If there were more demand for community-based, low-tech care, national decisions might take a new direction that would further reduce the threat of physical frailty to personhood and community participation.

Considering the influence visible in Clifden, Momence, and Botswana of the positive interaction between kinship and residential stability should lead us, in more personal domains, to examine assumptions about the weighting of the short run over the long term and the individual over the collective.

As the widows of Swarthmore can testify, following the cultural rules that lead to success in midlife may have less desirable consequences in old age. Viewed in the context of entire lives and whole families, decisions about work or education may look very different than those viewed in the moment and with a focus on one person. What is the "best" job or the "best" college are different questions asked in different time frames and from the point of view of one member versus the point of view of a family.

Our comparative study shows us both warnings and visions for an aging society. As individuals, we must learn to think about whole lives and whole families. As members of communities and societies, we must be alert to keep physical and cultural boundaries of age distinct. Overall we must be vigilant that cultural age barriers do not replace physical age barriers to full participation in our own aging society of the future.

Appendix:
Instructions on
Playing the Age Game

The following is the "script" used in Momence for interviewers administering the Age Game. In each site a similar script was developed. Following an introduction to the project, the interviewer was instructed to introduce the respondent to the Age Game and the sorting task. The remaining portions of the Age Game focused on the names and characteristics of age groups, an evaluation of age groups, and questions about people in the oldest groups who were doing especially well or having difficulties in old age.

Instruction Book: Project AGE, Momence, Illinois

Introduction to Project AGE

As we discussed before, the goal of our project is to learn about the meaning of age in various communities. Momence is one of three communities in which we are talking to people about their views of age. The other two are Swarthmore, Pennsylvania, a suburb of Philadelphia, and urban Hong Kong.

One of the ways we hope to learn about the meaning of age is by interviewing adults of all ages in each community. Although the focus of our study is on what about a community most affects its older members, we feel that the experiences and attitudes of people of all ages have important effects on what it is like to be old.

The interview includes questions about your views of different age groups and different stages of life. The interviews will be filed anonymously, so your name will not be attached to any of your answers. We do not think that there are any personal or embarrassing questions in the interview, but if there is anything you would rather not answer, please just tell me and we'll skip it.

Is there anything else you'd like to know about our study before we begin?

Our interview is in two parts. The first is the Age Game you may have read about in the newspaper. In the second part, we have a few questions about your life and about Momence.

Part I: Introduction to the
Age Game and Sorting of the Cards

We call the first part of our interview "The Age Game" because it involves cards and the sorting of cards.

We have cards describing people that we would like you to sort into age groups by making piles of cards that describe people that you think are about the same age.

We are very interested in the ways people in Momence look at age. There is no right or wrong way of organizing these cards. It is very likely that people with different points of view and with different experiences will organize them differently. What is most helpful to us is the way **you** arrange them and to know how you usually think about age groups in Momence.

The Sorting of the Cards

I have here two decks of cards. The white one describes women of different ages and the green one describes men of different ages.

Before we begin arranging the cards, I would first like you to think about the span of life from childhood to death and then to think of the different stages of life or age categories you see people moving through here in Momence. I'm going to give you the deck of cards describing people of different ages and I will ask you to sort them into these age groups.

Let us begin the Age Game with the _____ (men/women).

Would you please sort these into age groups or stages of life, based on your estimate of their ages.

INTERVIEWER:

Hand the cards of the same gender as the respondent to the respondent: Green if a man and white if a woman.

As Respondent begins the sort, talk about classification. These cards are to be classified by age, but people are also classified by other things. Give examples:

Gender—Men and Women
Race—Black, white, Asian, etc.
Ethnicity—Hispanic, Italian, Scandinavian, etc.

*If the respondent has difficulty in sorting, discuss mechanics, but **do not** sort the cards or give specific suggestions in sorting the cards. You can give examples from things that are not related to age.*

You can suggest that the respondent may want to put the age groups in order of increasing age by putting the youngest on the left and the older groups to the right.

Once the respondent is sorting, continue:

If you find some of the people a little more difficult to place in an age group, you may want to set them aside and come back to them later.

If a pile of more difficult cards is created, then once the sorting is done for that sex, ask what about that person made it difficult to place him or her in an age group. Record this in the recording booklet. Also record any commentary or observations about the sorting task (e.g., self-realizations, what characteristics respondent is using) in the space in the recording booklet.

Once the same-sex cards are sorted, hand the respondent the cards of the other sex. Have him or her repeat the sort. Let respondent do what he or she wants. If he or she makes parallel rows or puts one card on top of the other, that is fine.

After the Cards Are Sorted

Now I'd like to talk to you about the age groups you have made. Feel free to make any changes in the groups as we talk about them. Also feel free to recheck any of the age piles whenever you want.

Part II: Names and Characteristics of the Age Groups

I have several questions about each group, and we will write your answer on these cards and put it on top of your group.

At this point, make sure the age groups are in order of increasing age. Males and females are to be together in the groups, although there can be an exclusively male or exclusively female group. Ask questions 1 and 2 first for all groups, working your way from youngest to oldest.

Q-1. For each age group, would you tell me why you put these people together? What about the people in this group makes you feel they are close to each other in age? What do the people in this group have in common?

Q-2. What do you call this age group? Is there any name you give or term or phrase you use to refer to people in this group?

Once you have completed Q-1 & Q-2 and now have the yellow recording cards on top of each age group, go back to the youngest age group and ask Q-3 through Q-7 for each age group before moving on to the next age group. Record answers on Recording Card 1. If sex differences are noted, record below the line on the recording card and if necessary go to the back of the yellow card.

Now I'd like you to think of the piles you have made as age groups or stages of life. The individual cards are now less important than the age groups.

Q-3. What are the major concerns or issues facing people who are in _____ (use name of age group)?
Are they the same or different for men and women?

Q-4. What do you think is good about being a _____ (name of age group)?
What do you think is the best thing about being in this age group?
Is this the same or different for men and women?

Q-5. What do you think is undesirable about being a _____ (name of age group)?
What is the hardest thing about being in this age group?
Is this the same or different for men and women?

Q-6. How does one become a _____ (age group name)?
What marks the turning point at which a person enters this category?
Is this the same or different for men and women?

Q-7. Approximately what are the ages or the range of ages for the people called _____ (age group name)?
What is the age range for people in this category?
Is this the same or different for men and women?

Now move to the recording booklet to record the following two questions and continue the completion of Part II.

Q-8. In what age group would you place yourself? (RECORD IN RECORDING BOOKLET)

Q-9. How old are you? (RECORD IN RECORDING BOOKLET)

Part III: Evaluation of Age Categories

So far we have been talking about characteristics of your age groups. Now I'd like to talk about age groups more generally.

Now you move to the blue Recording Card 2. Fill in the number and name in the proper space. Place the blue recording cards on top of the yellow recording cards. You may keep these cards in order of increasing age for the purposes of recording the answers and, once Q-9 is complete, place them with their respective age groups.

Q-1. First, in which one of the age categories would you most like to be? Why?

Q-2. In which one of these age categories would you least like to be? Why?

Note: There is no Q-3.

Q-4. In which of these groups would you say you know the most people in Momence? (circle on Card 2 MOST/LEAST/NEITHER)

Q-5. In which of these groups would you say you know the fewest people in Momence? (circle on Card 2 MOST/LEAST/NEITHER)

Q-6. Which of these age groups is the easiest to get along with? (circle on Card 2 EASIEST/HARDEST/NEITHER)

Q-7. Which of these age groups is the hardest to get along with? (circle on Card 2 EASIEST/HARDEST/NEITHER)

Part IV: Older Age Groups

As you know, our research is focused on the meaning of old age in the communities we are studying around the world. Now I would like to ask you a few questions about the older age groups you have made.

Record the responses to the following questions on Card 2. The questions should only be asked for age groups which exceed 61 years of age and include people who are over 61. If an age group is bracketed 55-61, then it would be included as older. If a category includes people of a much younger age, ask for an example from the older end of the range.

Ask Q-1–Q-9 for the youngest of the older age groups, and if there are more older groups, repeat.

Q-1. Is there anyone in this age group that you know well here in Momence? (This means having more than a speaking acquaintance with.)

Write "Y" or "N" on the blue card.

If no, ask respondent to think of the last person in this group they saw or spoke to in Momence. If respondent can't do that ask him or her to think of the last person in this group he or she saw or spoke to anywhere.

Q-2a. Think about this person. *I DON'T NEED TO KNOW THEIR NAME, BUT* I would like to know if this person is a man or a woman and about what age they are (record on Card 2).

2b. Where do they live? (NEIGHBORHOOD OR, IF NOT MOMENCE, TOWN/STATE)

2c. When was the last time you spoke to this person who is included in this age group?

Q-3. What did you talk about? . . . do together?

Q-4. How long have you known him/her?

Q-5. How did you get to know each other?

Q-6. Do you ever help each other out in any way? How?

Q-7. What kind of relationship or contact would you say people who are in your age group in Momence *usually* have with someone who is in this group?

(Record on the back of card 2.)

If respondent has difficulty, prompt for quality, frequency, and content or basis of relationships.

Next I have a couple of questions about people you know who are doing especially well in the late years and about people who are finding old age to be a difficult time.

Q-8. Think of a person you know fairly well who is doing especially well in this stage of life. (*Name not necessary*)

a. Is this person a man or woman?

b. About how old is is person?

c. Why do they seem to you to be doing so well in this stage of life?

Q-9. Now, think of a person you know fairly well who is also in the same group but who is experiencing difficulties in this stage of life. **Again, I do not need to know their name.**

a. Is this person a man or a woman?

b. About how old is this person?

c. In what way do they seem to be finding _____(age group name) a particularly difficult stage in life?

For the oldest group, probe for others like the person having difficulty with this age to see if there is any name given to people experiencing difficulties in old age. Note term near "why" for Q-9 on the blue recording card.

Recording Cards

Since the units of reference were age groups with considerable variation in number differentiated, we faced some difficulty in recording respondents' responses. After discussing a number of alternatives, we settled on using what we called "elicitation cards." Where respondents used tables to sort the Age Game deck, we used two cards to record their answers for each age group. Examples of these cards are as follows. The numbers on the card refer to the questions outlined above. During the interview, the elicitation cards were placed on top of the piles of person cards. At the conclusion of the Age Game, both the person and the elicitation cards were secured together for each age group and placed in an envelope. In reviewing the interview, the interviewer recorded the ID numbers of the personae on the back of the first elicitation card.

Age Group Name _____ # _____ CD# 1(PTII)

| Q-1 | Q-1 |

Points of similarity (Q-2)   Major concerns/issues (Q-3)

Best thing about (Q-4)   Worst thing about (Q-5)

Entrance into (Q-6)

15..20..25..30..35..40..45..50..55..60..65..70..75..80..85..90..

(Q-7)

Age Group Name _____ _____# CD# 2 (PT III)

(Q-2)

Age Preference: (Q-8)   Know people (Q-4 & 5)

Rank: Most/Least/Neither

RE: (Q-9)

Get along with (Q-6 & 7)

Easiest/Hardest/Neither

OLDER GROUPS ONLY: (PT IV)

Age: M/F (Q-2 & 2a) Last time spoke to (Q-2)

Talk about/did (Q-3)   Person doing well (Q-8)

Age: RE:

How long known (Q-4)

How met? (Q-5)   Person experiencing difficulties (Q-9)

Age: RE:

Help out? How? (Q-6)

Q-7 on back

Endnotes

1. Multidimensional scaling (MDS) creates one-, two-, three- . . . five- or more dimensional graphs plotting each object ("people") in relationship to each other. Because of display issues, usually only the one-dimensional, two-dimensional, and possibly the three-dimensional solutions are presented. Cluster analysis creates branching tree diagrams in which the objects of greatest similarity are linked first and those of least similarity last. The image is one of branches, with high ones being the last joined and the most dissimilar and low ones being the most similar and clustered first.

Both techniques call for data in the form of a matrix of similarity or dissimilarity. A number of standard algorithms are frequently used and readily available. However, none of these was totally appropriate for our purposes. Three variables are important in calculating the matrices: (a) the age group of the first person, (b) the age group of the second person, and (c) the total number of age groups. By taking the difference between the two groups we have an indication of similarity. If they are in the same group, the difference is zero. If one is in the first group and the other is in the fifth group, the difference is 4. The absolute value is taken, thus eliminating the effect of negative numbers. We control for the variability in numbers of age groups differentiated by dividing our indication of similarity by the total number of age groups. If the similarity is perfect or zero, it will remain so because zero divided by any number is zero. If the similarity is 4 and the number of age groups is five, then the similarity score is .8. On the other hand, if the similarity is 4 and the number of age groups is 11, the similarity is .36. In the resulting matrix, the scores that are closer to zero indicate the most similarity and those closer to 1.0 the least similarity.

In the "Dimensions of the Life Course" section of Chapter 6, multidimensional scaling was used to examine the structure of the life course. In the "Stages of Life" section of Chapter 6, cluster analysis was used to compare the stages of life in five of our research locations.

2. The most direct way of accomplishing this is to actually sort the person cards into the four quadrants and to examine them for similarities and differences. A more systematic strategy is to enter the "people" and their attributes into a database management program (dBASE) and to order them by quadrants. With the attributes recorded as variables (i.e., children's status, work status, marital status, and the like), the differences and similarities are readily apparent. In any printed report, one scans each attribute one at a time for the prevalent pattern—such as "all are single" or "most have paid their mortgages."

3. In the coding of these data, we were very conservative in the boundaries of this category. For a response to be included, it had to make reference to the school level of the child. Otherwise, responses that referred to the ages of children or a more general status of children were coded as domestic roles.

4. Two statistical packages were used. The first was Johnson's Hierarchical Cluster Analysis. The second was the Cluster Program in SPSS. Comparison of a sample of dendrograms generated in both programs produced identical results. SPSS was selected primarily because of the graphic display. Each program requires a matrix of dissimilarities to be used for the generation of the dendrogram. The same matrices used in MDS were used for this analysis.

References

Aalen, F. H. A., Gilmore, D. A., & Williams, D. (1967). *West Wicklow: Background for development*. Dublin: Trinity College, Dept. of Geography.

Aldenderfer, M. S., & Blashfeld, R. K. (1984). *Cluster analysis*. Newbury Park, CA: Sage.

Almagor, U. (1978a). Gerontocracy, polygyny and scarce resources. In J. S. La Fontaine (Ed.), *Sex and age as principles of social differentiation* (pp. 139-158). London: Academic Press.

Almagor, U. (1978b). *Pastoral partners*. Manchester, U.K.: Manchester University Press.

Amoss, P. (1981). Coast Salish elders. In P. Amoss & S. Harrell (Eds.), *Other ways of growing old* (pp. 227-248). Palo Alto, CA: Stanford University Press.

Baltes, M. M., Wahl, H.-W., & Schmid-Furstoss, U. (1990). The daily life of elderly Germans: Activity patterns, personal control, and functional health. *Journal of Gerontology, 45*(4), 173-179.

Baltes, P. B., & Nesselroade, J. R. (1979). History of rationale of longitudinal research. In *Longitudinal research in the study of behavior and development* (pp. 1-39). New York: Academic Press.

Bearon, L. B. (1989). No great expectations: The underpinnings of life satisfaction for older women. *The Gerontologist, 29*(6), 772-778.

Bernardi, B. (1985). *Age class systems: Social institutions and polities based on age* (D. Kertzer, Trans.). Cambridge, U.K.: Cambridge University Press.

Blandford, A. A., & Chappell, N. L. (1990). Subjective well-being among native and non-native elderly persons: Do differences exist? *Canadian Journal on Aging, 9*(4), 386-399.

Botswana Meat Commission. (1991). *Annual Report*. Lobatse, Botswana: Botswana Meat Commission, Private Bag 4.

Bould, S., Sanborn, B., & Reif, L. (1989). *Eighty-five plus: The oldest old*. Belmont, CA: Wadsworth.

Campbell, A. (1981). *The sense of well-being in America: Recent patterns and trends.* New York: McGraw-Hill.

Campbell, A., Converse, P. E., & Rodgers, W. L. (1976). *The quality of American life: Perceptions, evaluations, and satisfactions.* New York: Russell Sage.

Campbell, R. T., Abolafia, J., & Maddox, G. L. (1985). Life course analysis in social gerontology. In A. S. Rossi (Ed.), *Gender and the life course* (pp. 301-318). New York: Aldine.

Cantril, H. (1965). *The pattern of human concerns.* New Brunswick, NJ: Rutgers University Press.

Cawley, M. (1979). Rural industrialization and social change in western Ireland. *Sociologia Ruralis, 19*(1), 43-57.

Cawley, M. (1980). *Aspects of rural-urban migration in western Ireland.* Unpublished manuscript.

Central Committee on Services for the Elderly. (1988). *Report of the Central Committee on Services for the Elderly.* Hong Kong: Hong Kong Government Printer.

Chappell, N. L., & Badger, M. (1989). Social isolation and well-being. *Journal of Gerontology, 44*(5), S169-176.

Chappell, N. L., & Havens, B. (1980). Old and female: Testing the double jeopardy hypothesis. *Sociological Quarterly, 21,* 157-171.

Chi, I., & Lee, J.-J. (1989). *A health survey of the elderly in Hong Kong.* Hong Kong: University of Hong Kong, Dept. of Social Work and Social Administration.

Colby, B. N. (1975). Cultural grammars. *Science, 187,* 913-919.

Costa, Jr., P. T., Zonderman, A. B., McRae, R. R., Cornoni-Huntley, J., Locke, B. Z., & Barbano, H. E. (1987). Longitudinal analysis of psychological well-being in a national sample: Stability of mean levels. *Journal of Gerontology, 42*(1), 50-55.

Covey, H. C. (1989). Old age portrayed by the ages-of-life models from the Middle Ages to the 16th century. *The Gerontologist, 29,* 692-698.

Cowgill, D. O. (1974). Aging and modernization: A revision of the theory. In J. Gubrium (Ed.), *Communities and environment policy* (pp. 123-146). Springfield, IL: Charles C Thomas.

Cowgill, D. O., & Holmes, L. (1972). *Aging and modernization.* New York: Appleton-Century-Crofts.

Daly, M. (1981). *Social and economic history of Ireland since 1800.* Dublin: Educational Company.

Diener, E. (1984). Subjective well-being. *Psychological Bulletin, 95*(3), 542-575.

Dowd, J. (1983). Social exchange, class and old people. In J. Sokolovsky (Ed.), *Growing old in different societies: Cross cultural perspectives* (pp. 29-43). Belmont, CA: Wadsworth.

Draper, P., & Glascock, A. (n.d.). *Can you ask it? Getting answers to questions about age in different cultures.* Unpublished manuscript.

Draper, P., & Keith, J. (1992). Cultural contexts of care: Caregiving for the elderly in Africa and the U.S. *Journal of Aging Studies, 6,* 113-134.

Estes, C. (1979). *The aging enterprise.* San Francisco: Jossey-Bass.

Estes, C., Swan, J., & Gerard, L. (1984). Dominant and competing paradigms in gerontology: Towards a political economy of aging. In C. Estes & M. Minkler (Eds.), *Readings in the political economy of aging* (pp. 25-36). Farmingdale, NY: Baywood.

Evans-Pritchard, E. E. (1940). *The Nuer.* London: Oxford University Press.

Featherman, D. L. (1981). *The life span perspective in social research.* New York: Social Science Research Council.

Finley, G. F. (1982). Modernization and aging. In T. Field, A. Huston, H. Quay, L. Troll, & G. E. Finley (Eds.), *Review of human development* (pp. 511-523). New York: John Wiley.

Foyle, H., & Newham, A. T. (1963). *The Dublin-Blessington Tramway* (Locomotion Papers No. 20). Dublin: Oakwood.

Fry, C. L. (1976). The ages of adulthood: A question of numbers. *Journal of Gerontology, 31,* 170-177.

Fry, C. L. (1986). The emics of age: Cognitive anthropology and age differentiation. In C. L. Fry & J. Keith (Eds.), *New methods for old age research* (pp. 105-130). South Hadley, MA: Bergin & Garvey.

Fry, C. L. (1990). The life course in context: Implications of comparative research. In R. L. Rubinstein (Ed.), *Anthropology and aging: Comprehensive reviews* (pp. 129-152). Dordrecht, the Netherlands: Kluwer Academic Publishers.

Fry, C. L., & Keith, J. (Eds.). (1986). *New methods for old age research: Strategies for studying diversity.* South Hadley, MA: Bergin & Garvey.

George, L. K. (1981). Subjective well-being: Conceptual and methodological issues. *Annual Review of Gerontology and Geriatrics, 2,* 345-382.

George, L. K., & Landerman, R. (1984). Health and subjective well-being. *International Journal of Aging and Human Development, 19*(2), 133-156.

George, L. K., Okun, M. A., & Landerman, R. (1985). Age as a moderator of the determinants of life satisfaction. *Research on Aging, 7*(2), 209-233.

Glascock, A. P. (1982a, February). *A categorization of death: An analysis of death and dying in non-industrial societies.* Paper presented at the Society for Cross-Cultural Research Annual Meetings, Minneapolis.

Glascock, A. P. (1982b). Decrepitude and death-hastening: The nature of old age in Third World societies. In J. Sokolovsky (Ed.), *Aging and the aged in the Third World, Part I. Studies in Third World societies* (Publication No. 22, December) (pp. 43-66). Williamsburg, VA: College of William and Mary, Dept. of Anthropology.

Glascock, A. P. (1987). The myth of the Golden Isle: Old age in pre-industrial societies. In C. Kagitcibasi (Ed.), *Selected Papers Volume of the Eighth International Congress of Cross-Cultural Psychology* (pp. 403-410). Lisse, Switzerland: Swets & Zeitlinger.

Glascock, A., & Feinman, S. (1981). Social asset or social burden: An analysis of the treatment for the aged in non-industrial societies. In C. Fry (Ed.), *Dimensions: Aging, culture and health* (pp. 13-31). New York: Praeger.

Glascock, A. P., & Feinman, S. (1986). Toward a comparative framework: Propositions concerning the treatment of the aged in non-industrial societies. In C. L. Fry & J. Keith (Eds.), *New methods for old age research* (2nd ed., pp. 281-296). South Hadley, MA: Bergin & Garvey.

Goldstein, M. C., & Beall, C. (1981). Modernization and aging in the Third and Fourth Worlds: Views from the rural hinterland in Nepal. *Human Organization, 40*(1), 48-55.

Graebner, W. (1981). *A history of retirement.* New Haven: Yale University Press.

Griffith, J. W., Jeffcott, H. H., & Griffith, J. P. (1921). *The River Liffey: Proposals for the utilization of its water power.* Dublin: Hodges & Figgis.

Guinnane, T. (1991). *The aged, the Poor Law and the 1908 Old Pensions Act in Ireland.* Unpublished manuscript.

Gubrium, J. F., & Lynott, R. J. (1985). Alzheimer's disease as biographical work. In W. A. Peterson & J. Quadagno (Eds.), *Social bonds in later life* (pp. 265-285). Beverly Hills, CA: Sage.

Gubrium, J. F., & Sankar, A. (1994). *Qualitative methods in aging research.* Beverly Hills, CA: Sage.

Guillemard, A. M. (1983). *Old age and the welfare state.* London: Sage.

Hagestad, G. O. (1990). Social perspectives on the life course. In R. H. Binstock & L. K. George (Eds.), *Handbook of aging and the social sciences* (3rd ed., pp. 151-168). New York: Academic Press.

Halperin, R. (1984). Age in cultural economics: An evolutionary approach. In D. Kertzer & J. Keith (Eds.), *Age and anthropological theory* (pp. 159-194). New York: Cornell University Press.

Halperin, R. (1987). Age in cross-cultural perspective: An evolutionary approach. In P. Silverman (Ed.), *The elderly as modern pioneers* (pp. 283-311). Bloomington: Indiana University Press.

Hannan, D. F. (1979). *Displacement and development: Class, kinship and social change in Ireland* (Institute Paper No. 96). Dublin: Economic and Social Research Council.

Harpending, H., & Pennington, R. (1991). *Herero mortality after early childhood* (Population Issues Research Center Working Paper 1991-20). Madison: University of Wisconsin, 1991.

Haynes, S., & Feinlaub, M. (Eds.). (1980). *Second Conference on the Epidemiology of Aging.* Bethesda, MD: National Institutes of Health.

Heikkinen, E., Waters, W., & Brzezinski, Z. (1983). *The elderly in eleven countries: A sociomedical survey* (Public Health in Europe No. 21). Copenhagen: World Health Organization.

Hendricks, J. (1982). The elderly in society: Beyond modernization. *Social Science History, 4,* 321-345.

Hendricks, J., & Calasanti, T. (1986). Social policy on aging in the United States. In C. Phillipson & A. Walker (Eds.), *Aging and social policy: A critical assessment* (pp. 237-262). Hants, U.K.: Gower.

Hong Kong Government Information Service. (1984). *Hong Kong 1984.* Hong Kong: Author.

Horley, J. (1984). Life satisfaction, happiness, and morale: Two problems with the use of subjective well-being indicators. *The Gerontologist, 24*(2), 124-127.

Ikels, C. (1983). *Aging and adaptation: Chinese in Hong Kong and the U.S.* Hamden, CT: Archon.

Ikels, C. (1991). Aging and disability in China: Cultural issues in measurement and interpretation. *Social Science and Medicine, 32*(6), 649-665.

Ikels, C., Keith, J., Dickerson-Putman, J., Draper, P., Fry, C., Glascock, A., & Harpending, H. (1992). Perceptions of the adult life course: A cross-cultural analysis. *Ageing and Society, 12,* 48-84.

Ishii-Kuntz, M. (1990). Social interaction and psychological well-being: Comparison across stages of adulthood. *International Journal of Aging and Human Development, 30*(1), 15-36.

Johnson, P. (1989). The structured dependency of the elderly: A critical note. In M. Jeffreys (Ed.), *Growing old in the 20th century* (pp. 62-73). London: Routledge.

Kaufman, S. (1986). *The ageless self.* Madison: University of Wisconsin Press.

Keith, J. (1985). Age in anthropological research. In R. Binstock & E. Shanas (Eds.), *Handbook of aging and the social sciences* (2nd ed., pp. 91-111). New York: Van Nostrand-Reinhold.

Keith, J. (1988). Participant observation: A modest little method whose presumption may amuse you. In W. Schaie, R. Campbell, W. Meredith, & J. Nesselroade (Eds.), *Methodological issues in aging research* (pp. 211-230). New York: Springer.

Keith, J. (1990). Age in social and cultural context. In R. Binstock & L. George (Eds.), *Handbook of aging and the social sciences* (3rd ed., pp. 91-112). New York: Academic Press.

Keith, J. (1994). The research process. In J. Gubrium & A. Sankar (Eds.), *Qualitative methods in aging research* (pp. 105-119). Beverly Hills, CA: Sage.

Kertzer, D. (1978). Theoretical developments in the study of age-group systems [review of Stewart, 1977]. *American Ethnologist, 5*, 365-374.

Kertzer, D., & Madison, O. B. B. (1981). Women's age-set systems in Africa: The Latuka of Southern Sudan. In C. L. Fry (Ed.), *Dimensions: Aging, culture and health* (pp. 109-130). New York: Praeger.

Kohli, M. (1986a). Social organization and subjective construction of the life course. In A. Sorensen, F. Weinert, & L. Sherrod (Eds.), *Human development and the life course* (pp. 272-292). Hillsdale, NJ: Lawrence Erlbaum.

Kohli, M. (1986b). The world we forgot: A historical review of the life course. In V. W. Marshall (Ed.), *Later life: The social psychology of aging* (pp. 271-303). Beverly Hills, CA: Sage.

Krause, N. (1991). Stressful events and life satisfaction among elderly men and women. *Journal of Gerontology, 46*(2), S84-92.

Kruskal, J. B., & Wish, M. (1978). *Multidimensional scaling.* Beverly Hills, CA: Sage.

Lance, C. E., Lautenschlager, G. J., Sloan, C. E., & Varca, P. E. (1989). A comparison between bottom-up, top-down, and bidirectional models of relationships between global and life facet satisfaction. *Journal of Personality, 57*(3), 601-624.

Langness, L. L., & Frank, G. (1981). *Lives: An anthropological approach to biography.* Novato, CA: Chandler & Sharp.

Larson, R. (1978). Thirty years of research on the subjective well-being of older Americans. *Journal of Gerontology, 33*(1), 109-125.

Larson, R., Mannell, R., & Zuzanek, J. (1986). Daily well-being of older adults with friends and family. *Psychology and Aging, 1*(2), 117-126.

Lau, S. K., & Kuan, H. C. (1988). *The ethos of the Hong Kong Chinese.* Hong Kong: The Chinese University Press.

Lawton, M. P., Moss, M., & Kleban, M. H. (1984). Marital status, living arrangements, and the well-being of older people. *Research on Aging, 6*(3), 323-345.

Lee, G. R., & Ellithorpe, E. (1982). Intergenerational exchange and subjective well-being among the elderly. *Journal of Marriage and the Family, 44*, 217-224.

Legesse, A. (1973). *Gada.* New York: Free Press.

Lewis, G. L. (1979). A Welsh rural community in transition. *Sociologia Ruralis, 10*, 143-159.

Liang, J., Asano, H., Bollen, K. A., Kahana, E. F., & Maeda, D. (1987). Cross-cultural comparability of the Philadelphia Geriatric Center Morale Scale: An American-Japanese comparison. *Journal of Gerontology, 42*(1), 37-43.

Liang, J., Lawrence, R. H., & Bollen, K. A. (1987). Race differences in factorial structure of two measures of subjective well-being. *Journal of Gerontology, 42*(4), 426-428.

Luborsky, M. (1987). Analysis of multiple life history narratives. *Ethos, 15*, 366-381.

Luborsky, M., & Rubinstein, R. (1987). Ethnicity and lifestyles: Self-concepts and situational contexts. In D. Gelfand & C. Barresi (Eds.), *Ethnic dimensions of aging* (pp. 35-50). New York: Springer.

McKenzie, B., & Campbell, J. (1987). Race, socioeconomic status, and the subjective well-being of older Americans. *International Journal of Aging and Human Development, 25*(1), 43-61.

Manton, K. G., & Soldo, B. J. (1985). Dynamics of health changes in the oldest old. *Milbank Memorial Fund Quarterly on Health and Society, 63*(2), 206-285.

Maxwell, E. K., & Maxwell, R. (1980). Contempt for the elderly: A cross-cultural analysis. *Current Anthropology, 21*(4), 569-570.

Maxwell, R., & Silverman, P. (1970). Information and esteem: Cultural considerations in the treatment of the aged. *International Journal of Aging and Human Development, 1*, 361-392.

Maxwell, R., Silverman, P., & Maxwell, E. K. (1982). The motive for gerontocide. In J. Sokolovsky (Ed.), *Aging and the aged in the Third World: Part I. Studies in Third World Societies* (Publication No. 22, December) (pp. 67-84). Williamsburg, VA: College of William and Mary, Dept. of Anthropology.

Mayer, J. W. (1986). The self and the life course: Institutionalization and its effects. In A. Sorensen, F. Weinert, & L. Sherrod (Eds.), *Human development and the life course* (pp. 199-216). Hillsdale, NJ: Lawrence Erlbaum.

Mayer, K. U., & Muller, W. (1986). The state and the structure of the life course. In A. Sorensen, F. Weinert, & L. Sherrod (Eds.), *Human development and the life course* (pp. 217-246). Hillsdale, NJ: Lawrence Erlbaum.

Minaker, K. L., & Rowe, J. (1985). Health and disease among the oldest old: A clinical perspective. *Milbank Memorial Fund Quarterly/Health and Society, 63*(2), 324-349.

Minkler, M. (1984). Introduction. In M. Minkler & C. Estes (Eds.), *Readings in a political economy of aging* (pp. 10-21). Farmingdale, NY: Baywood.

Modell, J., Furstenberg, F., & Hershberg, T. (1976). Social change and transitions to adulthood in historical perspective. *Journal of Family History, 1*, 7-33.

Mukherjee, R. (1989). *The quality of life: Valuation in social research.* New Delhi: Sage.

Myles, J. (1984). *Old age in the welfare state.* Boston: Little, Brown.

Myles, J. (1988). Decline or impasse? The current state of the welfare state. *Studies in Political Economy, 26*, 73-107.

National Council of the Aged. (1983). *Community services for the aged.* Dublin: Author.

National Council of the Aged. (1984). *Incomes of the elderly in Ireland.* Dublin: Author.

National Economic and Social Council. (1987). *Community care services: An overview* (Report No. 84). Dublin: Author.

Neapolitan, J. (1988). General symbolic definitions and subjective well-being. *Sociological Spectrum, 8*, 153-168.

Neugarten, B. L. (1968). *Middle age and aging: A reader in social psychology.* Chicago: University of Chicago Press.

Neugarten, B. L. (1982). *Age or need? Public policies for older people.* Beverly Hills, CA: Sage.

Neugarten, B. L., & Datan, N. (1973). Sociological perspectives on the life cycle. In P. B. Baltes & K. W. Schaie (Eds.), *Life span developmental psychology: Personality and socialization* (pp. 53-71). New York: Academic Press.

Neugarten, B. L., & Peterson, W. A. (1957). A study of the American age grading system. In *Proceedings of the 4th Congress of the International Association of Gerontology, 3*, 497-502.

Nydegger, C. (1977). *Measuring morale: A guide to effective assessment.* Washington, DC: Gerontological Society.

Nydegger, C. (1980). Measuring morale. In C. L. Fry & J. Keith (Eds.), *New methods for old age research* (pp. 177-203). Chicago: Loyola University, Center for Urban Policy.

Nydegger, C. (1983). Family ties of the aged in cross-cultural perspective. *The Gerontologist, 23*, 26-32.

Okun, M. A., & Stock, W. A. (1987). Correlates and components of subjective well-being among the elderly. *Journal of Applied Gerontology, 6*(1), 95-112.

Okun, M. A., Stock, W. A., Haring, M. J., & Witter, R. A. (1984). Health and subjective well-being: A meta-analysis. *International Journal of Aging and Human Development, 19*(2), 111-132.

Olson, L. K. (1982). *The political economy of aging.* New York: Columbia University Press.

Ortega, S. T., Crutchfield, R. D., & Rushing, W. A. (1983). Race differences in elderly personal well-being: Friendship, family, and church. *Research on Aging, 5*(1), 101-118.

Palmore, E. B., & Manton, K. (1974). Modernization and the status of the aged: International correlations. *Journal of Gerontology, 29*, 205-210.

Paul, R. E. (1965a). Class and community in English commuter villages. *Sociologia Ruralis, 5*, 2-23.

Paul, R. E. (1965b). *Urbs in Rue* (London School of Economics and Political Science Geographical Paper No. 2). London: London School of Economics and Political Science.

Pennington, R., & Harpending, H. (1993). *The structure of an African pastoralist community: Demography, history and ecology of the Ngamiland Herero.* Oxford: Oxford University Press.

Phillipson, C. (1982). *Capitalism and the construction of old age.* London: Macmillan.

Phillipson, C., & Walker, A. (1986). *Ageing and social policy. A critical assessment.* Hants, U.K.: Gower.

Powers, B. (1980). *Old and alone in Ireland.* Dublin: St. Vincent De Paul.

Press, I., & McKool, M. (1972). Social structure and the status of the aged: Toward some valid cross-cultural generalization. *Aging and Human Development, 3*, 297-306.

Quadagno, J. (1988). *The transformation of old age security.* Chicago: University of Chicago Press.

Radcliffe-Brown, A. R. (1929). Age organization terminology. *Man, 29*, 21.

Reinharz, S., & Rowles, G. (1988). *Qualitative gerontology.* New York: Springer.

Riley, M. W., Johnson, M. E., & Foner, A. (1972). *Aging and society: A sociology of age stratification* (Vol. 3). New York: Russell Sage.

Roberts, D. (1990). *Hong Kong 1990: Annual Report.* Hong Kong: Government Information Services.

Rubinstein, R. (1989). Temporality and affect: The personal meaning of well-being. In L. E. Thomas (Ed.), *Research on adulthood and aging: The human science approach* (pp. 109-125). Albany: State University of New York Press.

Ryff, C. D. (1989a). Beyond Ponce de Leon and life satisfaction: New directions in quest of successful aging. *International Journal of Behavioral Development, 12*(1), 35-55.

Ryff, C. D. (1989b). In the eye of the beholder: Views of psychological well-being among middle-aged and older adults. *Psychology and Aging, 4*(2), 195-210.

Sadler, T. U. (1928). The Manor of Blessington. *Royal Society of Antiquaries of Ireland, 58*, 128-132.

Sagy, S., Antonovsky, A., & Adler, I. (1990). Explaining life satisfaction in later life: The sense of coherence model and activity theory. *Behavior, Health, and Aging, 1*(1), 11-25.

Schultz, J. H., & Myles, J. (1990). Old age pensions: A comparative perspective. In R. Binstock & L. George (Eds.), *Handbook of aging and the social sciences* (pp. 398-414). New York: Van Nostrand-Reinhold.

Shanas, E., Townsend, P., Wedderburn, D., Friis, H., Milhoj, P., & Stehouwer, J. (1968). The psychology of health. In B. L. Neugarten (Ed.), *Middle age and aging: A reader in social gerontology* (pp. 212-219). Chicago: University of Chicago Press.

Shepard, R. N., Romney, A. K., & Nerlove, S. B. (1972). *Multidimensional scaling* (2 vols.). New York: Seminar.

Silverman, P. (1987). Comparative studies. In P. Silverman (Ed.), *The elderly as modern pioneers* (pp. 312-344). Bloomington: Indiana University Press.

Simmons, L. (1945). *The role of the aged in primitive society.* New Haven: Yale University Press.

Smeeding, T. (1990). Economic status of the elderly. In R. Binstock & L. George (Eds.), *Handbook of aging and the social sciences* (pp. 361-381). San Diego: Academic Press.

Smyth, W. J. (1970). Continuity and change in the territorial organization of Irish rural communities. Part I and II. *Maynooth Review, 1*(1, 51-78, and 2, 52-101.

Social Studies Course. (1982). *The development of Blessington and the surrounding areas.* Unpublished manuscript, St. Mark's Vocational School, Blessington.

Spencer, P. (1965). *The Samburu: A study of gerontocracy in a nomadic tribe.* London: Routledge & Kegan Paul.

Spencer, P. (1976). Opposing streams and the gerontocratic ladder: Two models of age organization. *Man, 11*, 153-174.

Stewart, F. H. (1977). *Fundamentals of age-group systems.* New York: Academic Press.

Thomas, L. E., & Chambers, K. O. (1989a). Phenomenology of life satisfaction among elderly men: Quantitative and qualitative views. *Psychology and Aging, 4*(3), 284-289.

Thomas, L. E., & Chambers, K. O. (1989b). "Successful aging" among elderly men in England and India: A phenomenological comparison. In L. E. Thomas (Ed.), *Research on adulthood and aging: The human science approach* (pp. 183-203). Albany: State University of New York Press.

Townsend, P. (1981). The structured dependency of the elderly: A creation of social policy in the 20th century. *Ageing and Society, 1*, 5-28.

Treiman, D. J. (1977). *Occupational prestige in comparative perspective.* New York: Academic Press.

Verbrugge, L. M. (1988). Unveiling higher morbidity for men: The story. In M. W. Riley (Ed.), *Social structures and human lives* (pp. 138-160). Newbury Park, CA: Sage.

Verbrugge, L. M. (1989). The dynamics of population aging and health. *Aging and health: Linking research and public policy.* Chelsea, MI: Lewis.

Villiers-Tuthill, K. (1986). *Beyond the Twelve Bens: A history of Clifden and the district 1860-1923.* Galway, Republic of Ireland: Author and the *Connacht Tribune.*

Walker, A. (1983a). Care for elderly people: A conflict between women and the state. In J. French & D. Groves (Eds.), *A labour of love* (pp. 106-128). London: Routledge & Kegan Paul.

Walker, A. (1983b). Social policy and the elderly in Great Britain: The construction of dependent social and economic status. In A. M. Guillemard (Ed.), *Old age and the welfare state* (pp. 111-133). London: Sage.

Wan, T. T. H., & Livieratos, B. (1978). Interpreting a general index of subjective well-being. *Health and Society, 56*(4), 531-556.

Weingarten, H., & Bryant, F. B. (1987). Marital status and the meaning of subjective well-being: A structural analysis. *Journal of Marriage and the Family, 49,* 883-892.

Whelan, B. J., & Vaughan, R. N. (1982). *Social circumstances of elderly in Ireland* (Economic and Social Research Institute Paper No. 110). Dublin: Economic and Social Research Council.

Whitbourne, S. K. (1985). The psychological construction of the life span. In J. E. Birren & K. W. Schaie (Eds.), *Handbook of the psychology of aging* (2nd ed., pp. 594-618). New York: Van Nostrand Reinhold.

Williamson, J. B., Evans, L., & Powell, L. A. (1982). *The politics of aging.* Springfield, IL: Charles C Thomas.

Wood, L. A., & Johnson, J. (1989). Life satisfaction among the rural elderly: What do the numbers mean? *Social Indicators Research, 21*(4), 379-408.

World Health Organization. (1980). *International classification of impairments, disabilities, and handicaps: A manual of classification relating to the consequences of disease.* Geneva: Author.

World Health Organization. (1985). *The uses of epidemiology in the study of the elderly: Report of a WHO scientific group on the epidemiology of aging* (Technical Report Series 706). Geneva: Author.

World Health Organization, Regional Office for Europe. (1982). *Epidemiological studies on social and medical conditions of the elderly: Report on a survey.* Copenhagen: Author.

Zautra, A., & Hempel, A. (1984). Subjective well-being and physical health: A narrative literature review with suggestions for future research. *International Journal of Aging and Human Development, 19*(2), 95-110.

Index

About the Authors

Jennie Keith received her Ph.D. in anthropology from Northwestern University, and she is Centennial Professor of Anthropology and Provost at Swarthmore College. Her research has been on the meanings given to age in various communities and societies. Her publications include *Old People, New Lives: Community Creation in a Retirement Residence, Old People as People: Social and Cultural Influences on Aging and Old Age, New Methods for Old Age Research* (with Christine Fry), and *Age and Anthropological Theory* (with David Kertzer), along with many chapters and journal articles. She is Co-Director, with Christine Fry, of Project AGE.

Christine L. Fry is Professor of Anthropology at Loyola University of Chicago. She received her Ph.D. in anthropology from the University of Arizona. As a graduate student she became interested in aging by moving into a retirement community and seeing the experiences of older people. Her interests have focused on age and social organization and comparative studies of the life course. She has edited *Age, Culture and Society*, and *New Methods for Old Age Research* (with Jennie Keith), as well as published articles on aging and the life course. She is Co-Director of Project AGE, with Jennie Keith.

Anthony P. Glascock is Professor of Anthropology and Head of the Psychology, Sociology, and Anthropology Department at Drexel University in Philadelphia. He received his Ph.D. in anthropology at the University of Pittsburgh in 1973 and taught at the University of Wyoming for 13 years, where he was founder and co-chair of the Program in Aging and Human Development. He has conducted research in Somalia, sponsored by USAID, on the relationship between health and aging and has published extensively on the status and treatment of the elderly in nonindustrial societies. He has been a Visiting Faculty Fellow at the Andrus Gerontology Center, University of Southern California, President of the Association for Anthropology and Gerontology, and a founding member of the Society for Cross-Cultural Research. He is currently Director of the Center for Applied Neurogerontology at Drexel, a Fellow of the Gerontological Society of America, and on the editorial board of the *Journal of Cross-Cultural Gerontology*.

Charlotte Ikels is an Associate Professor of Anthropology at Case Western Reserve University and a co-editor of the *Journal of Cross-Cultural Gerontology*. Her research interests focus on Chinese elderly, intergenerational relations, the life course, home health care, and urban life. She has conducted fieldwork in Hong Kong, China (Guangzhou), and the United States. Among her published works are *Aging and Adaptation: Chinese in Hong Kong and the United States* and two special issues of the *Journal of Cross-Cultural Gerontology*: *Policy and Aging in Contemporary China* (with Melvyn Goldstein) and *Home Health Care and Elders: International Perspectives*. She has just completed a manuscript on daily life in contemporary China entitled *The Return of the God of Wealth: The Transition to a Market Economy in Urban China*.

Jeanette Dickerson-Putman received her Ph.D. in anthropology from Bryn Mawr College. She is Assistant Professor of Anthropology at Indiana University and Purdue University at Indianapolis. In addition to her research in Ireland with Project AGE, she has done extensive fieldwork in Papua, New Guinea, and in French Polynesia with a focus on women's roles in development. She writes from a cross-cultural perspective about gender and community as well as about aging.

Henry C. Harpending received his doctorate in anthropology from Harvard University in 1972. He taught at the University of New Mexico until 1985, then moved to Pennsylvania State University, where he is Professor of Anthropology and Human Development. His research has been primarily about demography and population genetics of the !Kung and of Herero-speaking people of the Kalahari Desert. He has also written a number of papers with Patricia Draper about the evolution of human family organization and about sex differences, learning rules, and human reproductive strategies.

Patricia Draper received her Ph.D. in anthropology from Harvard University. She is Professor of Anthropology at Penn State University and President of the Society for Cross-Cultural Research. Her research with the !Kung focused on the earlier stages of life before she joined Project AGE, and she has published extensively in the areas of !Kung childhood socialization and relations between parents and children, as well of on the consequences of sedentarization for !Kung social life and more broadly of the evolutionary development of human family life.